ENOUGH ALREADY

Time to End the War on Terrorism

Scott Horton

Advance Praise for Enough Already

"If you only read one book this year on America's unending 'War on Terror,' it should be this persuasive and devastatingly damning account of how the United States created the original al Qaeda terrorism threat by its own actions and then increased that threat by orders of magnitude by its wanton killings in one country after another in the name of 'counter-terrorism.' Once I started reading it, I couldn't stop!" — Daniel Ellsberg, *Pentagon Papers* whistleblower and author of *The Doomsday Machine: Confessions of a Nuclear War Planner*

"Nothing has fueled the abuse of government power in the last 20 years like the 'War on Terrorism.' Scott Horton's essential new book, *Enough Already*, is the key to understanding why it's not too late to end the wars and save our country. Three administrations in a row have promised us a more restrained foreign policy. It is time we insisted on it." — Ron Paul, M.D., former congressman and author of *Swords into Plowshares: A Life in Wartime and a Future of Peace and Prosperity*

"With outstanding scholarship, research and analysis, Scott Horton's new book, *Enough Already*, lays bare the logical absurdity and self-defeating nature of America's permanent-war establishment. It might have taken its title from a line in the book's introduction: America's war policy since at least the Carter Administration has been 'a policy in search of a reason.' As Horton painstakingly lays bare, in virtually none of the military conflicts the United States has chosen to fight in since the 1970s was our security ever genuinely threatened. His ultimate solution is the only one that has any chance of preserving American security and giving us a chance to be ready in case we do face a genuine threat in the future: end the pointless and self-defeating forever wars. All of them." — Lt. Col. Daniel L. Davis, USA (Ret.) four-time combat deployer, two-time winner of the Bronze Star and author of *Eleventh Hour in 2020 America: How American Foreign Policy Got Jacked Up and What the Next Administration Can Do About It*

"This is it! Finally, we have a comprehensive, rigorously researched, beautifully written and unassailable argument to stop the 'endless wars' that virtually no Americans outside the foreign policy establishment want to continue. There is no better time for this book to appear and no better person to write it than Scott Horton, who has been the people's foreign policy expert for decades. If you want to save lives, buy it, read it and share it." — Thaddeus Russell, professor of history and philosophy at Willamette University and author of *A Renegade History of the United States*

"I finished reading *Enough Already* the same week I had to attend the funeral of a sailor from one of my Iraq deployments. He killed himself leaving behind a wife and three boys. Nothing in this book is simply historical or abstract to tens of millions of families. Scott Horton has written an incredible accounting of the wars of the last twenty years. This book should be used to hold accountable those who purposefully committed these crimes and to remember the generations of Iraqis, Afghans, Somalis, Yemenis, Pakistanis, Palestinians, Libyans, Iranians, Syrians, sub-Saharan Africans and Americans whose lives have been forever damaged and destroyed." — Capt. Matthew Hoh, USMC (ret.), former senior State Department official, Zabul Province, Afghanistan, senior fellow at the Center for International Policy

"Scott Horton is one of the best informed and hardest hitting critics of the War on Terror. His new book is a gold mine for anyone seeking to learn about the frauds and failures of U.S. foreign policy." — Jim Bovard, columnist at *USA Today* and author of *Public Policy Hooligan*

"Scott Horton's book courageously investigates the deception that is the 'War on Terror.' It provides an impressive and wide-ranging examination of the misguided and costly U.S. foreign policy decisions which led to morally indefensible, strategically useless and militarily catastrophic interventions and wars in Somalia, Afghanistan, Iraq and other parts of the world. *Enough Already* must be read by every American who cares about the future of his country because the cost of these imprudent wars has proven detrimental to the nation's moral compass, global reputation, economic well-being and, indeed, national security. *Enough Already* is an eloquently written book. Using accessible language, exhaustive research and indisputable arguments, Horton's latest volume is a damning and impassioned case against war." — Ramzy Baroud, editor of Palestine Chronicle and author of *These Chains Will Be Broken: Palestinian Stories of Struggle and Defiance in Israeli Prisons*

"Scott Horton has put together a devastating, deeply-researched account of how the U.S. war system betrayed the American people's trust in carrying out the so-called 'War on Terror.' He shows convincingly that it actually served other objectives and represents an unforgivable treachery that has inflicted incalculable harm on the United States. Readers across the entire deeply divided U.S. political spectrum will find truth in it that they can trust." — Gareth Porter, Martha Gellhorn Award-winning journalist and author of *Manufactured Crisis: The Untold Story of the Iran Nuclear Scare*

ENOUGH ALREADY

Time to End the War on Terrorism

Scott Horton

The
LIBERTARIAN
INSTITUTE

Published in the United States of America by
The Libertarian Institute
612 W. 34th St.
Austin, TX 78705

LibertarianInstitute.org

ISBN-13: 978-1-7336473-4-2
ISBN-10: 1-7336473-4-1

For Elizabeth Miller

Contents

Introduction

The Middle East, North Africa and South-Central Asia are in chaos. Populations have been riven by sectarian civil war in what remains of the former states of Iraq, Syria, Libya and Mali, across to Afghanistan and down into the Arabian Peninsula. More than a million people have been killed. Tens of millions more have been displaced, resulting in the massive refugee crisis that afflicted Europe in the last decade.

This is because the U.S. government has spent the last two decades waging wars and interventions against an endlessly shifting series of enemies across these regions. The government claims to be doing all this to defend the American people against international terrorist groups. In truth, the entire War on Terrorism has been at the expense of the actual security of the United States and the people of Africa and the Middle East. Membership in bin Ladenite terrorist groups is near its all-time high.

The reality is that the U.S. government got us into this mess in the first place and that virtually everything they have done in response to anti-American terrorism has only helped the terrorists grow in strength.

This is by design: the enemy's. As Osama bin Laden explained for years before the attacks of September 11, 2001, he was attempting to lure Americans into personally fighting the wars al Qaeda members believed the U.S. was already waging against them. They blamed America for the actions of its various proxy forces in the region, primarily the dictatorships in Saudi Arabia and Egypt as well as the Israeli occupation in Palestine.

By providing the American government a crisis to exploit, bin Laden guaranteed that the United States would set about accomplishing the terrorists' goals for them. Among these were the destabilization of U.S.-supported regimes in the region, religious and political radicalization of populations of Middle Eastern countries, and most importantly, the bankruptcy of the American treasury with the ultimate goal of forcing the U.S. from the region entirely.

Their plan was to provoke a U.S. invasion of Afghanistan so that they could attempt to replicate their 1980s war of attrition against the Soviet Union's military occupation of that nation. That effort, supported by the United States and their Saudi and Pakistani allies, by most accounts, did contribute to the final collapse of the USSR in the years 1988–1991.

Al Qaeda's mission was accomplished when America attacked Afghanistan in 2001. But, if the U.S. invasion of Iraq in 2003 was the

"hoped for, but unexpected gift to bin Laden," in the words of the former
chief of the Central Intelligence Agency's al Qaeda unit, the rest of
American policy since then must seem like they hit the lottery. The regimes
in Egypt and Saudi Arabia still stand, but America's wars in Iraq, Somalia,
Yemen, Libya, and especially the covert war against the Syrian government
from 2011–2017, have helped spread bin Ladenite political and religious
radicalism and violent conflict throughout the region and into northern
and western Africa. Groups declaring loyalty to al Qaeda or its Iraqi
splinter group ISIS now number in the tens of thousands.

A long-term proxy war between Saudi Arabia, Iran and their respective
Sunni and Shi'ite allies, which was worsened considerably by the U.S.
invasion of Iraq in 2003, has redrawn territorial lines of authority through
bloody conflict and guaranteed further violence for decades to come. Over
time, America has fought for and against all sides of this conflict,
sometimes at the same time.

Both radical Sunni al Qaeda, the American people's enemy, and Shi'ite-
led Iran, the American government's major strategic rival for dominance
over the Middle East, have only continued to make gains these last two
decades, at the expense of entire Middle Eastern civilian populations. As
many as two million fighters and civilians have been killed, wounded and
widowed — and tens of thousands of American soldiers, sailors, airmen,
marines, guardsmen and contractors with them.

Congress has passed thousands of new laws, established entire new
federal bureaucracies and granted spy agencies such as the CIA, NSA and
FBI vast new powers to collect information on all American citizens
without constitutional warrants. In the War on Terrorism era, federal
government lawlessness has made a mockery of the American values of
freedom and justice that our politicians have cynically invoked to justify
their destructive policies.

The government has spent trillions of dollars. Politically connected
interests have made massive fortunes, but American society at large has
gained nothing beyond, perhaps, increasingly necessary technological
advancements in the manufacture of prosthetic limbs.

The generals and hawks say we can never withdraw from any Muslim
country where U.S. forces are stationed because those spaces will then
become "safe havens" from which terrorists will be able to stage attacks
on American civilians. But it has been unwarranted American intervention
in other people's countries that has motivated terrorist attacks against us
all along. Meanwhile, American strategy and tactics against al Qaeda-loyal
forces have only been counterproductive, increasing the power and
influence of the targeted groups. When the U.S. has outright sided with
the enemy in Libya, Syria and Yemen, the results have been catastrophic.

In a perverse imitation of our enemies, the policy of American dominance in the Middle East amounts to murder-suicide on a mass scale. The treasury is empty, the infantry is exhausted, the Bill of Rights is in tatters and the American people do not believe in the war anymore.

Polls show that strong majorities of even the troops who have fought in Iraq and Afghanistan say these wars should never have happened in the first place.

Twenty years is enough already.

It is time to cancel the failed War on Terrorism.

It is time to just come home.

Chapter One:
Causing Problems

"Terror means killing and robbery
and coercion by people who
do not have state authority."
— Bill Clinton

"If we have to use force,
it is because we are America.
We are the indispensable nation.
We stand tall, and we see further
than other countries into the
future, and we see the danger
here to all of us."
— Madeleine Albright

"They hate our freedom."
— George W. Bush

Blowback Terrorism

On September 11, 2001, there were no more than a few hundred al Qaeda members hiding out in Afghanistan. Three months later, when the Central Intelligence Agency (CIA) paramilitaries, U.S. Army Delta Force and U.S. Air Force finished bombing them, and Osama bin Laden had escaped to Pakistan, there were not enough of the terrorists left alive to fill a 757.

Now, 20 years after that brief, one-sided victory, there are tens of thousands of bin Ladenite jihadists thriving in lands from Nigeria to the Philippines. Recently, and for almost three years, some even claimed their own divinely ordained caliphate, or Islamic State, temporarily erasing the border between Iraq and Syria. Local chapters of their group keep popping up all over the region. The State Department consistently reports a vast increase in the number of global terrorism incidents compared to the pre-September 11th era. Al Qaeda, the Islamic State in Iraq and Syria (ISIS) and their "lone wolf" copycats have carried out multiple, deadly attacks in more than a dozen major Western cities in the past decade, including Brussels, Paris, Berlin, London, San Bernardino, Orlando, New York City, Pensacola and Corpus Christi.

Something must be wrong.

The problem is that our government is ignoring and misrepresenting the real causes of the terrorists' war against the United States. It has then exploited the population's ignorance and fear to advance their own unrelated and counterproductive political agendas.

Two decades after the September 11th attacks, the War on Terrorism is still predicated on the false premise that al Qaeda and Islamic State terrorists want to kill Americans because their belief in "radical" Islam makes them hate and wish to destroy all innocent and virtuous people and things. Faced with such an implacable and irrational enemy, we are told there is only one option: "Fight them over there, so we don't have to fight them over here." When foreign-planned or foreign-inspired attacks then take place in the U.S. anyway, the answer remains: "Fight them over there some more." After all, even if the "collateral damage" from U.S. counter-terrorism efforts causes some "blowback," inspiring more terrorist attacks against our country, they still started it, right? What are we supposed to do, refuse to defend ourselves?

But this is all wrong. The truth is U.S. intervention in the Middle East long precedes al Qaeda's war against America and is the primary cause of our terrorism problem. Then, in a seemingly endless cycle, virtually everything the government has done in the name of defending us from terrorists has continued to make matters worse.

The September 11th attacks were no first assault by the "Muslim World," or even the forces of "Radical Islam," intent on invading the middle part of North America to overthrow the U.S. government, destroy our society and freedom and convert us to their religion. Instead, it was a last-gasp, desperate measure taken by a tiny group of formerly U.S.-backed Arab insurgent fighters, most of them from Saudi Arabia and Egypt, who had been exiled to the wilderness of Afghanistan's Hindu Kush mountains. Their strategy was to goad the United States government into helping accomplish their goals for them: destabilization, radicalization and revolution in *their* countries.

Leftist activist Saul Alinsky wrote that in all asymmetric, radical political operations, "the real action is in the reaction of the opposition." Bin Laden understood this well. And though his stated plans once seemed grandiose to the point of absurdity, it turns out that in the last 20 years, America's War on Terrorism has already accomplished more of al Qaeda's agenda than they could have ever dreamed of managing on their own.

For years before the September 11th attacks, bin Laden told the world precisely what his grievances were, what he would do about them and how he expected his plan to work. As he told Robert Fisk of the *Independent*, Peter Bergen and Peter Arnett of CNN, Abdel Bari Atwan of the newspaper *Al Quds al-Arabi* in London and others, his problem was U.S. military intervention in the Middle East. His plan was to wage war against the United States to force our military out of the region, thus making it possible to achieve al Qaeda's long-term goals of carrying out revolutions in their own countries without American interference.

John Miller, an ABC News reporter who later became a counter-terrorism agent for the Federal Bureau of Investigation (FBI), interviewed bin Laden at his mountain camp near the border between Afghanistan and Pakistan in 1998. Miller later described his incredulous reaction after hearing bin Laden declare his intentions for war against America and revolution throughout the region. "I thought, 'Yeah, you and what army?'"

Of course, it was America itself that had the only armed force powerful enough to accomplish bin Laden's far-reaching agenda. And one way or the other, the U.S. government has been doing the enemy's dirty work for them since al Qaeda's attack of September 11, 2001.

As "extreme" as al Qaeda and the Islamic State's version of Islam may be, what has motivated their war against the United States from the beginning are foreign policies they viewed as detrimental to their real-world political interests. Bin Laden repeatedly explained his motivations in his "fatwas" (religious edicts), speeches and media interviews leading up to the September 11th attacks. He claimed to be fighting a defensive war against significant American actions in their part of the world. Al Qaeda had not sworn to invade America to destroy democracy, freedom or depictions of adultery in Hollywood movies. From his 1998 "Declaration of War Against Jews and Crusaders":

First, for over seven years, the United States has been occupying the lands of Islam in the holiest of places, the Arabian Peninsula, plundering its riches, dictating to its rulers, humiliating its people, terrorizing its neighbors, and turning its bases in the Peninsula into a spearhead through which to fight the neighboring Muslim peoples. If some people have in the past argued about the fact of the occupation, all the people of the Peninsula have now acknowledged it. The best proof of this is the Americans' continuing aggression against the Iraqi people using the Peninsula as a staging post, even though all its rulers are against their territories being used to that end, but they are helpless.

Second, despite the great devastation inflicted on the Iraqi people by the crusader-Zionist alliance, and despite the huge number of those killed, which has exceeded one million ... despite all this, the Americans are once again trying to repeat the horrific massacres, as though they are not content with the protracted blockade imposed after the ferocious war or the fragmentation and devastation. So here they come to annihilate what is left of this people and to humiliate their Muslim neighbors.

Third, if the Americans' aims behind these wars are religious and economic, the aim is also to serve the Jews' petty state and divert attention from its occupation of Jerusalem and murder of Muslims there. The best proof of this is their eagerness to destroy Iraq, the strongest neighboring Arab state, and their endeavor to fragment all the states of the region such as Iraq, Saudi Arabia, Egypt, and Sudan into paper statelets and through their disunion and weakness to guarantee Israel's survival and the continuation of the brutal crusade occupation of the Peninsula.

There you have it. Foremost among al Qaeda's grievances against America were the U.S. Army and Air Force combat forces which had been stationed at Saudi bases since the beginning of preparations for the first Iraq war in 1990, and their presence in other countries on the Arabian Peninsula. National borders between these countries are a distinction without a difference to bin Laden and his followers. To them, the entire peninsula is not just their homeland, but holy land — birthplace of the Prophet Mohammed and the religion of Islam. The U.S. was using these military bases, bin Laden complained, to enforce the long-term sanctions policy against Iraq and the bombing of its "no-fly zones" throughout the 1990s.

Bin Laden also routinely cited America's unconditional support for Israel, which both controlled Jerusalem — considered to be the third holiest site in Islam — and also occupied the property of millions of Palestinian civilians in the West Bank and the Gaza Strip. Additionally, he objected to Israel's 1982 invasion and subsequent 18-year occupation of southern Lebanon and what he characterized as Israeli-centric plans to destabilize antagonistic states in the region, such as Iraq.

Another part of al Qaeda's public case justifying its war against America was U.S. support for corrupt dictatorships in the Middle East, which included Jordan, Saudi Arabia, Kuwait, the United Arab Emirates, Bahrain, Oman, Qatar, Yemen and Egypt. This support, bin Laden complained, came with the condition that these regimes keep oil prices artificially low and spend their profits on large purchases of American arms instead of using it for the people's benefit.

Is it a surprise then that all the September 11th hijackers were from countries with governments friendly to our own — Saudi Arabia, Egypt, Lebanon and the United Arab Emirates — and that none of them were from America's designated enemy states of Iran, Iraq or Syria?

Osama bin Laden was a mass-murderer, deserving the utmost contempt. Why should we listen to what he says? Why would anyone listen to him? The reality is that no matter what bin Laden really believed, this list of grievances was his successful recruitment pitch — the tale he told to motivate young men such as the September 11th attackers to carry out his war against America. The way he framed the conflict was that America was at war with Islam; that the U.S. was out to destroy Muslim people, occupy Muslim lands, devour Muslim resources and humiliate Muslim men — that we hate them for their freedom.

As former CIA bin Laden unit chief Michael Scheuer has emphasized, when Iran's Ayatollah Ruhollah Khomeini spent the 1980s denouncing America's corrupt popular culture, nobody was moved. Were conservative religious leaders concerned about American culture polluting young minds? Yes, of course. Was this enough to motivate men to want to kill and die in a war against the United States? Of course not. Bin Laden chose instead to harp on real, tangible, destructive U.S. government policies in Arab countries. This enabled him to recruit a small army of terrorists willing to do his bidding, even at the cost of their own lives.

For one example, as Lawrence Wright reported in *The Looming Tower*, in April 1996, after Israel launched their Operation Grapes of Wrath campaign in Southern Lebanon, future lead September 11th hijacker Mohammed Atta signed his last will and testament, a symbol of his willingness to die in the fight against those he blamed for the war. As journalist Terry McDermott explains in *Perfect Soldiers*, his book on Atta's so-called "Hamburg cell" of September 11th plotters, they had all agreed it was the Americans who were responsible for what Israel was doing since the U.S. government gives Israel so many billions of dollars in military equipment and other financial aid.

It was just a few months later, in August 1996, that Osama bin Laden released his first "fatwa" against the United States, entitled "Declaration of War Against the Americans Occupying the Land of the Two Holy Places." In it, bin Laden railed against the presence of U.S. military bases on the Arabian Peninsula, the bombing and blockade of Iraq from those bases and Israel's occupations — especially Operation Grapes of Wrath. This included what is now called the First Qana Massacre, during which Israeli forces shelled a United Nations compound, killing 106 Lebanese civilians who had sought shelter there.

> It should not be hidden from you that the people of Islam had suffered from aggression, iniquity and injustice imposed on them by the Zionist-Crusaders alliance and their collaborators; to the extent that the Muslims' blood became the cheapest and their wealth as loot in the hands of the enemies. Their blood was spilled in Palestine and Iraq. The horrifying pictures of the massacre of Qana, in Lebanon are still fresh in our memory. ...

> The youths hold you responsible for all of the killings and evictions of the Muslims and the violation of the sanctities, carried out by your Zionist brothers in Lebanon; you openly supplied them with arms and finance.

Bin Laden cited U.S. support for Israel's violence in the occupied territories and Lebanon again and again as motivation for al Qaeda attacks against American civilians. As he said in his 1997 interview with Peter Arnett of CNN,

> We declared jihad against the U.S. government because the U.S. government is unjust, criminal and tyrannical. It has committed acts that are extremely unjust, hideous and criminal, whether directly or through its support of the Israeli occupation of the Prophet's Night Travel Land [Palestine]. And we believe the U.S. is directly responsible for those who were killed in Palestine, Lebanon and Iraq. The mention of the U.S. reminds us before everything else of those innocent children who were dismembered, their heads and arms cut off in the recent explosion that took place in Qana.

When Atta and his best friend and co-conspirator Ramzi bin al-Shibh found out how closely Osama bin Laden agreed with their own view, they decided his war was to be their path. The next year, Atta and bin al-Shibh traveled to the training camps in Afghanistan to meet with bin Laden and volunteer their services. Their potential must have been obvious to al Qaeda; upper-middle-class graduate students studying engineering in Germany would have easy access to the United States.

These pilot hijackers cited U.S. military, financial, and diplomatic support, not simply for Israel's existence, but for its violence against the people of southern Lebanon — invaded and occupied by Israel between

1982 and 2000 — and against the occupied Palestinian population of the West Bank and Gaza Strip — areas conquered and ruled under Israeli military control since the 1967 Six-Day War.

This obviously does not mean al Qaeda leaders have ever indicated they would be happy to settle for a return to 1967 borders and a two-state solution for an independent Palestine. Bin Laden himself consistently railed against Israel's very existence. However, virtually every government in the region has said they would make a permanent peace with Israel on those terms, including Hamas, the fundamentalist militant movement that rules the Gaza Strip. This leaves little doubt that a considerable part of the controversy, as far as Palestine's value as recruitment material for al Qaeda, would completely dry up if the Palestinian people were truly granted independence under the proposed "two-state solution" for the West Bank and the Gaza Strip, or granted equal status as citizens of a single democratic state. Attacks from Hezbollah have almost entirely ceased since the Israeli military's withdrawal from Lebanon in 2000. It is the indefinite foreign military occupation of millions of Palestinian Muslims and Christians at the heart of the controversy in the region and in the motivation of anti-American terrorists who blame the United States for Israel's actions. The real costs and consequences of U.S. intervention in the region, then, extend far beyond the unnecessary billions of dollars spent on "Made in the U.S.A." brand F-16s and M-16s for Israel's military occupation over the Palestinians, to innocent American lives lost as well.

In fact, as Karen DeYoung explains in her book *Soldier: The Life of Colin Powell*, after the September 11th attacks, Secretary of State Powell believed President Bush's approval ratings were high enough, and the problem of anti-American terrorism was important enough, to move the issue of the creation of a Palestinian state in the Israeli-occupied West Bank and Gaza Strip to the front burner. He was soon disappointed to discover that the counter-narrative that the Israelis were simply innocent victims of Islamic terrorism — like us — was far more appealing to the president. "The JINSA crowd," as Powell called them, referring to the neoconservatives from the Jewish Institute for National Security Affairs, convinced Bush that "the road to Jerusalem runs through Baghdad." In other words, regime change in Iraq would be the panacea that would end all support for terrorism in the region and allow the U.S. and Israel to negotiate from a much stronger position in the future. According to the influential Israeli journalist Chemi Shalev, Prime Minister Ariel Sharon's aides reportedly "could not hide their satisfaction in view of Powell's failure. Sharon saw the white in President Bush's eyes, they bragged, and the President blinked first."

One may acknowledge this reality and yet persist in the belief that America should support Israel's occupation, keep troops stationed at bases in Arabia, continue to bomb Iraq and provoke terrorist enemies in various other ways. It is notable, though, when hawks occasionally admit the truth: al Qaeda's motives for attacking the United States are rooted in our government's foreign policies rather than the American people's freedom and innocence or lack of faith in the prophet Mohammed. The issue has always been the military occupations and support for dictatorships.

What does "radical Islamic extremism" have to do with anti-American terrorism? It plays some role, but not in the way the hawks claim. There are more than 1.6 billion Muslims, making up more than one-fifth of the planet's population. Of these, there are hundreds of millions of deeply committed believers in Islam in the world, including several million Americans. Sunni and Shi'ite Muslims — and several other, smaller schools — can be either fundamentalist or moderate, conservative or radical, and represent different nationalities and races from across the world. It is safe to say that since fewer than 100,000 bin Ladenite fighters and terrorists have emerged out of a global Muslim population of over one and a half billion, even in all the chaos of the U.S.-created Middle Eastern battlefields of the last 20 years and at the height of the so-called Islamic State in Iraq and Syria, there must be another explanation. The vast majority of even Salafi and Wahhabi fundamentalists — the Sunni extremist sects from which al Qaeda's leadership is primarily descended, and whose religious views themselves are often blamed for inciting terrorism — would prefer to solve problems peacefully and have no interest in supporting or engaging in terrorism. Bin Laden and his successors have tried to claim ownership of "true" Wahhabism and Salafism, but the rest of the world is not buying it. The vast majority of even these types of religious fundamentalists are "quietists" when it comes to earthly politics. They leave those questions to earthly authorities and focus on their devotion to God. The bin Ladenites are political radicals who, as John L. Esposito and Dalia Mogahed show in their 2008 Gallup Poll book, *Who Speaks for Islam? What a Billion Muslims Really Think*, have failed to inspire significant percentages of Muslims or Arabs to join them.

There is also the plain fact that many actual al Qaeda and ISIS terrorists are not religious fundamentalists or radicals at all. Over the last 30 years, many bin Ladenite terrorists have had a distinct lack of religiosity. This includes some of the perpetrators of the first World Trade Center bombing in 1993, at least a few of the September 11th hijackers and many Islamic State fighters in Iraq and Syria. The same is true for the Paris, Brussels and Nice attackers of 2015 and 2016. Though it rarely makes headlines, the Department of Defense, the RAND Corporation, the CIA, the Combating Terrorism Center at West Point, many think tanks, university studies and journalists have concluded the same: it is not religion, but politics, that motivates our enemies.

After September 11, Professor Robert Pape of the University of Chicago found evidence of suicide attacks on civilians and soldiers in many far-flung places and throughout recorded history, with no tie to Islam whatsoever. Examples range from the use of knives and swords by the Jewish Sicarii, or "dagger men," in resistance against the Roman occupation of antiquity, to the Shinto and Buddhist Japanese kamikaze pilots' attacks on the U.S. Navy in World War II, to the fierce Hindu-atheist-Marxist Tamil Tigers of Sri Lanka. In fact, for the last two decades before 2003, the Tamil Tigers were the "world leaders" in the use of suicide terrorist tactics against their Buddhist, Sinhalese enemies.

After studying every suicide attack on earth since 1980, Pape concluded that the single most significant factor in determining whether someone would commit an act of suicide terrorism was the presence of foreign combat forces on the attacker's home territory. For the perceived greater good, they sacrifice their own lives to kill others as part of a strategic campaign aimed at the target population to coerce the removal of foreign troops from their land.

As reported by the *Guardian*, a 2008 study by the British domestic intelligence service, MI-5, of those who became involved with terrorism, found that

> far from being religious zealots, a large number of those involved in terrorism do not practice their faith regularly. Many lack religious literacy and could actually be regarded as religious novices. Very few have been brought up in strongly religious households, and there is a higher than average proportion of converts. Some are involved in drug-taking, drinking alcohol and visiting prostitutes. MI-5 says there is evidence that a well-established religious identity actually protects against violent radicalization. ...

> The security service also plays down the importance of radical extremist clerics, saying their influence in radicalizing British terrorists has moved into the background in recent years. ... The MI-5 authors stress that the most pressing current threat is from Islamist extremist groups who justify the use of violence "in defense of Islam," but that there are also violent extremists involved in non-Islamist movements.

A 2010 report by the UK think tank Demos found that young Muslims, including religious radicals, rejected terrorism, and that, on the contrary, those who did embrace violence citing religious devotion tended to have a "simpler, shallower conception of Islam." They continued:

> [Religious] radicals refused to defend violent jihad in the West as religiously obligatory, acceptable or permitted. The same was true of the young Muslim sample. Young Muslims rejected al Qaeda's message and often use simple, catchy sayings from the Qur'an or

Hadith to express that rejection. However, there was widespread support among radicals and young Muslims for Iraqi and Afghan people "defending themselves" from "invaders," framed in the language of self-defense, just war and state sovereignty.

Even among those terrorists who can be considered fundamentalists or believers in radical branches of Islam, we again find explicit, repeated claims of secular motivations for attacks against the West, namely, revenge against Western governments for specific, violent foreign policies.

Religion's most important role in the situation is simply that it creates a shared identity, or basis for solidarity, between the victims of violence and those who fight in their names. None of the September 11th hijackers were Iraqi, but al Qaeda's Saudi and Egyptian ringleaders had made it clear for years that they were fighting the U.S. in part to defend or avenge the Iraqis — their fellow Arabs and Muslims — who were being slaughtered and starved under the American no-fly zones and blockade of the 1990s. They still saw Iraqi civilian victims as part of the "ummah," or greater Muslim community, regardless of where former European empires had drawn the modern national borders.

This is no different than the many American Christians, Jews, and, yes, Muslims, from Florida, Texas, Colorado and California who felt the need to join the American armed forces after the September 11th attacks against far-away New York and Washington, D.C., to defend their country from the terrorist enemy.

It is true that al Qaeda infuses their message with theology, citing scriptures and religious leaders to justify their positions and actions. It makes sense that those most committed to literalistic interpretations of scripture and belief in the afterlife might be some of the first to sign up to fight. But there is no reason to suppose this is unique to Christians, Jews or Muslims.

Abu Musab al Zarqawi, the first leader of al Qaeda in Iraq, and his successors in the Islamic State that grew out of it have had a far more apocalyptic religious view. They preach about the end of the world and an ideology that holds virtually genocidal views toward Shi'ites and other supposed heretics. And they act on them, ruthlessly massacring and enslaving minority civilians in areas where they have conquered. However, in practice, even the brutally sectarian Islamic State of Iraq and Syria (ISIS) — whose leadership was composed mostly of former Iraqi Ba'athist military officers and local insurgent leaders from the second Iraq war — fights first and foremost for territory here on Earth.

Of course, when it comes to religious doctrines, there is always a mix of charlatans and true believers among the leaders of the groups espousing them. Certainly, many al Qaeda and ISIS members have a deep devotion to their religion and various political doctrines about their people's place in the world. But it is the destabilizing chaos of war that makes the radical sidewalk preacher who calls for violence seem like he must be something other than a raving nut. American interventionists and the al Qaeda terrorists empower each other. Each group of radicals needs the violent chaos their enemies create to rally populations and portray themselves as the leaders of the new defensive war they are being forced to fight.

This is where the hawks on both sides benefit from highlighting the worst aspects of the other. ISIS complains about what they call the "Gray Zone," otherwise known as the modern West, where people's respect for individual rights — especially freedom of religion — allows millions of Muslims to live harmoniously among those of different faiths. This peaceful coexistence is anathema to the terrorist leaders. They explicitly order their followers to commit attacks against Western targets for the very purpose of forcing our governments to overreact — to clampdown upon and alienate Muslims in our societies where they have assimilated relatively well, especially in the United States.

It is unfortunate so many American hawks have found reason to abet such fringe criminals and murderers as al Qaeda and ISIS, legitimizing their claims to represent the true faith in their careless attempt to blame Islam for our terrorism problem. This has virtually criminalized the beliefs of more than a billion people in the minds of many in the West, possibly leading us further down the path to even worse conflict.

When attacks in the West occur, we always hear the hawks' refrain, "Where are the moderate Muslims denouncing this terrorism?" Yet, when Muslim leaders do denounce violence and terrorism, the major television media mostly ignore it, helping perpetuate the idea that terrorist violence has their broad support when, in fact, it does not.

According to former CIA counter-terrorism analyst Cynthia Storer, the agency's own internal "framework" for understanding what drives people to commit acts of terrorism is not religion-based at all but is instead political and universal. Terrorism is not about Islam; it is about virtually powerless people reacting — striking back — against governments they perceive to be oppressing them, governments they have cause to believe can never be reformed peacefully.

America's mission in the Middle East has never really been to "fight them over there, so we don't have to fight them here," but instead, in the words of the policymakers themselves, to achieve and maintain global dominance. Terrorism? Well, that is just a minor side effect — "a small price to pay for being a Superpower," as policy planners for the Joint Chiefs of Staff at the Pentagon were repeatedly heard to say by a "very senior" special operations commander in the 1990s. Fighting against terrorism then becomes a convenient cover for the further escalation of the kinds of interventionist policies that created the problem in the first place.

This was the dynamic bin Laden was betting on — that the American government was looking for and willing to exploit any excuse to expand its Middle Eastern empire, and that in doing so, it would sow the seeds of its own demise. This, all while helping to prepare the field for the growth of an eventual bin Ladenite Islamist state to dominate the region in the future.

As veteran intelligence beat reporter James Bamford explained,

> [Bin Laden's partner] Ayman al-Zawahiri argued that al Qaeda should bring the war to "the distant enemy" in order to provoke the Americans to strike back and "personally wage the battle against Muslims." It was that battle that bin Laden and Zawahiri wanted to spark [with their attacks on U.S. targets]. As they made clear in their declaration of war "against Jews and Crusaders," they believed that the United States and Israel had been waging war against Muslims for decades. Now their hope was to draw Americans into a desert Vietnam, with bin Laden in the role of North Vietnamese president Ho Chi Minh.

The CIA's Afghan Army

This "Vietnam trap" bin Laden was planning for the United States was not so original a concept. In fact, it is how Osama bin Laden ended up in Afghanistan in the first place. President Jimmy Carter's National Security Advisor, Zbigniew Brzezinski, boasted that when the Soviet Union invaded Afghanistan on December 24, 1979, he sent a memo to the boss: "We now have the opportunity of giving to the USSR its Vietnam war."

By 1979, "Vietnam" had already become a shorthand term for a bloody, no-win, far-flung quagmire that breaks the military and treasury, causes terrible disruptions to society back home and that everyone wishes had never happened. Badly burned by the experience, the American people were even said by the political establishment to have come down with the lamented "Vietnam Syndrome" — such a severe reluctance to engage in any further overseas military conflicts that it amounted to a form of mental illness. If such a disaster had been inflicted on the American people by previous administrations, the thinking went, perhaps rather than "containing" communism, the U.S. could instead bait it into over-expansion to inflict similar "self"-destruction on the Soviets. As Brzezinski and CIA officials like former director Robert Gates have boasted, Carter signed a finding — an order to the CIA — on July 3, 1979, authorizing the beginning of covert CIA aid to the Afghan mujahideen holy warriors in order to provoke the very invasion by the USSR that Carter later claimed necessitated U.S. intervention there.

Experts like Eric Margolis and Andrei Sakharov doubted that the American support really made the difference in the USSR's decision to invade. In fact, the Soviet's own Afghan puppet dictator, Hafizullah Amin, was destabilizing the country and provoking civil war. As soon as the Soviets invaded, the first thing the KGB did was shoot Amin and replace him.

Regardless, the Carter and then Ronald Reagan administrations, along with their Saudi and Pakistani allies, lent massive financial and material support to the mujahideen resistance fighters before and after the invasion. These included Afghans as well as the "International Islamic Brigades," composed of thousands of so-called "Arab-Afghan" fighters from across the Middle East, and even from America, who were sent by their governments to wage a holy war against the Communists' invasion of Muslim land. The U.S. eventually even provided advanced, guided, shoulder-fired, surface-to-air "Stinger" missiles, which helped the Afghan resistance level the fight against the attack helicopters of the technologically sophisticated Soviet air forces. President Reagan met and had his picture taken with mujahideen leaders in the White House's Oval Office. Hollywood even released the movie *Rambo III* in 1988 to explain the supposedly covert, but widely known, operation to the American people. In the film, the protagonist's mentor, Colonel Trautman, baits his KGB captor:

> There won't be a [Soviet] victory. Every day, your war machines lose ground to a bunch of poorly armed, poorly equipped freedom fighters. The fact is that you underestimated your competition. If you'd studied your history, you'd know that these people have never given up to anyone. They'd rather die than be slaves to an invading army. You can't defeat a people like that. We tried; we already had our Vietnam! Now you're going to have yours.

Sylvester Stallone's John Rambo, and therefore all right-thinking American patriots, revered the mujahideen for their dedication to their religious beliefs and heroic, selfless bravery in defending their land and people from foreign invasion.

The U.S. and Saudi Arabia, which agreed to match U.S. appropriations, contributed at least four billion dollars each to the operation. As many as 100,000 foreign fighters traveled to Afghanistan over the decade to join the cause.

The CIA, Saudi General Intelligence Directorate (GID) and Pakistan's Inter-Services Intelligence (ISI) directed money to the worst Afghan factions, such as that led by notorious warlords Gulbuddin Hekmatyar and

Jalaluddin Haqqani. In Egypt in 1980, U.S. Special Forces even trained them in terrorist tactics such as how to make and deploy car bombs. Some were brought to America and trained by the Green Berets at Camp Peary and Fort A.P. Hill in Virginia and another secret camp at Harvey Point, North Carolina. Navy SEALs also participated in training Afghan fighters at Fort A.P. Hill and Fort Pickett, Virginia. As John Cooley wrote in the book *Unholy Wars: Afghanistan, America and International Terrorism*, training

> included the use of sophisticated fuses, timers and explosives, automatic weapons with armor-piercing ammunition, remote-control devices for triggering mines and bombs (later used in the volunteer's home countries and against the Israelis in occupied Arab territory such as in southern Lebanon) ... strategic sabotage ... demolition and arson.

The project worked even better than its authors had anticipated. Neoconservative policy adviser Zalmay Khalilzad, then working under Paul Wolfowitz in the Defense Department, later wrote in the *Washington Post* that their "strangulation strategy" was only meant to increase the costs of the Soviet war in Afghanistan. They had not anticipated that they would lose outright. The mujahideen did deserve some credit. Communism was slowly falling apart due to the simple laws of economics. But the Americans, Saudis, Pakistanis and mujahideen — mostly the Afghans, but also the Arab and other foreign fighters — not only won the war, but also helped destabilize and further bankrupt the ramshackle Soviet empire, setting it up to be finished off entirely by the oil price crash of the late 1980s. At least that was what the Reagan Republicans and, more importantly, the Arab-Afghan mujahideen believed; with faith in God and their AK-47s, they had brought down the mighty USSR, one of the most powerful empires in history.

The Iranian Revolution

The other great crisis of 1979 was the Shi'ite Islamist-led revolution in Iran and its break from the United States. The CIA and State Departments long-ago released their archives admitting that the real story began much earlier, in 1953, when the American CIA and their partners in Britain's MI-6 overthrew the left-leaning, democratically elected government of Prime Minister Mohammed Mossadegh in Tehran after it had threatened to take control of British oil interests there. The U.S. then reinstalled and made an alliance with the dictator, the Shah, Mohammad Reza Pahlavi, helping to keep his brutal authoritarian dictatorship in power for another 26 years. It seemed like a great idea to the Eisenhower administration at the time, though it created the circumstances for "blowback" against the United States in the future. We are still dealing with the aftermath.

In fact, CIA analyst Donald Wilber coined the phrase *blowback* in a secret 1954 after-action report about the Iran coup. He advised, "Possibilities of blowback against the United States should always be in the back of the minds of all CIA officers involved in this type of operation."

Ironically, as Robert Dreyfuss shows in his book *Devil's Game: How the U.S. Helped Unleash Fundamentalist Islam*, the Americans had previously supported Mosaddegh's rise to power, hoping they could coax him away from the British and into the U.S. orbit before they turned on him after his assertion of independence in 1953.

The Americans may have supported the Shah, but the people of Iran hated him. In late 1978 through early 1979, a massive popular revolution broke out, leading to the overthrow of the dictatorship and allowing the Shi'ite Ayatollahs to come to power. They established the Islamic Republic in February 1979.

An often-neglected part of the story is that the Carter administration, on advice from the CIA and State Department, had given the go-ahead to the French to let the exiled Ayatollah Khomeini fly home from Paris to Iran to inherit the revolution. They considered him an old ally from back in 1953 when he had been part of a group of conservative Iranian clerics who had led protests against then-Prime Minister Mosaddegh, helping to soften up his government for the coup to reinstall the Shah. Ambassador William Sullivan had even compared Khomeini to India's Mahatma Gandhi. Neoconservative policy adviser Zalmay Khalilzad was inspired by the Iranian revolution, saying "the Khomeini regime also poses risks to the Soviets. The change of regime has encouraged similar movements in Iraq and Afghanistan."

The Carter administration, aware that the Shah was dying of cancer and judging that his regime could not survive without him, instructed the Iranian government to prepare for Khomeini's return, a move that ensured the success of the revolution and the Ayatollah's assumption of power.

Despite the errors of popular memory which blur these events together, the real crisis did not begin until nine months later, in November 1979, when riots broke out over Carter's decision to allow the exiled Shah into the U.S. for medical treatment against the advice of the U.S. embassy in Tehran. The Iranian people interpreted this as a signal that there would be a coup or a counter-revolution to reinstall him, which led to the riots and the seizing of the hostages at the embassy, complete with demands by the students that the U.S. turn the Shah over to them. That infamous hostage crisis became the foundation for the enmity between Iran and the United States ever since.

But it had been possible for the Americans to get along with the new Iranian revolutionary regime. The U.S. and Iran both saw the necessity of continued relations, mostly out of fear of what the USSR would do. After the February revolution, but before the November hostage crisis, the U.S. continued to work with the Iranians. The CIA passed them intelligence warnings about Saddam Hussein's intentions, the situation in Afghanistan and possible threats to Iran from the Russians.

A reporter brought up America's by then-publicly exposed 1953 Iranian coup to Carter in the context of the 1979 revolution and the related U.S. embassy staff hostage crisis. Carter replied that the 26-year-old CIA overthrow and installation of the dictatorship, which had only just come to an end, was "ancient history," and that "I don't think it's appropriate or helpful for me to go into the propriety of something that happened 30 years ago."

If the Iranian mullahs had overthrown President Bill Clinton a quarter-century ago, and replaced him with their hand-picked dictator, would we be used to it by now? To this day, Americans still cannot get over the Iranians' overthrow of the dictator our government had no right to install over them in their own country now more than 40 years ago. One might guess we would take an Ayatollah-installed autocrat in power on our shores much worse even than that. In any case, the Iranians were not over it when our government did it to them, even — or especially — after 26 years.

Nor did the Americans ever forgive the Iranians for their revolution. Since some of their friends and colleagues had been taken hostage in the crisis, the attitude of much of the State Department has remained solidly anti-Iranian in the decades since. Though the Reagan administration maintained a covert relationship with Iran through the 1980s, their overall policy was still based on reaction against Iran's revolution and declaration of independence from the United States.

The Carter Doctrine

After the disaster of the Iranian hostage crisis and the Soviet invasion of Afghanistan, President Carter decided there was nothing else to do but escalate. So he declared in his 1980 State of the Union Address that the nations of the "Persian Gulf region," which could be said to include the regimes of all the kings, emirs, sultans and sheikhs of Arabia would now be considered under the full protection of the United States. He added that any "attempt by any outside force to gain control of the Persian Gulf region will be regarded as an assault on the vital interests of the United States of America," which would be "repelled by any means necessary, including military force." Carter had deliberately attempted to provoke the Soviets to invade Afghanistan. After they did, Carter's team panicked, fearing the USSR would invade newly destabilized Iran next. From there, they could seek to dominate the Persian Gulf and its massive oil resources. The Americans would lose an important region to Soviet control. The new doctrine was meant to warn the USSR not to try it.

Even though America already had an alliance with the Saudis since Franklin Roosevelt's meeting with Ibn Saud in 1945 at the close of World War II, which was expanded upon by President Dwight Eisenhower in 1957, the Carter Doctrine was a claim of permanent American supremacy in the Persian Gulf. From then on, it would be considered an American lake. In practice, what it meant was the expansion of U.S. military bases in Saudi Arabia, Oman, Bahrain, and Qatar. This included what in the Reagan years was called "overbuilding and overstocking." This was when they pretended that bases were only full of U.S. troops because the Saudis had bought so much equipment, they needed the Americans to install and maintain it, when in reality that was just a cover story for the presence of American bases. This may have been a clever enough deception for the U.S. media, but it certainly did not fool the Saudi population.

Carter's government also established the new Rapid Deployment Force, which later grew into the military's Central Command (CENTCOM). This reaction made sense in terms of American presidential politics, as an attempt to look tough after these two embarrassing foreign policy setbacks, but it did not work. Carter was soundly defeated in 1980 anyway.

But ever since his administration declared it so, U.S. strategy has been that America absolutely must maintain its position as the dominant power in the Middle East, forever, or else someone else might take it. And then what? What harm do the American people face if our government loses its position of power and influence thousands of miles away? They rarely explain beyond mumbling vague slogans about the "values-based liberal world order" or sometimes the end of American access to Middle Eastern oil. As the first President Bush put it, "our jobs" and "our way of life" were on the line in the fight for control of Kuwait. That this makes no economic sense whatsoever apparently amounts to no objection at all.

The U.S. spends trillions more dollars "securing" Middle Eastern oil resources than the whole country spends on Middle Eastern oil. Some individual companies gain, but at the expense of the American taxpayer and energy consumer. The reality is that no matter who runs what regime in the Middle East, their first order of business must always be to provide security and stability for those who produce and export the oil. At one point, even Osama bin Laden joked to journalist Abdel Bari Atwan that "we are not going to drink it," and therefore oil would always be for sale on the world market even if the head terrorist himself ruled all of Arabia. Roger Stern, an economic geographer at Princeton University, published a study in 2010 which determined the U.S. had "misallocated" $8 trillion between 1976–2007 protecting the sea lanes in and out of the Persian Gulf when its safe transport was never really under threat. Former Reagan-era budget director David Stockman has emphasized time and again that "It doesn't matter who controls the oilfields ... the only effective cure for high oil prices is the free market. ... There is no economic case whatsoever for Washington's massive military presence in the Middle East."

American dominance of Middle Eastern oil is more about military imperatives, such as the ability to deny access to other major powers in a crisis or war, or political imperatives such as maintaining Saudi investments in U.S. government debt. These interests have much more to do with the policy than keeping prices low for U.S. consumers or even profits high for connected U.S. corporations. Ultimately, the American people get little out of the arrangement other than negative consequences.

The Iran-Iraq War

Evidently, the Carter administration was not opposed to invasions of revolutionary Iran in principle. They just preferred to see U.S. ally Saddam Hussein, the new dictator of Iraq, do it instead of the Russians. As journalist Robert Parry showed, after spending the better part of a year passing intelligence to the new Islamic Republic about the Iraqi threat, once the hostage crisis broke out, Carter turned around and gave Hussein the green light to attack.

Just after the Republicans took office in 1981, Ronald Reagan's secretary of state, Alexander Haig went to visit the Saudi Prince Fahd. The prince informed Haig that Jimmy Carter had a year earlier told him to forward on the go-ahead to Saddam Hussein to invade Iran in order to try to overthrow the new Shi'ite revolutionary regime. Haig evidently told Reagan, "It was also interesting to confirm that President Carter gave the Iraqis a green light to launch the war against Iran through Fahd."

As author Christopher Davidson shows in his book *Shadow Wars*, the U.S. had quite a long and complicated relationship with Saddam Hussein, dating back to his CIA-backed 1959 failed assassination attempt against Abd al-Karim Qasim, who had overthrown the old British-installed Hashemite King Faisal the year before. After the successful Ba'athist coup of 1963, Hussein was brought back from exile in Egypt and quickly became the head of the secret police, relying on CIA-supplied lists of suspected communists, ambitious officers and other troublesome individuals to be rounded up and murdered by the thousands.

The Ba'athists themselves were then overthrown within a year by another group of military officers but returned in 1968 with the American CIA again backing their counter-revolt. In 1979, Hussein pushed then-Iraqi President Hassan al-Bakr aside in his own violent coup, declared himself president and found common cause with the Americans and Saudis against the new Shi'ite revolution in Iran. Journalists Richard Sale and Patrick Cockburn have also written about this history in some detail, as has former National Security Council staffer and academic historian Roger Morris.

The Iranian Revolution was seen as a danger by Iraq, where Hussein's 20 percent Sunni Arab minority dominated the authoritarian, but secular-oriented Ba'ath Party government which ruled over the 60 percent super-majority Shi'ite Arabs (as well as another 20 percent Kurdish minority). The Shi'ites were predominant in the Iraqi south and east, much of the land bordering Iran. Concerned that the Iraqi Shi'ites might choose to side with their religious sect over their ethnic and national identities — some Shi'ite groups in Iraq were already celebrating the revolution — Saddam Hussein attempted to preempt the danger by conscripting them and sending them to war against Iran instead.

Iran's revolution represented a threat in the eyes of Saudi Arabia as well, where again the Shi'ites, in this case a small, powerless minority, happened to live on top of all the good oil deposits in the northeast of that country, the land almost adjacent to Iran. The Saudi royals quickly lined up behind the Iraqi effort. Kuwait and the United Arab Emirates also lent their support.

Hussein thought it would be a simple task to topple the mullahs' fragile new regime. The plan backfired. Despite all their physical losses, the new Iranian government's legitimacy was solidified by the public's reaction to Iraq's attack, and they were able to fend off the invasion.

Instead, the Iranians launched a massive counterattack that set the Iraqis back into their own territory, and the terrible, decade-long World War I-style permanent stalemate slaughter was underway. As the *New York Times* noted, since the Iraqis had bought so much equipment from the Soviet Union in decades past, "the war with Iran, particularly in its early phase, largely pitted Soviet arms wielded by [U.S.-backed] Iraq against the American weapons of the Iranian forces."

The incoming Reagan administration eagerly picked up Carter's policy, which by then had already failed, and ran with it. They sent Hussein's Iraq ever-larger amounts of money and intelligence and allowed regional allies Jordan, Saudi Arabia and Kuwait to sell Hussein American weapons. If the Ayatollah could not be defeated, he could at least be bled. A now-famous 1983 photograph and video clip shows one of then-Special Emissary Donald Rumsfeld's meetings with Hussein. His mission was to reopen official relations, share intelligence and provide nearly a billion dollars for the fight against Iran. This came after President Reagan's November 1983 National Security Decision Directive 114, which stated the United States government would do "whatever was necessary and legal" to prevent Iraq from losing the war with Iran.

For years Reagan's government backed Hussein, with the U.S. military and CIA even providing the Iraqis with satellite information to help them better target Iranian troops in the field with mustard and nerve gasses such as sarin and tabun. Tens of thousands of Iranian conscripts were killed by these chemical weapons. As even semi-official National Security State spokesman Shane Harris reported in *Foreign Policy*, CIA documents "are tantamount to an official American admission of complicity in some of the most gruesome chemical weapons attacks ever launched." The U.S. government looked the other way when American and western European companies sold necessary manufacturing facilities, precursor chemicals and germs for weapons to Iraq. As journalist Christopher Marquis showed, they also made it clear to the Iraqis that any public U.S. condemnations of their unconventional weapons use were strictly formalities, not to be considered prohibitive in any way.

Hussein attacked the Iraqi Kurds with these chemical weapons in the deadly Anfal Campaign of 1986–1989, including in the town of Halabja in 1988, which the Reagan administration initially tried to blame on Iran.

With their governments' approval, western corporations also helped build Iraq's 1980s-era rudimentary nuclear weapons program. The head of an Atlanta bank that made more than five billion dollars in U.S. government-backed "agricultural loans" to the Iraqi war effort credibly claimed when prosecuted in the "Iraq-gate" scandal that the project was approved by the governments of the United States, Britain and Italy.

The Reagan administration continued increasing support for Iraq when it appeared Iran was winning, but would turn around and authorize increased Israeli support for Iran when Iraq seemed to be gaining the upper hand. Each side would use its new equipment to improve its position, thus necessitating the next stage of intervention for the other side.

American hawks demonizing Iran these days have to go back to 1983 to say that Iran has attacked the United States, referring to the suicide bombing of the U.S. Marine barracks in Beirut, Lebanon. President Reagan sold Iran missiles just two years after that, but we are still supposed to think of this as some kind of unforgivable act that precludes our side from ever considering the Iranians as people to be dealt with in anything other than a violent or threatening manner almost 40 years later.

That attack is also taken as proof of Iranian religious irrationality and determination to provoke a violent conflict with the United States. But it has been since 1983, when Shi'ite militias — yes, backed by Iran — committed that attack. The American marines were combat forces intervening in a foreign conflict where they did not belong. The bombing itself was retaliation for the shelling, at Israeli instigation, of Beirut neighborhoods by the battleship *USS New Jersey*, which accomplished nothing but the killing of innocent people.

Of course, none of this justified the attack, but the proper context shows that it was not really terrorism, but a military attack against a military target. It was a tragedy, but it does not seem fair that the Americans get to hold the Iranians forever guilty for this attack on U.S. marines when in 1989 the U.S. shot down an Iranian civilian airliner over the Persian Gulf, mistaking it for an F-14 fighter that the U.S. had sold to them in the 1970s. They killed 290 people, and never apologized for it, much less for supporting Saddam Hussein's brutal eight-year war against their country.

President George H.W. Bush, who had been vice president under Ronald Reagan, later told the *Los Angeles Times*, "There was a lot of support at the time for Iraq as a balance to a much more aggressive Iran under Khomeini. So that was part of the policy of the Reagan administration. I was very proud to support that."

The regime change failed. As many as half a million people were killed on both sides of the eight-year war. But the outbreak of revolutionary Shi'ite Islam had been contained.

Iraq War I

When the bankrupt Soviet empire withdrew from Afghanistan and began disintegrating in 1989, Washington's war hawks, far from taking the lesson they had just helped to inflict to heart or running out of reasons for maintaining an empire, saw only opportunity. As President Bush put it, this was the dawn of the New World Order: "What we say goes."

So, they found a reason.

On July 25, 1990, Iraqi dictator Saddam Hussein summoned the American ambassador, April Glaspie, to discuss his worsening conflict with Kuwait over their overproduction of oil from the shared Rumaila oil field straddling the border between the two countries. Hussein explained to the ambassador that Iraq was $40 billion in debt and was going bankrupt from the cost of the war against Iran. The price of oil was so low that he saw no way repay the Kuwaitis, Saudis and Emirates the money Iraq had borrowed from them to pay for the war — a war which Hussein saw as being fought by Iraq partly on behalf of those kingdoms in the first place. On top of that, he accused the Kuwaitis of deliberately breaking their already-high OPEC oil cartel production quotas and agreements with Iraq over the shared field and of being difficult and grossly insulting and avoiding discussing these problems with his diplomats.

If the administration had plotted to set up Hussein and snare him in a trap in the first place, it would probably not have looked much different than what actually took place. Still, the simplest interpretation is that there was a massive failure to coordinate between the various U.S. government departments. Even though the Defense Intelligence Agency was warning that Hussein was "not bluffing," when it came to his threats against Kuwait, the State Department was signaling at least a yellow light to Iraq to proceed. Meanwhile, the CIA and military's Central Command decided to encourage the Kuwaitis to continue to take an intransigent stance against Iraq's demands for new negotiations. Secretary of Defense Dick Cheney and Undersecretary for Policy Wolfowitz, back at the Pentagon, had given a public warning to Iraq, claiming the U.S. was obligated to defend Kuwait. But their spokesman Pete Williams had walked it back. The darker hypothesis that this divided response was a deliberate trap set for Hussein does not seem to hold up, but as a prominent Kuwaiti businessman explained, "I think that if the Americans had not pushed, the royal family would never have taken the steps that it did to provoke Saddam."

Hussein clearly expressed desperation at the situation and made repeated, barely veiled threats of a military response. While Glaspie did express "concern" about Iraqi troops' movement toward the Kuwaiti border, she most certainly did not make it clear that the U.S. was opposed to any move against Kuwait or that they would do anything about it. It is much more likely the Iraqis thought Glaspie was indicating that the U.S. would instead look the other way.

As foreign policy analyst Stephen M. Walt put it,

> Even Glaspie's statement that President Bush is deeply interested in peace and stability in the Gulf can be read as something of a green light. If the president says he wants closer relations with Iraq but doesn't want war in the Gulf, might Saddam have seen that as suggesting that the United States wasn't about to fight to preserve Kuwaiti sovereignty? Remember: Saddam wasn't intending to fight a major war against Kuwait; he was just planning a *coup de main* [a single successful surprise attack]. Based on Glaspie's remarks, he might easily have concluded that Washington would ultimately acquiesce — however reluctantly — to his *fait accompli*.

Other statements made by State Department officials Margaret Tutwiler and John Kelly late that July expressed disinterest by the United States in the results of the crisis between Iraq and Kuwait and apparently also helped convince Hussein that he had received tacit permission to occupy Kuwait's northern oilfields, if not the entire country. Assistant Secretary of State John Kelly had testified before the House of Representatives in answer to a question about the Iraq dispute that "We don't have any defense treaty with the Gulf States. That's clear."

Joseph Wilson, the ambassador to Kuwait during the crisis, later wrote that "Despite the qualifiers that Kelly put into place about America's preference for peaceful solutions to disputes, the only thing the Iraqi regime heard was that we had no legal obligation or even any mechanism to react to an invasion. That had far more effect than anything April Glaspie may or may not have said in her meeting with Saddam Hussein."

Upon reading the dispatches from Ambassador Glaspie, Wolfowitz and some others at the Pentagon attempted to intervene and stop the delivery of a message to Saddam Hussein from President Bush on July 28, that the Defense officials worried was too conciliatory. After the message was delivered anyway, some of the hawks reportedly tried to have another, more strongly worded statement sent. But by then, it was too late.

In the official State Department notes, we see Ambassador Glaspie's staff's version of part of the discussion which Hussein claimed to interpret as permission to invade and occupy Kuwait's northern oil fields:

> Note: On the border question, Saddam referred to the 1961 agreement and a "line of patrol" it had established. The Kuwaitis, he said, had told [Egyptian leader Hosni] Mubarak Iraq was 20 Kilometers "in front" of this line. The Ambassador said that she had served in Kuwait 20 years before; then as now, we took no position on these Arab affairs.

The version released by the Iraqi government has Glaspie telling Hussein, "We have no opinion on your Arab-Arab conflicts, such as your dispute with Kuwait. Secretary [of State James] Baker has directed me to emphasize the instruction, first given to Iraq in the 1960s, that the Kuwait issue is not associated with America."

Glaspie later told the *New York Times*, "Obviously, I didn't think — and nobody else did — that the Iraqis were going to take all of Kuwait." Other "senior officials," possibly basing their thinking on an estimate from the Defense Intelligence Agency who guessed that Iraq would occupy just one oil field, confirmed that the administration thought Iraq would stop at a "limited invasion," that they "could live with." As another Bush administration official confirmed, "The crucial factor in determining the American response was not the reality but the extent of the invasion."

Hussein had plenty of reason to think that Bush would let him get away with it. Besides the State Department's conciliatory statements, his government had continued the Carter and Reagan administrations' policy of support for the Iraqi regime with money and weapons even after their war against Iran had ended. In fact, it lasted all the way up until the time of the invasion of Kuwait, as was later shown in the "Iraq-gate" scandal.

After Iraq invaded Kuwait on August 2, and occupied the entire country, the Bush Sr. administration still did not react harshly — possibly indicating that they still meant to let the invasion slide. That day, after the administration discussed embargoes on Iraqi and Kuwaiti oil, the meeting ended with Powell saying they should just draw the line at Saudi Arabia. Bush himself initially said he was "not contemplating" a military response. It was only after British Prime Minister Margaret Thatcher "performed a successful backbone transplant" on the president that he changed his mind. She warned Bush against "going wobbly" on August 3. H.W. Bush then sided with the hawks in his administration and chose to embark on the next chapter of mass violence in the Middle East to try to clean up the problems created by the last one.

The British had much more at stake in Kuwait than the United States did. They were heavily invested in Kuwaiti oil companies, and the Kuwaiti state in return held billions of dollars' worth of British government debt.

Economist Murray N. Rothbard pointed to the heavy influence of former Secretary of State Henry Kissinger — a long-time representative of Rockefeller family oil interests, which were extensive in Saudi Arabia. He concluded that the war was being waged not to protect the global oil supply, but only the profits of powerful politically connected companies' interests, at the expense of the rest of the country.

Though Secretary Baker's law firm later represented many of these same interests, he made it clear in multiple private conversations with later counter-terrorism chief Richard Clarke that he would not have launched Iraq War I at all if it had been his shot to call.

But it was Bush's decision. So, America's friend became its enemy.

And they lied. The administration pushed a hoax that a Kuwaiti nurse witnessed Iraqi soldiers murdering premature babies for their incubators in Kuwaiti hospitals and also claimed the Iraqis were lining up their army on the Saudi border in preparation for an attack on their capital city, Riyadh. This propaganda was made to break the American people's reluctance to go to war, their latent, so-called "Vietnam Syndrome," and scare the Saudi King into allowing the attack to be waged from Arabian soil.

In fact, the babies-thrown-from-incubators story was cooked up by a New York public relations firm called Hill and Knowlton, which was run by President Bush's former Chief of Staff from the Reagan years, Craig Fuller. This lie was presented in congressional hearings by the daughter of the Kuwaiti ambassador, who was not a nurse, had no ties to the hospital and had not even been in the country during the invasion. President Bush and other administration officials endlessly repeated this lie in the media to portray the Iraqis as rampaging, inhuman monsters, waging a total war to "dismantle" Kuwait.

The Bush administration's claim that there were 250,000 Iraqi troops and 1,500 tanks lining up on the Saudi border, preparing to conquer Riyadh and threaten global access to Gulf oil supplies was also a lie, as shown when the *St. Petersburg* (Florida) *Times* obtained Soviet satellite photos while attempting to confirm the story was true. Publishing ten days before the start of the war, the *Times* offered the story to the Associated Press, Scripps-Howard, CNN and other news services, but they all refused to run it.

The Bush Sr. administration also lied when they portrayed Iraq as a nuclear weapons threat to the United States. As Christopher Lane explained in *The Atlantic* a few months after the war:

> As early as last August [1990] conservative and neoconservative war hawks such as Frank Gaffney, Jr., Henry Kissinger, Richard Perle, A.M. Rosenthal, William Safire, and the *Wall Street Journal* claimed that smashing Iraq's military potential and destroying its capacity to develop nuclear weapons was America's overriding objective in the Gulf. Liberal supporters of Bush's policy also embraced the contention that the potential Iraqi nuclear threat to the United States was, as *The New Republic* put it, "the real reason there needs to be war against Iraq."

> The administration apparently discovered the Iraqi nuclear threat when it read the results of a *New York Times*/CBS poll last November which suggested that of all the reasons offered as justification for fighting Iraq, the only one resonating with the American public was the need to keep Saddam Hussein's finger off the nuclear trigger. Within days Bush was warning that Iraq was only a few months away from detonating a crude nuclear device and that the United States itself could be imperiled.

It turns out Iraq did have a nuclear weapons program, discovered in the aftermath of the war. But the hawks did not know that. They had only been bluffing, and the Hussein regime was still a long way from achieving a weapons capability. Even that was a reaction to the badly weighed Israeli decision to bomb their above-board Osirak nuclear plant in June 1981. Hussein had taken Iraq's civilian, internationally "safeguarded" nuclear program underground and turned it towards weapons production in response to Israel's airstrikes.

The Bush Sr. administration also lied that the war could not be avoided, even on America's terms. As soon as he realized how negative the Americans' reaction had been to the invasion, Hussein started to back down, promising not to invade Saudi Arabia and offering to negotiate.

Throughout the second half of 1990, Hussein tried to find a face-saving way to negotiate his withdrawal, but the U.S. government refused even to try.

Iraq was seeking only access to two small, uninhabited islands, Bubiyan and Warbah, in the Persian Gulf and a promise to negotiate over the still-disputed location of the Iraq-Kuwait border.

Even the United Nations resolution the U.S. had supported called for future negotiations over the border. But just a few days later, that "serious" and "negotiable" proposal was considered out of the question. The administration took the hard line on "unconditional withdrawal," with the American people none the wiser since the rest of the media went along with the government in ignoring the story.

Professor Noam Chomsky kept note of some of the different opportunities to negotiate an end to Iraq's occupation of Kuwait in the second half of 1990. They were

> [t]he August 12 Iraqi proposal concerning [U.S.] withdrawal from all occupied Arab lands; the August 19 proposal that the status of Kuwait be settled by the Arab states alone; the August 23 offer published by *Newsday*, and a "similar offer" ... that the *Times* kept under wraps at the same time; and the reported Jordanian and PLO proposals. Others continued to surface, receiving similar treatment. The business pages of the *New York Times* and *Wall Street Journal* reported a "near-panic of stock buying late in the day" on December 4, after a British TV report of an Iraqi offer to withdraw from Kuwait apart from the Rumaila oil fields, with no other conditions except Kuwaiti agreement to discuss a lease of the two Gulf islands after the withdrawal. Wire services carried the story, but not the news sections. News reports did, however, express uneasiness that proposed discussions with Iraq (actually, delivery of an ultimatum, according to the White House) "might encourage some European partners to launch unhelpful peace feelers."

Bush Sr. and his then-national security adviser Brent Scowcroft later wrote in their joint memoir that Soviet Foreign Minister Eduard Shevardnadze brought word of Saddam's repeated offer to withdraw in exchange for the concessions of control over the Rumaila oil fields and access to Bubiyan and Warbah. Bush insisted that Iraq would spin even these "face-savers" as "rewards," and that could not be tolerated.

But Hussein had a real reason to need to save face besides his ego. If he gave in too easily, the resulting perception of weakness on his part could lead to a coup against him from inside his own military.

At the beginning of January 1991, Saddam Hussein tried one last time to avoid war. As *Newsday* reported, the new offer included only vague conditions that Israeli withdrawal from the occupied territories be negotiated at some point in the future and that American and other foreign troops would withdraw from the region. Both Iraqi demands were so abstract they amounted to barely face-saving requests requiring no actual results. But the Americans insisted that there be "no linkage" between Iraq's occupation of Kuwait and any other issue.

To knowledgeable observers at the time, such as President Reagan's former secretary of the Navy and later-Senator Jim Webb, it was apparent Bush had no intention of following through with diplomacy. He wrote that "the supposed willingness to negotiate an Iraqi withdrawal from Kuwait was little more than veneer, a way to spin up the public's emotions and prepare the nation for a war the administration had already decided to fight."

By obscuring and burying the Iraqis' motives and pretending the invasion was just about abject conquest, instead of acknowledging the complicated story behind Iraq's war debts and shared oil wells, Hussein was then easily depicted as "So-damn Insane," a raving madman who could not be "appeased," only destroyed. The lie used on the Saudi King that Saddam's tanks were preparing to roll further south down to Riyadh was an effective part of the narrative inflicted on the American people as well. President Bush routinely compared Saddam Hussein to Germany's Nazi dictator Adolf Hitler, bent on regional and then even global domination. The American people's entire "way of life" was threatened, he claimed.

They launched a massive propaganda campaign. Americans were encouraged to tie yellow ribbons around every tree and light pole to show that their thoughts were with the troops. Brand new country music songs about the war were quickly produced and put on the radio. The excitement of the build-up and launch of the war was made for TV. As the great American comedian and social critic George Carlin said, "It was the first war that was on every channel — plus cable!" The message was that violence is usually wrong, but in this case, the president says it is all for a good cause, so go ahead and indulge your bloodlust. Almost all prominent political leaders in Washington got on board for the war. As Webb put it, "Many who had supported Vietnam were looking for a war to win. Many who had opposed it were looking for a war to support." Kuwait was almost irrelevant. This was about us.

The war itself, "Operation Desert Storm," launched January 16, 1991, was relatively short and seemingly decisive use of the American superpower's stealthy space-age technology against the aging Soviet-supplied army of the Iraqis. The U.S. quickly smashed their armor and infantry.

The U.S. military initially estimated 100,000 Iraqis were killed in the war, though they later revised these numbers downward. Still, tens of thousands were killed, including during the infamous moral if not legal war crime of the slaughter of thousands of Iraqi conscripts retreating from Kuwait on what later became known as the "Highway(s) of Death" and the so-called "'Battle' of Rumaila."

Journalist Patrick J. Sloyan estimated that thousands of Iraqi troops were buried alive in their trenches by U.S. tanks mounted with plows to drive by and entomb their victims. These tanks were then followed by Bradley Fighting Vehicles, with the gunners pumping the dying full of machine-gun bullets.

The Red Cross estimated that thousands of Iraqi civilians were killed as well. Much of the country's infrastructure was also destroyed. As the leaders of the war effort happily admitted, the Air Force had deliberately targeted Iraq's water, sewage and electrical facilities, crippling the infrastructure that sustained Iraq's civilian population. As the *Washington Post* reported, U.S. airstrikes

> deliberately did great harm to Iraq's ability to support itself as an industrial society. The worst civilian suffering, senior officers say, has resulted not from bombs that went astray but from precision-guided weapons that hit exactly where they were aimed — at electrical plants, oil refineries and transportation networks. Each of these targets was acknowledged during the war, but all the purposes and consequences of their destruction were not divulged.

> Among the justifications offered now, particularly by the Air Force in recent briefings, is that Iraqi civilians were not blameless for Saddam's invasion of Kuwait. "The definition of innocents gets to be a little bit unclear," said a senior Air Force officer, noting that many Iraqis supported the invasion of Kuwait. "They do live there, and ultimately the people have some control over what goes on in their country."

Though the official casualty count for the U.S. and its allies in the war was fewer than 400 dead, more than half of them in "friendly fire" or other accidents, and 350 wounded, the reality turned out to not be so simple. In the aftermath of Iraq War I, while occupying the south of the country, the U.S. found large caches of Iraqi conventional and chemical weapons. Most famously, they destroyed them at a site called Khamisiyah, where chemical warheads were filmed being destroyed in massive detonations, which exposed U.S. troops downwind to sarin and other poisons.

The government and media skeptics tended to dismiss the Gulf War Illnesses as a psychosomatic "syndrome," a mass hysteria describing diagnoses well within the expected ranges. However, credible evidence emerged over the 1990s that causes as varied as the Khamisiyah detonation, experimental anthrax vaccines, anti-sarin pills and exposure to dust from depleted uranium munitions may have contributed to the suffering of thousands of veterans of that conflict.

Not that it made any difference to the larger story. Once the short and seemingly easy Iraq War I was over and Kuwait's king, Jaber Al-Ahmad Al-Sabah, had been restored to his throne, President Bush declared, "It's a proud day for America. By God, we've kicked the Vietnam Syndrome once and for all!"

That was 30 years ago. The U.S. has been bombing Iraq ever since.

The New Order

Russell Kirk, one of the leading founders of the modern American conservative movement after World War II and author of *The Conservative Mind: From Burke to Eliot,* denounced the first Iraq war in a speech before the conservative Heritage Foundation in February 1991, while the war was still underway. He said that President George H.W. Bush, whom he had helped to secure the Republican nomination for president in 1988, was blowing America's late-1980s Cold War victory and peace dividend on a nonsensical mission to dominate the planet — hardly a "conservative" policy in any real sense. Kirk said that at the end of the Cold War with the Soviet Union,

> there remains an American Empire, still growing — though expanding through the acquisition of client states, rather than through settlement of American populations abroad. Among the client states directly dependent upon American military power are Japan, Korea, Taiwan, Israel, and El Salvador. ... Dependent upon American assistance of one kind or another, and in some degree upon American military protection, are the Philippines, the Dominican Republic, and Panama; and also, in the Levant, Egypt and Jordan, and formerly Lebanon. Now Saudi Arabia and Kuwait are added to the roster of clients. ... In short, although we never talk about our empire, a tremendous American Empire has come into existence — if, like the Roman Empire, in a kind of fit of absence of mind. No powerful counterpoise to the American hegemony seems to remain, what with the enfeebling of the USSR. ...
>
> Soon there sets to work a widespread impulse to pull down the imperial power. But that imperial power, strong in weapons, finds it possible for a time to repress the disobedient. ... In the long run, the task of repression is too painful a burden to bear; so the Communist Party of the Soviet Union has discovered in the past few years. ...
>
> [P]ower intoxicates; and, as Lord Acton put it, power tends to corrupt. The love of power tends to corrupt both speech and actions. It may corrupt a grave national undertaking into a personal vendetta. It may corrupt what began as a chivalric rescue into a heavy belligerent

domination. Talk continues to come to our ears of a "permanent American presence" in the Persian Gulf.

But the hawks, deaf to the warnings of wise men like Kirk, saw only "vacuums" to be filled with their own power and influence. It was time to celebrate. Army General Barry McCaffrey, whose forces had committed the atrocity at Rumaila, said that the war was "probably the single most unifying event that has happened in America since World War II. ... The upshot will be that, just like Vietnam had the tragic effect on our country for years, this one has brought back a new way of looking at ourselves."

Journalist Robert Parry believed that the defeat of the "Vietnam syndrome" had been the primary reason for the war. Americans had to be made to get over their reluctance to intervene in other nations' disputes. It seems that he was right. National Security Advisor Brent Scowcroft saw "a larger principle at stake" in the war, he later told journalist Bob Woodward. He wanted to dismantle the Powell-Weinberger six-point doctrine for avoiding wars that he saw as a legacy of the "Vietnam Syndrome."

Those in charge of the government had no intention of coming home after the fall of the Soviet Union and the end of the Cold War. They had a world to lead. A quick, easy win complete with lots of yellow ribbons and supersonic jets on TV was just what they needed to get the U.S. population out of its antiwar slump.

A year later, George H.W. Bush's defense secretary, Dick Cheney, had his staff members, neoconservative policy advisers Paul Wolfowitz and Zalmay Khalilzad, write the Pentagon's new "Defense Planning Guidance" for the coming decade. Though it was officially rescinded after being leaked to the *New York Times*, the rewritten version for I. Lewis "Scooter" Libby was essentially unchanged.

The document said that now that the U.S. was the lone superpower since the dissolution of the Soviet Union, "the world order is ultimately backed by the U.S.," and that America must never allow any power or any conceivable regional alliance of powers even to consider challenging American military dominance.

To this end, they wrote, the United States should expand its security commitments to former Warsaw Pact states in Eastern Europe, bolster other alliances in Asia, the Middle East and Latin America and be ready for war, "even outside ... traditional theaters of operation." This, of course, would necessitate increased military spending across the board, especially on naval and airpower and missile defense. "You've discovered a new rationale for our role in the world," a pleased Secretary Cheney told Khalilzad.

The most common objection cited by the press was the issue of American unilateralism in taking on all these burdens alone, rather than with the help of other nations. The legitimacy of the strategy of dominance itself was mostly considered outside reasonable debate.

But not all were convinced that America must seize the advantage and opportunity to expand. Ronald Reagan's former UN ambassador, Jeane Kirkpatrick, previously a neoconservative hawk, wrote in *The National Interest* in the autumn of 1990, that since the Cold War was over, the United States of America could revert to being a "normal country in a normal time," with a government focused on the security of its own people and with an intent to preserve our Constitution and sacred Bill of Rights for the ages. Kirkpatrick recommended that America "encourage" other nations to adopt democracy but dismissed claims of a mystical American mandate to control the fate of the world as self-destructive hubris:

> With a return to "normal" times, we can again become a normal nation — and take care of pressing problems of education, family, industry, and technology. We can be an independent nation in a world of independent nations.
>
> Most of the international military obligations that we assumed were once important are now outdated. Our alliances should be alliances of equals, with equal risks, burdens, and responsibilities. It is time to give up the dubious benefits of superpower status and become again a usually successful, open American republic.

But the hawks were intent on seizing what they called the post-Cold War "unipolar moment," at "the end of history," to inaugurate a "new American Century" of U.S. "predominance" and "benevolent hegemony" over the planet.

Uprising and Betrayal

Dick Cheney explained in a 2014 interview what it took to finally "close the deal" with Saudi King Fahd to allow the U.S. to build and occupy its massive new bases in the Saudi desert. He had agreed to the King's condition that the soldiers and airmen would be removed as soon as Iraq was driven from Kuwait and the alleged threat of an Iraqi invasion of Saudi Arabia had been thwarted.

But U.S. forces did not leave. Once the first Iraq war was over, a new reason for permanent occupation presented itself. During the war to expel Iraqi forces from Kuwait, Bush Sr. had released a radio message on Voice of America, and the military dropped leaflets over Iraqi army units and civilian populations, encouraging Shi'ite Arabs and Kurds to rise up and overthrow the primarily Sunni Arab-dominated dictatorship of Saddam Hussein. They took the chance and launched a revolt, believing the U.S.

would back their efforts. Not only did Bush then refuse to support them, but under the terms of Iraq's surrender in the war, the U.S. agreed to allow Hussein to keep his attack helicopters and use them to slaughter his opponents. According to journalist Barry Lando, the U.S. eventually even outright intervened on Saddam's side, landing American choppers on a highway to Baghdad to block an Iraqi army division that was marching on the capital to remove him.

This was the Great Stab in the Back in the Desert of 1991. The Bush Sr. administration really did want either a military coup or a popular uprising in which the Shi'ites and Kurds would overthrow Saddam Hussein. But Bush's war council suddenly changed their minds. This was due to the presence of the Badr Brigade, the militia of the Supreme Council for Islamic Revolution in Iraq (SCIRI). They were a group of Iraqi Shi'ites who had fled to Iran after Iraq invaded in 1980 or had been recruited from prisoner of war camps, and had fought on Iran's side in the Iran-Iraq war. This meant the U.S. was reversing the entire Reagan-era effort of backing Saddam Hussein in the 1980s Iran-Iraq war to contain the results of the 1979 Iranian Shi'ite revolution, importing it into Iraq instead. Bush Sr. quickly turned right around and betrayed the uprising in a massive Bay of Pigs-type debacle. Tens of thousands of Shi'ite Arabs and Kurds were slaughtered.

The U.S., Britain and France then announced permanent "no-fly zones" of allied air patrols in the south and far north of Iraq to protect those they had just sacrificed. The allies further proclaimed that the international economic sanctions policy imposed before the war would remain in place until regime change could be achieved.

As President Bush Sr. said in May 1991, "At this juncture, my view is we don't want to lift these sanctions as long as Saddam Hussein is in power." Robert Gates, who was then moving up to CIA director, added that "Iraqis will pay the price while he is in power. ... All possible sanctions will be maintained until he is gone." Gates said Iraq "will be nothing but a pariah state" as long as Hussein ruled, and that "Iraqis will not participate in post-crisis political, economic and security arrangements until there is a change in regime."

So the American military stayed in Saudi Arabia to protect the Iraqi Shi'ites and Kurds from their Sunni-led dictatorship and to enforce the deadly, decade-long United Nations blockade against them all.

Dual Containment

Soon after he took office, Bill Clinton's Iraq policy became constrained by a contrived plot against the life of former President George Bush Sr. during a visit to Kuwait in April 1993.

As journalist Seymour Hersh revealed, the CIA initially blamed the Kuwaitis for embellishing a local whiskey smuggling ring into an assassination plot in order to thwart any moves by the new administration to normalize relations with Iraq, as Clinton had previously indicated he was considering. But the new president went along with the hoax, launching cruise missile strikes against Iraq which killed eight civilians, including the famous artist Layla al-Attar. This brought the new process of bringing Iraq in from the cold to an end, just as intended. It turns out that the Kuwaiti ambassador whose daughter had lied to the U.S. Senate about the story of the babies murdered for their incubators in 1990 was the same man who was in charge of briefing the international press on the Bush assassination story three years later.

As *Newsweek* reported, after the U.S. occupied Iraq in 2003 and took possession of their intelligence documents, they never found a shred of evidence, or even an indication, that the plot had been real or that the Iraqi government had been behind it.

But under pressure from the hawks, such as his adviser Martin Indyk, to "do something" to look tough after the assassination story broke, in May 1993, the Clinton administration adopted a program of "dual containment" of both Iraq and Iran. Since Iraq War I had left the Iraqi regime too weak to contain Iran, the Israelis convinced Clinton both enemy states had to be contained by the newly empowered United States — from its permanent bases in Saudi Arabia. As Trita Parsi shows in his book *Treacherous Alliance: The Secret Dealings of Israel, Iran, and the United States*, the American Israel Public Affairs Committee (AIPAC) and other Israel affinity organizations made a massive and successful push for dual containment at Israeli Prime Minister Yitzhak Rabin's insistence. After the alleged plot against Bush, the Clinton government, which was mostly skeptical at first, went ahead with the policy anyway. Indyk, a former adviser to Israeli Prime Minister Yitzhak Shamir, gave a speech declaring the new doctrine at the Washington Institute for Near East Policy (WINEP), the AIPAC spin-off think tank which he had founded.

As Parsi shows, in 1991, as the Soviet Union was falling apart, the Pentagon, requiring a new rationale for their existence, settled on the threat of the last few "rogue states" outside the American-led international order who possessed ballistic missile technology. Iran was a target of this policy from the beginning.

Demonizing Iran was also a political ploy of Israeli Prime Minister Yitzhak Rabin. He had chosen to do so to help justify his abandonment of Israel's previous strategy of allying with powers on the far sides of their Arab neighbors, to keep them divided, to a new policy of negotiating with the Arabs, including the Palestinians. Just a few years before, in 1987, when he was the defense minister, Rabin had said that, "Iran is Israel's best friend and we do not intend to change our position in relation to Tehran, because Khomeini's regime will not last forever." He was right about that. Khomeini died in 1989. The far more moderate Ali Khamenei has been Supreme Leader of Iran since then. But instead of making even better friends, Israel turned on them. Iran had not changed. They did not start supporting Hamas until 1995, and they only did so in retaliation for Israel building this new coalition against them, as Indyk admitted years later.

After the Iranian Revolution of 1979, Israel and Iran had not broken their ties. And as America mostly backed Saddam Hussein during the Iran-Iraq war, the Israelis sided with the Iranians. That was why during the Iran-Contra operation, when Ronald Reagan's government sold missiles to Iran, they used the Israelis as cut-outs to do it. Israel still had the channels open. They had been selling weapons and providing intelligence to revolutionary Iran all along. It was not until the early 1990s that the Israelis decided to start demonizing the Ayatollah's regime. At the time, Israel's military, their foreign intelligence service, the Mossad, academic and security experts mostly resisted Rabin's new campaign against Iran, including future-prime minister and defense minister Ehud Barak, then army chief of staff, who remained an Iraq hawk.

Efraim Inbar, from the Israeli Begin-Sadat Center, revealed to Parsi another reason for the new strategy. In the 1990s, Rabin and his government were worried that with the smashing of Saddam Hussein's army and the fall of the USSR in 1991, they were running out of good reasons for the Israeli alliance with the United States. As a solution they focused on what they called "radical Islam" as represented by Iran. By "radical," they mean so caught up in irrational, fundamentalist beliefs that there could be no point in attempting to negotiate with them. Iran would be a permanent enemy that we could share. It was "new glue for the alliance" between the United States and Israel.

The Rabin government insisted that the Clinton administration go along, promising a deal with the Palestinians in exchange. Israel preferred U.S. dual containment over pressure by American on Iran to moderate its positions on Israel's occupation of the Palestinians. As Parsi writes, this was because the Israelis presumed that anything Iran did to soften their stances on Israel would be only a tactic by them to placate America, rather than a real strategic change. Israel was also worried that the U.S. and Iran had too many things in common, such as hatred of Saddam Hussein's Iraq and the Taliban's Afghanistan, and, of course, the oil business. America could end up leaning back toward their old ally and put Israel's interests on the back burner. So the Israelis feared a U.S.-Iran dialog more than Iran itself. Israeli Deputy Defense Minister Efraim Sneh explained, "We were against [U.S.-Iranian] dialogue ... because the interests of the U.S. did not coincide with ours." AIPAC and other pro-Israel organizations made a massive and successful push for the dual containment policy and new sanctions against Iran, at Rabin's insistence, to hedge against any second thoughts or new overtures. They were seeming to insist on being enemies with Iran by self-fulfilling prophecy.

After an Israeli settler assassinated Rabin in 1995, Shimon Peres became prime minister. As part of the new anti-Iran strategy, he launched the "Grapes of Wrath" attack on Iranian allies Hezbollah in southern Lebanon in 1996. This was the same operation that inspired Mohammed Atta and his friends in what became known as the "Hamburg cell" of September 11th hijackers to join al Qaeda's war against the United States.

Benjamin Netanyahu, who became Israeli prime minister the first time in 1996, picked up his anti-Iran strategy from Rabin and Peres. But for his government, scapegoating Iran was no longer part of a plan for negotiating with the Palestinians. Instead it became the excuse never to allow the West Bank and Gaza Strip to be a Palestinian state. Iran was a useful distraction every time another government or international body would complain about the occupation. This is a public relations strategy that continues to work. Shlomo Ben Ami, the foreign minister of Netanyahu's successor, Ehud Barak, admitted that their government also used Iran as a distraction from the disintegration of the Oslo agreement, which mandated a process toward the creation of a Palestinian state in the West Bank and Gaza Strip.

The American government has their own problems with Iran. They are still not over Iran's 1979 declaration of independence from the United States. That they have gotten away with it all this time sets a bad example for the other nations. It also raises the question of how America is supposed to dominate the Arab world without an alliance with the government in Iran to help hem them in. It is the big flaw in the U.S. quest for dominance of the region.

In this century, punishing Iran and containing their power has continued to be a significant motivation behind American policies in the Middle East — policies that have mostly empowered Iran instead.

Iraq War I 1/2

The project of American dominance in the Middle East was already what the military calls a "self-licking ice cream cone," meaning a policy in search of a reason for itself. In arguing against the hawks who lamented Bush Sr.'s alleged failure to "finish the job" against Saddam Hussein in 1991, Clinton Democrat Fareed Zakaria argued in a 1996 *Newsweek* piece entitled "Thank Goodness for a Villain":

> If Saddam Hussein did not exist, we would have to invent him. He is the linchpin of American policy in the Mideast. Without him, Washington would be stumbling in the desert sands. ...
>
> If not for Saddam, would the Saudi royal family, terrified of being seen as an American protectorate (which in a sense it is), allow American troops on their soil? Would Kuwait house more than 30,000 pieces of American combat hardware, kept in readiness should the need arise? Would the King of Jordan, the political weather vane of the region, allow the Marines to conduct exercises within his borders? ...
>
> [T]he end of Saddam Hussein would be the end of the anti-Saddam coalition. Nothing destroys an alliance like the disappearance of the enemy. ... Imagine American policy in the Middle East if we didn't have Saddam Hussein to kick around anymore.

"Dual containment" was surely an improvement over the previous policy of arming Iraq and Iran against each other in war, as the U.S. had done during the 1980s. However, what the policy really meant was no real peace could be reached with either country. No end to the cold war against Iran or the "warm" one against Iraq would be possible for the remainder of the 20th century — and beyond. The U.S. would also need to keep all their new and expanded bases in Arabia to do the containing. The war President George Bush Sr. had sworn would "not be another Vietnam" continued, albeit mostly from the Treasury Department in Washington and 30,000 feet in the sky over Iraq.

Americans think of the Bill Clinton years as a time of peace and prosperity. His wars, and news of them, rarely received much popular attention. But as journalist Jeremy Scahill and the *Washington Post* have reported, during Clinton's presidency, the U.S. and British air forces bombed Iraq an average of three to four times per week. They told the American people each of these bombings represented an attempted radar lock by Iraqi ground stations, an act of "aggression" against U.S. combat aircraft flying over a foreign nation. However, after 1998, radar and other military installations were deemed legitimate targets of self-defense even if they had taken no action at all. Not one U.S. or UK plane was ever hit, much less shot down, by Iraqi anti-aircraft fire during the entire decade after Iraq War I. However, hundreds of innocent civilians the U.S. and UK were supposedly protecting were killed in these allied bombings.

The 1990s United Nations blockade was an even more tragic story. The global sanctions regime on Iraq destroyed what was left of the Iraqi economy after the Iran-Iraq war and Iraq War I. The U.S., which had been happy to look the other way when Hussein was importing "dual-use" items to manufacture chemical and biological weapons to use against Iran a few years before, now, in addition to banning Iraqi oil sales, was forbidding the importation of "possible dual-use" spare parts for repairing delivery trucks and the country's electrical grid. As author Joy Gordon showed in her book *Invisible War: The United States and the Iraq Sanctions*, even chlorine for disinfecting civilian water supplies was banned under the pretense that the Iraqis must only want it to make prohibited chemical weapons. Essential medicines that were cheap and plentiful elsewhere in the world became impossible to obtain. Malnutrition was widespread. There were deadly epidemics of cholera and typhoid. It was a ruthless economic war against all Iraqi men, women and children. The American people, diverted by euphemisms such as "sanctions" in place of "blockade" and comparisons to the full-scale air and tank war that had just been waged, may not have realized the new status quo was a permanent, global trade embargo that was starving and strangling the entire civilian population of the country. Any doubts they may have had were apparently sufficiently smothered in political partisanship, racism and nationalism.

Study after study conducted throughout the 1990s, including those by the U.S. Air Force, World Food Program, Harvard University and the *New England Journal of Medicine*, and the UK's *Lancet*, showed the unbearable suffering of the Iraqi population. But this only proved the success of the program. Civilian deaths were a prime feature, not a bug, of the sanctions policy. As Pentagon officials explained to the *Washington Post*, "People say, 'You didn't recognize that [bombing civilian infrastructure] was going to have an effect on water or sewage[?]' Well, what were we trying to do with sanctions — help out the Iraqi people? No. What we were doing with the attacks on infrastructure was to accelerate the effect of the sanctions." And "Big picture, we wanted to let people know, 'Get rid of this guy, and we'll be more than happy to assist in rebuilding. We're not going to tolerate Saddam Hussein or his regime. Fix that, and we'll [allow you to] fix your electricity.'"

The infamous 1995 United Nations report claiming that more than 500,000 children had died due to the sanctions was tainted by bad data and retracted. But Dr. Richard Garfield of Columbia University concluded that a more conservative and accurate estimate was still more than 300,000 "excess deaths" of children in Iraq during the sanctions period, in what Americans called "peacetime." Even this was comparing to the previous decade when Iraq had been at war with Iran, hardly ideal economic conditions for a baseline. Two UN officials overseeing the sanctions,

Denis Halliday and Hans Von Sponeck, resigned in disgust at the devastation they had helped to cause. Halliday told the author that though they were allowed to spend Iraqi oil revenue on infrastructure in northern Iraqi Kurdistan, he was forbidden to do anything to help the people of the south get clean water, repair their sewage facilities or anything that could improve the quality of life for the people because the U.S. "wanted to continue the punishment."

Finally, in 1996, the UN Oil for Food program was introduced. However, it was common knowledge in foreign policy circles during this period that despite the strict rules governing the program, Hussein's regime was diverting the profits from the oil sales for its own needs. Saddam was "spending it all on his palaces," as the saying went then. The Iraqi people's suffering was not being alleviated. Yet this was seen only as another useful talking point for the effort to demonize the dictator. The idea of lifting the embargo on the Iraqi people and figuring out a better way to proceed was never seriously considered.

The 1990s was also an era of endless UN weapons inspections under the terms of the ceasefire at the end of the war. These were done under the pretense of ridding Saddam Hussein's Iraq of the chemical weapons Iraq had used against the Iranians with U.S. assistance and against the Iraqi Kurds without the slightest hint of opposition only a decade before. The fact that these weapons were virtually all destroyed by the end of 1991, and that the UN inspectors were completely satisfied of this fact by the end of 1995, had no apparent effect on the massive global sanctions regime other than to change its goal from pretended arms control to outright regime change. Hussein wanted the sanctions regime lifted far more than any desire he held for unconventional weapons.

When the United Nations Special Commission on Iraq was ready to declare the country free of weapons of mass destruction in 1997, they were preempted by Clinton's secretary of state, Madeleine Albright. She gave a speech announcing that no matter what, the sanctions regime would persist until the people of Iraq overthrew Saddam Hussein. The fact that the Iraqi people were starving, dying and getting weaker under the sanctions in relation to their formerly U.S.-supported government, and that the U.S. had encouraged and then betrayed the Iraqi majority when they had had their chance to overthrow Saddam Hussein during the 1991 uprising, seemed to mean nothing to the Clinton government. Nor was there any reason, beyond wishful thinking, to believe there would be a revolution from within the Ba'ath Party or the military. A CIA-backed 1995 revolt by Kurdish and Iraqi exile forces and a 1996 coup attempt orchestrated by the CIA and their British counterparts in MI-6 both ended in disaster.

When asked about the reported 500,000 children who had been deprived to death as a result of the embargo, Secretary Albright infamously told CBS News, "We think the price is worth it." It was "worth it" to the Clinton government to continue this ruinous policy even though it was officially based on a plain absurdity. This number represented more children, as her interlocutor put it, "than died at [the nuclear bombing of] Hiroshima," in World War II. Albright has since repeatedly apologized for saying what she did in such a crude manner but has still not been asked whether she is sorry for actually enforcing the policy that killed so many innocent people and enraged so many new enemies. She has certainly not volunteered to do so.

The U.S. and UN coalition's endless 1990s war, coupled with America's decision to stay in Arabia to maintain its war footing against Iraq, was all it took to turn the Arab-Afghan mujahideen against the United States. Osama bin Laden was the wealthy son of a powerful Saudi construction magnate who had contributed large sums of money and equipment to the 1980s war effort in Afghanistan and had been wounded in battle against Communist forces there. Believing the Americans had tricked Hussein into attacking Kuwait, he was incensed that they had received the Saudi king's writ to force the Iraqi army back out. Bin Laden had attempted to volunteer his men for the cause.

He was even more enraged by the expanded and indefinite presence of "crusader" U.S. combat forces during and after the war on what he considered to be the holy territory of the Arabian Peninsula. The Arab-Afghan mujahideen, the U.S. government's once-friendly, even heroic, "freedom fighter" allies from the great anti-Soviet holy war of the 1980s, had become the enemies of the American people. With the Soviet invaders gone from Afghanistan, they were now determined to drive U.S. combat forces from the Arabian Peninsula by any means necessary.

As a senior official in the George W. Bush administration later surprisingly admitted,

> [F]atwas from Osama … cited the effects of sanctions on Iraqi children and the presence of U.S. troops as a sacrilege that justified his jihad. In a real sense, September 11 was part of the cost of containing Saddam. No containment, no U.S. troops in Saudi Arabia. No U.S. troops there, then bin Laden might still be redecorating mosques and boring friends with stories of his mujahideen days in the Khyber Pass.

Deputy Secretary of Defense Paul Wolfowitz later even cited the necessity of removing U.S. combat forces stationed in Saudi Arabia as one of the benefits of invading Iraq:

There are a lot of things that are different now [that the U.S. occupies Iraq], and one that has gone by almost unnoticed — but it's huge — is that ... we can now remove almost all of our forces from Saudi Arabia. Their presence there over the last 12 years has been a source of enormous difficulty for a friendly government. It's been a huge recruiting device for al Qaeda. In fact, if you look at bin Laden, one of his principal grievances was the presence of so-called crusader forces on the holy land, Mecca and Medina. I think just lifting that burden from the Saudis is itself going to open the door to other positive things. I don't want to speak in messianic terms. It's not going to change things overnight, but it's a huge improvement.

Former CIA officer John Kiriakou wrote in his book, *The Reluctant Spy: My Secret Life in the CIA's War on Terror*, that in the summer of 2002 the CIA's director of Iraq operations told him in a meeting at their headquarters:

Okay, here's the deal, we're going to invade Iraq next spring. We're going to overthrow Saddam Hussein. We're going to establish the largest air force base in the world, and we're going to transfer everybody from Saudi Arabia to Iraq. That way, al Qaeda won't have that hanging over us, that we're polluting the land of the two holy cities.

In fact, as soon as the United States invaded Iraq in the spring of 2003, they began closing the major air bases remaining in Saudi Arabia. The *New York Times* explained:

The drastically reduced American profile could simplify the government's position among Saudis who espouse Osama bin Laden's contention that the American military foothold was an affront to the kingdom's sovereignty. For years, the American presence not far from Islam's two holiest sites, at Mecca and Medina, has provided al Qaeda with an important rallying cry.

The Far Enemy

In the early 1990s, Dr. Ayman al-Zawahiri, a former surgeon who was one of the leaders of Egyptian Islamic Jihad, began to merge his group with bin Laden's group. All were veterans of the U.S.-backed effort against the Soviets in Afghanistan in the 1980s. They agreed that the local revolutions they would someday like to wage, particularly against the regimes in Egypt and Arabia and ultimately leading to the creation of a new Islamic caliphate, would be impossible as long as the powerful American military was there to support the governments of its client states. The "far enemy" would have to be driven out of the region first. "We must move the battle to the enemy's grounds to burn the hands of those who ignite fire in our own countries." The "only language understood by the West," Zawahiri said, was "maximum casualties."

This is not to say that they had the slightest chance to succeed against their local despots even without U.S. intervention, only that they saw American support for their enemies as their biggest obstacle. As confirmed to the author by former CIA analyst Cynthia Storer, at the time of the September 11th attacks, there were only about 400 true members of al Qaeda in Afghanistan, and not many more around the Middle East.

Their strategy was fairly simple, as bin Laden and Zawahiri repeatedly explained. They wanted to replicate their success against the Soviet Union by provoking America to invade the region outright, bog the U.S. military down and bleed its treasury dry, ultimately forcing complete imperial collapse and withdrawal from the Middle East.

Some of their colleagues had already started attacking. In 1990, the groups that were then beginning to merge into what we now call al Qaeda assassinated the radical rabbi Meir Kahane, founder of the Israeli Kach Party, in New York City, over his support of settlement expansion in the West Bank. This was followed by the targeting of American marines in the botched Yemen hotel bombings of December 1992. According to journalist Peter Bergen, the CIA was aware of Osama bin Laden's role in the attempted Aden, Yemen attacks by April 1993.

Next was the first hit on the World Trade Center with another — thankfully failed — bombing in February 1993, which killed six people but could have been much worse. The bombers fell short in their attempt to topple one tower over into the other, which, at midday, could have instantly killed tens of thousands of people. Notably, the ringleader of the plot, "the blind Sheikh," Omar Abdel Rahman of Egyptian Islamic Jihad, had been allowed into the country only with the assistance of CIA officials who considered him and his co-conspirators old friends from the 1980s Afghan jihad, as reported by the *New York Times* and *Boston Globe*. Still, the terrorists' conspiracy could have been thwarted entirely, as the FBI had an undercover informant inside the plot in a position to create a fake bomb with inert explosives. But the FBI supervisor, Carson Dunbar, refused to cooperate with his agents' efforts, leading the informant, Ahmed Salem, to bail out of the operation. Salem was then replaced by the ultimate bomb maker, Abdul Basit, better known as Ramzi Yousef. No one at either agency was held accountable. The story was told by the journalist Ralph Blumenthal in the *Times*.

The letters Yousef sent to New York newspapers before fleeing to the Philippines and his eventual trial statements made clear he was motivated to join this group and attack the United States by America's support for

Israel's wars in Lebanon and Palestine and the continuing U.S.-UN economic sanctions against Iraq. At Yousef's eventual sentencing hearing, the convict went into an extended tirade about America's "terrorist" foreign policy. The federal judge, Kevin Duffy, then completely ignored Yousef's statement and instead refuted only what the government had claimed about his motives: "You weren't seeking conversions. The only thing you wanted to do was to cause death. Your God is not Allah. You worship death and destruction."

Next came the thwarted plots against the Lincoln and Holland Tunnels and United Nations headquarters in New York by the same cell that had done the 1993 attack on the Twin Towers. Then followed a string of attacks planned by Ramzi Yousef in the Philippines in 1995, where he fled after the World Trade Center attack. Following an accidental fire at his Philippines apartment, two of Yousef's co-conspirators were arrested, and police confiscated his laptop computer. The computer revealed plans to assassinate Pope John Paul II and President Bill Clinton on their scheduled trips to the Philippines and a plot called "Bojinka," a scheme to time bomb ten or more airliners over the Pacific Ocean. A test run of this plan failed to destroy the plane but did kill the Japanese businessman underneath whose seat Yousef had planted a small bomb. There was also a plot to hijack airliners and crash them into multiple targets on both U.S. coasts — the "planes operation," which later became the September 11th plot in the hands of Yousef's uncle, Khalid Sheikh Mohammed.

Then came the Saudi National Guard bombings in 1995, which killed five Americans training their internal security forces, and the Khobar Towers attack in 1996, near Dhahran, Saudi Arabia, which killed 19 U.S. airmen in their barracks. For political reasons, the government decided to blame the Khobar attack on "Iranian-backed Saudi Hezbollah." What if the story had been told straight to the American people that it was this former "freedom fighter," Osama bin Laden, who keeps demanding the U.S. withdraw its troops from his country, "holy land," no less, who just bombed 19 of our airmen stationed there? There would have at least been an opportunity for the American people to see such an important example of the trouble brewing at the time. Instead, they blamed it on Iran, across the Persian Gulf, which was not being occupied, thus obfuscating the reality of the motive behind the tragic event (and further preventing rapprochement with Iran). It was later shown that the Khobar Towers attack was almost certainly orchestrated by Osama bin Laden and Khalid Sheikh Mohammed of al Qaeda. Bin Laden himself took credit for the attack to journalist Abdel Bari Atwan.

On August 7, 1998, in Nairobi, Kenya, and Dar es Salaam, Tanzania, al Qaeda struck again with devastating dual truck bomb attacks against the U.S. embassies there, killing hundreds of people. Atwan later wrote, "al

Qaeda explained that these cities had been chosen because they each housed a large U.S. military presence and because both the Kenyan and Tanzanian governments backed U.S. aggression against Iraq and had close links with Israel."

The African embassy attacks were followed up by the thwarted "millennium attack" on Los Angeles International Airport in 1999, a failed attack on the Navy ship *USS The Sullivans* in January 2000, a foiled plot against the Radisson Hotel in Amman, Jordan, and finally, the rubber-dinghy bomb attack on the *USS Cole* at port in Aden, Yemen, which killed 17 sailors in October of that year.

In the years and months leading up to the September 11th attacks on New York and Washington, D.C., the Clinton administration seemed completely unwilling to confront the enemy they had provoked. The only exceptions were his cruise missile strikes on an essential antibiotics factory in Sudan — a move that was based on false claims that it was a chemical weapons plant — and some empty Afghan training camps in the "Monica missiles" episode of August 1998, while his mistress was testifying before a federal grand jury. Former CIA bin Laden unit chief Scheuer later told the author his team had given Clinton ten different chances to kill bin Laden in Afghanistan before his term ended in 2001. A U.S. Senate report later put the number at 13.

The last chance the U.S. had under Clinton to kill bin Laden was in April 2000 when an unarmed Predator drone spotted him walking across a field at his "Tarnak farm" outside of Kandahar City in southern Afghanistan. Authority for the Navy to strike was denied.

The Hand That Fed Them

Perhaps the lax attitude toward this dangerous anti-American terrorist group was because the U.S. and its allies still considered them useful for accomplishing other foreign policy goals, even though these "Arab-Afghans" had long since turned against their American patrons. While bin Laden had claimed to target America in part for its tacit support for Russia, China, Uzbekistan and India in their violent suppression of Muslims, the truth was more complicated. The U.S. and their Saudi allies had covertly favored al Qaeda's Islamist allies in Chechnya in their fight to secede from the Russian Federation, as shown in reports by the influential private intelligence firm Stratfor and former FBI lawyer Coleen Rowley. The Saudi role was admitted by the *Washington Post* in 2003. The Clinton administration, along with their Saudi and British partners, also backed mujahideen affiliates in Bosnia in the mid-nineties, where September 11th ringleader Khalid Sheikh Mohammed earned his stripes, as well as the al

Qaeda-tied Kosovo Liberation Army in the Kosovo War of 1999. In both the Bosnia and Kosovo wars, the U.S. knowingly supported the mujahideen fighting against the Russian-aligned Serbs. In the latter conflict, this was based on the outright lie that they had exterminated 100,000 Kosovar ethnic Albanian civilians. Just two months before September 11th, journalist Eric Margolis witnessed Chinese Uighurs training in CIA-sponsored camps in Afghanistan for use against the regime in Beijing. All this was taking place despite Clinton's declaration that terrorism was "the enemy of our generation," one against which "we must prevail." Clinton's chief Balkans negotiator, Richard Holbrooke, later told the *Los Angeles Times*, "I think the [Bosnian] Muslims wouldn't have survived without" this help from the Arab mujahideen veterans of the 1980s Afghan war. Similarly, the British MI-6, with CIA help, supported the Libyan Islamic Fighting Group, formed by the Libyan veterans of the 1980s Afghan war, to try to assassinate their dictator, Colonel Moammar Gaddafi, in 1996 as revealed by the MI-5 whistleblower David Shayler.

The Saudis also continued to donate hundreds of millions of dollars to al Qaeda in the form of protection money. After the attacks on U.S. forces in Saudi Arabia in 1995 and 1996, an agreement was made that Saudi charities would continue to fund the terrorists if they would cease their attacks inside Saudi Arabia itself.

In the book *Dollars for Terror*, Richard Labeviere quotes a former CIA analyst as saying in the 1990s, "The policy of guiding the evolution of Islam and of helping them against our adversaries worked marvelously well in Afghanistan against the Red Army. The same doctrines can still be used to destabilize what remains of Russian power, and especially to counter the Chinese influence in Central Asia."

Back in August 1993, Gina Bennett, an intelligence analyst at the State Department's Bureau of Intelligence and Research (INR), wrote a classified memo titled "The Wandering Mujahideen: Armed and Dangerous." It warned that the 1980s Afghan war's

> melting pot gave the militant Islamists numerous ideological and logistical ties with fighters from other countries. Victory over the Soviet Union has inspired many of them to continue their jihad against other infidels, including the U.S., Israel and more secular Middle East regimes.

She explained that these radical fighters were returning to Egypt, Algeria, Yemen and the Philippines, among other places, and moving on to new battlefields such as Bosnia, Somalia and Kashmir. "The perception that the U.S. has an anti-Islamic foreign policy agenda raises the likelihood that U.S. interests increasingly will become targets for violence from the former mujahideen," she wrote. Bennett also warned of the danger of the wealthy Saudi sheikh and religious zealot, Osama bin Laden, and his ties to Egyptian Islamic Jihad, citing his funding of Omar Abdel Rahman, the "blind sheikh" whose cell was responsible for the first World Trade Center bombing in February 1993. She continued:

> The alleged involvement of veterans of the Afghan war in the World Trade Center bombing and the plots against New York targets are a bold example of what tactics some former mujahideen are willing to use in their ongoing jihad. U.S. support of the mujahideen during the Afghan war will not necessarily protect U.S. interests from attack.

> The growing perception by Muslims that the U.S. follows a double standard with regard to Islamic Issues — particularly in Bosnia, Algeria and the Israeli-occupied territories — heightens the possibility that Americans will become the targets of radical Muslims' wrath. Afghan war veterans, scattered throughout the world, could surprise the U.S. with violence in unexpected locales.

Perhaps the Clinton administration got the message but read it wrong. They did seem to reason back then that it was important for the U.S. to take Muslims' side in a fight somewhere to undermine their motive to attack the United States. After the September 11th attacks, former President Bill Clinton and two of his congressional allies, Democratic Senator Tom Lantos and Representative Brad Sherman, were incredulous that bin Ladenite terrorists would want to attack America after everything the administration had done for them, such as supporting their efforts in Bosnia and Kosovo.

But why should the Democrats have expected a group of professional terrorists to be impressed by these efforts on their behalf? None of the rest of America's Mideast policies had changed, and al Qaeda's war against the U.S. had only continued to worsen during that time. President Clinton had helped to further build up jihadist forces, but he could not buy their loyalty.

In 1998, Zbigniew Brzezinski did a now-infamous interview with the French magazine *Le Nouvel Observateur*. When asked whether he had any regrets about the rise of the Taliban fundamentalist regime which had taken hold of much of Afghanistan in 1996 following America's efforts on behalf of the mujahideen in the 1980s — and, implicitly, its sheltering of international anti-Western terrorists such as Osama bin Laden — Brzezinski replied:

> What is most important to the history of the world? The Taliban or the collapse of the Soviet empire? Some stirred-up Muslims or the liberation of Central Europe and the end of the Cold War?

In the same year, Republican Senator Orrin Hatch of Utah, who also supported the effort to back the mujahideen in the 1980s, told NBC News' Robert Windrem that, even considering the growing list of al Qaeda attacks against the United States, "It was worth it."

"Those were very important, pivotal matters that played an important role in the downfall of the Soviet Union," he said. Hatch seemed to assume that the USSR would not have fallen otherwise and that the innocent people killed by the rising generation of terrorists and the millions of victims of the eventual wars justified by their deaths would share his same value judgment on the issue.

Not everyone was so blind. On November 19, 1997, Republican Congressman Ron Paul of Texas wrote a letter to President Clinton, stating in part:

> Policy toward Iraq is ... not designed to protect U.S. national security. It is instead a threat to our security because it may lead to war and loss of American lives, increase terrorism and is certainly an additional expense for the U.S. taxpayer. The hyped rhetoric coming from Washington which describes Hussein as the only evil monster with which we must deal in the world is a poor substitute for wise counsel.

In February 1998, during a peak period of no-fly zone bombings, Dr. Paul addressed the House of Representatives:

> Mr. Speaker, the Saudis this past week expressed a sincere concern about an anti-American backlash if we start bombing Baghdad. We should not ignore the feelings of the Saudis. If a neighbor can oppose this bombing, we should be very cautious.

Later that year, when Clinton launched the cruise missile attacks on the al-Shifa antibiotics factory in Sudan and empty al Qaeda training camps in Afghanistan, Dr. Paul again spoke from the floor of the House. He warned the Congress and the public that our policy was making enemies of our former friends, the mujahideen fighters of the Afghan war (whom he had opposed funding in the first place during his stint in Congress in the 1980s):

> Osama bin Laden and his Afghan religious supporters were American allies throughout the 1980s and received our money and training and were heralded as the Afghan "Freedom Fighters." Even then, bin Laden let it be known that his people resented all imperialism, whether from the Soviets or the United States. ...
>
> [T]he region's Muslims see America as the imperialist invader. They have deeply held religious beliefs, and in their desire for national sovereignty many see America as a threatening menace. America's

presence in the Middle East, most flagrantly demonstrated with troops and bases in Saudi Arabia, is something many Muslims see as defiling their holy land. Many Muslims — and this is what makes an extremist like bin Laden so popular — see American policy as identical to Israel's policy; an affront to them that is rarely understood by most Americans.

Far too often, the bombing of declared (or concocted) enemies, whether it's the North Vietnamese, the Iraqis, the Libyans, the Sudanese, the Albanians or the Afghans, produces precisely the opposite effect to what is sought. It kills innocent people, creates more hatred toward America, unifies and stimulates the growth of the extremist Islamic movement and makes them more determined than ever to strike back with their weapon of choice — terror.

On December 16, 1998, the night before the full House of Representatives was to begin debating his articles of impeachment, Clinton launched his massive "Operation Desert Fox" bombing campaign against Iraq. Rep. Paul complained that this week-long air war was "an outrage ... much worse than anything being considered under the impeachment [hearings]," and again warned that "we are [now] more likely to have attacks by terrorists."

During all this time leading up to the September 11th attacks on New York and Washington, D.C., the Clinton administration was thankfully too bogged down in the president's personal and domestic political scandals to react for the worse. However, while Clinton did not take the bait and invade Afghanistan, neither did he reconsider the policies motivating al Qaeda nor confront the enemy he had provoked in any meaningful way.

The Whirlwind

Then, finally, came the attacks of September 11, 2001.

The American population had been completely distracted by stock market bubbles, tabloid-style news and syndicated *Seinfeld* reruns during the "peacetime" years of Bill Clinton. They largely looked on the new millennium as another beautiful "morning in America," and politics under the new George W. Bush administration as not much more than a slight distraction until that point. So the broadcast images of the attack could not have been more misleading: the planes came out of the clear blue sky — just like in the cliché. A stunned population did not know what to make of it. This was "blowback" as properly defined — consequences of secret or unknown foreign policies, which catch the population off guard and leave them open to false interpretations about the nature of the conflict.

George W. Bush's vice president, Dick Cheney, was being truthful when he stated just five days later that bin Laden and al Qaeda's real motive for attacking the United States was "to force us to withdraw from that part of the world." But he was wrong that the attack was meant to make America withdraw our military forces from the world immediately. Instead, it was meant to give the U.S. administration a crisis to exploit, to provoke an overreaction that would encourage our government to invade, to run our country into the ground, like a Soviet Army officer on a fool's errand.

American hawks have often cited bin Laden's taunts that U.S. withdrawal after the Beirut truck bomb attack on U.S. marines in 1983 and the disastrous "Black Hawk Down" events in Somalia in 1993 proved America was a paper tiger that could easily be scared into withdrawal from the region with just a few more similar attacks. The interventionists, like Reuel Marc Gerecht and Jonah Goldberg, then concluded that America needed to "go big" this time instead. Bin Laden may well have understood that forcing America to retreat from its overall policy of dominance in the region was a far different matter than chasing the military out of minor missions in places like Lebanon and Somalia. Or perhaps the strategy of scaring the U.S. off with foreign "pinprick" attacks had already been deemed to have failed. Regardless, the attacks of September 11th, which killed nearly 3,000 people, but could have killed many thousands more, were clearly designed to provoke — to give the U.S. government reason to launch a full-scale war in Afghanistan and beyond to "bleed us to bankruptcy," as bin Laden put it in 2004. Only the U.S. government, manipulated into overreacting — more accurately, given an opportunity to take advantage of a horrible situation — could accomplish this tiny group of terrorists' seemingly impossible goals. These included ending American dominance of the Middle East through imperial overstretch and self-destruction, along with the further political and religious radicalization of the region, increased division between the West and Islamic societies, destabilization of U.S.-supported dictatorships and an increase in the terrorists' own power and influence over the future. By attacking New York and Washington, al Qaeda succeeded in making America, in the words of ex-CIA analyst Scheuer, its "indispensable ally" in their scheme.

But government and TV said America had been attacked because it had been an inward-looking "sleeping giant" as the Terror Juggernaut was closing in. They were provoked and emboldened by American weakness and isolationist indifference, so the government would need to begin to take a much more activist approach to world affairs now that everything had changed.

This was just as the enemy had planned.

As Vice Admiral Thomas R. Wilson, the director of the Defense Intelligence Agency, testified to the U.S. Senate Committee on Intelligence in February 2002, "The strategic intent [of the September 11th attacks] was to deliver a blow that would force the U.S. to either alter its Middle East policies or goad America into a 'disproportionate response' that would trigger an apocalyptic confrontation between Islam and the West."

In 2010, when Osama bin Laden was still living free in Pakistan, *Rolling Stone* magazine published an interview with his non-terrorist son, Omar.

> My father's dream was to bring the Americans to Afghanistan. He would do the same thing he did to the Russians. I was surprised the Americans took the bait. I so much respected the mentality of President Clinton. He was the one who was smart. When my father attacked his places, he sent a few cruise missiles to my father's training camp. He didn't get my father, but after all the war in Afghanistan, they still don't have my father. They have spent hundreds of billions. Better for America to keep the money for its economy. In Clinton's time, America was very, very smart. Not like a bull that runs after the red scarf.

> I was in Afghanistan when Bush was elected. My father was so happy. This is the kind of President he needs — one who will attack and spend money and break the country. I'm sure my father wanted [Sen. John] McCain more than Obama [in the 2008 election]. McCain has the same mentality as Bush.

This may be a naïve view of Clinton and Obama, but the point remains that the more the Americans want to fight in their enemy's part of the world in the short term, the better it helps to achieve Osama bin Laden's goals in the long term.

The reporter asked Omar bin Laden if he thought his father would launch any more attacks in the United States. He replied, "I don't think so. He doesn't need to. As soon as America went to Afghanistan, his plan worked. He's already won."

Chapter Two:
Afghanistan

"I prefer peace. But if trouble must
come, let it come in my time, so
that my children can live in peace."
— Thomas Paine

"This is my fifth deployment. It's
[my son's] first. We're fortunate to be
in the same unit now, so I know
Mom's pretty excited about that."
— CSM Michael Kirby

"So we are continuing this
policy of bleeding America
to the point of bankruptcy."
— Osama bin Laden

"No Negotiations"

The longest war in American history never had to happen. Even after the September 11th attacks, the U.S. did not need to invade Afghanistan. Despite all the propaganda conflating the two, the Taliban regime's leader, Mullah Omar, hated and resented bin Laden and his destabilizing presence there. He told the *Washington Times* in the summer of 2001 that bin Laden was like "a chicken bone stuck in his throat that he can't swallow or spit out." Omar had been negotiating the terrorist's handover since after the African embassy attacks in 1998 and had given the Americans several opportunities to kill the al Qaeda leader in the meantime. They had even sent their foreign minister to try to warn the U.S. of the impending attack, though they were ignored.

The Clinton administration had supported the Taliban's rise to power along with Saudi Arabia and Pakistan back in 1996. Neoconservative policy adviser Zalmay Khalilzad defended the Taliban at the time, writing that "the Taliban does not practice the anti-U.S. style of fundamentalism practiced by Iran." He was advising the firm Unocal, which sought to build an oil pipeline from Turkmenistan to the Pakistani port of Karachi. They wanted to see a total Taliban victory over their Northern Alliance enemies so they could provide the necessary security for the pipeline.

For example, U.S. officials were pleased when the Taliban seized the ancient city of Herat in far western Afghanistan in 1995. And when they sacked the capital of Kabul in 1996, an American diplomat told journalist Ahmed Rashid it would be great if the Taliban went ahead and conquered the whole country. "The Taliban will probably develop like the Saudis did. There will be Aramco, pipelines, an emir, no parliament and lots of Sharia law. We can live with that." Sheila Heslin, an energy expert from the Clinton White House's National Security Council, told Congress, "U.S. policy was to promote the rapid development of Caspian energy. ... We did so specifically to promote the independence of these oil-rich countries, to in essence break Russia's monopoly control over the transportation of oil from that region, and frankly, to promote Western energy security through diversification of supply." Another high-ranking diplomat admitted, "The U.S. acquiesced in supporting the Taliban because of our links to the Pakistan and Saudi governments who backed them. But we no longer do so and we have told them categorically that we need a settlement."

While some believed the Taliban never truly meant to hand bin Laden over, former CIA station chief Milton Bearden, who ran the covert Afghan war in the 1980s, told the *Washington Post*, "We never heard what they were trying to say. We had no common language. Ours was, 'Give up bin Laden.' They were saying, 'Do something to help us give him up.' ... Every time the Afghans said, 'He's lost again,' they are saying something. They are saying, 'He's no longer under our protection.' They thought they were signaling us subtly, and we don't do signals. ... I have no doubts they wanted to get rid of him. He was a pain in the neck."

Alex Strick van Linschoten and Felix Kuehn wrote in their book, *An Enemy We Created: The Myth of the Taliban-Al Qaeda Merger in Afghanistan*, that the Taliban government and their Saudi and Egyptian al Qaeda guests had a strained and "segregated relationship." There were major differences in Taliban leader Mullah Omar and al Qaeda leader bin Laden's schools of Islamic thought and political priorities, as well as the history of distance and personal animosity between the two. The two "were from different worlds, with different beliefs, different customs, different agendas, and — until the September 11th attacks — different paths for the future. The evidence by no means shows a joint agenda or any interest on bin Laden's part in sharing operational details with the Taliban."

After September 11th, the Taliban offered to extradite bin Laden, first to any Muslim country, after some evidence of his guilt be provided. Then they said they would turn him over to the Pakistanis, again, if some evidence would be provided toward establishing bin Laden's responsibility for the attack. But President Bush was adamant: there would be no negotiations. Once the bombs started falling on October 8, the Taliban finally offered to give bin Laden up to any third country and dropped their demand to see evidence of al Qaeda's involvement in the plot. Obviously, at that point, just about any third country in the world would have turned bin Laden and al Qaeda over to the U.S. immediately. This was just the slightest face-saving for the Taliban's surrender on the issue, but it was too little and too late for the Bush administration. As the *Guardian* reported on October 16, 2001,

> For the first time, the Taliban offered to hand over Bin Laden for trial in a country other than the U.S. without asking to see evidence first in return for a halt to the bombing, a source close to Pakistan's military leadership said.
>
> But U.S. officials appear to have dismissed the proposal and are instead hoping to engineer a split within the Taliban leadership.
>
> The offer was brought by Mullah Wakil Ahmed Muttawakil, the Taliban foreign minister and a man who is often regarded as a more moderate figure in the regime. He met officials from the CIA and Pakistan's ISI intelligence directorate in Islamabad on Monday. ... [U]ntil now the Taliban regime has consistently said it has not seen any convincing evidence to implicate the Saudi dissident in any crime.

"Now they have agreed to hand him over to a third country without the evidence being presented in advance," the source close to the military said. ... The U.S. administration has not publicly supported the idea of a trial for Bin Laden outside America and appears intent on removing from power the Taliban leader Mullah Mohammed Omar and the hardliners in the regime.

The era of legal extraditions and trials for al Qaeda members was over. The War on Terrorism had begun.

The Great Escape

This is not to say that the Bush administration was especially determined to capture or kill Osama bin Laden. This author makes the case in *Fool's Errand: Time to End the War in Afghanistan* that the Bush administration must have deliberately let bin Laden escape to Pakistan. When the Delta Force and CIA had bin Laden and the other al Qaeda leaders pinned down at Tora Bora in Afghanistan's eastern Nangarhar province in December 2001, they did call in some massive airstrikes and kill a few hundred al Qaeda fighters there. It was possible that they could have killed bin Laden that way. However, the Bush administration absolutely refused to commit the available ground forces to seal off the border and make sure al Qaeda did not escape. Thousands of Army Rangers were already occupying the Bagram air base north of the capital city of Kabul, just 100 miles or so from Tora Bora. A detachment of Green Berets was fighting the Taliban in the north of the country. And then-Marine General James Mattis, later the secretary of defense under President Donald Trump, had 4,000 marines nearby in the Kandahar Province. He later claimed to have requested permission to get into the fight. None of them were allowed to back up the Delta Force and their local "Eastern Alliance" militia proxies at Tora Bora despite repeated requests from the commanders in charge of the mission on the ground.

It has since been shown in the literature by military professionals that they definitely had enough men available to do a "block and sweep" operation to stop bin Laden and his men from crossing the border. But the top of the chain of command would not allow it.

Gary Berntsen, the second CIA commander in the field in charge of the early part of the war, wrote in his book *Jawbreaker* that he and his superiors "begged" for reinforcements for weeks and weeks, and were consistently told no. His boss, Henry Crumpton, laid out a map on the Oval Office desk, explained the situation and why his men needed support from the Rangers. The president himself turned him down. Berntsen and others, such as Delta Force commander Thomas Greer (a.k.a. "Dalton

Fury"), author of *Kill Bin Laden,* repeatedly complained that they just "could not understand" what were "some of the strangest decisions [they] have ever encountered."

At a press conference in March 2002, President Bush virtually outright confessed that he had called off the operation and allowed bin Laden to escape:

Question: Mr. President, in your speeches now you rarely talk [about] or mention Osama bin Laden. Why is that? Also, can you tell the American people if you have any more information, if you know if he is dead or alive? Final part — deep in your heart, don't you truly believe that until you find out if he is dead or alive, you won't really eliminate the threat of —

Bush: Deep in my heart I know the man is on the run if he's alive at all. Who knows if he's hiding in some cave or not; we haven't heard from him in a long time. And the idea of focusing on one person is — really indicates to me people don't understand the scope of the mission.

Terror is bigger than one person. And he's just — he's a person who's now been marginalized. His network, his host government has been destroyed. He's the ultimate parasite who found weakness, exploited it, and met his match. He is — as I mentioned in my speech, I do mention the fact that this is a fellow who is willing to commit youngsters to their death and he, himself, tries to hide — if, in fact, he's hiding at all.

So I don't know where he is. You know, I just don't spend that much time on him, Kelly, to be honest with you. I'm more worried about making sure that our soldiers are well-supplied; that the strategy is clear; that the coalition is strong; that when we find enemy [Taliban] bunched up like we did in Shahikot Mountains, that the military has all the support it needs to go in and do the job, which they did.

And there will be other battles in Afghanistan. There's going to be other struggles like Shahikot, and I'm just as confident about the outcome of those future battles as I was about Shahikot, where our soldiers are performing brilliantly. We're tough, we're strong, they're well-equipped. We have a good strategy. We are showing the world we know how to fight a guerrilla war with conventional means.

Question: But don't you believe that the threat that bin Laden posed won't truly be eliminated until he is found either dead or alive?

Bush: Well, as I say, we haven't heard much from him. And I wouldn't necessarily say he's at the center of any command structure. And, again, I don't know where he is. I — I'll repeat what I said. I truly am not that concerned about him. I know he is on the run. I was concerned about him when he had taken over a country. I was concerned about the fact that he was basically running Afghanistan and calling the shots for the Taliban.

But once we set out the policy and started executing the plan, he became — we shoved him out more and more on the margins. He has no place to train his al Qaeda killers anymore. And if we — excuse me for a minute — and if we find a training camp, we'll take care of it. Either we will or our friends will.

Though it is impossible to know for certain what U.S. political leaders were thinking, the president could hardly have been more explicit about his intent in this statement. The hunt for the chief perpetrator of the September 11th attacks had been canceled. It had only been six months. Bush later admitted to Bob Woodward that he "was not on point" and did not "feel that sense of urgency" to focus on al Qaeda in his eight months on the job as president before September 11th. In fact, he had ignored forty CIA Presidential Daily Briefs mentioning al Qaeda before the attacks. Here it was just six months later and the president had already changed the subject entirely. The bad guys were long gone, but the war would continue, in Afghanistan and beyond.

It was better for the government that Osama bin Laden still lived so that he could serve as an Orwellian "Emmanuel Goldstein" enemy figure lurking out there somewhere where he could attack us any time. And who would care about Saddam Hussein's alleged alliance with bin Laden if the al Qaeda leader were already dead? National Security Council meeting notes reported by Woodward in his book *Bush at War* make the administration's intentions quite clear. They wanted to go on to Iraq and openly worried that if they got the bad guys too soon, the American people would think the war was over before they had a chance to expand it.

When the National Security Council met at the White House on Tuesday, September 25, two weeks after the attacks and more than a week before the bombing of Afghanistan had even begun, Bush declared, "'We can't define the success or failure in terms of capturing UBL.'" Secretary of Defense Donald Rumsfeld agreed, saying, "We ought to have a broad beginning and an ending. It ought to focus on al Qaeda — it shouldn't focus on UBL ... It's not over if we get his head on a platter. And the failure to get his head on a platter is not failure." Combining an almost perfectly satirical take on the incentives of bureaucratic expansion with the preconceived plan to take the war to Iraq, Rumsfeld went on to suggest, "As part of the war on terrorism, should we be getting something going in another area, other than Afghanistan, so that success or failure and progress isn't measured just by Afghanistan?"

Woodward dryly, perhaps entirely without irony, notes that on the day after the attack, "Rumsfeld worried that a coalition built around the goal of taking out al Qaeda would fall apart once they succeeded in that mission, making it more difficult to continue the war on terrorism elsewhere." In other words, if we won by defeating the enemy, the war would be over. So, to avoid that problem, they would have to be far more ambiguous about just who was to be included as targets in the war.

The evidence is circumstantial but convincing that the Bush administration deliberately withheld the resources that the Delta Force needed to capture or kill bin Laden. Instead, they took most of the fight to the Taliban — which had not attacked us — determined to change the regime in Kabul and Kandahar City instead of focusing on the actual enemy. But as van Linschoten and Kuehn explained, the Taliban leader Omar could not stand bin Laden. He resented the radical terrorist's threat to his fledgling regime, putting it in the crosshairs of the American superpower. As medieval as many of the Taliban's customs were, the previous American administration had helped put them in power only five years before. And believe it or not, the laws of the Taliban's Hanafi Rights sect of Sunni Islam are actually quite a bit more progressive than the ancient Pashtun tribal code, especially concerning the rights of women.

A limited mission, focused on Osama bin Laden and his few hundred men, could have been over by the end of 2001. Even Gary Berntsen has conceded the likelihood of this. "The war could have been over pretty quickly," he told reporter Michael Hirsh in 2016, lamenting Bush's refusal to allow the Rangers and marines to reinforce the CIA and Delta Force in their attempt to kill bin Laden at Tora Bora in December 2001. "We could have had the entire al Qaeda command structure had we done that. Also, the terrorism that metastasized into Pakistan might not have happened. It's impossible to prove any of this. It's a what-if. But, sadly, we lost the opportunity."

The author makes the case in *Fool's Errand* that Bush could have negotiated al Qaeda's extradition and that the U.S. did not have to go to war at all. But if the reader is incredulous about that possibility or believes that al Qaeda deserved to be bombed and shot, rather than arrested and prosecuted, then still, the war could have been directed at the guilty — bin Laden, Zawahiri and their 400 closest Arab lackeys and followers — not the Taliban government of Afghanistan who had not participated in the attack against us. But if the reader thinks that no, the Taliban still deserved to be bombed for harboring al Qaeda for five years leading up to the attack and not giving up bin Laden, no-questions-asked on September the 12th, then still, we all must admit that Bush did not have to create a new government in Kabul to replace the one he destroyed. The Taliban had given up and withdrawn their forces by the end of the year. The U.S. then installed a new government in power in the capital. It then made enemies out of all the new regime's enemies, allies out of its allies and enemies out of their enemies too. This is the war the U.S. has been fighting in Afghanistan for the last 20 years.

Warlords and Sectarian Conflict

The new government the U.S. installed was primarily made up of the Northern Alliance that the Taliban had been fighting. Some of its most prominent leaders had been former puppets of the Soviets, including General Rashid Dostum, a notorious war criminal, torturer, rapist and murderer. Dostum was the perpetrator of the November 2001 Kunduz massacre, where hundreds of Taliban prisoners were locked in shipping containers and then machine-gunned to death or drowned in the blood of those who had been. He became vice-president and then defense minister. The Kabul government has recently named Dostum its military's "marshal," supposedly their highest honor. The new regime was also largely a coalition government of ethnic minorities, the Tajiks, Uzbeks and Hazaras, being leveraged against the 40 percent plurality Pashtuns, dominant in the east and south of the country where the Taliban are from.

The new American-installed president, Hamid Karzai, chosen by neoconservative policy adviser Zalmay Khalilzad, was a Pashtun and the son of an influential tribal leader from Kandahar Province, but he did not really represent the Pashtun people, nor did they ever have any real representation inside the government. If anything, installing Karzai just helped warlords like Gul Agha Sherzai and Pasha Khan Zadran ("PKZ"), and heroin kingpins like President Karzai's half-brother Wali Karzai and his successor Abdul Raziq, who were imposed on the people by Kabul. These newly empowered criminals ruthlessly murdered, raped and exploited the locals. So, the fact that there is some Pashtun representation in the government does not really change its character. Nor does it change the fact that attempting to foist this mostly minority coalition government from another part of the country on this plurality Pashtun tribal population that will absolutely not accept their rule simply has not worked.

There is no reason why it would have. As then-Army General David Petraeus himself admitted, the Taliban's systems of criminal and civil justice — the people's basic security needs — are more in tune with their culture and preferences. And they are not as corrupt as the criminals that the American and Kabul government continue to put in power as mayors, judges, police chiefs and governors.

In a perfect damned-either-way situation, the U.S. chose to marginalize the powerful Pashtun warlords, Gulbuddin Hekmatyar and Jalaluddin

Haqqani, both of whom had been favorites of the CIA in the 1980s due to their effective murderousness. Perhaps it would have been a terrible idea to bring them into the new government. Maybe they could have accepted the new order and attempted to work within it. Instead, they were both turned into allies of the Taliban and deadly enemies, with Hekmatyar's Hizb-e-Islami group and the Haqqani network both responsible for many deaths among American and Afghan soldiers and civilians as well. Hekmatyar made a deal and finally came back to Kabul in peace in 2016.

Pakistan's Role

Afghanistan's eastern border with Pakistan is called the "Durand Line," named for the British bureaucrat who drew it there to divide the unruly Pashtun tribes back in the 19th century. This has been successful, but only to a degree. Ties still run very deep. Importantly for America's Afghan war, Pakistan's intelligence agency, ISI, has been backing the Afghan Taliban's renewed insurgency since 2005, especially in providing the Taliban with safe haven on the Pakistani side of the border from which to wage their war. The Americans did not even really catch up to what was going on until 2007. But there was really nothing they could do about Pakistan's double game anyway since they are so dependent on Pakistan for logistical support for their efforts there.

The Pakistanis have an important reason for their treachery. The Afghan government has a strong military and intelligence relationship with the government of India. The Pakistanis' concern is that the government in Afghanistan would truly consolidate power over the entire country and form a strong alliance with their rival India, leaving them surrounded. To Pakistan, Afghanistan is their "strategic depth" in the event of a nuclear war with India, allowing the government to retreat across the Khyber Pass to safety. Even though the Pakistanis are friends with the Americans who are creating and foisting this Kabul government on the country, they have worked all along to prevent it. They cannot overthrow the Kabul government, but they have consistently, for more than 15 years, backed America's Afghan enemies to at least keep them in play and prevent it from establishing a real monopoly on force.

Ever since the Bush years, America has asked India to help support the Kabul government in its fight against the Taliban. India has taken the opportunity to spend billions of dollars ingratiating themselves with the U.S.-installed government, mainly on domestic infrastructure projects, but in military affairs as well. They have supplied hundreds of trucks and armored personnel carriers for the Afghan army, Russian Mi-25 and Mi-

35 helicopters for their air force, plus all sorts of small arms and training for their soldiers and national police. Of course, one of the main reasons Kabul has needed this help to fight against the Taliban is because the Pakistanis are backing the Taliban because the Indians are helping support the government against them. So around and around the war goes, for years on end.

The Afghan Taliban is not only not diminished but is stronger than ever. That is partially because they have a safe haven across the border in Pakistan. The Taliban's leadership is said to mostly live in the southern Pakistani city of Quetta, where on Obama's third day in office, Director of National Intelligence Mike McConnell told him that the U.S. cannot attack due to the population density. Even when the Obama administration fought the drone war in Pakistan, it was mostly not against the U.S.'s Afghan enemies. Instead, the CIA war there was directed against a few leftover al Qaeda fighters and the Pakistani government's enemies, the Pakistani Taliban, or Tehrik-i-Taliban, an entirely separate group. [See Chapter 6.]

Great Games

"The Long War" is the Pentagon's phrase for their planned indefinite counterinsurgency war from West Africa to Central Asia to the Philippines. The plan is to fight "in dozens of countries for many years to come," as they put it in 2006. But what is the purpose? They boast that bases in Afghanistan put American forces adjacent to Iran and Russia's southern frontier, as well as right in the path of presumed future Chinese expansion. This is perceived to be to America's strategic advantage. Now that we have bases there, how could we ever leave? Yet, one could look at America's presence in Afghanistan as a tripwire for a possible conflict with Iran, Russia or China that the American people otherwise would prefer to avoid at all costs. Military domination of Eurasia by the United States could destroy us before it secures a thing for us.

The war is not about mineral wealth, though hawks such as Gen. Petraeus have brought that issue up as an excuse to stay. The reality is that the geography, topography and security situation just will not allow for such expensive and long-term investments in that country in any near term. This is not to say that theft would justify the occupation, only that the excuse is just an excuse since no theft worth the price could possibly be won anyway.

It is just hubris to think, as Brzezinski wrote in *The Grand Chessboard*, that even though our naval power is absolutely dominant on earth, since we are from way over here in the New World, the U.S. desperately needs a foothold in Central Asia to add to our bases in Europe and East Asia. We must establish military hegemony in the center of Eurasia because this is the "pivot point" on our way to dominance in Eastern Europe and the rest of the world. This is all allegedly necessary because if we did not dominate it, then supposedly the Russians would.

The news is that Central Asia is Russia's near-abroad. It is not ours. And Russian President Vladimir Putin or his successors would be fools to follow in America's footsteps on the path of the old Soviet Union's imperial suicide mission in Afghanistan. They would have no reason to intervene there at all other than keeping bin Ladenites down, the same reason they have supported U.S. efforts and the new Kabul government in Afghanistan since 2001. That they would try to replicate the USSR's 1980s attempt to dominate the country is not a serious concern. These antiquated, originally British, imperial doctrines are policymakers' justification for our permanent war in Afghanistan, though the policy is clearly more of a risk than potential benefit. This is especially true for the civilian populations caught in the middle of foreign powers' Great Games. [More on Afghanistan in Chapter 5.]

Chapter Three:
Iraq War II

"Truth is the first casualty in war."
— Ethel Annakin

"One of the hardest parts of my job is
to connect Iraq to the war on terror."
— George W. Bush

"The way you do hope is
through a form of government."
— George W. Bush

"Every ten years or so, the United States
needs to pick up some small, crappy little
country and throw it against the wall, just to
show the world we mean business."
— Michael Ledeen

Taking Advantage

From the moment President George W. Bush delivered his statement from the Oval Office on the night of the September 11th attacks, the die was cast. There was no mention of al Qaeda, even though the government already knew who had been responsible for the attack.

In his speech to Congress nine days after the attack, Bush declared war on "terrorism," a mandate so broad it could include the targeting of almost any violent political group on earth. Now, we were told, everything had changed. It was the dawn of a new era of war to "end evil" on Earth. It is clear why the administration framed the conflict the way they did: The president and his men had already decided, the very day of the attack, that they would be launching a project far greater than a mere hunt for the leaders of the group that was responsible. The Terror War, like the Cold War with the Soviet Union, would serve as a larger framework for numerous smaller wars. "There are thousands of these terrorists in more than 60 countries," Bush claimed. "Our war on terror begins with al Qaeda, but it does not end there. It will not end until every terrorist group of global reach has been found, stopped and defeated."

Before the sun had gone down on September 11th and anyone could even be sure the attacks were completely over, Secretary of Defense Donald Rumsfeld was already telling his staff to plan for war against Iraq. Undersecretary of Defense for Intelligence Stephen Cambone took notes:

> Hard to get good case. Need to move swiftly. Near term target needs — go massive — sweep it all up, things related and not. ... Best info fast. Judge whether good enough [to] hit SH [Saddam Hussein] at same time — not only UBL [Osama bin Laden]. Tasks. [Pentagon General Counsel] Jim Haynes to talk with PW [Deputy Secretary of Defense Paul Wolfowitz], for additional support [for] connection with UBL.

Over at the White House, Richard Clarke, the head of counter-terrorism, was doing everything he could to keep the focus on Osama bin Laden in Afghanistan, forcefully debunking Deputy Secretary of Defense Paul Wolfowitz's immediate conflation of bin Laden's group with the government of Iraq. Wolfowitz had long associated himself with the mainstream conspiracy crank Laurie Mylroie. She blamed Iraq for secretly orchestrating the entire al Qaeda war against the United States. Mylroie claimed that Saddam Hussein was behind the first World Trade Center bombing in 1993 and the deadly shooting outside CIA headquarters later that year, which in reality was a lone-wolf attack tied to neither Iraq nor bin Laden. She even blamed Iraq for the 1995 Oklahoma City bombing and all the al Qaeda strikes overseas in the years since. The CIA, FBI and the other intelligence agencies had dismissed her ravings, which all hung on the provably false claim that al Qaeda operative Ramzi Yousef was actually an Iraqi secret police agent who had stolen Yousef's identity. But for Wolfowitz, former Clinton-era CIA director James Woolsey, influential neoconservative Richard Perle and a few of their fellow travelers, it was the ultimate case of confirmation bias, if not simply lying in the pursuit of other agendas.

By November 2001, Rumsfeld and CENTCOM commander General Tommy Franks were working on plans for invading Iraq, including floating proposed excuses for it, such as showing an Iraqi link to September 11th or the anthrax attacks, or an alleged violation of international restrictions against their possession of weapons of mass destruction. Gen. Franks briefed President Bush about the plan on December 28.

In the words of the CIA's Michael Scheuer, the 2003 invasion of Iraq was America's "hoped for, but unexpected gift" to Osama bin Laden and his movement. The American people had given the President the writ to get the men responsible for the attack on the U.S., "dead or alive." Bush had other plans. Like the bootleggers and Baptists of last century, the American politicians and the terrorists did not need to secretly be in league to remain strategic allies. Both sides have continued to benefit from each other at the expense of the people of America and the Middle East.

General Wesley Clark, who had been the supreme allied commander of NATO forces in Europe under President Clinton's administration, later told a story about going to the Pentagon a few weeks after September 11th. He was shown a memo by an officer from the Pentagon's Joint Staff explaining, "This is a memo that describes how we're going to take out seven countries in five years, starting with Iraq, and then Syria, Lebanon, Libya, Somalia, Sudan and, finishing off, Iran."

Not one of those governments had an alliance with al Qaeda, nor the slightest thing to do with the September 11th attack. But the administration decided that rather than being diverted from their long-term goal of regime change in Iraq and the other countries on the list due to the danger of anti-American terrorism, they would just use terrorism as their excuse to go ahead and go through with it anyway. They thought it was going to be easy. In this case, the entire thing completely blew up in the hawks' faces, costing the United States much of the influence that it had in the region, rather than strengthening their position. The Iraq invasion of 2003 also fatefully touched off a regional sectarian war that for various reasons will probably last, in one form or another, for the rest of our lifetimes.

In January 2002, Bush announced in his State of the Union speech that an "Axis of Evil" threatened the U.S. and peace in the world and that this gathering danger would have to be dealt with sooner than later. Marvel at the blatant lie that bin Laden's al Qaeda, Hussein's Iraq, Khamenei's Iran and Kim's North Korea were an "axis," comparable to Hitler's Germany, Mussolini's Italy and Hirohito's Japan in World War II — an alliance at war against the United States of America, no less. It was just nonsense. In fact, Iraq and Iran were enemies of each other and al Qaeda. North Korea's only connection to any of the above was having sold some medium-range missiles to Iran years before. Just five months after al Qaeda's attack on the U.S., President Bush was announcing an entirely new aggressive foreign policy that had nothing to do with fighting those who had attacked the United States or the terrorism that threatened American civilians' lives whatsoever. It was just a giant bait-and-switch. The administration claimed to be so concerned that these countries could pass "the world's most dangerous weapons" to terrorist groups like al Qaeda, but all three countries were members of the Non-Proliferation Treaty, and, despite administration claims, were verified not to have nuclear weapons programs at the time, much less a working relationship with Osama bin Laden. Any supposed threat from any of the three could have easily been contained without violent conflict.

It is remarkable that the government was able to announce a year and a half before starting a war that they were going to attack this country, Iraq, and that they were going to come up with whatever propaganda was necessary to get the people to allow them to do it. It did not matter that Iraq was a small, poor country that the U.S. had already been bombing for 12 years straight, which had a gross domestic product the size of northern Arkansas, possessed no navy, no air force and no ability to project power beyond its borders whatsoever. Nor did it matter that secular Saddam Hussein, with his clean-shaven chin, Western suit and French beret, was no ally of the fundamentalist radical bin Laden. The Bush government and the media's narrative was that the lesson of September 11th is that we must start all the wars from now on ourselves. That way, no one can ever attack us because we already attacked them first. This was just an excuse for aggression. This was certainly the case with Iraq, which had no means, motive or plans to attack the United States for Bush to "preempt" at all.

The White House Iraq Group (WHIG), led by Bush political adviser Karl Rove, decided that "preemption" of an impending Iraqi attack would be their sales pitch to average Americans. They just had to repeat it enough times, and the people would start to repeat it back as if it was their own idea. "You think we should just wait around for Iraq to attack us?!" they would ask, the false conclusion assumed.

There is no question that they knew they were lying about Iraq's alleged "threat" to America. In early 2001, Secretary of State Colin Powell and National Security Advisor Condoleezza Rice had both stated that Saddam Hussein could easily be contained. Saddam "has not developed any significant capability with respect to weapons of mass destruction. He is unable to project conventional power against his neighbors," stated Powell in February. In April, Rice admitted, "Saddam does not control the northern part of the country. We are able to keep his arms from him. His military forces have not been rebuilt."

Bush's real motive for launching the war was to guarantee his own reelection and to prove that he was smarter and tougher than his father, or at least good enough for him. As then-Texas Governor Bush told his biographer Mickey Herskowitz in 1999,

> One of the keys to being seen as a great leader is to be seen as a commander-in-chief. My father had all this political capital built up when he drove the Iraqis out of [Kuwait] and he wasted it. If I have a chance to invade Iraq, if I had that much capital, I'm not going to waste it. I'm going to get everything passed I want to get passed and I'm going to have a successful presidency.

His former press secretary Scott McClellan later wrote that "As I have heard Bush say, only a wartime president is likely to achieve greatness, in part because the epochal upheavals of war provide the opportunity for transformative change of the kind Bush hoped to achieve. In Iraq, Bush saw his opportunity to create a legacy of greatness." Bush's first secretary of the treasury, Paul O'Neill, the former CEO of Alcoa, the powerful aluminum firm, later confirmed that from the very first two cabinet meetings, the administration's entire agenda surrounded the question of how to start a war against Iraq. He said the president's attitude was, "Go find me a way to do this."

As for Vice President Cheney, he had done a horrible job as CEO of the oil services firm Halliburton in the 1990s. He lost billions of dollars after buying the firm Dresser Industries right as they were being held liable for years of asbestos-caused cancer claims. Going to war was a convenient way to pay them back by putting the company and their subsidiary, Kellogg, Brown and Root (KBR), on the dole building bases for the army, working the Iraqi oil fields and providing fuel, food and other services to soldiers. In the ten years after the invasion, KBR received more than $39 billion in Pentagon contracts. Cheney also had a conservative ideological bent toward "privatizing" — really, contracting — as much of the grunt work as possible to free up fighting forces. All indications are that Cheney agreed with the neoconservatives' claims about how easy the war would be and that it would enhance American dominance of the region and its oil and gas resources. His previously stated concerns from the Desert Storm era about pieces of Iraq "flying off" under the dominance of regional players were the Baghdad regime to fall had evidently been successfully allayed. The war would also be a great way to demonstrate the principles of the old Defense Planning Guidance that was now the official National Security Strategy of the United States. America was the world hegemon and any nation which tested that premise would find out the hard way. Iraq's weakness, not its strength, was what made it a prime target. Iraq was "doable," as Paul Wolfowitz put it.

Many war opponents misunderstood the role of oil in Cheney and the hawks' thinking. Sure, profits for connected oil companies were meant to be a nice side benefit and payoff to political supporters, but this was not central to the plan, nor was cheap gasoline to benefit American consumers. The primary role of oil in the plan for war was a hare-brained neoconservative scheme, dreamt up by Ariel Cohen and Gerald P. O'Driscoll, Jr. at the Heritage Foundation. They wanted to privatize Iraqi oil to as many firms and as rapidly as possible in order to depress the global price and break Saudi Arabia's OPEC cartel. James Baker III, Bush Sr.'s former secretary of state whose law firm Baker-Botts represented Exxon and just about every other oil company in America and Saudi Arabia, quickly put an end to this plan as soon as the war began. Iraq would have a national oil company, and it would work with Saudi Arabia and OPEC after all, thank you very much. The other significant role oil played in the motive for the war was in terms of military hegemony. As Cheney had testified to Congress back in 1991, whichever power controlled the Middle East's "choke points" for petroleum has the ability to shut off energy supplies to enemies in times of war. The U.S. is not dependent on Persian Gulf oil, but our allies and adversaries in South and East Asia are. Power, not money, was the end the vice president and the Pentagon had in mind.

Donald Rumsfeld, who had previously been defense secretary under President Gerald Ford, was determined to transform the military's war doctrines to emphasize airpower, special operations forces and light and fast strikes against enemy regimes. Iraq was to serve as the primary test-case for his strategy.

Though TV portrayed attacking Iraq as the only logical consensus of the American foreign policy community, this was not true. The president, vice president and secretary of defense were leading the charge, surrounded by a chorus of neoconservative hawks in the administration and in the media. While the Republican Party establishment and a great many liberal-Democratic hawks jumped on board for the cause, many leftist, progressive, libertarian, realist and paleo-conservative thinkers, writers and activists opposed the war from the beginning. So did millions of Americans who joined antiwar protests from coast to coast in February and March 2003. On September 26, 2002, 33 international relations scholars of the realist school signed an open letter in the *New York Times*, asking for the Bush government to rethink its decision to go to war. Later, Bush Sr.'s former national security adviser and close friend, retired

General Brent Scowcroft, even wrote an essay for the *Wall Street Journal* entitled "Don't Attack Saddam." Back during the Bush Sr. years, one of Scowcroft's jobs as national security adviser had been to "keep the crazies in the basement," that is, the neoconservatives away from Middle East policy. Now, as a favor to the father, Scowcroft was trying to warn the son not to listen to them. H.W. Bush's second secretary of state, Lawrence Eagleburger, also chimed in with "Msg. to Bush: Don't Attack Iraq" for ABC News.

But it was too late. George W. Bush, Cheney and Rumsfeld had stacked the government with the men his father had labeled "the crazies." Former leftists and Cold War Democrats, the neoconservatives were highly ideological about the beneficence of American military power and, in many cases, close to the nationalist Likud Party in Israel. They were determined to spread the War on Terrorism into Iraq as quickly as possible. It had been a major priority of the neoconservative "cabal" — their term — in Washington for years.

The *New York Times*'s Thomas L. Friedman, an Iraq war supporter but not a part of the neoconservative group, talked to the Israeli daily *Haaretz* just after the war began. They wrote, somewhat paraphrasing:

> Is the Iraq war the great neoconservative war? It's the war the neoconservatives wanted, Friedman says. It's the war the neoconservatives marketed. Those people had an idea to sell when September 11 came, and they sold it. Oh boy, did they sell it. So this is not a war that the masses demanded. This is a war of an elite. Friedman laughs: I could give you the names of 25 people (all of whom are at this moment within a five-block radius of this office) who, if you had exiled them to a desert island a year and a half ago, the Iraq war would not have happened.

A Clean Break

Neoconservative thinker and apparatchik David Wurmser was the primary author of two important studies in 1996. He, along with Richard Perle, Douglas Feith and a few other neoconservatives, signed on to the first essay, which was done for the Israeli Institute for Advanced Strategic and Political Studies' "Study Group on a New Israeli Strategy Toward 2000." It was titled "A Clean Break: A New Strategy for Securing the Realm." Wurmser also wrote a companion piece called "Coping with Crumbling States: A Western and Israeli Balance-of-Power Strategy for the Levant." These were followed by his 1999 book, *Tyranny's Ally: America's Failure to Defeat Saddam Hussein*. Wurmser argued that Israel's primary foreign adversary was the Lebanese Shi'ite militia and political party, Hezbollah.

The group, "The Party of God," was founded in 1982 by Lebanese Shi'ites in reaction to Israel's invasion and occupation of Lebanon, where they sought to expel the Palestinian Liberation Organization (PLO). Since Iran armed Hezbollah by way of Syria, the goal was to weaken Syria and Iran's position in the region to limit the power and the threat of Hezbollah to Israel. Unbelievably, Wurmser said the way to accomplish this was to "focus on removing Saddam Hussein from power in Iraq — an important Israeli strategic objective in its own right — as a means of foiling Syria's regional ambitions."

The idea was that if they deposed Saddam, the then-king of Jordan, King Hussein bin Talal, could take over Iraq. In this case, the Jordanian King Hussein was a Sunni and would be attempting to rule over the Iraqi super-majority Shi'ite Arabs. But Wurmser was convinced that King Hussein, from the Hashemite clan, who claimed to be descended from the prophet Mohammed, would command the allegiance of the Iraqi Shi'ite clergy in the southern Iraqi city of Najaf. Based on the smoke the Iraqi exile Ahmed Chalabi had been blowing, Wurmser started hallucinating. From "A Clean Break":

> Were the Hashemites to control Iraq, they could use their influence over [Shi'ite religious leadership in the city of] Najf [Najaf] to help Israel wean the south Lebanese Shia away from Hezbollah, Iran and Syria. Shia retain strong ties to the Hashemites: the Shia venerate foremost the Prophet's family, the direct descendants of which — and in whose veins the blood of the Prophet flows — is King Hussein.

So once Iraq gets its Jordanian king, the Sunni and also the Shi'ite Arabs, the latter in the thrall of their religious leaders in Najaf, would fall in line with the king's, and therefore Israel's, will. Iraq would join the American-Jordanian-Turkish-Israeli alliance system in the Middle East. These clerics could then be used to claim Lebanese Hezbollah's loyalty away from Iran, thus weakening their threat to Israel. This thinking was hilariously and tragically stupid. The Shi'ite religious leadership in Najaf had no allegiance to the Hashemites whatsoever. If they had revered that line of supposed descendants of the prophet — which they did not — that would in no way have bound their loyalty and deference to a new king. The Najaf clergy even had a fatwa banning religious Shi'ites from supporting the Hashemites from 1922–1937. The idea that they would just obey the Jordanian king, sever their kinship with Iran and somehow command Hezbollah to bow down to Israel was simply ridiculous. As it turned out, after the invasion of 2003, Jordan proved to have little influence there. Wurmser further elaborated on this fantasy in "Coping with Crumbling States":

A Hashemite presence in Iraq, especially within the Shia centers in Najaf, could break Iran's and Syria's grip on the Shi'ite community of Lebanon. Were Jordan to prevail in Iraq, then Najaf's elite, with its veneration of the prophet's family, would be tied to King Hussein, and pro-Jordan Iraq Shi'ites [such] as Ahmed Chalabi ... would define the Iraqi Shi'ite community after Saddam's removal. Close cooperation between Israel and Jordan could undermine Syria's pressure on Israel's northern border as the local Shia are weaned from Hezballah's domination. In short, developments in Iraq could potentially unravel Syria's structure in Lebanon by severing the Shia-Syrian-Iranian axis.

Wurmser believed that once the new Hashemite-ruled Iraq became allies with Israel and Turkey, they would isolate Syria and Lebanese Hezbollah from Iran, cut off all financial support for Hamas and other Palestinian groups and thus relieve the Israelis of the necessity of giving any of the Golan Heights back to Syria or the West Bank back to the Palestinians. Instead of "land for peace," they could achieve "peace through strength." Why, the new Iraq would even rebuild the old British oil and water pipeline to the Israeli city of Haifa, the Iraqi exile Chalabi had promised.

In "Coping with Crumbling States," Wurmser suggests after toppling Saddam Hussein in Iraq, that Israel and the U.S. should also "expedite the chaotic collapse" to Syria so that they could remake that society in a way closer to our liking as well:

> The issue here is whether the West and Israel can construct a strategy for limiting and expediting the chaotic collapse that will ensue in order to move on to the task of creating a better circumstance. ...

> If ... Jordan wins, then Syria would be isolated and surrounded by a new pro-western Jordanian-Israeli-Iraqi-Turkish bloc, the first of which can help contain and manage (through its more solid and traditional regime) the scope of the coming chaos in Iraq and most probably in Syria.

Wurmser admits that these policies could lead to an increase of Islamist terrorism. However, since he denied that secular Ba'athism in Iraq or Syria could do anything to contain it, the only other choice had to be regime change.

> Secular-Arab nationalism, particularly Ba'athism, undermines regional stability and damages the West's interests not only in its active role as a threat, but also in its more passive role as an obstacle to introducing more formidable, and beneficial, intellectual defenses among Arabs with which to stem fundamentalism. ... The West and its local friends must engage fundamentalism with better associates than Ba'athists.

It is clear that this bill of goods was sold to the neoconservatives in the 1990s by Ahmed Chalabi, the Iraqi exile and convicted embezzler whose CIA- and later Pentagon-funded Iraqi National Congress (INC) had been trying to depose Hussein for years. The INC later supplied many of the defectors who falsely claimed Iraq still possessed weapons of mass destruction in the run-up to the invasion of 2003. Chalabi is referred to numerous times in the three Wurmser papers.

These were the very same neoconservatives — David Wurmser, Richard Perle and Douglas Feith — prominent among them, in George W. Bush's first term, who led the push to launch Iraq War II to accomplish these goals. Wurmser himself went from the Defense Department to the State Department, and later became Dick Cheney's foreign policy adviser. Perle was made chairman of the Defense Policy Board, and Feith got the job as deputy secretary of defense for policy. Perle and Feith's close associate Paul Wolfowitz was made deputy secretary of defense.

Perle, the self-proclaimed "Prince of Darkness," was one of the most important neoconservative ringleaders of that era. A former student of the influential philosophy professor Leo Strauss at the University of Chicago, Perle entered politics working for Democratic Senator Henry "Scoop" Jackson of Washington State, a Cold Warrior popularly nicknamed "the senator from Boeing," along with Paul Wolfowitz, Douglas Feith and Elliot Abrams. Perle helped lead the neoconservative move from the Trotskyite and Democratic left to the Republican right in the 1970s and into the Ronald Reagan administration's Defense Department in the 1980s. He had been investigated multiple times by the FBI for passing classified information to Israel, but was never prosecuted. His seat on the Defense Policy Board did not give him direct access to the levers of power, but it did give him the ability to put all of his best friends and fellow-travelers in the right positions to carry out his agenda regardless.

The certain-to-be-roaring success of the regime-change operation, the neoconservatives claimed, would inspire the envious Iranian population to rise up and overthrow their government so they could have an America-friendly democracy too. Wurmser assumed that Iran abandoned the 1991 Iraqi Shi'ite uprising because of their fear of Iraqi Shi'ite authority and influence, rather than the obvious fact of the uprising's doomed fate after being backstabbed by the United States. He insisted in *Tyranny's Ally* that, "A free Iraqi Shi'ite community would be a nightmare to the theocratic Islamic Republic of Iran." All of this completely backfired. It is Iranian power in Iraq that has been enhanced above all, permanently altering the regional balance of power in their favor and leading to even worse American policies in response to that failure.

The true neoconservatives have probably never counted more than 100 men and women among their ranks. But during the run-up to the invasion of Iraq, they divided themselves almost perfectly into newspaper, magazine, think tank, and undersecretary positions across the national security bureaucracy. In the Bill Clinton years, they had congregated at the major conservative foundations and think tanks in preparation for the coming Republican era. Perle, Wurmser and "Clean Break" co-signer Robert J. Lowenberg wrote a series of articles promoting regime change for the *Wall Street Journal* and *Washington Times* in 1996. Neoconservative policy advisers Zalmay Khalilzad and Paul Wolfowitz, who had worked together in the Defense Department during the first Iraq war, wrote a piece called "Overthrow Him" for *The Weekly Standard* in December 1997. They founded the Project for a New American Century (PNAC) in 1998, immediately writing an open letter to President Clinton demanding regime change in Iraq. It was signed by neoconservatives Khalilzad, Perle, Elliot Abrams, William Kristol, James Woolsey, Robert Kagan and Francis Fukuyama, among others. They succeeded in getting Congress to pass the Iraq Liberation Act of 1998, which made it official American policy to seek regime change against Saddam Hussein.

As the group stated in their influential paper, "Rebuilding America's Defenses," dominance of the Middle East was the heart of their strategy:

> Since the collapse of the Soviet empire, this [American security] perimeter has expanded slowly but inexorably. ... In the Persian Gulf region, the presence of American forces, along with British and French units, has become a semipermanent fact of life. Though the immediate mission of those forces is to enforce the no-fly zones over northern and southern Iraq, they represent the long-term commitment of the United States and its major allies to a region of vital importance. Indeed, the United States has for decades sought to play a more permanent role in Gulf regional security. While the unresolved conflict with Iraq provides the immediate justification, the need for a substantial American force presence in the Gulf transcends the issue of the regime of Saddam Hussein.

Israel's interests had always been the purpose of the neoconservatives' advocacy of American militarism. As one of the movement's most important founders, Norman Podhoretz, explained in 1979,

> There was, to be sure, one thing that many of even the most passionately committed American Zionists were reluctant to do, and that was to face up to the fact that continued American support for Israel depended upon continued American involvement in international affairs — from which it followed that an American withdrawal into the kind of isolationist mood that prevailed most recently between the two world wars, and that now looked as though it might soon prevail again, represented a direct threat to the security of Israel.

This same thinking was at the heart of the neocons' strategy to lie the American people into war with Iraq. As the journalist Jim Lobe wrote two months before the war,

> Indeed, the strongest advocates for attacking Iraq both inside and outside the administration — Deputy Defense Secretary Paul Wolfowitz, Perle and other [Defense Policy Board] members, respectively — have been the neoconservatives.
>
> In their view, the interests of Israel and the United States are virtually identical, or as one of them, former Education Secretary William Bennett, noted last year, "America's fate and Israel's fate are one and the same."

In George W. Bush's first term, a dozen or so neoconservatives spread throughout the government while reporting directly back to the vice president, Dick Cheney. Then-Secretary of State Colin Powell later described the neoconservative network as "a separate government" inside the government. I. Lewis "Scooter" Libby was the chief of staff to the vice president and special adviser to the president. John Hannah was Cheney's assistant national security adviser and the Iraqi National Congress's point of contact for passing along their WMD propaganda straight to the highest levels. Eric Edelman, Cheney's deputy national security adviser, had been part of the group that wrote the 1992 Defense Planning Guidance. On the National Security Council was neoconservative policy adviser Zalmay Khalilzad, who had also helped write that document in 1992, along with Elliot Abrams, Robert Joseph and Steven Hadley. According to journalist Barton Gellman, Hadley was known as "Cheney's mole" at the NSC.

Along with Wurmser at the State Department was the foreign policy hawk John Bolton. Bolton, a lifelong Barry Goldwater conservative, is not an actual neocon, but his brand of right-wing nationalism has always fit well with their agenda. He and Wurmser's job was to act as the vice-president's leash on Secretary of State Powell and his deputy Dick Armitage, ramming through Cheney's policy and attempting to limit Powell's comparatively restraining influence on President Bush. Mark Groombridge, an aide to Bolton at the State Department, later told the media, "Everyone knew that Bolton was Cheney's spy." Another official explained, "John almost regards Israel as part of the United States. He thinks our interests and their interest are identical."

In the Defense Department were Paul Wolfowitz, the deputy secretary of defense, and Douglas Feith, the deputy secretary of defense for policy, who set up a group called the Office of Special Plans (OSP). This "expanded Iraq desk" was run by neoconservative academic and former Perle aide Abram Shulsky and retired Navy officer and former Cheney aide

William Luti. Staff included Michael Rubin from the American Enterprise Institute (AEI), David Schenker from the Washington Institute for Near East Policy (WINEP), a spin-off of the powerful American Israel Public Affairs Committee (AIPAC), retired Colonel William Bruner, a former Gingrich aide, and Michael Makovsky from the Jewish Institute for National Security Affairs (JINSA). Iran-Contra scandal figure and neoconservative radical, Michael Ledeen, was brought on as a paid consultant. Their job was essentially to pick through the CIA's trash and collect the INC exiles' tall tales of illicit weapons production. They would then funnel the lies that led to war up the "stovepipe," straight to the White House and mainstream media in ready-made talking point format. We know so much of that story due to the efforts of the heroic Pentagon whistleblower, Air Force Lieutenant Colonel Karen Kwiatkowski. After the war began, it was revealed that by the summer of 2002, an INC official boasted in an internal memo that they had already succeeded in placing 808 stories in the American and British press pushing their lies and arguments for war. They also noted that they passed their propaganda straight to William Luti at the Pentagon and John Hannah in the vice president's office, confirming Kwiatkowski's account.

Also in the Pentagon, under the auspices of Douglas Feith's policy department, David Wurmser set up the Policy Counter-Terrorism Evaluation Group (PCTEG) with Michael Maloof, another former aide of Richard Perle's. They pushed the Salman Pak training center hoax, which claimed that Iraq was training terrorist hijackers, as well as the lies about Iraqi government support for the group Ansar al Islam hiding safe up in American-protected Iraqi Kurdistan. They also pushed the fake story about an Iraqi official meeting with September 11th hijacker Mohammed Atta in Prague, Czech Republic, shortly before the attack. (More on these below.) When asked by a reporter about the CIA's complaints regarding his sloppy work, Maloof shot back, "This is the same crowd that worked with the mujahideen in Bosnia, that couldn't give us any heads up on the worst intelligence failure in U.S. history?" Good point. They were still right about him though.

At the Pentagon's Office of Net Assessment, Harold Rhode helped the neocons to purge actual Middle East experts from their positions and replace them with loyal hawks from the think tanks.

The influential neoconservatives Richard Perle, Kenneth Adelman, James Woolsey and Jeane Kirkpatrick, along with their allies former House Speaker Newt Gingrich and former secretary of state and national security adviser Henry Kissinger, led the Pentagon's Defense Policy Board. They all recommended attacking Iraq as early as September 19, 2001. Kirkpatrick had given up on her idea that America could be a normal country in a normal time, now that everything had changed.

Like Cheney and Libby, Gingrich made repeated visits to CIA headquarters to pressure analysts for more dirt on Iraq. He also waged a personal campaign to try to discredit the idea of weapons inspections being even possible under the Hussein regime. For example, Gingrich wrote in the *Washington Times* that inspections were a "clever arrangement" meant to "slowly undermine the Bush administration's policy on Iraq while having the appearance of cooperation. The danger is that the State Department will fall for the proposal, and in the process make replacing Saddam Hussein more difficult, if not impossible." Inspections could undermine the case for war over weapons they would not be able to find, because they would be so well hidden of course.

Outside of government, the neoconservative movement dominated the Washington, D.C. think tanks, such as PNAC, JINSA, AEI, WINEP, the Center for Security Policy (CSP), Heritage Foundation and the Hudson Institute. Their liberal-hawk allies dominated at the Brookings Institution and the Council on Foreign Relations (CFR). The neocons also dominated the major magazines, newspapers and cable TV networks where they pushed ceaselessly for invading Iraq. These included William Kristol, William Safire, Norman and John Podhoretz, Gary Schmitt, William J. Bennett, Danielle Pletka, Charles Krauthammer, Robert Kagan, Daniel Pipes, Francis Fukuyama, David Brooks, Jonah Goldberg, Michael Ledeen, David Frum, William Bennett, Fred Hiatt, Cliff May, Bret Stephens, Michael Novak, Eli Lake, Reuel Marc Gerecht, David Horowitz, Frank Gaffney, Marvin Olasky, Stephen Schwartz, Joshua Muravchik, Eliot Cohen, Laurie Mylroie, Michael Weiner (a.k.a. "Savage") and Max Boot, in alliance with conservative writers and TV and radio hawks like Andrew McCarthy, Rich Lowry, Stephen Hayes, Francis Brooke, Ann Coulter, Glenn Harlan Reynolds, Victor Davis Hanson, George F. Will, Cliff May, Michelle Malkin, Bill O'Reilly, Sean Hannity, Rush Limbaugh, Glenn Beck, Neal Boortz and Mark Levin. The political right was joined in urging an attack by their counterpart liberal hawks, journalists and "humanitarian interventionists" like Jeffrey Goldberg, Christopher Hitchens, Thomas L. Friedman, Will Marshall, Matthew Yglesias, David Rose, Chris Hedges, Ivo Daalder, Michael McFaul, Andrew Sullivan, Robert Kerrey, George Packer, Peter Beinart, Michael Kelly, Lawrence F. Kaplan, Marty Peretz, Juan Cole, Ken Pollack and Michael O'Hanlon, the anchors of the PBS *Newshour* and National Public Radio — and of course the big three: Dan Rather, Peter Jennings and Tom Brokaw, legendary anchors of the major networks' nightly newscasts. Rather later complained that CBS had "regulatory needs" in Washington, D.C. that he needed to consider before telling the American people the truth about the war. (Peter Beinart and Andrew Sullivan later sincerely apologized.)

Not only the neoconservatives but the broader Israel Lobby, especially AIPAC, pushed for war as well. As their semi-official ombudsman Jeffrey Goldberg later wrote in the *New Yorker*, "AIPAC lobbied Congress in favor of the Iraq war." Their then-executive director Howard Kohr also bragged that the group had lobbied Congress to vote for the war authorization. The *Washington Post* found that while AIPAC did not have an "official position" on the war, due to fears about stoking American anti-Semitism, unofficially, there was no question that they supported and argued for the war. AIPAC promoted the war in print too. Their "briefing book" from 2002 included the statement that "As long as Saddam Hussein is in power, any containment of Iraq will only be temporary until the next crisis or act of aggression," and went on to accuse the Iraqi government of maintaining an alliance with Osama bin Laden.

In February 2002, Israeli Prime Minister Ariel Sharon warned Bush that war against Iraq would unleash chaos and empower Iran. However, Sharon's primary rival in the Likud Party, Benjamin Netanyahu, whose faction the neoconservatives more closely represented, wanted to hit Iraq first and foremost. In September, Netanyahu testified before the U.S. Congress that Israeli intelligence knew for a fact that Hussein had a secret uranium enrichment program and that, "If you take out Saddam, Saddam's regime, I guarantee that it will have enormous positive reverberations on the region."

It was not long before Sharon was convinced. As Julian Borger and Robert Dreyfuss separately reported, he even created his own group inside the prime minister's office to manufacture bogus intelligence in English to stovepipe up to the top of the Bush administration to help make the case for war. Sharon would push for the U.S. to attack Iran immediately afterward.

Haaretz reported:

> Senior IDF officers and those close to Prime Minister Ariel Sharon, such as National Security Advisor Ephraim Halevy, paint a rosy picture of the wonderful future Israel can expect after the war. They envision a domino effect, with the fall of Saddam Hussein followed by that of Israel's other enemies.

Six months before the war, National Security Advisor Rice's assistant Philip Zelikow admitted what experts understood, but average Americans were never told. This war was to be fought primarily to protect the interests of Israel, not the United States.

> Why would Iraq attack America or use nuclear weapons against us? I'll tell you what I think the real threat [is] and actually has been since 1990 — it's the threat against Israel. And this is the threat that dare not speak its name, because the Europeans don't care deeply about that

threat, I will tell you frankly. And the American government doesn't want to lean too hard on it rhetorically, because it is not a popular sell. Don't look at the links between Iraq and al Qaeda, but then ask yourself the question, "Gee, is Iraq tied to Hamas and the Palestinian Islamic Jihad and the people who are carrying out suicide bombings in Israel?" Easy question to answer; the evidence is abundant.

But nobody told the American people this. They said Iraq was going to attack us with weapons of mass destruction if we did not stop them first. It did not help much that the only antiwar guests allowed on cable TV news was the actor that played B.J. Honeycutt on M*A*S*H and the secretary from the Larry Sanders Show. Hosts Phil Donahue and the former Navy SEAL and Minnesota governor Jesse Ventura were quickly fired from MSNBC before they could do too much to undermine the war party's narrative.

Lying Us Into War

The administration claimed that Iraq maintained stockpiles of chemical and biological weapons of every description and active programs to make more. They said Hussein had restarted his nuclear weapons program as well, and that it was only a matter of time before the mad dictator handed these weapons to Osama bin Laden's al Qaeda terrorists to attack the United States. And that we had to stop them before it was too late. But they knew they were lying.

The CIA and White House were pretending to believe that intercepted aluminum tubes were for uranium enrichment centrifuges rather than short-range rockets. The actual nuclear experts in the Energy and State departments, as well as the IAEA, rocket scientists from the Defense Department and independent experts, had repeatedly discounted the tale long before the war. One State Department INR analyst said the tubes were such a poor fit for centrifuges that if Iraq genuinely wanted to use them this way, "we should just give them the tubes." IAEA inspectors had observed the same kind of tubes being used for Iraqi rockets back in 1996. The *Washington Post* had debunked the story in September 2002 — on page A18 — four months before Colin Powell lied about it in his UN speech and six months before the invasion began. The government and the rest of the media just went with it anyway.

Iraq's alleged attempt to buy yellowcake uranium from Niger was another major pillar in the story that they were developing nuclear weapons. The CIA had debunked this disinformation more than a year before the war, intervening repeatedly to prevent the hawks in the vice president's office from including it in his speeches, until finally allowing it in President Bush's all-important State of the Union address in 2003. The IAEA discredited the forged documents supporting the accusations with internet searches in 30 minutes. The Bush administration knew there was not a secret Manhattan Project-like attempt to build atomic weapons in Iraq. That was why they had to resort to public relations tricks such as having Bush, Rice, Powell and Cheney all invoke the phrase "we can't wait for proof that could come in the form of a mushroom cloud," simultaneously certain of the threat, but hiding behind the excuse that we could all die if we tried to make them prove that it was real.

It is the same for the mobile biological weapons laboratories. The CIA knew the source, "Curveball," an Iraqi defector to Germany tied to the Iraqi National Congress, was a liar. They used his fake claims anyway. In his UN address, Secretary of State Powell actually showed drawings of what these mobile biological weapons trucks would look like if anyone on Earth could see them, which they could not since they did not exist. After the war, the closest thing the Iraq Survey Group could find to a mobile lab were two trailers with equipment for making hydrogen for use in weather balloons. One British member of the inspection team, a former army officer and biological weapons expert, said, "The equipment was singularly inappropriate" for making germ weapons. "We were in hysterics over this. You'd have better luck putting a couple of dust bins on the back of the truck and brewing it in there."

Powell twisted intercepts that only proved compliance into evidence of a coverup by deliberately embellishing the transcript of the audio. Powell claimed a transcript of Iraqi soldiers read, "We sent you a message yesterday to clean out all of the areas, the scrap areas, the abandoned areas. Make sure there is nothing there." But the actual transcript never said, "clean out all of the areas" nor "make sure there is nothing there." Without these elaborations, the intercepts were far less incriminating.

In the ultimate demonstration of the logical fallacy of "begging the question," Powell, echoing the CIA, complained that Iraq's 12,200-page dossier on the entire history of their weapons programs that they had turned over to the United Nations was "rich in volume, but poor in information and practically devoid of new evidence." That is, the U.S. would only accept Iraq's declarations of innocence on the charges if they would prove their honesty by admitting their guilt, which would remain a foregone conclusion.

Even the most ridiculous claims from Ahmed Chalabi's INC defectors got spots in the speech, including the obviously preposterous lie that important files proving Iraq's guilt, and even banned weapons themselves, were in government cars being driven around in circles somewhere out in the desert to dodge the UN inspectors. Clearly attempting to implicate Iraq in the U.S. anthrax attacks without directly accusing them, Powell mentioned the attacks along with references to Iraq's 1980s stockpile. It was considered no important matter that Powell had been Ronald Reagan's national security adviser when the U.S. was abetting Hussein's chemical and biological weapons programs and his use of chemical weapons against Iran. Powell then falsely claimed that Iraq's anthrax was all unaccounted for. This was not true. The UN had shown back in the 1990s that Iraq's anthrax had already been destroyed.

Powell then pointed to a nondescript building with a guard shack and water truck next to it and then just laid on the interpretation, claiming proof of chemical weapons:

> How do I know that? How can I say that? Let me give you a closer look. Look at the image on the left. On the left is a close-up of one of the four chemical bunkers. The two arrows indicate the presence of sure signs that the bunkers are storing chemical munitions. The arrow at the top that says "security" points to a facility that is the signature item for this kind of bunker. Inside that facility are special guards and special equipment to monitor any leakage that might come out of the bunker. The truck you also see is a signature item. It's a decontamination vehicle in case something goes wrong.
>
> This is characteristic of those four bunkers. The special security facility and the decontamination vehicle will be in the area, if not at any one of them or one of the other, it is moving around those four, and it moves as it needed to move, as people are working in the different bunkers.
>
> Now, look at the picture on the right. You are now looking at two of those sanitized bunkers. The signature vehicles are gone, the tents are gone, it's been cleaned up, and it was done on the 22nd of December, as the U.N. inspection team is arriving, and you can see the inspection vehicles arriving in the lower portion of the picture on the right.
>
> The bunkers are clean when the inspectors get there. They found nothing.

Has a less convincing case for starting a war ever been presented?

All of Bush and his cabinet's claims — hundreds of them — that Iraq had hidden warehouses full of mustard gas, VX and sarin nerve gas, anthrax (just like that used in the mysterious unsolved 2001 attack on the United States) and facilities ramping up production of it were all false. There were no weapons left for them to give up. As former chief UN weapons inspector Scott Ritter confirmed to the author, the United Nations inspectors knew in 1995 that all Iraqi WMDs had been destroyed by the end of 1991, and they had spent the better part of the last decade overseeing the destruction of the last of Iraq's capacity to produce unconventional weapons. The former director of the Iraq Nuclear Verification Office, Jacques Baute, confirmed Ritter, saying that everything the Iraqis had given them after 1995 "was pretty accurate." President Clinton had only pulled the inspectors out in 1998 before his Operation Desert Fox bombing campaign. There were no new programs, just new lies told by INC defectors and their neoconservative enablers, along with the CIA.

The WHIG, the CIA and Pentagon neocons worked overtime to drum up talking points and consensus about Iraq's alleged unconventional weapons threat. Compliant reporters like the *New York Times's* Judith Miller, Michael Gordon and David Sanger dutifully passed on their lies, seeming to "confirm" that the claims were independently verified by printing them.

On the eve of war, in February 2003, the government instructed Americans to run out and get plastic and duct tape to cover their windows and doors to protect our houses from a possible imminent biological or radiological dirty bomb attack by al Qaeda. This was just two days after President Bush threatened that Iraq had seven mobile biological weapons labs and could somehow strike the "Homeland," possibly with their unmanned drones that somehow must have a range of 7,000 miles. In some places, especially in Washington, D.C. and its suburbs, people actually believed this stuff and did so, cleaning out their local Home Depot shelves in a panic. The reality was that Iraq's "drones" were made of balsa wood and string and were for local aerial surveillance if they could be used at all. They were never designed to spray anyone with poison gas or germs. Those were just lies.

Many careers were made helping lie the country into war. The National Geospatial-Intelligence Agency, under Lieutenant General James Clapper, was eager to label any old structure with a roof as a possible weapons site. The post-invasion inspectors found no such thing in any of the areas the analysts had identified as suspect locations. So Clapper pushed the completely fake story, originated by the Israelis, that Hussein had arranged for Russia to help smuggle his chemical stocks out of the country to Syria at the last minute. He would continue to be promoted and later make himself famous for committing perjury in front of Congress when he lied about the extent of the National Security Agency's data collection on American citizens as Director of National Intelligence. He is now an analyst for CNN.

One of the most blatant lies was one that Cheney told the Veterans of Foreign Wars in his August 2002 speech. He claimed that Saddam Hussein's son-in-law, Hussein Kamel al-Majid, who had defected to Jordan in 1995 and spilled his guts to the CIA, MI-6, UN inspectors, IAEA and even CNN, had admitted that Saddam's regime had cheated and continued to possess banned weapons. This was simply not true. What Kamel had said was that Hussein had kept some mustard gas after the ceasefire in 1991, but that after being caught, they destroyed every last bit of it by the end of the year. "All chemical weapons were destroyed. I ordered destruction of all chemical weapons. All weapons — biological, chemical, missile, nuclear — were destroyed." He brought with him documents to prove it. After Kamel's defection, Hussein had panicked and ordered his government to turn over every last scrap of documents they had on his unconventional weapons — 12 trunks full — to make sure the U.S. and UN could not claim that he was holding out on anything. The UN inspectors were satisfied that Kamel and the dictator were both telling the truth by the end of 1995. In 1996, Kamel returned to Iraq and was executed by Saddam Hussein.

Not only did the Bush administration know that Hussein's old unconventional weapons stocks had all been destroyed, everyone else who was paying attention did too. Iraq allowed the UN inspectors back into the country in the fall of 2002. They spent months searching suspicious sites and came up empty everywhere the U.S. sent them to look. In early December, still four months before the invasion, UN inspectors went to the sites where the U.S. claimed Iraq was reconstituting their old nuclear program and found nothing of the kind. The inspectors determined right away that the aluminum tubes really were for rockets, as the Iraqis had claimed, and that the warehouses full of chemical weapons were no such thing at all.

José Bustani, a Brazilian who headed the Organization for the Prevention of Chemical Weapons (OPCW) tried in 2001–2002 to negotiate Iraq's adoption of the Chemical Weapons Convention, which would have mandated inspections of Iraq's suspected unconventional weapons infrastructure. Once the Iraqis agreed, the Bush administration intervened to stop it. Cheney's agent at the State Department, John Bolton, demanded Bustani resign and threatened the man's children when he refused. Bolton confirms demanding the resignation but denies threatening Bustani's family. However, since John Bolton has proudly explained on Fox News that lying is an essential part of his job, the tie will have to go to Bustani, the otherwise-seemingly honest man who was trying to stop a war through negotiations and increased transparency into Iraq's military capabilities. Weeks later, a year before the war, Bustani was removed in a special session of the OPCW at the insistence of the United States, which threatened to cut off funding for the organization if they did not comply. There was no mystery about the reason for his ouster. New inspections would have undermined the case for war.

In the fall of 2002, Iraq turned over a 12,000-page dossier to the UN. Since the conclusion was already presumed, the fact that they did not confess to having revamped programs was taken only as proof that they were still lying. For years since the war, its supporters have attempted to rationalize that Hussein's government was pretending to still have weapons to intimidate Iran, and that somehow the U.S. was accidentally fooled as well. To tell themselves and us this story, they only have to ignore Iraq's multiple protestations of innocence, virtually carte blanche permission to UN inspectors to search for them, and this massive dossier which included the entire history of Iraq's unconventional weapons programs, none of which survived past the year 1991. The U.S. Iraq Survey Group, tasked with finding the weapons and examining Iraq's papers after the invasion, determined that since the Iraqis were so confident nothing would be found, they thought that by allowing inspectors in after UN Security Council Resolution 1441, not only would they stave off the attack, but finally prove the negative and get the sanctions lifted altogether.

The U.S. also had at least two high-level spies inside the Iraqi government, the Foreign Minister Naji Sabri and Tahir Jalil Habbush al-Tikriti, who was the head of intelligence and one of Hussein's top diplomats. Both men assured the U.S. that all of Iraq's WMD really had all been destroyed long before the invasion. This was kept secret from the American people before and for years after the war.

When the Iraq Survey Group later did its study of Iraq's former programs, they insisted that Saddam Hussein must have planned to be able to one day try again to manufacture these weapons. They say this was because he would have wanted to deter Iran next door, and to a lesser extent, Israel. That Hussein would pass off unconventional weapons to Osama bin Laden to use against the people of the United States of America? The idea was apparently so laughable that the inspectors were too embarrassed even to bring it up to debunk it in their report.

After Bush reportedly scoffed at the weakness of CIA Deputy Director John McLaughlin's Oval Office presentation of their best evidence of Iraq's illegal weapons, CIA Director George Tenet told President Bush not to worry, the case is a "slam dunk." Tenet later denied saying that he meant Iraq definitely had the weapons. He just meant he thought Bush had a convincing enough story to make the American people believe it, that was all.

For years, a viral email went around which claimed that soldiers found the weapons of mass destruction after all, and it was just too bad that George W. Bush was too honorable to take credit for being right. But that is not true. All you need to do is read the actual article the emails' authors cherry-picked from. It is a *New York Times* piece from 2014 called "The Secret Casualties of Iraq's Abandoned Chemical Weapons." It tells the story of how the military covered up the fact that soldiers deployed in Iraq were finding mustard and sarin gas shells, as well as being attacked by Iraqi insurgents with them. Even though the chemicals were way past their shelf life for effective weapons, they were still somewhat toxic, so men were getting sick. But the Army clamped down on their stories, which meant that these soldiers were denied proper medical treatment for their exposure. It was an important story in its own right, beyond being the basis for an otherwise tall tale about Bush's vindication.

Why would the Bush government clamp down on this truth that supposedly proved they were right all along? The answer is that none of these recently discovered shells had been manufactured after the first Iraq war in 1991. So none of this story supported Bush's claim that there were active chemical weapons programs of any kind in Iraq at the time of the 2003 invasion, nor had there been in more than ten years. These munitions were all left over from when President Ronald Reagan and the president's father, George Bush Sr., helped Hussein purchase and use chemical weapons against Iran and the Iraqi Kurds back when he was a loyal client of the U.S. in the 1980s. All the article said was that soldiers and insurgents had found old duds out in the desert, virtually all of which had already been declared to the United Nations, even if the local GIs out on patrol had not been warned in advance that old mustard gas shells were buried out there. Back in the 1990s, the UN had simply decided it would be more dangerous to try to move them than to just leave them out there in the desert to decay. The *Times* reported:

> The United States had gone to war declaring it must destroy an active weapons of mass destruction program. Instead, American troops gradually found and ultimately suffered from the remnants of long-abandoned programs, built in close collaboration with the West. ...
>
> The discoveries of these chemical weapons did not support the government's invasion rationale. ...
>
> [D]uring the long occupation, American troops began encountering old chemical munitions in hidden caches and roadside bombs. Typically 155-millimeter artillery shells or 122-millimeter rockets, they were remnants of an arms program Iraq had rushed into production in the 1980s during the Iran-Iraq war. All had been manufactured before 1991, participants said. ...
>
> Participants in the chemical weapons discoveries said the United States suppressed knowledge of finds for multiple reasons, including that the government bristled at further acknowledgment it had been wrong. "They needed something to say that after Sept. 11 Saddam used chemical rounds," Mr. Lampier said. "And all of this was from the pre-1991 era."

Others pointed to another embarrassment. In five of six incidents in which troops were wounded by chemical agents, the munitions appeared to have been designed in the United States, manufactured in Europe and filled in chemical agent production lines built in Iraq by Western companies.

The same thing happened with an Associated Press story from July 2008, "Secret U.S. Mission Hauls Uranium from Iraq." The hawks were right, after all, they claimed. This was false. First of all, it was "yellowcake" uranium, meaning half-refined ore that is useless as any kind of weapon until converted into a gas, enriched up to weapons-grade purity and then machined into a warhead, which Iraq had no capability of doing whatsoever in 2003. This uranium, left over from Iraq's pre-1991 nuclear program, had all been officially declared to inspectors and had been sitting in a storage facility under IAEA lock and seal. It in no way justified the claim that Hussein had a nuclear program of any kind at the time of the invasion. This also meant that if Hussein had wanted any yellowcake uranium, he would not have needed to buy it from Niger. He could have simply broken open the warehouse door where he already had some in his country. Instead, it was still sealed and unused. But it made for a great headline for those who wished to take the story out of context to rationalize their belief in things that were not true.

It remains unclear why the CIA did not just make up lies about Saddam Hussein's supposed ties to al Qaeda. Instead, they tortured Ibn al-Shaykh al-Libi, not even a true member of al Qaeda, but associated with them, as well as Abu Zubaydah, another man they falsely believed to be a high-level al Qaeda operative, into making claims about that group's relationship with Saddam Hussein's Iraq. The Iraqis had an airplane fuselage at a police training facility used to train them in anti-hijacking operations in a town called Salman Pak. The CIA and Egyptian secret police tortured al-Libi into claiming that it was for training hijackers how to take over planes instead. Al-Libi also said under torture that the Iraqi regime had trained al Qaeda on chemical weapons production. Documents later showed CIA analysts did not believe the claims the agency's operators had tortured out of al-Libi, nor did the DIA. This did not stop them from making sure they were featured prominently in the public case for war, including in Colin Powell's infamous January 2003 United Nations address. Zubaydah, under torture, also claimed that Hussein's government had a relationship with the Jordanian terrorist Abu Musab al-Zarqawi.

This was another major lie about Iraq and al Qaeda that Secretary Powell invoked in his UN presentation. He claimed that Zarqawi was a member of al Qaeda and that he was supported by Saddam Hussein, representing a significant tie between the two. In fact, Zarqawi had declined to join bin Laden's group, as the Pentagon's Defense Intelligence

Agency (DIA) had said in July 2002. The DIA had also concluded that if Hussein had infiltrated Zarqawi's group Ansar al Islam (a.k.a. Jama'at al Tawhid w'al Jihad), it was for protection or for intelligence efforts against Kurds. After all, Hussein had a warrant out for the terrorist's arrest.

The neoconservatives and the Iraqi National Congress were claiming that Zarqawi had been wounded fighting in Afghanistan and that Saddam Hussein's government had given him treatment in a Baghdad hospital, including giving him a fake wooden leg. This, of course, turned out to be a lie. Further, Zarqawi was hiding safely in the American-protected, autonomous region of northern Iraqi Kurdistan, far outside of Baghdad's reach. But Colin Powell told the American people and the world he was in "Iraq," which proved al Qaeda's connection to the Iraqi government. It was a blatant deception. Worse, the military had repeatedly requested permission from the Bush administration to target and kill Zarqawi and his group hiding in Kurdistan before the war began and were repeatedly denied permission. The administration needed their talking point. As soon as the war started, Zarqawi and his group moved south to join the insurgency. More than a year and a half after the war began, at the end of 2004, Zarqawi finally named his group al Qaeda in Mesopotamia (or Iraq) (AQI) and declared his loyalty to Osama bin Laden. His group became a menace to U.S. forces there. Just as he had planned, with a little more help from their enemies, it later grew to become the "Islamic State." [See Chapters 10–11.]

The most famous lie about Iraq's connection to al Qaeda began with a claim by Czech intelligence that a source recognized September 11th hijack ringleader Mohammed Atta as having met with an Iraqi diplomat, Ahmad Khalil Ibrahim Samir Ani, in Prague shortly before the attack. The Israelis quickly put a story in the German *Bild* newspaper that their intelligence agents had coincidentally been there and, in fact, witnessed the Iraqi agent hand over a flask of anthrax to Atta. This was a ridiculous hoax. The FBI and CIA quickly debunked the story. Yet it was repeatedly raised by Vice President Cheney, the Pentagon neocons, William Safire at the *New York Times* and Stephen Hayes and his associates at the *Weekly Standard* and Fox News in the run-up to the war. Douglas Feith even briefed President Bush on the story in the Oval Office.

Iraqi intelligence had met with bin Laden's men a few times over the years. But nothing had ever come of it, as the CIA had previously determined and repeatedly told the White House — when they were not passing on the lies they had tortured out of Zubaydah and al-Libi. The CIA's spies inside the Hussein regime, Sabri and Habbush, had also confirmed this. CIA officer John Kiriakou later wrote that, "At the agency, the alleged partnership between this odious pair was widely known as the Big Lie."

Journalist Charles Lewis later counted 935 false statements concerning accusations of Iraq's possession of banned weapons and support for al Qaeda terrorists made by the top seven officials of the Bush administration on at least 532 separate occasions in the year before the war.

In 2002, Joe Biden was the chairman of the Senate Foreign Relations Committee. He and his aide Antony Blinken, later to become President Biden's secretary of state, called just two days of sham hearings on the question of invading Iraq. Only hawks were permitted to testify and serious experts who could have cast doubt on the cause for war were excluded. Biden's colleagues, Senators Hillary Clinton and John Kerry — all three heavyweight Democratic politicians who would end up being nominated for the presidency — along with the majority of Senate Democrats (not to mention the virtually unanimous Senate Republicans) also made the obviously political decision to support Bush's war. Nancy Pelosi and the majority of Democrats in the House, to their credit, along with a handful of antiwar Republicans like Reps. Ron Paul and Jimmy Duncan, opposed it.

Biden did not just support the war. He served as Bush and Cheney's Senate gatekeeper and whip, guaranteeing a majority vote for the war in the upper chamber while controlled by the opposition party. If Biden had any moral courage at all, he could have stopped that war. All he would have had to do was bring in real experts like former UN weapons inspection chief Scott Ritter and former CENTCOM commander General Anthony Zinni to debunk the case that Iraq was stockpiling banned weapons or had programs that necessitated war. The senator could have asked Gen. Scowcroft to testify. He could have held up the authorization vote and refused to support an aggressive war. Instead, Biden conspired with the White House to force the authorization through. He also continued to endorse the war publicly for years after that, though he has since spent the better part of a decade denying he ever did, lying that he only wanted the inspectors back in the country and that he had denounced the war immediately after it started.

The president's refrain that the U.S. had to attack Iraq "because of September 11th," and the endless claims of certainty about an alliance between Iraq and al Qaeda by the government, its spokesmen such as Ari Fleischer, the leaders of the opposition party and all the neoconservative media myna birds were more than enough to convince the majority of Americans to support the war.

Polls showed that all the propaganda about Iraq's alleged alliance with al Qaeda succeeded in convincing as much as two-thirds of the American people that Iraq had helped carry out the September 11th attack against our country by the time of the invasion in March 2003.

It was not just the weapons and terrorist ties. The George W. Bush-era war party spent an extraordinary amount of effort pushing the narrative that "the Islamic world" was a single, cohesive, "radical" civilization that was beginning a new era of massive expansion at our expense. In fact, the U.S. had been attacked by people whose countries were under total American dominance. Stateless bandits, al Qaeda had to hijack our jets to even have a weapon to use against us.

But what a death toll. Comparable to Pearl Harbor in casualties, the shock of September 11th was severe enough to allow the government to persuade the American people that there was some force comparable to Imperial Japan out there behind the effort. To anyone experienced enough to know better, this was all a transparent attempt to exploit our families' and neighbors' fears. It worked. That time was truly terrifying for many Americans. Though they were in no real danger, their fear was cultivated by the government and its interested parties located in the think tanks and media. Combined with the average citizens' disbelief that the government could possibly be so cynical as to manipulate their fear in such a fashion and their consequent deferral to the Bush administration's leadership, it was enough to start a war. Numerous times Americans were heard to reason that self-defense simply must be the reason: Of course Iraq did 9/11, or else why would we be attacking them?

"Imagine those 19 hijackers with other weapons and other plans — this time armed by Saddam Hussein," Bush threatened. What patriot could deny their leader the right to protect them?

This became a terrible mark of division in the country, mostly along partisan lines. There were those who were indignant with rage that the other half of the population were so weak and unpatriotic that they would refuse to support their country defending itself against merciless terrorists who had shed so much innocent American blood, while the other side could only marvel at and insult the former's ignorant credulity. As the writers of the TV show South Park observed, the division was hardly about Iraq at all, but the right-left divide, country versus rock 'n roll. Whose side are you on? Americans have had the hardest time hearing each other speak ever since that time, even long after most who supported it changed their mind.

Surrender Denied

Some Americans wondered, why not negotiate? No, we cannot talk to "evil" regimes. That would "legitimize" them, the administration claimed. But Bush's secretary of state at the time was former four-star General Colin Powell. If Powell was not tough enough, they could have sent

Hussein's old acquaintance from the Reagan years, the gruff old Secretary of Defense Donald Rumsfeld over there to read Hussein the riot act and put his regime in line. The terms could have been as simple as they were obvious: keep al Qaeda down and out, stop sending money to Hamas and we will lift the blockade and let Iraq rejoin the international community. And no massacres.

It could have been. Eight months after the war began, the *New York Times* published a story about how Saddam Hussein had offered to surrender on virtually "unconditional terms." Meeting with important neoconservative ringleader Richard Perle in London, Hussein's emissary, Lebanese-American businessman Imad Hage, revealed that the Iraqis were not even sure what the problem really was, so they offered to concede on every imaginable point. Perle was told that if the conflict is truly about weapons, the U.S. can send in the FBI to look wherever they want. If the problem was Iraq's role in the Israel-Palestine crisis, they offered "full support for any U.S. plan." If the dispute was about mineral rights, they offered to make oil concessions to U.S. companies. If Bush's motive was Hussein's dictatorship itself, they even promised to hold elections under international supervision. On top of all this, the Iraqis promised to work with the U.S. in fighting against al Qaeda. Instead, Perle told Hussein's representative to tell the dictator and his men, "we will see them in Baghdad." In a separate story, journalist Seymour Hersh reported that Perle had been approached with an Iraqi peace offer by a Saudi industrialist named Harb Zuhair. He ignored it. Attempts by Hussein's regime to negotiate "were all non-starters because they all involved Saddam staying in power," a senior administration official told Knight-Ridder newspapers.

The Bush administration refused to accept victory without war. The president announced in his "48 hours" speech of March 17, 2003, that Hussein and his sons had two days to leave Iraq, but that even if they did so, the new regime would be expected to allow the "peaceful entry" of U.S. troops, making it clear that the U.S. was going to invade no matter what.

How could it be that if Saddam and his two sons left Iraq and moved to Cairo, and there was a brand-new general in charge in Baghdad, the administration would not give the guy a chance to dig through the records to see if he could come up with some mustard gas canisters? It was never really about the weapons. Why else would it be that Saddam and his sons leaving town would not be enough even to buy the Iraqis another few weeks' delay on their death sentence?

As Paul Wolfowitz later admitted in an interview with *Vanity Fair*, for "bureaucratic reasons" the administration settled on weapons of mass destruction as the cause for launching the war. In other words, the lawyers in the U.S. State Department and British Foreign Ministry were afraid that some of them might go to prison for starting an aggressive war, which is against the law. They had to be able to pretend that the Iraqis were in violation of United Nations resolutions, that America was supporting the rule of law, and that it was invading not as an act of aggression, but as an act of fulfilling the UN's mandates. This was not true. The U.S. refused to allow a Security Council vote on a resolution authorizing the attack because Russia, China and France would have not only abstained but voted no and vetoed it. So, they just went ahead anyway.

The traditional conservative criticism of the United Nations was that it infringed on American independence and made other countries' small problems and disputes into international ones, constantly laying tripwires for intervention and causing the United States to get into disputes outside of, and even contrary to its interests. But the neoconservatives, like Richard Perle, were just mad that the UN Charter makes it a crime to start a war without the agreement of the Security Council. Shortly after the Iraq invasion, Perle wrote in the *Guardian*:

> Saddam Hussein's reign of terror is about to end. He will go quickly, but not alone: in a parting irony, he will take the UN down with him. Well, not the whole UN. The "good works" part will survive, the low-risk peacekeeping bureaucracies will remain, the chatterbox on the Hudson will continue to bleat. What will die is the fantasy of the UN as the foundation of a new world order. As we sift the debris, it will be important to preserve, the better to understand, the intellectual wreckage of the liberal conceit of safety through international law administered by international institutions.

Why bother with liberal-minded "governance" as an excuse for global hegemony when you have total power in the form of the Army's 3rd Infantry Division at your service, at war against a tactic and anyone you claim might use it?

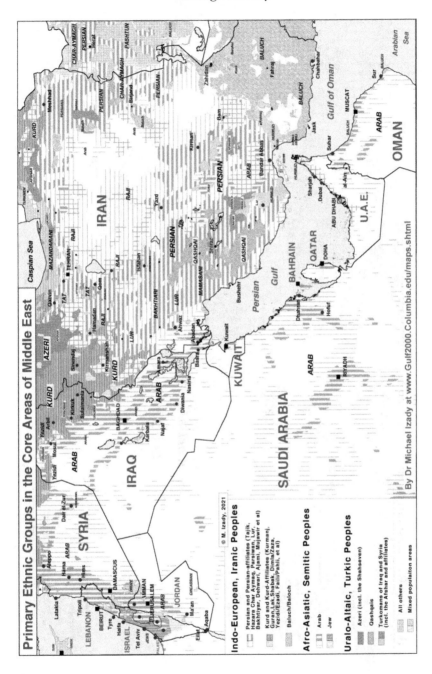

Primary Ethnic Groups in the Core Areas of Middle East

© M. Izady, 2021

By Dr Michael Izady at www.Gulf2000.Columbia.edu/maps.shtml

Indo-European, Iranic Peoples

Persian and Persian-affiliates (Tajik, Hazara Char Aymaq, Parsiwan, Lur, Bakhtiyar, Dehwari, Ajami, Mujawir et al)

Kurd and Kurd-Affiliates (Kurmanj, Guran, Lak, Shabak, Dimla/Zaza, Yezidi/Ezadi, Faili/Pahli, et al)

Baluch/Baloch

Afro-Asiatic, Semitic Peoples

Arab

Jew

Uralo-Altaic, Turkic Peoples

Azeri (incl. the Shahsaven)

Qashqais

Turkomans of Iraq and Syria (incl. the Afshar and affiliates)

All others

Mixed population areas

89

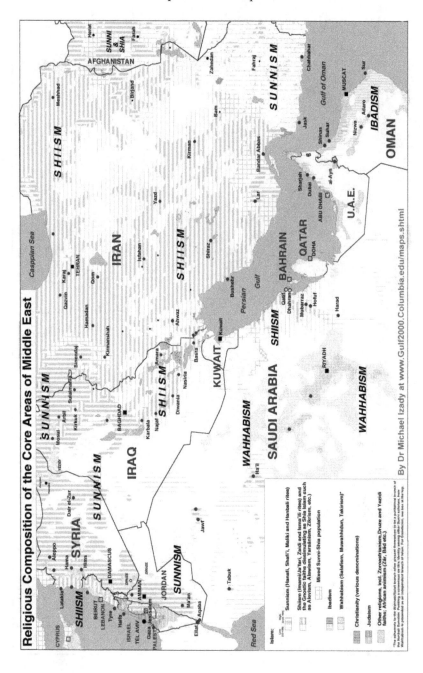

Religious Composition of the Core Areas of Middle East

By Dr Michael Izady at www.Gulf2000.Columbia.edu/maps.shtml

Islam:

Sunnism (Hanafi, Shafi'i, Maliki and Hanbali rites)

Shiism (Imami/Ja'fari, Zaidi and Isma'ili rites) and the Gnostic faiths dissimulating as Shia Islam such as Alevism, Alawism, Yarsainism, Zikrism, etc.)

Mixed Sunni-Shia population

Ibadism

Wahhabism (Salafism, Muwahhidun, Takirism)*

Christianity (various denominations)

Judaism

Other religions, incl. Zoroastrianism, Druze and Yazidi faiths; African animism (Zâr, Bâd etc.)

Lay of the Land

Shi'ites are a minority of Muslims on earth, but the split is about fifty-fifty in the Middle East. They are dominant in Iran and in southeastern Iraq, more or less the land from Baghdad down to Kuwait and over to Iran.

Jordan, Saudi Arabia, UAE, Bahrain, Qatar and Egypt are — excepting Bahrain — predominantly Sunni populations, and all are ruled by Sunni kings, "emirs," and "presidents." Yemen is a somewhat different matter. [See Chapter 12.] Bahrain has a majority Shi'ite population ruled by a Sunni king. Turkey is also a predominantly Sunni country and part of the American alliance system in the region, as well as being an official member of NATO. Of course, Middle Eastern politics are messy, and relationships hang on more than simple ethnic and religious divisions or loyalty to America's interests for that matter. [See Chapter 7.]

Take a special note of the city of Baghdad, the capital of Iraq, a formerly mixed city on the edge of that crucial religious fault line.

Iran is primarily Persian and Shi'ite, though it also has many Arabs, Kurds, Balochis, Azeris and other ethnic and religious minority groups as well.

Also, please observe the size of Kurdistan. It is a region that has never been an independent nation, and is currently divided between Iran, Iraq, Syria, Turkey and even a bit by Azerbaijan and Armenia. They are mostly Sunni, though are said to be a distinct ethnicity from their Arab and Turkic neighbors. The Kurds have had somewhat autonomous sovereignty in northern Iraq since 1991 and did in Syria between 2011 and 2019, though their political factions remain sharply divided.

The point here is not to reduce all these conflicts to some ageless and permanent sectarian conflict over there, as those who would prefer to absolve U.S. policymakers of their responsibility for the current crises often choose to do. It is meant only to help the reader understand the basic outlines of who is who on the various sides of the regional civil war playing out in the Middle East today.

Overall, it is the U.S., Saudi Arabia, UAE, Bahrain, Qatar, Egypt, Jordan, Turkey and Israel in the U.S.-Sunni alliance (still including differences between them) versus the Shi'ite-based Iranian so-called "crescent" alliance: the Ayatollah, the Shi'ite-aligned Ba'athists in Syria, and Hezbollah in Southern Lebanon (each with their own interests as well). Bush's 2003 invasion simply moved Baghdad to the Iranian side of the ledger.[*]

---

[*] See Michael R. Izady's magnificent, detailed, full color ethnic and sectarian maps of the entire Middle East and Pakistan at https://libertarianinstitute.org/enoughalready and https://gulf2000.columbia.edu/maps.shtml.

Who's Zoomin' Who?

Iraq War II turned out to be, as General William Odom called it, "the greatest strategic disaster in United States history." Those seeking to impose heightened American dominance in the region instead drove U.S. power and influence into the ground, wasting trillions of dollars and more than a million lives and achieving nothing but an escalating series of disasters.

For the entire eight years of Iraq War II, 2003–2011, the government and TV narrative depicted the Americans and the Iraqi people on one side versus "the terrorists" on the other. The U.S.A. was trying to help the nice citizens create a democracy, but on the other side were the bad guys attempting to thwart America's effort to secure freedom for the people.

But there was no such thing as al Qaeda in Iraq at the start of the war. Abu Musab al Zarqawi had been hiding up in American-protected autonomous Kurdistan, out of Hussein's reach. Though he quickly joined the fight on the side of the Sunni-based insurgency, Zarqawi and his men did not swear their loyalty to and join al Qaeda until after the second battle of Fallujah in the autumn of 2004, more than a year and a half into the war. For all the propaganda depicting the Jordanian terrorist Zarqawi and his group as the leaders of the insurgency, those who initially led the armed resistance against the United States were mostly former military men fighting on their own ground. In other words, they were local, indigenous forces, not international bin Ladenite terrorists who had signed on to this war to attack the United States. It just was not true, but the "terrorists" narrative prevented the Bush government and Pentagon from ever having to explain who was who and whose side the U.S. was on.

What the U.S. military was actually doing was causing a massive civil war by taking the side of the Shi'ite super-majority. These were the same people that George Bush Sr. had encouraged to rise up and then backstabbed and abandoned in 1991. In 2003, George W. Bush came in and picked up where his father left off, taking them all the way to Baghdad. But remember why Bush Sr. abandoned them: Iranian-based Iraqi militias were arriving to take over the campaign against Saddam. The same thing happened again. The Supreme Council for Islamic Revolution in Iraq (SCIRI), their Badr Brigade militia and their counterparts from the Da'wa Party, who had been living in Iran since the start of the Iran-Iraq war in 1980, came right across the border on the heels of the American invasion. President Bush had not only destroyed Iran's greatest enemy in Hussein's Ba'athist regime, but he had also put the U.S. military on a mission to install the Ayatollah's loyal friends in power in Baghdad. That was who America was fighting for more or less throughout the whole war.

Mixed in with Iraq's Sunni and Shi'ite Arabs and Kurds were small sects of Chaldean and Assyrian Christians, Turkmen, Yazidis and others. The Sunni Arabs had been the dominant class inside Hussein's Ba'athist state. There were Shi'ites who were part of the government and ruling party, and there were mixed populations in the major cities. People lived together in ways that were sometimes compared to relations between Catholics and Protestants in America: most hardly noticed or cared to which sect their neighbors belong. Still, the power at the top of the Ba'ath Party was at the hands of the minority Sunni tribes. That is how it had been since the dissolution of the Ottoman Empire after World War I.

But the U.S. invasion changed all that. First, the deputy secretary of defense for policy, Douglas Feith, and senior adviser to the Iraqi Coalition Provisional Authority, Walter Slocomb, insisted that U.S. "Viceroy" Paul Bremer dismiss the entire Iraqi army. They then outlawed Saddam Hussein's Ba'ath Party and decreed that no former member of it could hold a government job of any kind under the new regime. This gave an extra advantage to the Shi'ite factions vying for power in the capital. However, other than getting out of the country immediately, the Bush government had left itself little choice. If the Americans had not abolished the army and previous government so entirely, they might have been forced to support them in another massive effort to crush newly empowered Shi'ite forces. The latter were determined to take President Bush and Deputy Secretary of Defense Wolfowitz up on their claims that this invasion was all about spreading democracy to the people of Iraq and the region.

The Clean Break crew had caused the war, but their goal of installing Ahmed Chalabi to rule (in place of King Hussein of Jordan, who had died two years before) had fallen apart. Bush did not trust Chalabi, but it would not have mattered anyway. The highest-ranking Shi'ite cleric in the world was and is the Iranian-born Grand Ayatollah Ali al-Sistani, who had lived for decades in southern Iraq. Viceroy Bremer had planned to create a "caucus system" where the U.S. would handpick leaders from various Iraqi communities to come together to write the new constitution and form a new government. But al-Sistani had other ideas. In January 2004, he put out a statement saying that the faithful should go outside and demand one-man, one-vote, majority-rule democracy. They did, by the millions, in Basra, Najaf and Baghdad.

That was it. What was the U.S. going to do now, start the war all over again against the Shi'ite super-majority that had thus far stood aside and watched as our army got rid of Saddam's Sunni dictatorship for them? No. Bush backed down, and the Shi'ite political parties, the "United Iraqi Alliance," made up of SCIRI, Da'wa and working-class cleric Muqtada al-Sadr's group, has in one form or another been in power ever since. The

Bush administration, unable to just admit they had been wrong and withdraw, instead became the Shi'ite forces' humble servants, helping them to crush the Sunni-based insurgency that was primarily made up of officers and soldiers from the former regime.

That fall, the Shi'ite coalition wrote the constitution for the new "Islamic Republic of Iraq." A few months later, in January 2005, the U.S. held the first mass elections for the new Iraqi parliament. American TV was extremely impressed with the women voting and proudly displaying the purple ink on their fingers. What they were really doing was pouring napalm on a smoldering fire. Sunni leaders, anticipating a significant defeat, had urged a boycott of the vote in an attempt to undermine the legitimacy of the process. This was a huge strategic mistake on their part because their abstention did not subvert the election since its results were being backed up by American guns. Instead, they ended up with even fewer seats and less influence in the new government than they were already destined to have under the rules of apportionment in the constitution. The new parliament was then dominated by the Iranian-backed Shi'ite parties and their Kurdish allies, who had done so well in the election. "*Ayatollah you so*," wrote Billmon, legendary anonymous blogger of that era.

The Shi'ite United Iraqi Alliance, led by the Da'wa Party and SCIRI, had taken control of approximately 70 percent of the new parliament. Provincial elections in the nine southern provinces in Iraq all fell into the hands of religious Shi'ite parties, mainly the Supreme Council for Islamic Revolution in Iraq. They renamed the group the Islamic Supreme Council of Iraq (ISCI) after the U.S. won their revolution for them. They had taken over the country at the provincial level and had won a super-majority in the parliament. Though Prime Minister Ibrahim Jaafari — chosen by neoconservative policy adviser Zalmay Khalilzad — was from the Da'wa Party, the interior minister, minister of petroleum and the other executive leaders came from ISCI. Like Jaafari, his successors Nouri al-Maliki — also chosen by neoconservative policy adviser Zalmay Khalilzad — and Haider Abadi were from the Da'wa Party. The fourth Iraqi prime minister, Adil Abdul-Mahdi, was from ISCI. Mustafa Al-Kadhimi, sworn into power in May 2020, is the first Prime Minister who does not come out of Da'wa or ISCI, though he remains heavily dependent on their support for his power.

It was revealed after the war began, that Iraqi National Congress chief Ahmed Chalabi, according to the CIA and DIA, had not only notified Iran that the U.S. had broken their secret codes and told them about American plans for Iraq, but he had also been working for Iran all along to lie us into war against the Ayatollah Khamenei's hated enemy and strategic rival Saddam Hussein. The fact that INC headquarters were in Tehran might have been considered a major tip-off, but apparently not. About those chemical and germ weapons stocks and Iraq's "reconstituted" nuclear weapons program? I guess we were just "heroes in error," Chalabi later told the *Daily Telegraph*.

The *Financial Times*'s John Dizard wrote a devastating take on the whole affair in 2004, called "How Chalabi Conned the Neocons." About a year after the war began, it finally started to dawn on the hawks how easily their enemy had manipulated them. They wanted then to try to tilt to the Kurds or the Sunnis, but they were overruled. It was too late. Feith's law partner, Marc Zell, whose firm represented Israeli settlers on the West Bank, raged to Dizard:

> Ahmed Chalabi is a treacherous, spineless turncoat. He had one set of friends before he was in power, and now he's got another. He said he would end Iraq's boycott of trade with Israel and would allow Israeli companies to do business there. He said [the new Iraqi government] would agree to rebuild the pipeline from Mosul [in the northern Iraqi oil fields] to Haifa [the Israeli port and the location of a major refinery]. … He promised that. He promised a lot of things.

Chalabi had not only given those assurances to the neoconservatives privately but had vowed the same in a June 1997 speech at JINSA and in a 1998 interview with the *Jerusalem Post*. Even Benjamin Netanyahu bought the bit about the pipeline, Reuters reported in June 2003. Dizard wrote that, "With Chalabi's encouragement, the Israeli Ministry of National Infrastructure, which is responsible for oil pipelines, dusted off and updated plans for a new pipeline from Iraq." However, he continued:

> Chalabi's Arab admirers say they knew he'd never make good on his promises to ally with Israel. "I was worried that he was going to do business with the Zionists," confesses Moh'd Asad, the managing director of the Amman, Jordan-based International Investment Arabian Group, an industrial and agricultural exporter, who is one of Chalabi's Palestinian friends and business partners. "He told me not to worry, that he just needed the Jews in order to get what he wanted from Washington and that he would turn on them after that."

In 2004, the FBI launched an investigation to determine who had informed Ahmed Chalabi that U.S. intelligence agencies had cracked Iran's communications. But the probe was not limited to the Chalabi leak. The *Washington Post* reported that the FBI was also looking into Douglas Feith, Paul Wolfowitz, David Wurmser, Richard Perle, Harold Rhode "and others at the Pentagon." This was in regards to the FBI's investigation of Pentagon Iran expert Larry Franklin's passing of classified information on Iran to Israel through the American Israel Public Affairs Committee.

Secretary Powell's then-chief of staff, Colonel Lawrence Wilkerson, told the author that while all the neoconservatives were strong supporters of Israel, he always believed that Douglas Feith and David Wurmser were acting as literal agents of influence for the Israeli government. Perle and Wolfowitz had both been investigated by the FBI back in the 1970s for passing classified information to Israel. Franklin, who worked under Feith in the policy department, was prosecuted, but none of the neoconservatives were held accountable.

But it was Iran and not Israel that was getting what they wanted out of America's war in Iraq. The Bush administration argued that creating a parliamentary democracy to provide a venue for all Iraq's problems to be worked out politically was the solution to the violence. In fact, it had only provided the opportunity for entirely new groups to seize and consolidate power over their former overlords, driving those on the losing end to violent insurgency, rather than away from it. In the West, "democracy" by definition includes protections of individual rights, property rights, minority rights, freedom of religion, speech, association and so forth. But boiled down, democracy simply means majority rule, and God help the minority.

The reader may recall the common refrain from that time, "Well, even if we should not have invaded, we cannot leave now because the violence will get worse." It was remarkably effective propaganda, especially for those who had supported the war in the first place and were trying to withhold judgment on the consequences for as long as possible. But the presumption that whatever we are doing there is making things more peaceful and that the fighting would have gotten worse if we left was completely false. Not only had our government introduced over 100,000 combat forces into the theater, they had essentially put them at the disposal of the Shi'ite factions. The way they spun it was that the Americans were using the Shi'ite militias to hunt down the leaders of the Sunni-based insurgency, but who was really using who? The answer is both, of course, but think of the perverse incentives and moral hazards involved when a local sectarian militia like ISCI's Badr Brigade has the U.S. Army and Marine Corps at their beck and call to use against their enemies. The Americans were not tamping things down. They were making things worse.

Part of the problem is that in Iraq, all the oil is in the far north near Kirkuk, which is territory mostly shared by Kurds and Shi'ite Arabs, and in the south near the city of Basra, deep in eastern Iraqi Shiastan. There are few developed oil resources in the predominantly Sunni, western regions of the country. When these Sunni tribal groups and Ba'athists lost their dominance over the central government in Baghdad, they lost their power to run away with all that oil wealth. They were in danger of being left out while the Kurds and Shi'ites kept all the money for themselves. This is, in fact, what happened. It was an important reason why the predominantly Sunni insurgency fought so hard against the American effort to install the Shi'ites in power in the capital.

As experts like Robert Dreyfuss explained, Iran exploited Bush's Iraq War II not just to extend their influence, but to support in power the most bigoted anti-Sunni type extremists from ISCI and a "strong federalism" policy which essentially meant "cleansing" and seizing the capital of Baghdad, then cutting the predominantly Sunni regions off from the patronage of the central state. This plan of the Iranians to divide Iraq, similar to that advocated by Senator Joe Biden and his aide Antony Blinken during Iraq War II, played a significant role in setting the stage for the rise of the Islamic State a few years later.

Demographic maps from before and after the war show that Baghdad's formerly mixed areas are now virtually all Shi'ite-dominated. The Sunnis have been pushed almost entirely out of the capital city except for its far southwest. It is hard to imagine what could reverse it. Baghdad is a more than 85 percent Shi'ite city now. It took the American army and marines and six years of fighting to give the Shi'ites control of an Arab capital for the first time in a thousand years. The bin Ladenites may fling suicide bombers at it from now unto eternity, but they will never be able to take it back for the Sunnis.

In December 2004, as he was predicting an overwhelming victory for the Shi'ite slate in the upcoming Iraqi election, King Abdullah of Jordan coined the term "Shi'ite crescent" to describe the newly empowered Iranian alliance system in the region. The Saudi King Abdullah shared his frustration. A State Department document leaked by U.S. Army Specialist Bradley (now Chelsea) Manning summarizes the Saudi king's frustrations with the second Iraq war as he explained them to neoconservative policy adviser Zalmay Khalilzad:

> King Abdullah promised Saudi cooperation, but was deeply skeptical of the chances of success and even appeared to question the bonafides of U.S. policy in Iraq. He commented that whereas in the past the U.S., Saudi Arabia, and Saddam Hussein had agreed on the need to contain Iran, U.S. policy had now given Iraq to Iran as a "gift on a golden platter."

So much for securing the realm.

A Golden Opportunity

The Iranians held a million-man vigil in Tehran on September 12, 2001. They saw America's catastrophe as their opportunity to normalize relations since the U.S. now had their primary enemies, the Taliban in Afghanistan and Saddam Hussein's Ba'athist regime in Iraq, as well as bin Laden's group, in common. They thought they had a chance to create a new relationship with the United States. As reported by journalist Gareth Porter, in April 2003, just after the invasion of Iraq, Iran delivered to the United States what is now known as the "golden offer." Iran's government sent this proposal to the Americans by way of the Swiss ambassador Tim Guldimann. When he brought it to the State Department, he got a dressing down for daring even to make the delivery.

The offer said that the Iranians were willing to negotiate on everything: their nuclear program, support for Hamas and Hezbollah in Palestine and Lebanon, a new policy of officially ignoring Israel, working together with the U.S. against the Taliban in Afghanistan and on the future of Iraq. They also offered to trade information on al Qaeda fighters they had captured fleeing Afghanistan for information on members of the Mujahideen-e-Khalq (MEK), then under American protection in Iraq.

As has been documented in numerous places, even including the Pentagon's RAND Corporation, MEK is a formerly Communist, extremely cultish Iranian terrorist group that had killed Americans in Iran before and during the 1979 revolution. They then worked with the mullahs for a time before betraying them for Saddam Hussein, where they fought on Iraq's side in the Iran-Iraq war of the 1980s and helped to crush the post-Iraq War I Shi'ite and Kurdish uprising in 1991. After the invasion of Iraq in 2003, they had fallen into the hands of the Americans and the Israelis. Iran was offering to trade information on bin Laden's son, Hamza, Saif al-Adl and some other prominent al Qaeda prisoners they were holding on house arrest for information on the MEK in exchange.

The Bush administration refused the opportunity to make peace with Iran and possibly gotten their hands on important al Qaeda figures at the same time. The hawks preferred confrontation. After a May 2003 al Qaeda bombing in Riyadh, the Defense Department pretended to believe that it must have been orchestrated out of Iran under their government's supervision, falsely putting them on the opposite side of the war against al Qaeda from the United States.

After the U.S. invaded Iraq and inherited the MEK from Saddam Hussein, Cheney and Rumsfeld began using them for intelligence missions inside Iran. According to journalist Seymour Hersh, they were even brought to the U.S. for military training. Israel famously used them to launder the revelation of construction of the Iranian nuclear centrifuge facility at Natanz, which had, in fact, already been publicly revealed. Since then, MEK has often proclaimed other "intelligence" about Iran's nuclear program, usually unreliable, such as the so-called "smoking laptop" which they provided to the IAEA in 2004. They have also made various false claims about nuclear facilities in Iran, such as in 2015, when they released a stock photo of a vault door in an attempt to show proof of a secret uranium enrichment site in Tehran. During Obama's first term, the Israelis started using MEK cultists to murder Iranian nuclear scientists in an assassination campaign between 2010–2012. They killed four, including a graduate student, and narrowly missed an attempt on the director of their Atomic Energy Organization. Finally, the Obama administration leaked a story about it to NBC News, essentially burning the operation and demanding its end. MEK was very likely involved in the assassination of another Iranian nuclear scientist in November 2020 as well.

The common propaganda campaign has it that Iran is "the world's leading state sponsor of terrorism." This is simply laughable. They back Hamas in the Gaza Strip and Hezbollah in southern Lebanon. But though both have used terrorist tactics in the past, both groups are now elected political parties. And while they provide determined armed resistance to Israel, neither is an international terrorist group nor do either of them target the United States of America.

Claims that Iran backs al Qaeda are lies pushed by hawks like Donald Trump's secretary of state Mike Pompeo and neoconservative groups like the Foundation for Defense of Democracies. They have been discredited by in-depth studies by the Combating Terrorism Center at West Point, the New America Foundation and Reuters and official statements by the CIA and Pentagon. There is also the fact of multiple attacks by al Qaeda and associated groups against Iran over the years. Former Bush NSC official Flynt Leverett has confirmed to the author that Iran was opposed to al Qaeda and was very cooperative with the War on Terrorism until the administration turned on them. They targeted the Iranians with new sanctions, named them as an enemy in Bush's official national security strategy, putting them on the shortlist for regime change, and pretended for years to believe they were in violation of their sworn forbearance of the pursuit of nuclear weapons in the Non-Proliferation Treaty, a possible tripwire for war.

The worst thing one can accuse the Iranian government of in the last 20 years is that after Bush rejected their overtures, they implemented their own Iraq policy based on "strong federalism," which helped tear that country apart. Iran's strategy was mostly centered around having their favored groups cooperate with America's war. We were fighting it for them.

Sectarian War

The first Battle of Fallujah began at the very end of March 2004. The trouble started when the Israelis assassinated the leader of Hamas, Sheikh Ahmed Yassin, in the Gaza Strip. This caused a riot in Fallujah where four Blackwater mercenaries were killed, their burnt corpses left hanging from a bridge. In retaliation, Marine Gen. James Mattis launched two massive attacks on the city, one almost immediately that spring, and another just after President Bush's reelection in November. The rules of engagement were overly broad, including vast free-fire zones where all people were to be considered enemy combatants. Many innocent civilians were killed as a result.

It may be worth quoting the Commander in Chief's statement to the generals before the spring assault began. According to Lieutenant General Ricardo Sanchez, George W. Bush told them:

> Kick ass! If somebody tries to stop the march to democracy, we will seek them out and kill them! We must be tougher than hell! This Vietnam stuff, this is not even close. It is a mindset. We can't send that message. It's an excuse to prepare us for withdrawal. There is a series of moments, and this is one of them. Our will is being tested, but we are resolute. We have a better way. Stay strong! Stay the course! Kill them! Be confident! Prevail! We are going to wipe them out! We are not blinking!

U.S. military forces are very strong. So, there is nothing they cannot accomplish with firepower, right? Rather than crushing the insurgency, Gen. Mattis's marines just turned Fallujah into a "Remember the Alamo!"-type battle cry and helped to energize the predominantly Sunni-based insurgency against the U.S. in towns and cities across Iraq. Perhaps this is part of what Mattis had in mind when he said in 2013 that, "I paid a military-security price every day as the commander of CENTCOM because the Americans were seen as biased in support of Israel."

As the great war reporter Dahr Jamail documented, another part of the attack's consequences were that many of the refugees from predominantly Sunni Fallujah fled to Baghdad to go and stay with their friends and family. This led to some disruption, fighting and backlash among the local Shi'ite residents.

The U.S. then went to Ramadi to hunt Sunni insurgents, causing reprisal attacks against some Shi'ites and their displacement. This process kept being repeated. Because of the large attacks on these cities, many refugees would always be driven out. Those displaced people would then displace others wherever they sought shelter. This helped drive tit-for-tat and revenge attacks between the opposing sides.

General Ray Odierno, as head of the fourth infantry division, further provoked massive insurgency in Anbar Province. In 2004, the Sunni tribal leaders offered a ceasefire under the same terms that Petraeus later accepted during the "Awakening." Instead, Odierno tried to defeat them by cracking down on the entire population, rounding up "fighting-aged males" by the thousands and driving even more people into the arms of the insurgency. The Army themselves later confirmed that 90 percent of the people arrested by their forces were completely innocent.

Army Gen. David Petraeus got his start in Iraq stationed in Mosul in the predominantly Sunni Arab northwest of the country. He had launched a major initiative to arm and train Sunni fighters to serve as the local police force there. This program collapsed when the entire group of more than 3,000 took their weapons and joined the insurgency against U.S. forces. The second battle of Fallujah, in November 2004, also only created more resistance in response.

The Pentagon then doubled down on support for Shi'ite forces to fight the insurgency in predominantly Sunni towns in Iraq's west. The culmination of this strategy was the "Salvador Option," named for policies implemented against leftist insurgents in El Salvador in the 1980s. In practice, this meant Gen. Petraeus and his special advisers, retired colonels James Steele and James Coffman, hired Shi'ite death squads, primarily ISCI's Badr Brigade, to hunt down and kill the leaders of the Sunni-based insurgency. They also wanted to make the Sunni population pay the price for their resistance to U.S. and Shi'ite forces. In fact, before he made his name as the famous leader of the Iraqi "surge" of 2007, Gen. Petraeus's job was training and arming up the Badr Brigade to serve as the core of the new Iraqi army and Iraqi National Police, as well as running their private death squads through Steele and Coffman. An investigation by the *Guardian* and BBC Arabic demonstrated that Steele and Coffman, both of whom worked directly for Gen. Petraeus, were implicated in overseeing the torture of Iraqi prisoners.

This Salvador Option played a large role in the outbreak of full-scale sectarian civil war in Iraq. Not only had the Shi'ite parties won the elections, now they were working in full alliance with the Americans to attack the Sunni Ba'athist and tribal forces. Iraq war logs revealed by Manning and Wikileaks show how the Badr Brigade was acting as an extrajudicial death squad, engaging in widespread torture against Sunni Arabs. One of the biggest stories to come out of the Iraq War Logs was about a "fragmentary order," Frago-242. It instructed American troops that they were not to report and were forbidden from interfering with the Badr and Wolf Brigades and other Shi'ite militias taking Sunni captives off to be tortured unless given specific orders to the contrary from higher up the chain of command. This was long after the torture at Abu Ghraib prison had been exposed, and new orders banning such abuse by U.S. military members had been issued.

Readers may be familiar with the 2014 Clint Eastwood Iraq war film *American Sniper*, where the protagonist saves innocent victims from enemy terrorists torturing them with power drills. In the real world, it was the American-backed Shi'ite militias such as the Badr and Wolf Brigades whose signature was torturing Sunnis to death with drills through their hearts, brains and eyeballs. That is who the U.S. military fought the war for, not who they saved the Iraqi people from.

Zarqawi's men attacked the Shi'ite al-Askari "Golden" mosque in the city of Samarra in February 2006. This bombing represented an effort by Zarqawi to do everything he could to turn the Sunni-based insurgency against the U.S. occupation and new Baghdad government into a war against Shi'ite civilians. This was because reprisal attacks by Shi'ites against other Sunni civilians helped drive more into his camp in response. It was the so-called "strategy of savagery," meant to terrorize the enemy and empower their own forces as well. Al Qaeda leaders hiding back in Pakistan tried to advise him against it, but he would not stop. He was trying to destroy the modern Iraqi state so that it might be replaced by something much worse.

American politicians, generals and pundits, flustered by the rise of the new generation of jihadist fighters in Iraq, began to push the "flypaper theory": sure, maybe they had spread chaos to a formerly stable, secular country, but that was a good thing because it was drawing all the would-be terrorists from around the region to the "flypaper" that was Iraq's sectarian war. This simply allowed the U.S. Army to meet them and kill them there in Iraq, far away from innocent American moms and babies. However, that argument presumed there was a finite number of Sunni "fighting-age males" who could ever get mad enough about others being killed to choose to join the fight. This was wishful thinking at best. Desperate spin put out to undermine the rising new consensus was a more likely explanation.

A 2004 report by the Defense Science Board two National Intelligence Estimate (NIE) of the combined American National Intelligence Council (NIC) from 2005 and 2006 showed that the war was increasing the influence of bin Ladenite terrorists in Iraq and across the region as they rallied against the U.S. and the rise of Shi'ite power in Baghdad.

Saudi and Israeli studies from 2005 concluded that virtually all the foreign fighters who traveled to fight under Zarqawi's al Qaeda in Iraq and allied groups there were young new recruits. None of them were mujahideen from the war against the Russians in Afghanistan. The only role the older terrorists were playing was in recruitment and sending new volunteers off to fight. An entirely new generation of not just local Sunni insurgents but international fighters came from around the region to fight, just as they had gone to Afghanistan to fight the Russians twenty years before. The foreign fighters tended to be the most radical and aligned with Zarqawi's al Qaeda in Iraq, engaging in terrorist attacks against soldiers and civilians alike. They were radicalized by the war itself, not before it.

And the Saudis should know. One of the most important buried stories of Iraq War II is that when Bush failed to put another Sunni strongman in power but instead took the side of the Shi'ites in the creation of the new Iraqi state, the Saudis, outraged and panicked, began financing the Sunni-based insurgency and sending jihadists off to join the fight against their American friends. The CIA and NSC complained to their friends in the newspapers a few times, but the Bush administration apparently never insisted the Saudis cease this betrayal.

David B. Low, primary author of the 2006 NIE, told the *Washington Post* the invasion of Iraq provided the bin Ladenites with

> a training ground, a recruitment ground, the opportunity for enhancing technical skills. ... There is even, under the best scenario, over time, the likelihood that some of the jihadists who are not killed there will, in a sense, go home, wherever home is, and will therefore disperse to various other countries.

The report itself said that, "The al Qaeda membership that was distinguished by having trained in Afghanistan will gradually dissipate, to be replaced in part by the dispersion of the experienced survivors of the conflict in Iraq."

The "Surge"

In 2007, the administration and military launched the Iraq "surge." All this escalation accomplished was the near-completion of the brutal sectarian cleansing of Sunni Arabs from Baghdad and the consolidation of power in the hands of the Shi'ite forces in the capital city. We cannot know what would have happened if the U.S. had withdrawn just after deposing Hussein's government, or even later, say in 2006 when Secretary of Defense Rumsfeld wanted to end the war before finally being forced out himself. But if they had pulled the troops out, then there certainly would have been much more incentive remaining for the Shi'ite parties to negotiate. Perhaps there would have been a horrible civil war no matter what.

We do know what happened when Shi'ite factions had the Americans at their disposal. It was a bloodbath. Instead of using Rumsfeld's position as cover to back out, Bush fired him and brought in the former CIA director Robert Gates to be the new secretary of defense. Gen. David Petraeus would take over the war and implement his and Gen. Mattis's newly revised and rewritten counterinsurgency manual for how to win the hearts and minds of the Iraqi people.

The result was not the reconciliation in the "benchmarks" for victory stated at the beginning of the year. Instead, all they did was predictably remove the last incentive that the Shi'ite factions had to compromise with the Sunnis. Their militias, and indeed the new Iraqi army, which was drawn primarily from their ranks, doubled down on their sectarian cleansing campaign. The U.S. was giving the Shi'ite factions a total victory in the capital city.

Petraeus also announced the policy of supporting the "Sahwa" or "Awakening" movement. This meant that he compromised with the different Sunni tribal factions in the western Anbar province, allowing them to patrol their own neighborhoods and bribing them with cash and guns to stop attacking American troops and instead to marginalize the worst of the al Qaeda forces who had been fighting with them in the Sunni insurgency. Neoconservative policy adviser Zalmay Khalilzad had first proposed a deal with the Sunni insurgency to President Bush, who turned it down, at the end of 2005.

In fact, the local Iraqi Sunnis were sick and tired of the jihadis' antics and had already started marginalizing them around the time Khalilzad wanted to make the change — more than a year before Petraeus ever showed up at the front of that parade. AQI, at that time mostly led by Egyptians and Saudis, had worn out their welcome. Local Sunnis betrayed Zarqawi to U.S. forces, who promptly killed him with an airstrike, that summer. At its lowest point, after his death, Zarqawi's group renamed itself the "Islamic State of Iraq" in what was simultaneously a moment of then-comedic self-ridicule and what turned out to be an ominous portent of the years ahead. Though they had no power to make it happen, they were making their goals as clear as could be. All the while, more and more Shi'ites were being expelled by these Petraeus-sanctioned Sunni militias out of the western Anbar province, east toward the new Shi'ite lines. Divisions were getting sharper than at any time since the fall of the British-backed king.

Petraeus bribed the tribes to continue expelling the bin Ladenites while all along promising them a place in the new Iraqi system that he could never provide. Many jihadis were killed. Many more simply went home to cause trouble later. Al Qaeda in Iraq was practically decimated by their former allies among the Iraqi Sunni-based insurgency.

The U.S. military was quickly backing down from their stated goals. "The surge is working, we're going to achieve those benchmarks, you watch," the administration said in the winter and spring of 2007. By the summer, with body counts in the civil war coming in at more than 3,000 per month, it was announced that Gen. Petraeus's report to Congress would be delayed. Then the military and media suddenly quit mentioning "benchmarks" at all. The whole narrative was reduced to an empty banner slogan: "The surge is working! The surge is working!" What it was working at was no longer defined. By the fall, the talking point was updated to "The surge worked!" It no longer mattered what the "surge" was ever supposed to achieve. It just worked. Virtually the entire political and media class bought it. It cost them nothing.

But the benchmarks were supposed to be political reconciliation between major factions in the now-secure, newly 85 percent Shi'ite capital of Baghdad. Instead, they created a situation where the Shi'ite parties had no reason left to compromise with the Sunnis. Petraeus's promises to the "Sons of Iraq" and the "Concerned Local Citizens" — the Sunni insurgents who had quit their fight against U.S. forces — that they would be incorporated into the police and military and into patronage positions in the ministries, never happened. They were just left high and dry.

Once the U.S. helped make Baghdad an almost entirely Shi'ite city, there was a lot less fighting among factions in the capital. Peace was what they called it, but they were leaving the country open wide for the next conflict to break out a few years later due to the unresolved question of the now-powerless factions of western Iraqi Sunnistan.

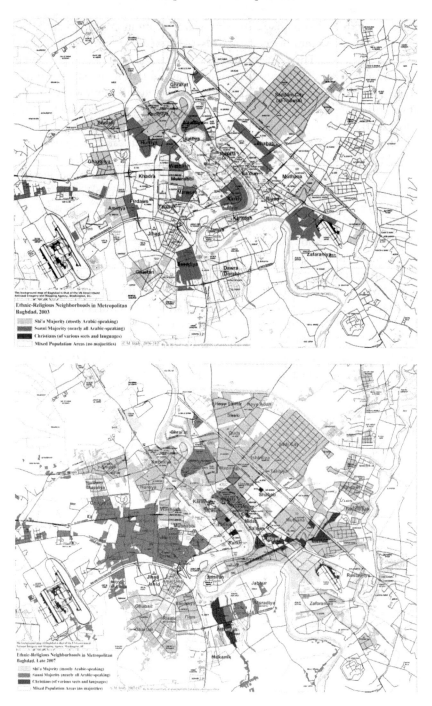

Soda Straws and EFPs

During the Iraq "surge," the U.S. also fought a small war against one major Shi'ite faction as well. The infamous "Collateral Murder" video leaked by Chelsea Manning and published by Wikileaks shows a July 12, 2007, Apache helicopter gunship attack and kill a group of civilians, including two Reuters reporters, Saeed Chmagh and Namir Noor-Eldeen. They were covering the U.S. Army fighting in East Baghdad against the Shi'ite forces of Muqtada al-Sadr.

Sadr, however, was part of the United Iraqi Alliance that the Americans were supporting and fighting so hard to enthrone in power in Baghdad. "Muqtada! Muqtada! Muqtada!" the mob had chanted at Saddam Hussein's hanging in 2006. The son and son-in-law of two powerful Shi'ite clerics who had both been murdered by Saddam Hussein, Sadr had an incredible amount of political legitimacy among the Shi'ite masses in southern Iraq. As soon as U.S. troops entered the capital in 2003, the people of the eastern Baghdad slum "Saddam City" renamed it "Sadr City" in his family's honor. Initially dismissed as just a "minor cleric" and nuisance by U.S. occupation forces, Sadr has been one of the major kingmakers behind the Da'wa Party and ISCI leaders that America has put in power since 2005. Prime ministers Jaafari, al-Maliki, Abadi, Mahdi and Al-Kadhimi have all gotten the job with, and only with, Sadr's support. Yet in 2007, America was taking the fight to him at the same time as his sometimes-enemies in the Sunni-based insurgency.

Secretary of Defense Gates said that the problem with the public seeing the "Collateral Murder" video was that they "end up looking at the war through a soda straw," and so could not understand the proper context or meaning.

So, what was the context? Why was the U.S. fighting to weaken one of the three central pillars of the faction they were fighting the whole war to install in power? It was to weaken his influence compared to the Supreme Islamic Council and the Da'wa Party, his major partners in the United Iraqi Alliance group. But to what actual end, and at what cost? The Americans claimed that Sadr was a puppet of Iran and was serving their interests by insisting that the U.S. withdraw all forces from the country. This was despite the fact that since the start of the war, Sadr had positioned himself as an Iraqi nationalist, willing to cooperate with the Sunnis — when his forces were not helping to cleanse them from their neighborhoods — and had repeatedly denounced both the U.S. and Iran for their interference in the country. During the first battle of Fallujah in the spring of 2004, the Sadrists had also risen up in response to the shutting down of one of their newspapers in eastern Baghdad. In the middle of that fight, he sent Shi'ite fighters in pickup trucks to Fallujah in the predominantly Sunni west to show nationalist solidarity and fight on their side against Gen. Mattis's marines.

Sadr had also routinely condemned the far more Iran-tied ISCI and Da'wa factions for their emphasis on the Iran-friendly policy of "strong federalism" for Iraq. Sadr wanted an alliance with Sunnis and a strong central Iraqi government with the ability to limit foreign intervention in Iraq by the U.S. or their neighbors.

The assault on Sadr's forces during the 2007–2008 surge killed many people, but if anything, it accomplished the opposite of the mission's goals. Sadr himself escaped the assault by fleeing to Iran, where he received further religious instruction and gained a higher clerical rank. In response to Petraeus's assault, many members of Sadr's militia, the Mahdi Army, traveled to Iran to be trained by the Iranian Quds force, supposedly the reason the U.S. launched the attack against them in the first place. Republican Senator John McCain famously accused Iran of taking in al Qaeda fighters for training until his friend Sen. Joe Lieberman stepped up to correct him to just call them "militants." This revealed that McCain, one of the biggest proponents of the 2003 invasion and the 2007 "surge," did not have the first clue who was fighting who in Iraq nor what Iran's role in the conflict was. Sadr also continued to insist on American withdrawal as a condition for continuing to support the al-Maliki government the U.S. had installed.

In 2006, President Bush and the military began to claim that all their Iraq problems were Iran's fault. But in 2007, with the launch of the "surge," the administration started a whole new media campaign to reinforce this narrative. Any time an American soldier was killed fighting in a predominantly Shi'ite part of the country, typically in eastern Baghdad or the southern city of Najaf, the U.S. would blame it on Iran, particularly if they were killed by an Explosively Formed Penetrator (EFP) roadside bomb. EFPs were a distinct improvement over other forms of Improvised Explosive Devices (IEDs) in that they were shaped charges with copper cores that could cut through American armor. More than 500 out of the 4,500 Americans killed in Iraq War II lost their lives fighting Sadr's Mahdi Army, many of them by these EFPs. A major propaganda campaign was launched by Gen. Petraeus and the American media. Michael Gordon of the *New York Times*, the same man who co-authored many of Judith Miller's worst tall tales about Saddam Hussein's weapons of mass destruction programs in 2002 and 2003, took the lead pushing this story on the public. They claimed that all of these bombs had Iranian origins and had been sent as part of a plot to kill American troops. But it was shown repeatedly in reports by Gordon's *New York Times* colleague, Alissa Rubin, Reuters staff, Andrew Cockburn in the *Los Angeles Times*, Yochi J. Dreazen in the *Wall Street Journal*, Ellen Knickmeyer in the *Washington Post*,

David Hambling in *Wired*, Sam Dagher of the *Christian Science Monitor*, Seymour Hersh in the *New Yorker* and Gareth Porter in Interpress Service that the EFPs were not Iranian weapons. They were made in Iraq by Iraqis. Further, Porter demonstrated that the Iraqi Shi'ites had picked up the technique from Lebanese Hezbollah, who in turn had first learned it from the Irish Republican Army, not Iran.

Retired Marine Captain Matthew Hoh, regimental engineer in 2006 and 2007 for the 7th and then 2nd Marines and who was stationed at the Joint IED Defeat Organization (JIEDDO) in 2008, confirmed to the author that "Yes, the EFPs were all made in Iraq, in workshops by Iraqis."

James Aragon, at the time an Air Force Master Sergeant-select, was then an augmentee for 5th Special Forces Group when that unit took command of Combined Joint Special Operations Task Force-Arabian Peninsula (CJSOTF-AP). He was the Combined Intelligence Cell night-shift Non-Commissioned Officer in Charge (NCOIC) and lead analyst for concerns related to Iranian influence in Iraq. Aragon "lived and breathed the secret side of the war for over 2,600 hours" and "read over 4,000 intelligence summaries from all intelligence agencies" during the 2007–2008 period. He told the author in an email that Iranian Quds Force commander, Qasem Soleimani "denied to Iraq Minister of Interior Jawad al-Bulani that he had any knowledge of EFPs in Iraq. I never saw any intelligence that proved otherwise."

That is no surprise because there was no evidence proving that the EFPs came from Iran, much less that they were all sent as part of an Iranian military operation against the United States. Petraeus scheduled a big press conference to lay out his accusations, but they canceled it when the assembled reporters started looking critically at the pile of random hardware laid out for display. They noticed that some had "Made in the UAE" printed on them in English, and others read in Arabic, "Made in Haditha," that is, Iraq. This again indicated that these parts were bought on the open market and assembled there. "The truth is, quite frankly, we thought the briefing overstated, and we sent it back to get it narrowed and focused on the facts," National Security Advisor Stephen Hadley admitted. They never tried again. The CIA, Chairman of the Joint Chiefs General Peter Pace, Secretary of Defense Robert Gates and the British army all backed down from claims about Iranian involvement in the Sadrist resistance and the supplying of roadside bombs.

Even if the military had proven the Iranian origin of these weapons — which they never did — they certainly did not show that the Iranian government was behind the effort at all. Due to the war, the border was essentially left wide open to arms dealers and black marketeers of all descriptions. Also, the only reason Sadr's Mahdi Army was fighting and killing any Americans at all was because Petraeus had decided to pick an ultimately meaningless fight.

The EFP narrative was a lie, one that the hawks used throughout the spring of 2007 to try to push President Bush into striking Iranian Quds Force targets inside Iran, which he thankfully refused to do. This was apparently based on sound advice given to him by the Joint Chiefs of Staff that if the U.S. were to start a war with Iran, they could not promise "escalation dominance." While America's technically sophisticated armed forces far outmatched the Iranians, they also did not have confidence that they could control every stage of the war. It was not clear what Iran might do to retaliate, but they knew they would not be able to prevent it. In the event of a real war with Iran, the U.S. had tens of thousands of troops and a vast array of military targets vulnerable to missile attack in Iraq, Afghanistan, Kuwait, Qatar and Bahrain. This was especially true in Iraq where the U.S. had more than a hundred thousand troops stationed at the time, and which could be expected to "light up like a candle," because, as a four-star general told Seymour Hersh, "the Iranians could take Basra with ten mullahs and one sound truck." Abdul Aziz al-Hakim, leader of the Supreme Islamic Council of Iraq (ISCI) told a journalist that if the U.S. attacked Iran, "Then, we would do our duty." In other words, their Badr Brigade, and for that matter the new Iraqi army, would turn on their American allies and fight on Iran's side of the war in an instant.

At this point, the neoconservatives were desperate. None other than David Wurmser, the man who said invading Iraq would tame the wicked Iranian mullahs, was among those most determined to spread the war to Iran to try to correct for his massive error. It was Wurmser, then-Vice President Cheney's deputy assistant for national security affairs, who told a group of hawks in late spring 2007 that due to Bush's reluctance to attack, Cheney was considering having the Israelis provoke a conflict with Iran as an "end run" around the president, to trap him into going to war. They would force Iran to hit U.S. naval forces in the Gulf in retaliation for Israeli missile strikes against the Natanz nuclear facility, thus starting a full-scale war. This wild-sounding claim by Washington, D.C. liberal think tank official Steven Clemons was confirmed by the *New York Times*, *Time* magazine and *Washington Post* reporter-author Barton Gellman in his book *Angler*.

The commander of CENTCOM, Admiral William "Fox" Fallon, finally made it known publicly that the U.S. would attack Iran "over his dead body," and that the administration had better cool their harsh rhetoric. He was clearly insubordinate, but it sure is ironic how America's permanent standing military is so often the restraining force on their own civilian commanders. As America's founders knew, the military itself has the most substantial incentive to find things to do to keep itself going at the people's expense. But thankfully, they sometimes also pull the brakes on the civilians' worst political agendas. In this case, it seems that the Joint Chiefs and CENTCOM commander were the most important factors in stopping the war in the spring and summer of 2007.

There may be some truth to the claim that the Iranian Quds Force helped to coordinate Shi'ite resistance to the U.S. in East Baghdad and Najaf. Iran had reason to let the Americans know that their stay was only temporary and that the Shi'ite majority was only tolerating them for short term help in defeating their Sunni Arab enemies. But it was never proven. The claim that they were behind the EFP roadside bombing campaign is demonstrably false. The idea that they were behind everything that had gone wrong with the war was only as true as U.S. forces made it for them.

The book *The Good Soldiers* by Dexter Filkins tells the story of these soldiers who were killing and dying in this war in East Baghdad during the "surge," fighting against one of the exact same factions that their army was fighting for in the larger war. At only one point each do the local commander and the journalist-author muse about the irony of fighting a war against their ally before dismissing those concerns and getting back to the work of leading and chronicling that fight.

The leader of the brigade profiled in that book, Sadr City "surge" commander U.S. Army Lieutenant Colonel Ralph Kauzlarich, was credibly accused by two of his soldiers, Ethan McCord and Josh Stieber, of ordering them to commit war crimes against civilians in that unnecessary subset of an unnecessary war. Retired Army Major Danny Sjursen, the influential antiwar writer and activist, lost his best friend Alex Fuller and many others fighting these pointless battles against the Shi'ites of eastern Baghdad during Petraeus's failed "surge." None of this succeeded in marginalizing the power of Muqtada al-Sadr, who remains one of the most powerful political figures in Iraq to this day, where he still rails against American and Iranian interference in Iraqi affairs.

No Nukes!

The important context to Gen. Petraeus's repeated accusations against Iran for their interference in Iraq was the role he was playing in Vice President Cheney's plan to extend the war to Tehran despite Bush's reluctance. Before and after the EFP subterfuge was the scandal of Iran's civilian nuclear program.

It is important to emphasize not only that Iran has never tried to make nuclear bombs, but that we all have been told the opposite about this supposed threat for the last 30 years. Even the American National Intelligence Council and Israeli Mossad have both conceded that Iran gave up their preliminary research into nuclear weapons production in 2003 and never had a program to develop a nuclear weapon at all.

When the NIC released their National Intelligence Estimate (NIE) on the issue in 2007, in which they made this judgment with "high confidence," it was widely seen as a rebuke to the administration's attempts to gin up a crisis. Bush later lamented in his memoir:

> The NIE's conclusion was so stunning that I felt certain it would immediately leak to the press. As much as I disliked the idea, I decided to declassify the key findings so that we could shape the news stories with the facts. ...

> Both [Israel and the Arabian states] were deeply concerned about Iran and furious with the United States over the NIE.

President Bush described meeting with the Saudi king:

> "Your Majesty, may I begin the meeting?" I asked. "I'm confident every one of you believes I wrote the NIE as a way to avoid taking action against Iran."

> No one said a word. They were too polite to confirm their suspicion aloud.

> "You have to understand our system," I said. "The NIE was produced independently by our intelligence community. I am as angry about it as you are."

> The NIE didn't just undermine diplomacy. It also tied my hands on the military side. ... After the NIE, how could I possibly explain using the military to destroy the nuclear facilities of a country the intelligence community said had no active weapons program?

But in the book *Manufactured Crisis: The Untold Story of the Iran Nuclear Scare*, journalist Gareth Porter shows that even those claims about preliminary research before 2003 are overblown. They are based only on the previously mentioned, Israeli-forged "smoking laptop" documents and some fair-but-mistaken guesses about the meaning of some Iranian purchases of dual-use items that were later shown to have been for their originally claimed civilian purposes at Sharif University.

As Porter showed in his article, "When the Ayatollah Said No to Nukes" in *Foreign Policy*, Ayatollah Khomeini had forbidden the creation or use of chemical or nuclear weapons back during the 1980s, even at the height of Hussein's U.S.-enabled mustard and tabun nerve gas attacks on his troops. When the Reagan administration increased support for Iraq's chemical weapons attacks on Iranian soldiers and civilians in the late 1980s, the Iranian Revolutionary Guard Corps (IRGC) asked permission to pursue the creation of their own chemical weapons. The Ayatollah forbid it. "It doesn't matter whether [Iraq's attacks are] on the battlefield or in cities; we are against this," Khomeini told the IRGC. "It is haram [forbidden] to produce such weapons. You are only allowed to produce protection." The second and current post-revolution supreme leader, Ali Khamenei, has reaffirmed that edict. We should not take their word for it, but we can see their order's implementation. They have not sought to make nuclear weapons.

In the Bush years, the Israelis and their associates in America pushed the lie that the Iranians had a secret, parallel nuclear weapons program that the U.S. and international inspectors did not know about. They were simply bluffing. Certainly, now a decade and a half after the CIA and Mossad admitted Iran had no nuclear weapons program, regular updates from the CIA reaffirming that conclusion, and with three years of expanded inspections before President Trump took the U.S. out of the 2015 nuclear deal, it is clear that it was never the case. What they have is a known, open, "declared," civilian electricity program. David Sanger of the *New York Times* and George Jahn of the Associated Press have continued for years to claim as a proven fact that Iran does have a nuclear weapons program. They are either liars or lousy journalists.

In 2007, at the height of the threat of war between the U.S. and Iran over their nuclear program, first-generation neoconservative leader Norman Podhoretz admitted that, "If we were to bomb the Iranians as I hope and pray we will, we will unleash a wave of anti-Americanism all over the world that will make the anti-Americanism we've experienced so far look like a lovefest." Apparently remembering the camera, he quickly added, "On the other hand, that's a worst-case scenario."

And for what are Americans supposed to make this sacrifice? Israeli Prime Minister Benjamin Netanyahu and his then-defense minister, the former prime minister Ehud Barak, admitted in 2010 that even if Iran were hypothetically to gain atomic weapons, the Israelis were not afraid the Ayatollah would attack them in a first strike, as they constantly tell the public. Instead, they were merely concerned that it would limit their "freedom of action" against other regional adversaries, such as Hezbollah, and could cause a "brain drain" of talented young Israelis to the United States. Netanyahu's immediate predecessor, Prime Minister Ehud Olmert told the *New York Times* that, "Just as Pakistan had the bomb and nothing happened, Israel could also accept and survive Iran having the bomb." Former Clinton administration State Department official Jamie Rubin also explained in *Foreign Policy* that the problem was never an Israeli fear of a first strike by Iran, but "Israel's real fear — losing its nuclear monopoly and therefore the ability to use its conventional forces at will throughout the Middle East — is the unacknowledged factor driving its decision-making toward the Islamic Republic." Despite years' worth of war party propaganda about Iran to credulous American TV audiences, Rubin emphasized that

> for Israeli leaders, the real threat from a nuclear-armed Iran is not the prospect of an insane Iranian leader launching an unprovoked nuclear attack on Israel that would lead to the annihilation of both countries. It's the fact that Iran doesn't even need to test a nuclear weapon to undermine Israeli military leverage in Lebanon and Syria.

Remember that the next time you and your family are being told the U.S. has to go to war with Iran to protect Israel because the theocrats in Tehran are so hell-bent on destroying the Jewish state that they would be willing to start a suicidal nuclear war to get it done. Israeli leaders and their partisans sometimes happily admit they are not in danger of anything but losing the ability to start violent conflicts "at will." Everyone in the U.S. government knows but is forbidden to say what has been publicly reported since the Israeli whistleblower Mordechai Vanunu revealed their nuclear weapons arsenal in 1986: Israel is the nuclear hegemon of the Middle East. Their government possesses more than 200 nuclear weapons and has refused to sign the Non-Proliferation Treaty. Vanunu confirmed that number to the author in 2018.

American Enterprise Institute hawk Danielle Pletka did as much as anyone to support Ahmed Chalabi and his group's claims about Iraq's weapons. She conceded in 2011 that the real threat was that if Iran made nuclear weapons, and then refrained from using them, it would undermine the Israelis' and neoconservatives' narrative of how crazy and irresponsible they are. These are very movable goalposts.

Iran's strategy after America announced their inclusion in the "Axis of Evil" and claimed they had a secret nuclear weapons program was to put their hands up, open their books wide and shout to the whole world that they have signed the Non-Proliferation Treaty, have a Safeguards Agreement with the International Atomic Energy Agency (IAEA), and remain within their international obligations. The IAEA regularly inspects all their facilities and "continues to verify the non-diversion of nuclear material" for military purposes, which renders America's pretext for regime change null and void. The U.S. and the Israelis confronted the Iranians with 15 years of accusations, threats and "crippling" sanctions over their nuclear program until President Obama finally negotiated the Joint Comprehensive Plan of Action (JCPOA) (a.k.a. "the nuclear deal") in 2015.

Iran did not require a new deal to prevent them from obtaining nuclear weapons because we already had one — the Non-Proliferation Treaty — and they were already adhering to it. Legally speaking, all the new deal really did was add an "additional protocol" and some "subsidiary arrangements" to Iran's Safeguards Agreement with the International Atomic Energy Agency. Still, the deal locks down Iran's civilian nuclear program beyond any other program in history. They poured concrete into the core of their heavy water reactor at Arak, completely disabling it and eliminating the production of potential weapons-grade plutonium waste, which they never had the necessary facility for reprocessing anyway. They scaled back the number of operating centrifuges, accepted new limits on the amount of low-enriched uranium they can stockpile, expanded IAEA access to include their uranium mines and centrifuge facilities and signed up for processes that even allow inspection of their military bases. For this, they got some of their own money returned which had been seized and "frozen" by the Treasury Department mid-weapons purchase during the 1979 revolution and some limited sanctions relief. Yes, those famous pallets of cash were what America had owed Iran for 40 years. None of it was American tax money. Iran got the short end of that deal and signed it anyway.

So, all the accusations you have heard in the last 25 years on this subject have been overblown. Iran is not making nukes. Their nuclear electricity program is simply based on opportunity costs. There is little demand on the international market for Iran's natural uranium deposits. But they can satisfy their domestic electric power needs with their nuclear facilities and sell their oil — when they are not under blockade, anyway.

The worst one could honestly claim is that Iran has a latent nuclear weapons capability since they have mastered the nuclear fuel cycle and so could potentially make an atom bomb if they thought there was no choice. This is the same semi-ambiguous stance as the Japanese currently have. But Iran's policy has essentially been that as long as the U.S. does not attack them, they will not make the mistake of trying to make a nuke which they know would provoke the U.S. to attack them. They have a civilian nuclear energy program, wholly "safeguarded" by the International Atomic Energy Agency. We should all be happy to leave it at that.

Yet without the fake threat of an Iranian A-bomb serving as such a major obstacle, the U.S. has no real excuse for its continuing cold war against them. That is why the hawks were so opposed to the nuclear deal of 2015. It was only a first step but put a real reduction of tensions back on the table.

Torture

The author's 2017 book, *Fool's Errand*, has a much more thorough section on the George W. Bush and Barack Obama administrations' torture programs. In order to avoid too much repetition here, the brief version of the story is that the mandates and protections that President Bush gave to the CIA to engage in the brutal torture of al Qaeda suspects at their "black sites" in Poland, Romania, Morocco, Thailand, and their secret annex at Guantánamo Bay, Cuba immediately bled over to the military in Guantánamo, Afghanistan and Iraq. U.S. military forces were instructed that the Geneva Conventions did not apply. "The rules are 'Grab whom you must. Do what you want,'" a former intelligence official explained to journalist Seymour Hersh. At least five men were murdered by the CIA: one in the "Salt Pit" dungeon in Afghanistan, one in Abu Ghraib prison in Iraq and three at the CIA's secret annex, "Camp No," or "Penny Lane," in Guantánamo. Former CIA officer John Kiriakou has said, "people were just sort of dying in-process. I always wondered if we were killing people off the books." They brutally tortured a British citizen named Binyam Mohamed, including slicing his genitals with a razor blade until he made up a story accusing American al Qaeda member Jose Padilla of plotting to attack the U.S. with a radioactive "dirty bomb." Padilla was illegally held by the military for years over this lie until Bush backed down before his detention case could be heard by the Supreme Court. A Florida jury gave him life in prison anyway.

Torture in the Bagram prison in Afghanistan continued for years into the Obama era. His administration even "rendered" people to Afghan prisons who had never before stepped foot in the country, just to keep them from American courts, which by then had already intervened in the case of Guantánamo Bay.

By the time America was in the heat of fighting the Sunni-based insurgency in Iraq, they were torturing people by the tens of thousands. It was not just the scandal revealed at Abu Ghraib prison, where at least one man was tortured to death and children were raped in front of their mothers. U.S. military forces were torturing Iraqis in their homes, on the side of the road, at military bases — including later-Afghan war commander General Stanley McChrystal's "Camp NAMA," which stood for Nasty-Ass Military Area — and all over Iraq. According to then-Secretary of State Colin Powell's chief of staff, Col. Lawrence Wilkerson, at least 108 men were tortured to death or otherwise killed in military custody, a number later confirmed by the Associated Press. No one officer-level or higher was ever held accountable.

Retired Army Colonel Arnaldo Claudio, the 18th Airborne Corps Provost Marshal in command of U.S. military police conduct in Iraq, investigated human rights abuses of Iraqi detainees in the town of Tal Afar in 2005, in a camp commanded by then-Colonel H.R. McMaster, whom Claudio says he threatened to arrest. Claudio told the author that detainees were kept in extremely overcrowded conditions, handcuffed, deprived of food and water, and were left to rot in their own urine and feces in the hot desert sun. A so-called "good behavior program" was implemented by McMaster that held detainees indefinitely (beyond a rule requiring release after two weeks) unless they provided "actionable intelligence," which, of course, most did not have. McMaster was promoted instead of court-martialed. He ended up becoming President Donald Trump's second national security adviser.

Great credit goes to the American torture whistleblowers Claudio, Ian Fishback, Joe Darby, Anthony Lagouranis, Joseph Hickman, Todd Pierce, Brandon Neely, John Kiriakou, Steven Kleinman and Anthony Camerino (a.k.a. Matthew Alexander) for sticking their neck out to tell the truth on this vital matter.

The U.S. government continues to successfully argue in court against releasing the rest of the pictures and other evidence from Abu Ghraib under the reasoning that they could provoke terrorism. They have claimed the same thing in their case against Wikileaks founder Julian Assange and the secrets he exposed about America's role in Iraqi torture.

This is a reasonable fear if not a reasonable reaction. Torture, and reports of it, certainly drives terrorist recruitment. It is not our freedom that they hate. As Iraq War II Air Force interrogator Tony Camerino reported, huge numbers of foreign fighter insurgents who had traveled to Iraq to fight said they did so in reaction to the published photos of the torture at Abu Ghraib prison.

Ayman al-Zawahiri, Osama bin Laden's former partner and current leader of al Qaeda, was not involved with the assassination of Egyptian President Anwar Sadat in 1981 but was a member of the Muslim Brotherhood at the time. Zawahiri, a prominent Cairo surgeon, was rounded up and tortured with the rest of them. But being tortured by the new Hosni Mubarak regime was what led him to break from the conservative old Egyptian Muslim Brotherhood and instead join the more radical Egyptian Islamic Jihad, which he then later merged with bin Laden's al Qaeda.

As Italian journalist and author Loretta Napoleoni showed in her 2005 book, *Insurgent Iraq*, Abu Musab al-Zarqawi was just a two-bit criminal until the "royal" regime in Jordan mercilessly tortured him in prison. After suffering that brutality, Zarqawi became deeply committed to his religion and his fight against the king of Jordan — America's client — and after the U.S. invasion of Iraq, the Americans themselves.

It is now shown in defense department documents that Zarqawi's successor, Abu Bakr al Baghdadi, the eventual leader of the Islamic State (or ISIS), was imprisoned at Abu Ghraib during the period in which the notorious torture pictures were taken. He, therefore, was likely subject to the same abuses depicted in those photos.

So, there is every reason to believe that three of the very worst terrorists of our era were made by the Americans themselves or American-backed client dictatorships by torturing them. Call it the "setting a ticking time-bomb" scenario.

Destroying a Nation

It can hardly be overstated: America destroyed Iraq. Destroyed not just the government, but their society — completely ruined it. At least a million people were killed because of the war, certainly more in the aftermath. The Assyrian and Chaldean Christian communities who had been living in Iraq for 2,000 years have been virtually eradicated. There were almost a million and a half Iraqi Christians before the invasion. Now there are fewer than 250,000 left.

The Yazidis, Turkmen, Marsh Arabs and other religious and ethnic sectarian groups — some with their own languages and religions, people most in the West have probably never even heard of before — have been severely damaged by the war, and may never recover. As of 2008, there were only eight Jews left in Baghdad compared to a few dozen before the war. (Many Iraqi Jews had fled back in the 1950s due to Israeli false-flag terrorist attacks against them, waged to convince them to move to Israel.)

Throughout Iraq War II, the Iraqi Kurds kept their alliance with the Iraqi Shi'ite factions and avoided much of the violence because the Americans were not occupying the population in their northern mountains. Kurdish forces committed plenty of violence of their own, though, kidnapping and purging Arabs out of Kirkuk by the thousands in an attempt to take it for their own — a policy which failed. Kirkuk remains in the hands of Baghdad's Shi'ite Arab government.

Under Saddam Hussein's secular tyranny, women could wear blue jeans and no scarf while teaching college. Iraq was arguably the most westernized and secularized country in the region after Egypt. If American officials meant anything they said about trying to liberalize societies around the world, Iraq might have been a good place to start. After the September 11th attacks, they could have normalized relations with Hussein again and make him promise to do his part to keep al Qaeda down. The U.S. would not have had to support Iraq, but they could have let them come back into the so-called international community's good graces. Hussein's post-war CIA interrogator John Nixon later explained that, far from plotting with bin Laden to attack America with nuclear or germ weapons, the dictator was terrified of al Qaeda, semi-retired and busy writing a romance novel at the time of the U.S. invasion in 2003.

For the predominantly Shi'ite southeast of the country, they did establish a parliamentary democracy in form, but no one pretends Iraq is governed under a real rule of law. It is now an Islamist theocracy in all but name. The only thing restraining official oppression is that the government is so corrupt that its agents are thankfully too busy stealing most of the time to whip women for smiling or beat men for selling alcohol or giving someone the wrong haircut.

None of this had to happen at all. It may be difficult, especially for people who spent the 2000s defending the war and believing that it was all a great effort to fight for our and the Iraqi people's freedom, to really understand the level of pain that they have put that society through. But it happened. Some of it is still happening.

One important book from that era is *Collateral Damage: America's War Against Iraqi Civilians*. It is the words of American soldiers and other veterans bearing witness to the moral and legal war crimes that they participated in and witnessed during the war, and what it has been like for them to deal with the fact that their government sent them to fight, not against an enemy army, but the population of a country.

Regretful soldiers told the BBC:

> An IED goes off, and you just zap any farmer near you.

> You get so into it.

> When I first got there, you could basically kill anybody you want. If you see anybody out here at night, shoot 'em. Just drop [plant] a shovel [i.e., evidence of an IED].

> That's why they call them Hajis. You have to desensitize yourself to it. They're not people, they're animals. ... Hajis, Hajis. They beat it into your head. These aren't people.

Of course, Haji is an honorific for a Muslim who has made his mandatory pilgrimage to Mecca. But to American troops in the war it meant someone you can kill. In March 2008, Iraq Veterans Against the War hosted an event called "Winter Soldier: Iraq & Afghanistan," that featured numerous testimonies of veterans telling their stories of atrocities they had witnessed and participated in during the wars.

The Iraq War Logs, leaked to Wikileaks by Spc. Chelsea Manning, showed that the military did, in fact, do body counts — which they had denied — and that the real number of civilians killed was at least 15,000 higher than they had previously admitted. Spc. Manning was driven to leak the Iraq War Logs in 2010 after being ordered to help process the arrest of a man — certain to be tortured, possibly killed — who was guilty of no worse crime than writing a newspaper column critical of the corruption of America and Iran's chosen Iraqi prime minister, Nouri al-Maliki.

The Bush administration was allowed to get away with this because the American media, political class and overall culture during that era said that lowly American citizens could not question the president or his decisions during wartime. Bush was even reelected after deliberately lying the country into war (albeit running against the very weak candidate and Iraq war supporter Senator John Kerry).

The sanctimony of Iraq War II's promoters and propagandists was legendary. They pretended to own all patriotism and denounced anyone who knew better than them as traitors to America. Citizens got on board with little flag stickers on their cars which conflated loving the country with support for attacking Iraq. Some Protestant ministers cynically encouraged their flocks to believe that the war against the Ba'athists was necessary to fulfill the Biblical prophecy of the Rapture and the second coming of Christ at the turn of the millennium. Talk radio was unanimous. CNN and MSNBC raced to try to be as pro-war as Fox News, where Bill O'Reilly and Sean Hannity easily shouted down all scripted, weak, liberal opposition. Rumsfeld's Pentagon used more than 75 retired generals as "message force multipliers" to saturate cable news channels with the war party's point of view on every aspect of the invasion. The people loved it. Not since alcohol prohibition had so many people been so certain and so wrong. Nor were they ever again — until the war in Syria a few years later.

Only in Bush's second term, after hurricane Katrina drowned more than 1,000 people in New Orleans in the summer of 2005 while the Louisiana state guard, along with guard units from neighboring states, was off in Iraq and unavailable to carry out their primary responsibilities, did the proverbial dam break. The media finally admitted that perhaps Bush's team were not the most competent leaders and administrators in world history after all. Until that point, the standard narrative had been that it was a mortal sin to question our political leaders' grave national security decisions to protect us from terrorism and avenge the September 11th attacks. Their cover for his errors and crimes had gone on for four years. By the time the tune began to change, it was already far too late.

Thanks, Sucker

Once the Shi'ite parties and their militias, which included the Iraqi army, were done winning the civil war in 2008, they told President Bush the U.S. would have to leave. Bush said he would like to have 56 military bases. The Iraqis said no. Bush then tried for 40. The response was the same. As Patrick Cockburn covered for *The Independent*, over and over through the summer of 2008 the administration tried to figure out a way to stay in Iraq. Prime Minister Nouri al Maliki simply smiled and delayed. Bush had won the war for the Da'wa Party. They did not need him anymore. Besides, Maliki's position and those of many of his parliamentary coalition were dependent on the support of Muqtada al Sadr, who was sticking with his demand for full U.S. withdrawal no matter what.

The method the Iraqi government found for forcing American withdrawal was their refusal to sign a new Status of Forces Agreement (SOFA), which granted immunity to American forces if they committed war crimes against Iraqi civilians. The Iraqis claimed that they were a sovereign nation and had the right to prosecute U.S. troops in their own courts for such deeds. That was the deal-breaker for the Americans. The administration could never agree to such a stipulation. But the UN resolution legitimizing the occupation was set to expire. Without one or the other document signed, the U.S. military no longer had legal authority to stay.

It was Bush's last year in office. He was out of time, and so he signed onto the Iraqis' plan. The U.S. would withdraw the last of its forces by the end of December 2011.

This was the greatest debacle imaginable. The hawks' dream of global hegemony was blown to bits in that desert. The groups America fought five hard years and spent trillions of dollars to put in power in that country had no further use for the U.S. military at all. And they had no intention of letting the U.S. keep an air base there with which to threaten their primary patrons, Iran. David Wurmser had said that Saddam Hussein's oppression prevented the Iraqi Shi'ites from rising up to their true height of power to lord it over the Iranians and force them into compliance with American wishes. Instead, America installed the parties closest to the government in Tehran to rule in Baghdad.

Over the length of the entire war, the U.S. had constructed a massive imperial "embassy" compound in Saddam Hussein's former Green Zone palace district in Baghdad, approximately the size of the Vatican in Rome. The Bush administration imagined it would be the headquarters of their permanent American military colony. Its peak of operations was in 2011. As the troops were withdrawn, so was the 16,000-person embassy staff. Run by a skeleton crew, the campus remains only as a monument to American hubris and the occasional target of rocket fire from Shi'ite militias.

In Iraq's west, the Sunni-based insurgency had been quelled temporarily, but the score in their eyes had not been settled. [See Chapters 10–11.] In 2010, as he abided by the deal Bush had signed, President Obama had a chance to lessen the sectarian divisions in the country, but he squandered it. Ayad Allawi was a former Ba'athist, former CIA asset and former U.S.-appointed prime minister of the country after viceroy Paul Bremer left in 2004. Amazingly, his party had won the plurality of votes in the parliamentary elections in the spring of 2010. Under the constitution, he had the right to have the first chance to form a new government. If anyone had a chance at leading a real move towards reconciliation, it might have been Allawi. As a former Ba'athist but also a Shi'ite, he had associations on both sides and may have been able to seek compromise.

But the Iranians insisted on keeping Nouri al-Maliki as prime minister. Rather than use U.S. influence to push the Iraqi government to follow the law, Obama sent then-Vice President Biden to resolve the situation. Biden threw his weight behind Maliki, even calling Allawi personally to tell him to give it up. The U.S. would continue to support Iran's friends in power in the vain hope that someday the Iraqis would need us more than them. Obama and Biden would be back to kick Maliki out of power in a few years, but only after absolute disaster struck.

The prime minister's attitude toward the Sunnis was just to cut them loose, treating them as outlaws and foreigners. All of Gen. Petraeus's big promises that they would be integrated back into the Iraqi police, military and patronage systems meant nothing. They would get virtually no oil money, no jobs and no place in the new order at all. While some important Sunni tribesmen sat in the parliament, they had no real power to deliver for their people.

There is no guarantee that Allawi could have done any better. After all, the sectarian cleansing of Baghdad and many other cities was already complete. But he could have tried to split the difference and find a way forward. It was clear that he wanted to attempt it. Instead, under Maliki, the predominantly Sunni areas of western Iraq were just left adrift — and wide open for another regime change.

In the meantime, America's War on Terrorism was still raging on other battlefields.

Chapter Four:
Somalia

"You have no choice."
— James Mattis

Freedom Works

The name "Somalia" has somehow become a slur against Americans who prioritize political liberty. "Oh, you think freedom works, huh? Well, why don't you just move to Somalia?" This nonsense may have originated from the fact that some libertarian economists, such as Michael van Notten and Peter T. Leeson, noticed that when Somalia's government ceased to exist after various warlords had exhausted themselves fighting over control of the country in the late 1990s, freedom was working. No power in the country had a monopoly on force, so traditional tribal methods of dispute resolution were being used instead. There was no authority to collect tariffs at the ports of Kismayo or Mogadishu, so the economy was booming. The cell phone industry, which was a huge marker of progress, was also growing rapidly in Somalia, greater than anywhere else in that part of Africa.

As Mary Harper wrote in her book *Getting Somalia Wrong?: Faith, War and Hope in a Shattered State,*

> Although living standards in Somalia were low by Western standards, they compared fairly favourably with those in other countries in Africa. … Telecommunications have improved dramatically since the fall of central authority, with Somalia moving from twenty-ninth to eighth position in the list of African countries.

> One positive side of "statelessness" is that Somalia has benefited from the absence of restrictive and over-bureaucratic business laws and other regulations that are so prevalent in other parts of Africa, stifling the spirit of entrepreneurship and inhibiting growth. … Many commentators have noted that the Somali civil war ironically resembled, in its outcomes, a radical structural adjustment program: it entirely freed the economy from state regulation — liberalizing foreign trade, freeing exchange rates, eliminating subsidies, destroying the public sector, and privatizing parastatals.

No, it was not perfect. It was Somalia. They had been ruled by the brutal American-backed Communist dictator Siad Barre until 1991. The country was essentially coming up from nothing. And in the scheme of things, they were doing okay without any single power leading it all.

But the U.S.A. canceled all that back in 2001.

Much of the violence and chaos there since that time has been the result of intervention by the U.S. military and CIA. American intervention, not freedom, has brought this small, poor country out of anarchy and back into chaos and destruction.

Even if there had been a strong central government in Mogadishu, they obviously could not have held off the U.S. and its allies in the Ethiopian army, which invaded in 2006. In fact, it was the eventual consolidation of a central government in reaction to the CIA's violence which had provoked the invasion and Somalia's destruction.

A Vicious Cycle

Just after the September 11th attacks, the CIA and Joint Special Operations Command (JSOC) — that is top tier special operations forces — went to Somalia and started hiring the very warlords who had been America's antagonists during the infamous "Black Hawk Down" disaster of 1993. In that case, local fighters assisted by Osama bin Laden's men took revenge against the Americans for horrifying war crimes committed against Somali civilians, including children, by United Nations "peacekeepers" from Canada, Belgium and Italy. But with the advent of the War on Terrorism, Hussein Mohamed Aideed, the son of then-enemy Mohamed Farrah Aidid, and other local thugs, were hired by the CIA to hunt down and kill Islamist terrorists. What happened instead was the warlords took the money and guns and did whatever they wanted, fighting against their own enemies and for their own power at the expense of the Somali people. That is why they are called warlords. They may have turned up with the scalp of a jihadist here or there, or claimed so to the Americans every once in a while, but they were mostly using the money and weapons to fight amongst each other and oppress the locals. The situation grew progressively worse in a cycle where local militias would fight against these warlords and drive them back. The warlords would then come back to the CIA, claiming the resistance to their criminality only proved how many enemies there were out there. They would then receive more money and weapons for the effort. This pattern continued until finally, in 2005, 13 separate groups joined together into the Islamic Courts Union (ICU). They succeeded in driving the warlords across the border into Ethiopia later that year.

It should be noted here that virtually all of this story takes place in southern Somalia. The northern regions of Somaliland and Puntland have their own problems, including piracy, but nothing like this.

In the summer of 2006, the CIA renamed their favored warlords the Alliance for the Restoration of Peace and Counterterrorism (ARPCT). This provoked a massive popular reaction in favor of the insurgents. All across southern Somalia, tribal leaders, businessmen and the traditional courts united into the new ICU, renamed the Supreme Council of Islamic Courts (SCIC).

It is possible the SCIC had some aspirations toward Talibanism. They were accused of closing a local movie theater in Mogadishu and banning female employment outside the home, but they had no power to enforce a real authoritarian state. Also, it turned out that the movie house rule only applied in the morning because kids had been skipping school and had nothing to do with Islamism, and the rumors about women being banned from working were false. Somalia is a Muslim country, but their traditions are nothing like the Hanafi Muslim Pashtun culture in Afghanistan or the Wahhabist absolutism of America's Saudi allies. There were no real al Qaeda members around, but the SCIC had the word "Islamic" in their name. That was enough for George W. Bush.

Ethiopia Invades

The U.S. encouraged the Ethiopians to invade and smash the SCIC at the end of December 2006. The CIA and special operations forces backed up the invading army with C-130 gunships, strafing and bombing innocent people, a war crime. Americans also labeled anyone who was running for any border to escape the violence as a terrorist, some of whom were subject to "extraordinary rendition" to Ethiopia, including one American citizen.

The *Washington Post* claimed that this was all justified not because the Islamic Courts Union has the word "Islamic" in it. That would be overkill. No, the war was launched because the FBI said there were three al Qaeda "suspects," who were "wanted for questioning" in the case of al Qaeda's 1998 African Embassy attacks, Fazul Abdullah Mohammed, Saleh Ali Saleh Nabhan and Abu Talha al-Sudani. Back in the 1990s, terrorism was still considered a job for the Justice Department and the FBI. Federal agents were even being deployed overseas to try to arrest and prosecute al Qaeda plotters. After September 11th, Dick Cheney decided the days of filing criminal charges and empaneling grand juries were over. But these three guys, still wanted by the criminal justice system, were cited by the government as their excuse to launch a devastating war of regime change in Mogadishu with Ethiopian proxy forces.

The war against the Islamic Courts was over very quickly. But a new enemy is the target in Somalia now. When the 13 groups came together to compose the ICU-SCIC government, the least-influential of all the groups had been the youth, "al-Shabaab." The elders and local authority figures were in charge. But when the Ethiopian army invaded, backed by the United States, and destroyed the fledgling state, who picked up rifles to fight? The youth.

Al-Shabaab are not really international terrorists, but they are sworn bin Ladenites, in word if not in actual form. Though they have not targeted the United States, they have grown from nothing into something that is certainly dangerous to the people of Somalia and the region. They are the effect of, and now the ongoing reason for U.S. intervention in the country.

Somalia expert Bronwyn Bruton wrote of the American role in the war:

> From the beginning, the United States was viewed as a not-so-hidden partner of Ethiopia. Besides its public support for the Ethiopian invasion, the United States launched a series of missile attacks on fleeing SCIC leaders in January 2007. The missiles failed to hit their targets, but caused scores of civilian casualties, and inextricably linked the United States to Ethiopia's occupation and subsequent human rights abuses by the TFG [Transitional Federal Government], Ethiopian, and African Union forces. These abuses included rape, kidnapping, mortar fire on civilian hospitals and media houses, and indiscriminate shelling of civilian crowds in response to insurgent attacks.

It has been a bitter war. Tens of thousands have been killed in the violence. At various times al-Shabaab has even ruled the major cities of Mogadishu and Kismayo.

In 2008, with the clock running out on the Bush administration, Secretary of State Condoleezza Rice announced that Sharif Sheikh Ahmed, former leader of the Islamic Courts Union, could go ahead and be the president after all. But he would have to accept the role of president of the "Transitional Federal Government" that the U.S. and UN had created for Somalia instead of the old ICU-SCIC. "It would be preferable to co-opt a weak Sharif Sheikh Ahmed, to prevent hardliners from rallying around him," Assistant Secretary of State Jendayi Frazer explained. America had launched and fought a two-year war up to that point just to say that the guy they overthrew can actually go ahead and be in charge anyway. Sharif took the deal. The U.S. kept him as the president through 2012. He is now known, at least in the West, as "The Father of Modern Somalia." The whole war had been for nothing. Not that it is over yet. Al-Shabaab quickly denounced Sharif as a traitor for bowing down to America and their Ethiopian proxy and vowed to fight on.

Starving

Sadly, the worst part of the war has been the weather. Drought came in 2010–2012 and again in 2015–2017. Crops failed across the whole Horn of Africa, but Somalia was hit the hardest because they were at war. The farmers had not had a chance to sow their crops or to harvest them. They had no transportation, so whatever crops could be grown could not reach the market, which was closed anyway because no one had any money. The entire system of food distribution and services in Somalia completely broke down. People were lying down and dying in refugee camps on the sides of the highways. A quarter of a million of them had starved to death by the beginning of 2013. The Famine Early Warning Systems Network (FEWSNET), a U.S. and UK-backed non-governmental organization (NGO) that keeps track of global famines, said that more than half of the 250,000 who had died were children under five years old. The elderly were also among those hit hardest by the mass starvation. A million people had been driven from their homes.

America helped to reduce Somalia to the most desperate state. Then in 2011, President Obama sent President Bill Clinton's old friend and national security adviser, Anthony Lake, to take charge of distributing international food relief. These efforts fell far short. The food relief did not get to the starving people out in the countryside. The warlords seized it all to feed their soldiers and sell the rest. Also in 2011, the Kenyan invasion disrupted the distribution of food aid. This has been one of the worst humanitarian crises of this century, inflicted by the most powerful nation in history against one of the weakest — people who have done nothing to us. In 2017, FEWSNET reported that mortality and under-five mortality rates remained at emergency levels. In 2020, the Cost of War Project estimated that 46 percent of Somalia's population have been displaced since the U.S. began its latest intervention at the dawn of the War on Terrorism.

'No Choice'

Al-Shabaab seized the southern port city Kismayo in 2008 and began clear-cutting for their industry in black market charcoal which contributed to the famine as well. In 2012, Kenyan troops took Kismayo from al-Shabaab and drove them out. However, separating them from their revenue had the perverse effect of forcing them to turn to funders in Saudi Arabia and elsewhere for support. They finally declared their allegiance to al Qaeda, six years into the war, to secure Saudi donors. There is no real reason to consider al-Shabaab to be actual bin Ladenite international terrorists. Though they have hit targets across borders in Kenya and Ethiopia, these represent military and reprisal attacks against their direct opponents in the war.

Two separate "black sites" — secret, illegal prisons — have been revealed by American journalists, one in the capital of Mogadishu and one in the northern province of Somaliland. In both cases prisoners were reported to have been tortured. Both are run with the help and cooperation of U.S. intelligence agents and officers.

The Ethiopian army was driven out of Somalia in 2009, but have since returned along with Burundi, Ugandan and Kenyan forces acting under the auspices of the African Union, with America footing the bill. Al-Shabaab's terrorist attacks against civilian targets have expanded to Kenya and Ethiopia in response.

All through the Obama years, he used CIA and Air Force drones, special operations forces and even fired cruise missiles from submarines, killing women and children, in the effort to fight al-Shabaab. Hundreds of innocent people were killed. Dozens of Somali-Americans have reportedly traveled back to their home country to fight with al-Shabaab. Fortunately, none have yet decided to wage their part of the war here in America. In late 2020, the Justice Department charged and accused a Kenyan member of al-Shabaab of, they claimed, training to fly an airliner for the purpose of attempting a September 11th-type suicide attack on the United States.

President Trump escalated the war, expanding the number of airstrikes, special operations forces — both those fighting and training the Somali national army — and sent regular infantry there as well. He also signed orders designating Somalia as an active war zone, devolving strike authority lower down the military chain of command and removing some restrictions on who can be targeted.

But, at least according to the *Washington Post*, this was all despite the fact that Trump did not want the U.S. there at all. He complained about the Army's useless mission in far-flung Somalia. "Can't we just pull out?" the president repeatedly asked his staff in 2017. "You have no choice," replied then-Secretary of Defense Mattis. So, Trump escalated the war, killing many but accomplishing nothing. In his term, Trump's administration launched more drone attacks on Somalis than Bush and Obama's combined. Terrorist attacks and territory held by al-Shabaab only increased.

Jason Hartwig, a former military assistance coordinator for the U.S. mission to Somalia, told the author there is no way the U.S.-created government in Mogadishu can defeat al-Shabaab without a massive, cost-prohibitive effort. The reality is that the situation, like Afghanistan, is worse than a stalemate. The initiative is with the indigenous insurgents. The mission to train up a new army has failed. Without the African Union Mission in Somalia (AMISOM), made up of Ethiopian, Ugandan, Kenyan and Burundian troops there to support the regime, it would fall to al-Shabaab, "very quickly." That is because the government the U.S. has installed has little popular support. Mary Harper writes that the government "is known by the derogatory Somali nickname *daba dhilif*, which translates roughly as a 'government set up for a foreign purpose' or a 'satellite government.'" Bronwyn Bruton explains that the U.S.-installed regime uses false accusations of association with the terrorists as an excuse to do whatever they want. "The Somali government often uses the al-Shabaab charge to wipe out people either to get the land they want or out of clan rivalry." Ugandan and Burundian troops have been credibly accused of raping Somali women and young girls. The current president was working at the Department of Transportation in Buffalo, New York, before the CIA dropped him in place to be the face of the national government. The people there are not going to submit to this any more than we would.

Ahmed Abdi Godane, leader of the al-Shabaab faction with the most extensive ambitions, was killed by a drone strike back in 2014. The war in Somalia is really a civil war and should be treated as one. America and its allies should simply withdraw and let the negotiations begin.

Without foreign intervention creating the pressures that hold the al-Shabaab alliance together, it is more likely that clan-based conflict resolution would return as the dominant tradition. As Bruton wrote,

> Previous attempts by jihadist groups to govern Somalia have foundered against the Somalis' hostility to restrictive, non-Somali religious edicts and the inability of foreigners to operate within the clan system. During the 1990s, an al Qaeda-linked group called al-Ittihad controlled a significant portion of southern Somalia, but quickly faced resistance and became defunct — without any intervention by the United States.

Even if al-Shabaab ends up taking over the whole southern part of the country, they would have every incentive to try to get along with America. The ICU had tried to deal with the U.S. back in 2005, and many members of the current government are former ICU and SCIC members. Victory against their forces is not in the cards. So what are we still fighting for?

It does not matter one bit to the American people, or even "U.S. interests," broadly defined, who rules the Horn of Africa. It is in no one's interest to close the gates of the Red Sea, nor could any force on this planet resist the U.S. Navy if it came to a contest of arms.

Before the 2020 election, Trump's staff leaked to Bloomberg News that he wanted to withdraw from Somalia. He could have simply commanded it to be so. Instead, after the election, in December 2020, Trump's Defense Department announced they were pulling "the majority" of troops out of Somalia. They quickly clarified, "While a change in force posture, this action is not a change in U.S. policy." The troops are being moved to Djibouti and Kenya instead. Anti-al-Shabaab missions are to continue indefinitely.

Chapter Five:
Escalating Afghanistan

"When I am President, we will wage
the war that has to be won."
— Barack Obama

"Now, thanks to the extraordinary sacrifices
of our men and women in uniform, our
combat mission in Afghanistan is ending,
and the longest war in American history is
coming to a responsible conclusion."
— Barack Obama

"From now on, victory will have a
clear definition: attacking our enemies,
obliterating ISIS, crushing al Qaeda,
preventing the Taliban from taking
over Afghanistan, and stopping mass
terror attacks against America before
they emerge."
— Donald Trump

The COINdinistas

When Barack Obama came to power in 2009, the common narrative was that George W. Bush had botched the Afghan war by diverting our military assets to Iraq instead. Accordingly, the narrative was that it was now time to do the right thing by doubling down in a new "surge" in Afghanistan to finally get it right. Obama had campaigned on sending a few brigades. But as soon as he was sworn in, a massive public relations campaign was launched by the generals, think-tankers, congressional Republicans and all the usual suspects in the media demanding a massive escalation and the adoption of the Pentagon's newly updated counterinsurgency strategy (COIN).

These self-described "COINdinistas" included Center for a New American Security (CNAS) cofounder Michèle Flournoy, who was named deputy secretary of defense for policy and put in charge of implementing the "surge" she had pushed so hard to get approved; as well as former Army Ranger Andrew Exum; Robert Kagan's brother Frederick and the latter's wife Kimberly; retired Army general Jack Keane of Fox News and the Kagans' Institute for the Study of War; Australian COIN theorist and Petraeus adviser David Kilcullen; John Nagl, the "Johnny Appleseed of COIN" and former military adviser to Paul Wolfowitz; Stephen Biddle of the Council on Foreign Relations, who had previously championed the "Sunni turn" in Iraq; "CNAS journalists," Thomas Ricks of *Foreign Policy* and the "totally co-opted by the military" Robert Kaplan of *The Atlantic;* with Army generals David Petraeus and Stanley McChrystal leading the choir.

They demanded a tripling of deployed troop strength and for the application in Afghanistan of their counterinsurgency theories. The new Counterinsurgency Field Manual — written by Gen. Mattis along with Petraeus and his staff during the worst part of the second Iraq war — was said to contain the magic words that would help America achieve victory, or at least "success" as they called it, in Afghanistan.

The CNAS group may not have known the first thing about winning a war of any kind, but what a public relations coup. The cult of the military expert was in full swing. Never mind those dim-witted, Bush-era incompetents, the real war-scientists were in charge now, and they knew what to do.

A State Department whistleblower named Matthew Hoh publicly resigned and dissented against the "surge" in the late summer of 2009, giving interviews to the *Washington Post* and PBS *Newshour*, and publishing his resignation letter. A decorated former Marine captain who had fought in Iraq War II and was then a member of a Provincial Reconstruction

Team in Afghanistan, Hoh knew the war could not be won and that the lives lost under a new escalation would simply be wasted.

As Hoh told the *Post*, "I want people in Iowa, people in Arkansas, people in Arizona, to call their congressman and say, 'Listen, I don't think this is right.'" Hoh's resignation letter concluded:

> The dead return only in bodily form to be received by families who must be reassured their dead have sacrificed for a purpose worthy of futures lost, love vanished and promised dreams unkept. I have lost confidence such assurances can anymore be made.

Then-Vice President Joe Biden and "war czar" General Douglas Lute favored a partial escalation, with an emphasis on "counter-terrorism," even though al Qaeda was long gone, rather than a full counterinsurgency campaign against the Taliban. With Hoh's honesty, and the dissent of his boss, Ambassador Karl Eikenberry, who had previously been a former Army general in charge of the war, this should have been all the cover President Obama needed to refuse Petraeus's "surge."

Winning Hearts and Minds

Instead, Obama rolled over under the pressure. He sent an extra 65,000 troops, bringing the total up to 100,000, plus another 40,000 from NATO countries and Australia, to a war that he already knew was wrong and could not be won.

The "surge" did not accomplish any of the goals proposed at its start. U.S. forces never took the Helmand province in any tangible way, much less Kandahar. They occupied some firebases spread out here and there, and the guerrillas withdrew temporarily. But the U.S. never ruled the place. Nor did they provide a new 21st century, technocratic "government in a box," as Gen. McChrystal called it, to take over and provide security services to the local population, pacifying them and winning their loyalty as promised.

War commander McChrystal himself described the reality of Afghan "insurgent math" to reporter Michael Hastings: "If you killed two out of ten insurgents, you don't end up with eight insurgents. You might end up multiplying the number of fighters aligned against you. More likely, you're going to have something like twenty." As McChrystal's intelligence chief, then-Colonel Michael Flynn complained, ongoing airstrikes without good intelligence were strictly counterproductive. Their solution of escalating ground troop numbers did not help at all, but the effort was at least based on recognizing the difficulty of targeting the "right" people while avoiding angering anyone else with the "collateral damage" that comes from hitting the wrong ones.

As soon as the army and marines withdrew two years later, everything went right back to normal again. Thousands had been killed in bitter fighting. After failing in Helmand, they did not even try their new strategy in Kandahar, which was supposed to have been the showcase proof-of-concept for COIN.

British naval intelligence officer Frank Ledwidge talked about his experience while stationed in the Helmand province in southern Afghanistan during the "surge." "Ninety-two percent of Helmanis have never heard of 9/11. And when they are told that some Arabs crashed a plane in the village of New York in a valley far away, they ask, 'So what has that got to do with us?'"

In Lashkar Gah, the capital of Helmand Province, in Kandahar City, and in the other provincial capitals, government-friendly forces still reign. The Taliban has not taken the provincial capitals because they do not want to lose a big set-piece battle against American airpower, but they have ruled virtually all of the countryside in the predominantly Pashtun eastern and southern provinces for more than a decade. As researcher Ashley Jackson has shown, the Taliban's shadow government, the "Islamic Emirate of Afghanistan," is, in fact, the only government in more than half the country.

The typical TV news narrative has been that the only problem with the Obama surge was that it was too small and too short. One might have thought the term "surge" itself implied a short-term escalation, but apparently not. As Army COIN critic, Colonel Gian Gentile and journalist Robert Kaplan have written, according to the counterinsurgency experts' math, to win the war America would need to put between 300,000–500,000 men on the ground in Afghanistan for about 25 more years to keep killing Afghans until their culture is remade into a good one, that is, one cooperative with American goals. There is no reason to believe this would accomplish anything either, but it raises the question of why the generals would insist on a strategy they did not have enough men to implement by their own reckoning.

Another alleged major flaw in Obama's surge strategy was his administration's announcement that the escalation was on a timeline: You never tell your enemy that you are ever going to leave because then they will just wait you out. This makes sense on the face of it, but as the saying goes, "the Americans have watches, the Taliban have time." They know that ultimately the U.S. is on the other side of the planet. The Americans cannot wait them out, but they can wait the Americans out. There is nothing that can be done about it.

The insurgents will not give in. As one Pashtun Pakistani general told journalist Patrick Cockburn, "Hating foreigners is at the core of Pashtun culture." But Afghanistan is no aggressive empire. They are always the ones defending themselves. The country is in the middle of Eurasia's central transit point near the old Silk Road and the Indian Subcontinent. It has been invaded and occupied repeatedly over the millennia. There is no foreign al Qaeda terrorist enemy to fight in Afghanistan. The Taliban insurgency is made up of local Pashtuns fighting for their own territory. For years, the Americans have talked about the Taliban as though they were the foreign invaders of the country that our forces were helping the locals protect themselves from. That is, of course, exactly backward. They are strongest in Helmand, Kandahar and Nangarhar provinces because that is where they live. As long as the U.S. fights the Afghans to protect them from themselves, our troops will always have an enemy.

Perhaps there are some cultures in the world that would submit to American rule, but the Pashtuns will clearly not give in to foreign invaders, and certainly not to a bunch of people who have a completely different skin color, different culture, different language, different religion, and are from as far on the other side of the planet as you could possibly get from Afghanistan.

America's strategy for training up the Afghan National Army to be able to fight the Taliban was always destined for failure. The soldiers are desperately poor people fighting for pay only, with no real intention to dominate other parts of the country. Worse, the Taliban figured out that it is easy enough to infiltrate their loyalists into the ANA and local and national police forces to wait for the right moment to attack and kill their comrades and trainers. In one case, three marines were killed by the child sex slave of a local police chief they were installing in power in Helmand Province. A lawsuit by the whistleblower, Marine Major Jason Brezler, showed that Navy and Marine officials knew of the local tyrant's abuses, and ignored them — before his victim turned on and killed the three marines.

The Pentagon calls these "insider attacks" or "green on blue" attacks. What they are and have been is a deal killer. American soldiers train troops while their "guardian angel" buddies oversee the whole area through their sniper scopes in case one of their charges turns his rifle on his trainer. This has meant that the U.S. has had to take a far more hands-off role in the ANA's training and that their ability to take on the Taliban has been further diminished as a result.

The U.S. has also paid the Taliban quite literally billions of dollars in protection money to allow their convoys of fuel and supplies get through to troops at their remote bases. The Taliban use that money to buy weapons from corrupt interests in the Afghan National Army. They then turn around and use those weapons against the ANA and the Americans who supplied them. There is an entire book explaining this process called *Funding the Enemy* by Douglas Wissing.

Americans may not want to hear it, but it is a fact that U.S. forces, special and otherwise, along with special operations forces from allied countries such as the British Special Air Services (SAS) and the Australian Special Forces, have committed atrocities against innocent Afghan civilians, torturing and murdering prisoners, executing farmers in their fields and children sleeping in their beds. This is not to mention the tens of thousands of innocent victims of U.S. airstrikes or the CIA's lawless "counter-terrorism pursuit teams" sectarian death squads that rampage across the countryside slaughtering people.

American plane and drone forces have adopted the voodoo pseudo-science of "link analysis." This is just conspiracy theory software that manufactures "links" between people and can supposedly interpret to some degree of confidence the nature of these connections, usually based on cell phone SIM card data alone. Gareth Porter won the Martha Gellhorn Award for his journalism documenting the fact that the vast majority of targets in these strikes were innocent civilians. "The Drone Papers," allegedly leaked to journalist Jeremy Scahill by a National Security Agency analyst whistleblower named Daniel Hale and published as the book *The Assassination Complex*, later provided further evidence that Porter was correct. They showed that in Afghanistan, from 2012 to 2013, out of 200 people killed by drone strikes only 35 were the intended targets, or "jackpots," as they called them. The rest of those innocent civilians? They were just EKIAs — Enemies Killed in Action. If no one proves they were innocent after they are killed, then the dead are presumed guilty and their killers innocent.

It is impossible that these people could somehow be made to see American and allied forces as liberators. They are not. Our side would sooner support al Qaeda terrorists again after what they have done to us. [See Chapters 8–12.]

The current "National Unity Government" is a post-constitutional, ad hoc arrangement cooked up by Secretary of State John Kerry after the botched elections of 2014. Ashraf Ghani was made president, while his competitor and would-be assassin, Abdullah Abdullah, insisted on being the co-president. After the elections of 2020, Abdullah lost again — though there has never been anything like a free and fair election in Afghanistan in all these years of American-administered democracy — but he insisted on swearing himself in as president anyway. The two presidents continue to try to reconcile as they are supposed to be in the middle of coming to peaceful terms with the Taliban.

Some fighters, who mostly came in from Pakistan during the Obama years, but are still essentially indigenous militia forces, began claiming to be part of the Islamic State (ISIS) in 2014. [See Chapter 6.] They are now being invoked as a whole new excuse to stay in Afghanistan forever. But "ISIS-K" (for "Khorasan Province") are not international suicide terrorists. They are just local insurgent fighters, in this case using the ISIS brand name for the notoriety.

"Precipitous Withdrawal"

Donald Trump was against the expansion of the Afghan war in the Obama years. He even publicly supported the president he hated in 2012 when Obama was facing down the generals and insisting on drawing down the "surge."

When Trump came to power in 2017, he stalled for months while his national security adviser, General H.R. McMaster, and defense secretary, Gen. James Mattis, pushed hard for another escalation. In August, he finally did give in for the same reason that Obama did: he thought it was good for his political future. Both presidents knew that the war could not possibly "succeed." In the book *Fire and Fury*, Dina Powell, Gen. McMaster's deputy on the national security council, said that withdrawal "left Donald Trump with having lost a war, an insupportable position for the president." In the Bob Woodward book, *Fear*, Defense Secretary James Mattis is portrayed as virtually blackmailing Trump, threatening to publicly blame him for anything bad that were to happen in Afghanistan after he withdrew the last soldiers and marines. Trump submitted. He sent 10,000 more troops and massively escalated the air war, leading to thousands more civilian deaths. Americans, mostly special operations forces, continue to fight there as well.

The best news to come out of U.S. foreign policy under Donald Trump was his deal with the Taliban, negotiated by neoconservative policy adviser Zalmay Khalilzad. He had picked Hamid Karzai to be the first Afghan president after Bush's regime change of 2001. Now, named Special Representative for Afghan Reconciliation, Khalilzad was given the mandate to negotiate America's exit from Afghanistan based mainly along the lines the Taliban demanded. The peace deal signed in February 2020 does not mandate any agreement with the Kabul government, only a Taliban promise to talk to them during and after the U.S. withdrawal. The Taliban's only other obligation is their vow to prevent international terrorist groups such as al Qaeda or ISIS from returning to the country or launching attacks from it. This is something they have promised for years and have an obvious long-term interest in abiding by. The U.S. is scheduled to finish the withdrawal by May 2021. It remains to be seen whether the Biden administration will follow through.

In December 2019, the *Washington Post* published "The Afghanistan Papers," made up of more than 400 interviews of officials from various levels by the office of the Special Inspector General for Afghan Reconstruction (SIGAR). The various generals and bureaucrats in charge of the war were perfectly happy to admit, when they believed their candid statements would remain secret, that they knew all along that the project was a lost cause.

The revelation had no larger effect on the overall status of the war in Washington. The foreign policy establishment is solidly against Trump's withdrawal deal. The Taliban will be sure to increase their territory if we leave, the think tank experts all tell the media, but they never explain how staying does anything beyond delaying the inevitable. H.R. McMaster, whose job it had been to abolish corruption in Afghanistan during his meal ticket David Petraeus's failed "surge," compared Trump to British Prime Minister Neville Chamberlain in his appeasement of German dictator Adolf Hitler at Munich for negotiating an exit from a 19-year-long war that McMaster personally had a significant hand in losing. The American people, on the other hand, agree that McMaster has already had his chance and failed. Polling in 2019 and 2020 show the public and military veterans alike support ending the Afghan war by supermajorities.

After the presidential election of 2020, Donald Trump finally purged the Defense Department of Mark Esper, its Raytheon lobbyist secretary he had appointed, and replaced him with a former Green Beret and head of counter-terrorism, Christopher Miller. More importantly, he named the conservative non-interventionist Colonel Douglas Macgregor to be the secretary's senior adviser. Disappointingly, Trump never could close the deal. His final order was for the Pentagon to draw down to 2,500 men each in Afghanistan and Iraq. This represented a reduction of 2,000 troops in Afghanistan, but only about 500 from Iraq. In neither case did it reveal a genuine change in strategy. Trump would leave the war to Joe Biden and his vice president, Kamala Harris, in much the same way he inherited it from Obama and Biden just a few years before.

President Biden is opposed to the withdrawal deal. He wants to stick to his 2009 plan to leave thousands of "counter-terrorism" troops there indefinitely. He has also suggested moving bases into Pakistan to hit terrorists in Afghanistan. American troops will remain in Central Asia indefinitely if the president and National Security State have their way.

But al Qaeda is long-gone from Afghanistan. In recent years there have been more claims of al Qaeda fighters' presence but with a notable lack of evidence. Pentagon assertions along those lines tend to have no details at all, for example whether the people they are talking about are even foreign to Afghanistan. Many cite UN reports claiming al Qaeda has returned, but they do not provide any evidence for their assertions either. They only cite "member states" and "information." More likely this is propaganda by vested interests meant to undermine the withdrawal deal based on claims that the Taliban are not living up to their end of the bargain.

In 2018, the military news site Task & Purpose reported that Gen. McChrystal was recorded while recalling his advice to Secretary of State Mike Pompeo to find a way to stay in Afghanistan: "Just muddle along."

> [I]f we pull out and people like al Qaeda go back, it's unacceptable for any political administration in the U.S. It would just be disastrous, and it would be a pain for us.
>
> If we put more troops in there and we fight forever, that's not a good outcome either. I'm not sure what the right answer. My best suggestion is to keep a limited number of forces there and just kind of muddle along and see what we can do.
>
> But that means you're gonna lose some people, and then it's fair for Americans to ask, "Why am I doing this? Why am I putting my sons and daughters in harm's way?" And the answer is, there's a certain cost to doing things in the world, being engaged. That's not as satisfying. That's not an applause line kind of answer, but that's what I think, the only thing I could recommend.

That might be good enough for some. But in the last months of Trump's presidency, many veterans of Iraq and Afghanistan wrote articles and made TV appearances trying to somehow convince Donald Trump to finally end the wars before the chance was lost for another 20 years.

The hawks argue that to leave Afghanistan is simply unthinkable until someday when they have finished winning the war. But they lost the war more than a decade ago, and no one who protested against Trump's draw-down had a single coherent thing to say about how staying there is supposed to somehow change the reality of Taliban power in that country. As Chairman of the Joint Chiefs General Mark A. Milley explained in late 2020, "We have been in a condition of strategic stalemate where the government of Afghanistan was never going to militarily defeat the Taliban, and the Taliban, as long as we were supporting the government of Afghanistan, is never going to militarily defeat the regime." He claimed that this amounted to a "modicum of success," when he was actually conceding that the Kabul government, after 20 years, cannot stand without support from the American superpower. They have not succeeded at all. President Ashraf Ghani has himself admitted that, "We will not be able to support our army for six months without U.S. support and U.S. capabilities."

In late 2020, there was a breakthrough when the Kabul government and Taliban announced an agreement for the framework for future talks. It can be considered a hopeful sign, and possibly a rebuke to those who said that the U.S. must stay to protect the Afghan national government to the bitter end. Perhaps a credible threat of withdrawal was what they needed to stop procrastinating and make a deal while they still could.

Then again, things could get very ugly in Afghanistan after the U.S. finally leaves, whether sooner or later. The government has a slim chance of survival without American support. On the other hand, the Taliban is not as likely to try to conquer the capital of Kabul without the U.S., Saudi and Pakistani support they had in 1996. May all sides of the war embrace decentralization and peace.

Colin Jackson, a former Pentagon official who worked on Afghanistan, opposed the idea of withdrawal, telling the *Washington Post*, "We don't have a single example where pulling the plug has gone well — Vietnam, Iraq, not one." If America had won those wars, it could have withdrawn with friends in power. But they ended in failure. Pulling the troops out was just conceding to the fact of the failure. It was not the failure itself. Perhaps defending this nation in war is a more reasonable goal than overthrowing and attempting to remake someone else's entirely alien society.

In fact, America gets along with Communist Vietnam just fine now, and as will be shown in subsequent chapters, it was American intervention in Iraq and Syria by George W. Bush and Barack Obama which caused the disastrous rise of the Islamic State, not a lack of it.

As the Cato Institute scholar Doug Bandow put it in 2020, "The U.S. has been involved longer in Afghanistan than in the Civil War, Mexican-American War, Spanish-American War, World War I, World War II, and Korean War combined. For what?"

Americans should do everything they can to make the truth the common narrative in our country in a way that the media and politicians cannot ignore: It is time to end the war in Afghanistan.*

---

* For a more thorough treatment of this subject, see the author's 2017 book, *Fool's Errand: Time to End the War in Afghanistan*. Details at FoolsErrand.us.

Chapter Six:
Pakistan

"Turns out I'm really
good at killing people."
— Barack Obama

"I think we're looking
at kind of a 30-year war."
— Leon Panetta

Swat Team

Along with Barack Obama's escalation of the war in Afghanistan from 2009–2012, he also massively increased the already-growing CIA drone war in Pakistan that resulted in terrible consequences for the Pakistanis, Afghans and the broader fight against al Qaeda and related groups. This air war focused not on the Afghan Taliban leaders taking shelter across the border, but on the last members of the original al Qaeda group hiding out there, many of whom were being sheltered by the Pakistani Taliban, the Tehrik-i-Taliban. As al Qaeda targets dwindled, they began to target lower-level Afghan Taliban fighters hiding in the border region, also with devastating consequences for civilians.

The reason the U.S. was also targeting the Pakistani Taliban in the tribal areas was that they had to make a side deal with the Pakistani government that in exchange for their letting U.S. forces drone bomb al Qaeda targets, the Americans would also help destroy Tehrik-i-Taliban targets for them. In 2009 and 2010, the Pakistani army invaded the Swat Valley in Pakistan's Northwestern "Federally Administered Tribal Territories" to remove Tehrik-i-Taliban forces from power there, causing significant casualties and displacing thousands of people.

Terrorizing Civilians

On the third day of his presidency, Barack Obama ordered two CIA drone strikes in Pakistan that killed 20 civilians. In effect, his administration was setting a new baseline. Just as in Afghanistan, they took care of the public relations problem caused by so-called "collateral damage" by simply classifying all dead civilians as terrorists. As the *New York Times* explained,

> Mr. Obama embraced a disputed method for counting civilian casualties that did little to box him in. It in effect counts all military-age males in a strike zone as combatants, according to several administration officials, unless there is explicit intelligence posthumously proving them innocent. ...

> "It bothers me when they say there were seven guys, so they must all be militants," the [senior intelligence] official said. "They count the corpses and they're not really sure who they are."

Since the CIA was never tasked with proving its own officers guilty of killing non-combatants, that posthumous evidence was never collected. They must be guilty, or else why would we be killing them?

In 2012, Stanford Law School put out a report called "Living Under Drones" that described life for the Pakistanis of Waziristan and the Swat Valley. Pakistan's tribal territories may feel too far away to relate to or compel much interest. But this study makes it easy to see the drone war from the point of view of the people on the ground. It describes the sheer terror of life below a sky of prowling robot assassins. Children were growing up afraid of the sun and blue sky because that meant the drones would be out killing people. Only cloud cover or rain could help them feel a little bit safe. People were being panicked out of their minds by the CIA's buzzing Predator and Reaper drones loitering in their skies day after day for months and years on end, killing innocent men, women, children and elderly, striking without warning, and without any apparent rhyme or reason to the victims or survivors. These civilians, killed by the thousands, are all just so-called "collateral damage" to the Americans killing them, or worse, "bugsplat."

What sort of warriors sit in bunkers in New York and Nevada, hiding behind the entire diameter of the Earth from their civilian targets below, who they hunt and target with killer droids? Even a B-1 bomber pilot could conceivably run out of fuel or have engine trouble — maybe a bird strike? But there seems to be a unique callousness to fighting a war while putting yourselves at literally no risk whatsoever. Gen. McChrystal himself warned that "The resentment created by American use of unmanned strikes ... is much greater than the average American appreciates. They are hated on a visceral level, even by people who've never seen one or seen the effects of one." He said it worsens a "perception of American arrogance that says, 'Well we can fly where we want, we can shoot where we want, because we can.'"

British human rights lawyer Clive Stafford Smith has highlighted the problems of paid informants getting innocent people killed in the CIA's Pakistani drone war. Locals were given considerable incentives to implicate someone, anyone, for supposed "ties" to al Qaeda fighters with no accountability for getting it wrong. Even more innocents were hurt and killed when the Taliban falsely accused and attacked people for selling them out. Former U.S. Navy Commander Leah Bolger reported about life in Waziristan before and after the Reapers came. She said there were drastic negative changes to the locals' previously tight-knit communal society. Living under the drones, people became afraid to travel in groups of more than two or three, go to school or hold large group events like weddings and funerals. Citizens began to live in permanent suspicion of each other for being informants, like in Romania or East Germany under the Soviet Communists.

White House counter-terrorism adviser turned CIA director John O. Brennan would meet with President Obama once a week for their "Terror

Tuesday" ritual of deciding who to assassinate with their armed drones. This was the Democrats' way of dealing with the question of the imprisonment of al Qaeda suspects: just kill them. That way, President Obama would not have to figure out how and where to hold them, how to try them nor whether or not they were actually guilty of anything. The administration did continue to "rendition" alleged terrorists to their home countries as well as to the Bagram prison in Afghanistan, but it was clear that the increase in the drone war was decided partly to relieve the government of the need to hold more prisoners at Guantánamo Bay or try them in civilian courts in the United States.

In his 2020 memoir, *Promised Land*, Obama wrote that he had no choice but to escalate the drone wars because his first chief of staff, Rahm Emanuel, had "spent enough time in Washington to know that his new, liberal president couldn't afford to look soft on terrorism." After killing so many people, the former president had lost track of what could possibly serve as a justifiable reason for doing so. Picking up a few seats in the mid-terms, or keeping John McCain, whom he had just soundly defeated, quiet in the Senate might not seem like justifiable grounds for thousands of homicides. But to the Democrats, there was never any question about it.

The CIA and Obama adopted a policy of "signature strikes." While this might sound as if it means the president himself had to sign off on strikes with his signature, what it actually meant was that he gave the CIA permission to kill people who followed the "signature" of a terrorist's "pattern of life." Even members of the Obama administration criticized the CIA's methods, "joking" that they would kill innocent people for exercising or carrying a bag of fertilizer, which was, in fact, accurate.

Obama's first Director of National Intelligence, Admiral Dennis Blair, was forced out over his opposition to Obama and Brennan's drone war. He later complained to the *Times* that

> it is the politically advantageous thing to do — low cost, no U.S. casualties, gives the appearance of toughness. It plays well domestically, and it is unpopular only in other countries. Any damage it does to the national interest only shows up over the long term.

Of course, they lied. Brennan tried to claim that he "has not found credible evidence of collateral deaths resulting from U.S. counter-terrorism operations outside of Afghanistan or Iraq." Later he was forced to admit that was not true. Chris Woods and his teams from the Bureau of Investigative Journalism, and later Airwars.org, found between 2,515–4,026 total killed in the Pakistan drone war, with at least 424–969 civilians killed, 172–207 of them children. These are conservative estimates. In just one attempt to kill al Qaeda leader Ayman al-Zawahiri, the CIA killed 108 civilians, 76 of them children. Pashtun culture has such conservative restrictions on releasing any information regarding women, it has surely led to an inaccurate count of how many of them were killed in these strikes.

Al Qaedaizing the Locals

As Pakistani reporter Saleem Shahzad, who was later murdered by the Pakistani Inter-Services Intelligence agency (ISI), told the author, one of the effects of these campaigns was that they were giving al Qaeda an opportunity to align with the local Pakistani militant factions. He presciently warned that this helped give these small groups broader dreams of Islamist states and international power that they had never really entertained before. The war was "al Qaedaizing" local Pakistani fighters, as Shazad put it, making them more dangerous.

According to journalist Steve Coll, in 2014 some Pakistani navy officers, linked to members of al Qaeda, almost succeeded in a mutiny, temporarily seizing a navy ship that, according to Indian intelligence, had nuclear weapons aboard.

The mutineers were thwarted by a commando team on the ship, but if they had succeeded in seizing the vessel and had found the nukes, they could have destroyed Mumbai, India. This is the kind of fire that our government is playing with and carelessly spreading. Rather than extinguish the terrorist threat, the American way of war seems to just provide it more fuel.

These results should be no surprise. In the Pakistani drone war, the CIA quite deliberately used the terrorist "double-tap method" that Eric Rudolph, the abortion clinic bomber and Olympic Park bomber of 1996, often used, hiding a second bomb to kill the medics when they arrive to tend to the survivors of the first. This was also a major part of American anti-Sunni insurgency propaganda during Iraq War II. It was true; al Qaeda in Iraq and other Sunni groups did sometimes use this same double-tap method. They would bomb a group of Shi'ite civilians, then when the rescuers arrived, they would bomb them as well. It is a terrorist tactic. That is what Barack Obama's CIA did to the Pakistanis: double-tap strikes, killing the first responders. As revealed in "The Drone Papers," the reasoning goes that anyone they bomb must be guilty of being armed terrorist militants unless proven otherwise. Therefore, any first responder to the bombing of terrorists must be a terrorist too.

The CIA has also deliberately bombed Pakistani funerals under the same reasoning as their bombing of EMTs. If someone attends the funeral of a person the U.S. accuses of being a bad guy, then they must be a bad guy too. The issue is not only that it is wrong, but also that these tactics tend to leave an impression on people.

Fighting Them Over Here

We have seen backdraft terrorist attacks from these policies already. If *blowback* means long-term consequences of secret or unknown foreign policies that catch the population off guard and leave them open to false interpretations about the nature of the conflict, *backdraft* means the short-term consequences of overt policies blowing up right in our face. This is borrowed from the term for when a firefighter kicks in a door, providing oxygen to a heated and fuel-filled room causing a massive explosion. For example, one consequence of America's Pakistani drone war was the failed Times Square bombing of May 2010. The Pakistani Taliban had never tried to attack the United States, but after the drone war against them began, they recruited a Pakistani-American to attempt this act of revenge against civilians in New York. The perpetrator, Faisal Shahzad, pleaded guilty, calling himself a "Muslim soldier." At his sentencing, the judge challenged him over his willingness to kill innocent women and children. Shahzad responded:

> Well, the drone hits in Afghanistan and Iraq, they don't see children, they don't see anybody. They kill women, children, they kill everybody. It's a war, and in war, they kill people. They're killing all Muslims. … I am part of the answer to the U.S. terrorizing the Muslim nations and the Muslim people. And, on behalf of that, I'm avenging the attack. Living in the United States, Americans only care about their own people, but they don't care about the people elsewhere in the world when they die.

Then there was the Benghazi attack of September 11, 2012, which is covered in detail in Chapter Eight. That attack was also backdraft caused by the drone war in Pakistan. But that was the least of it.

The New Threat

The entire existence of the so-called Islamic State-Khorasan Province (ISIS-K or ISKP), the ISIS group in eastern Afghanistan, is backdraft from the wars waged by the U.S. and Pakistani state in the northwestern tribal territories during the early Obama years. The men who formed ISIS-K sought safe haven on the Afghan side of the border. Perhaps it should be no surprise that the Afghan National Directorate of Security (NDS), and therefore presumably the CIA, for a time recruited these men to launch tit-for-tat revenge strikes against Pakistani targets as revenge for their harboring the Afghan Taliban on their soil. They also tried to use them

146

against the Afghan Taliban in Afghanistan as well. But then these men hoisted the black flag and declared their loyalty to ISIS in Iraq and Syria.

The ISIS-K group is virtually all from one Pakistani tribe, but since they have adopted the ISIS brand name, the Afghan safe haven myth has been reinforced again. As President Trump said in his 2017 speech announcing his Afghan escalation, withdrawal would "create a vacuum that terrorists, including ISIS and al Qaeda, would instantly fill." In reality, ISIS-K are still only local Pashtun tribesmen from the far side of nowhere rather than international Arab terrorists in the Levant. For a time, they were vying for power with the Afghan Taliban and Afghan National Army in the country's east, although the Taliban seemed to have mostly made relatively short work of them. According to the *Washington Post*, operators from the top-tier Joint Special Operations Command (JSOC) joke that they are now the "Taliban Air Force," flying drones and planes as air cover for their effort against ISIS-K. Under the February 2020 withdrawal deal, the Taliban are sworn to keep al Qaeda and ISIS out forever. It is clearly in their own interests to do so.

The good news is that President Obama reduced the CIA drone war in Pakistan in 2015. President Trump did six strikes in 2017 and 2018. But the damage had already been done.

Obama's CIA drone war was relatively effective against the original al Qaeda leadership hiding in Pakistan, but at a high cost, especially for the Pakistani people and the eventual Afghan victims of ISIS. But not only them. Many of the core al Qaeda members who had been living in exile in the Swat Valley with the Pakistani Taliban when the drone campaign began, instead fled home to Yemen, Libya and other places in the Middle East where they could cause more trouble.

Al Qaeda was initially made up of fighters who had come home from the American-backed war against the Soviets in Afghanistan in the 1980s. Now the next generation of bin Ladenites began returning home from Iraq War II and the Pakistani drone war as well, helping to spur the creation of new jihadist groups and conflicts.

Chapter Seven:
The Arab Spring

"Made in the U.S.A."
— Egyptian tear gas canister

Manning and Bouazizi

At the beginning of 2011, U.S. troops had not even been withdrawn from Iraq yet, and would not be for another year. But the significant blowback from Iraq War II was already beginning in the Middle East. One of the major consequences of the war, just as bin Laden had hoped, was that many countries in the region became destabilized. Their U.S.-backed leaders had lost legitimacy by association with the invaders, and due to the dollar's dominance in the international system, they were forced to print money to match America's efforts to inflate away the costs of the war. This meant that the poorest people in the region were seeing their minimal incomes reduced in real terms. This made necessities unaffordable and led to mass dissatisfaction. In the Arab Spring revolts, small bread riots culminated in multiple major political uprisings across the region. The American and Saudi-led counter-revolution then turned the Arab Spring into an unbelievable catastrophe, spreading war across Africa, the Levant and back into Mesopotamia.

It began in 2010, when Army Spc. Chelsea Manning, who was stationed in Iraq, leaked the American war logs and State Department cables, which were published online by WikiLeaks that fall. One of the first consequential reactions was in Tunisia, where the population knew very well that their dictator Zine al-Abidine Ben Ali was corrupt. But when the State Department cables showed American diplomats describing his corruption to each other in the starkest terms, it blew up into a huge scandal. During that political crisis, a young man named Mohamed Bouazizi failed to bribe the right officials to be allowed to operate a vegetable stand on the side of the road in the city of Sidi Bouzid. The local bureaucrats came and harassed him, shut down his stand and confiscated his scales. In an act of desperate protest, Bouazizi burned himself to death on the steps of the local regulatory office. That fire touched off a revolution. Massive demonstrations and riots broke out. Soon Ben Ali was overthrown and forced to flee the country for Saudi Arabia. Just like that, Tunisia's dictatorship was a thing of the past.

In the years since, Tunisia seems to be the most successful transition to come out of the Arab Spring protests and revolts. They have created a democratic state with regular elections and peaceful transfers of power. There have been terrorist attacks and retaliatory raids by U.S. special operation forces, but they do seem to have emerged in a better position than before the changes of 2011.

End of an Era in Egypt

When the Tunisian despot fled, the Egyptian people — nearly all of them — looked up from their TVs and exclaimed in unison, "You can do that?" They then went outside, nationwide from Alexandria to Giza to Cairo and all points in between, demanding an immediate end to the regime of military dictator "President" Hosni Mubarak, an American client and Secretary of State Hillary Clinton's "family friend." The right, left, young, old, town, country, union workers, Coptic Christians and Islamist Muslim Brotherhood were all united in this demand. The regime the U.S. supported with $1.3 billion worth of military aid every year looked vulnerable.

So-called "Day of Rage" protest movements broke out across the Middle East and North Africa, including in Algeria, Libya, Yemen, Saudi Arabia, Oman, Bahrain, Kuwait, Iraq, Jordan and Syria.

In Egypt, after weeks of protest, the junior officers made it clear that they would mutiny against their commanders before they would fire on the civilians occupying Cairo's Tahrir Square. At that point, the Americans and the generals finally forced Mubarak to step down.

The Obama administration was doing everything it could to promote Mubarak's head of intelligence and chief torturer, Omar Suleiman, to be the Americans' next Egyptian pharaoh, but the consensus in the street was absolutely against it. They were not going to get their way. Instead, the U.S. sent the non-governmental organizations (NGOs) to try to intervene on behalf of the supposed "liberals," mostly socialist students and labor union members, only to see their agents unceremoniously arrested and deported. Democracy would have a chance in Egypt despite America's best efforts — for a little while.

Back in the George W. Bush years, recognizing that Mubarak was getting old and that his son Gamal was considered an unsatisfactory figurehead by the military, the government started planning for what might come next in Egypt. Vice President Cheney's daughter Liz, now the U.S. representative from Wyoming, was then principal deputy assistant secretary of state for near eastern affairs and coordinator for broader Middle East and North Africa initiatives. There she spent tens of millions of dollars to train up young pro-American, pro-democratic forces in Egypt. The National Endowment for Democracy (NED), International Republican Institute, National Democratic Institute and the influential NGO Freedom House all soon joined in. When the Tahrir Square protest movement began, the "civil society" groups the U.S. had been supporting were some of the very first ones to take to the streets to issue demands. Rather than a fake, CIA-controlled "color-coded revolution" being forced upon Egypt by the U.S., however, this seemed more representative of an interventionist policy blowing up in the American government's face. The primary evidence of this is President Obama's extended support for Mubarak and then Suleiman before finally greenlighting their removal. It seems he realized there was no longer a choice in the matter. The people's insistence would be enough. The Qatari government-owned al Jazeera network gave huge amounts of coverage and support to the revolution. While it is true that the Qataris favored the Muslim Brotherhood, and likely saw the revolution as a chance to expand their influence, there is no denying that their coverage reflected the popular will of the country at the time.

After the revolution, Egypt held two elections without U.S. interference. They were mostly fair ones, according to international monitors. In the parliamentary elections of 2011 and the presidential election of 2012, the Muslim Brotherhood won, barely.

It is important to note that though Islamist, the Brotherhood is not equivalent to al Qaeda, at least not in Egypt. Its leadership was made up of doctors, lawyers, academics and wealthy, state-connected business community leaders. The group had renounced violence many years before, and were composed of the religious but conservative, not radical right. As detailed in Robert Dreyfuss's book *Devil's Game*, the Brotherhood's more violent days in the 1960s, when they worked for the British, Americans and Saudis against the Nasserite nationalists, were long behind them. Even neoconservative hawks Robert Kagan and Daniel Pipes went on the record saying that the United States ought to give them a chance.

The Brotherhood's government lasted about a year and a half. They never wielded any real power in office because the permanent bureaucratic state, from the generals to the garbagemen to the cops and civil servants of every kind, would never obey the politicians' directives. They instead engaged in work slowdowns and mass insubordination which greatly stymied the new regime. This is not to say that the Brotherhood would or could have done much better otherwise, only that they never had the opportunity to fail. As Vijay Prashad wrote in *Arab Spring, Libyan Winter*, "If Mubarak had to go, then Mubarak's regime had to remain in place, and the public outcry had to be slowly silenced. The Egyptian military, well-financed by the U.S., came in to do the work." They had help.

In 2013, Saudi Arabia began financing a pale imitation of the original Tahrir Square protests of 2011. They paid mobs to reoccupy the square to protest against the Muslim Brotherhood's fledgling regime. Within America's Sunni Kingdom-dominated alliance system in the Middle East, there is a rift between the Turkish-Qatari coalition and the Saudis and their partners in the United Arab Emirates. This has much to do with Turkish and Qatari favoritism toward the Brotherhood, which is currently out of favor with the Saudis, at least in Egypt. Reportedly, these differences were somewhat smoothed over after the death of Saudi King Abdullah and his replacement with King Salman in 2015. But they were certainly at odds in Egypt during the Arab Spring revolt.

The Saudi-backed demonstrations achieved nothing like the turnout of the original Tahrir Square protests, but the Egyptian military took advantage of the pretended crisis to claim they had to intervene to prevent a civil war from breaking out. The army overthrew and arrested the Muslim Brotherhood president, Mohamad Morsi, and massacred more than 1,000 pro-Brotherhood protesters in the streets. If this had happened in Russia or Iran, it would have been considered a terrible atrocity, but in this case, it was an American ally killing people the U.S. government wanted them to kill, so it was ignored, just as Mubarak's 30-year tyranny had been before.

The Egyptian liberals threw away a tremendous opportunity. They had won a democratic system in a bloodless revolution against a military dictatorship — a virtual miracle. But instead of capitalizing on and defending the new form of government they had created and mobilizing their constituents to try harder to beat the religious right in the next elections, they sided with the military against their conservative party opponents. In the most short-sighted fashion, they played the pressure from below, demanded intervention, and gave the generals and foreign interventionists all the pretext they needed to cancel the revolution entirely, restoring the military dictatorship. Morsi was replaced by the head of the military, Field Marshall Fatah al Sisi. In 2018, al Sisi's reign was ratified by an utterly fake election which showed a Saddam Hussein-style victory of 97 percent for the tyrant against his opponent, who was a self-described "Sisi supporter." The chance of anything approaching self-government for the people of Egypt had been delayed indefinitely. Then-Secretary of State John Kerry declared that this bloody military coup against the only honestly elected government in the history of the country was the "restoration of democracy."

There is no common description of the Muslim Brotherhood. In Qatar, they sit in the parliament. In Syria, they are indistinguishable from bin Ladenite terrorists. It is a large and widespread movement — one that unsurprisingly owes much to the CIA, British MI-6 and the Saudi royal family for early support against regional socialists and nationalists during the Cold War. The 2013 coup against their elected regime was unnecessary, even presuming the U.S. and Saudi Arabia had the right to meddle at all. The Morsi government had made no significant breaks with Mubarak's foreign policy agreements with the U.S. and Israel, such as the Camp David Accords. He spoke with Iran and slightly loosened up on the joint Israeli-Egyptian siege of the Palestinians in the Gaza Strip, which angered the Saudis and Israelis, but the new government was not threatening independence from the American order in the Middle East. They were certainly attempting to tread very cautiously. But doing nothing was not good enough. They were rewarded with total destruction.

Al Qaeda leader Ayman al-Zawahiri soon put out a recording gloating at the Muslim Brotherhood's failure. He ridiculed them as stupid old fools for participating in Western-style democratic elections and thinking that the Americans would ever let a vote that does not go their way stand. The coup, he asserted, proved that al Qaeda was right again about America. He said the U.S. did not really mean what they said about spreading democracy in the region, and that the only way to achieve independence was to fight.

Now that all the old Muslim Brotherhood leaders have been imprisoned or killed, younger, bolder men have taken their place. There is a new Islamist uprising in Egypt's Sinai Peninsula, and there have been terrorist attacks in Cairo and Alexandria in recent years where there had been none for decades. The military police state is even more oppressive than before. As Trump's secretary of state, Mike Pompeo, admitted on the occasion of approving more military aid to the Sisi regime, "The overall human rights climate in Egypt continues to deteriorate." According to Human Rights Watch, the regime has returned to the use of torture, disappearances (i.e., murder), mass trials for accused terrorists and all the worst aspects of a lawless, authoritarian dictatorship.

Crushing Protest in Saudi Arabia and Bahrain

In predominantly Sunni Saudi Arabia, there is a substantial minority Shi'ite population. They just happen to live in the Eastern Province above all the best oil deposits. While certainly no threat to the rule of the Saudi royal family or the clerical rule of the nation's imams, from time to time they protest against the absolute authority of the monarchy and are crushed by the country's national guard. "Crushed," in this context, means the Saudis hold fake mass trials, behead dissident leaders with swords and then sometimes crucify the headless corpses for all the locals to see what will happen to them if they try to insist on fairness and justice too.

As John R. Bradley wrote in *Foreign Affairs* in October 2011,

> If the Arab Spring had any hope of ushering in greater freedom and democracy, it would have had to challenge from the beginning the influence of Saudi Arabia, the region's Washington-allied superpower and its most antidemocratic, repressive regime. That is a tall order indeed. The tragic irony of the uprisings is that the exact opposite happened.

153

In the tiny Persian Gulf island nation of Bahrain, home of the U.S. Navy's Fifth Fleet, the Arab Spring took off with huge protests in what was called the Pearl Roundabout in the capital city of Manama — their version of Cairo's Tahrir Square. Though Bahrain has a minority Sunni monarchy ruling over a super-majority Shi'ite population, the protesters took great pains to be clear that they were only calling for a constitutional monarchy. They wanted a semblance of a rule of law: some rules the government would have to abide by and rights they would have to respect. There was no talk of overthrowing the king. Nor were they chanting for the triumph of Shi'ite-Iranian power or any such thing. All they were asking for was the slightest semblance of a fair shake.

Instead, the Bahrain government cracked down. At the king's request, the Saudis rolled their trucks and tanks right across the causeway which connects the two countries to help end the protests. Thousands of people were tortured and killed. Security forces used birdshot, leaving the protesters with signature wounds. This made it easier to arrest and torture not only the protesters, but all the doctors who treated them to make an example out of them too.

Not only was dissent in Bahrain crushed, but the lesson was driven home to the Saudi Shi'ites as well: stick your neck out, and you will get it cut off, literally. Their protests were quickly quelled.

At the same time this was happening in Bahrain, America was launching a war in Libya in the name of joining their Arab Spring protests and freeing the oppressed people of that country from the evil dictatorship of Col. Moammar Gaddafi. When Admiral Mike Mullen, then-Chairman of the Joint Chiefs of Staff, was asked about the discrepancy, why do we side with insurgents in one nation and the king in another? Mullen simply replied, "We haven't had a relationship with Libya for a long, long time." Bahrain, however, "has been a critical ally for decades."

America must keep supporting these Arabian monarchies because they host so many military bases and assets, including the Navy base in Bahrain and the massive Al Udeid Air Force base in Qatar, forward headquarters of the U.S. Air Force Central Command. That way we can use these assets to fight the terrorists who are supported by these monarchs and who are motivated to attack the United States due to our governments support for them and military bases in their countries.

Protest movements in Morocco, Algeria, Kuwait and Jordan were also quickly crushed or dispersed.

But the American and Saudi-led counter-revolution against the Arab Spring was just the beginning. Next they would move to hijack it for their own purposes in Libya, Syria and Yemen.

Chapter Eight:
Libya

"We had a war in Libya?"
— Apocryphal

"Senator McCain assured Muatassim
[Gaddafi] that the United States wanted
to provide Libya with the equipment it
needs for security. He stated that he
understood Libya's requests regarding
the rehabilitation of its eight C130s
and pledged to see what he could do to
move things forward in Congress."
— U.S. State Department Cable, 2009

"Gaddafi must go."
— John McCain, 2011

A Deal with The Devil

Col. Moammar Gaddafi, dictator of Libya, was expendable. The U.S. relationship with Gaddafi was only eight years old. He had been brought back into America's good graces in 2003 when President Bush needed a publicity stunt to try to make it seem as though Iraq War II had accomplished something. The administration adopted the narrative that the attack on Iraq had frightened the international outlaw into compliance. In fact, as former senator Gary Hart has written, Gaddafi had been begging to come in from the cold since 1996. All he had done differently this time was buy some old first-generation centrifuge parts from A.Q. Khan, the Pakistani black-market nuclear equipment supplier, to have a bargaining chip to trade away. In reality, Libya had no nuclear weapons program or expertise to create one. It was mostly old junk still in its crates. He had only bought the equipment to give the American president a victory and make a friend out of a former enemy. Luckily, Bush needed a win, so he took the opportunity to make peace.

But the Bush administration made not just friends, but allies out of Gaddafi, helping him and using his help to fight against al Qaeda. The *Wall Street Journal* called it a "tight working relationship." For example, when the CIA and Egyptian secret police were finished torturing Sheikh Ibin al-Libi into inventing fake connections between Iraq and al Qaeda and needed him to be disposed of, they rendered him home to Libya where he promptly "committed suicide" in his prison cell. Intelligence sources told the *Washington Times* that the Libyan government was "pretty helpful" when it came to capturing high-value al Qaeda targets, "because there were so many Libyans in al Qaeda and they had a unique window into that."

Senators John McCain, Lindsey Graham and Joe Lieberman, the three most outspoken hawks in the U.S. Senate at the time, made a big point of making friends with Gaddafi and going over to Libya to try to sell him armored personnel carriers and other equipment. But that would not last.

A PR Stunt

With the 2011 Arab Spring revolutions in Tunisia and especially Egypt, the U.S. had a severe public relations crisis. Even on CNN and other news channels, it was impossible to avoid the reality that the heroic, peaceful civilian protesters in Cairo were overthrowing a military dictator who had been backed by America. The tear gas canisters even had "Made in the U.S.A." printed right on them. The story that the purpose behind America's imperial global hegemony was the selfless export of freedom and democracy to the people of the world was starting to strain the credulity even of American TV news anchors.

Ben Ali, the dictator of Tunisia, had also been backed by America. In fact, the United States supported — provided financial, military and other aid to, or had basing agreements with — the unelected governments of Algeria, Libya, Tunisia, Egypt, Yemen, Oman, the United Arab Emirates, Bahrain, Qatar, Saudi Arabia, Kuwait and Jordan. The only governments that America was not supporting in the Middle East in 2011 were Syria and Iran.

Using the war as a public relations stunt was clearly a significant part of the Obama administration's motivation in launching the attack against Libya. As several State Department officials confirmed to journalist Michael Hastings, when a coalition of Egyptian groups refused to meet with her, Hillary Clinton decided that America's credibility was threatened by the Arab Spring. So she decided, "We didn't get off to such a great start with Egypt — let's reverse that with Libya." Anne-Marie Slaughter, Hillary Clinton's former Director of Policy Planning at the State Department, urged her to support the attack, claiming the Libya war "will change the image of the United States overnight." It will "impress the young people across the Middle East," she promised.

The State Department and its allies were desperate to try to change the story from America being a hypocritical supporter of brutal dictators to being supporters of scrappy, overmatched "rebels" against the renewed hate figure and tyrant Moammar Gaddafi. Sarah Lee Whitson from Human Rights Watch said she thought that "the dynamic for the U.S. government was: Things are changing fast, Tunisia has fallen, Egypt has fallen, and we'd better be on the front of this, supporting a new government and not being seen as supporting the old government."

The Americans were also concerned about Libya's promotion of African alternatives to the International Monetary Fund and International Criminal Court along with resistance to the rise of the Pentagon's new African Command (AFRICOM).

Maximilian Forte, in his book, *Slouching Towards Sirte: NATO's War on Libya and Africa,* wrote that America's reasons for war included the potential for infrastructure contracts for American corporations, "warding off" Chinese and Russian oil companies, bolstering AFRICOM at the expense of the African Union and advancing the narrative that the U.S. is there because it cares, fighting for the little guy against unjust oppressors.

French President Nikolas Sarkozy had accepted millions of euros in campaign funding from Gaddafi and so had a motive to obscure that relationship by making hawkish noises against him. His government had also been embarrassed by their support for Ben Ali's regime in Tunisia, even after it was already falling apart. Secretary Clinton's unofficial adviser

Sidney Blumenthal wrote to her that the Libyans planned to challenge French currency dominance in its former African colonies in part by introducing a new gold-backed dinar to compete with the franc. However, it is not clear how advanced that plan was or how much of a threat the French honestly considered it to be. It remains unclear why the British were so intent on starting the war. According to an aide of Gaddafi's son Saif, the Libyan government had reneged on arms deals and oil deals with both the French and British not long before the war. The Libyan revolutionaries also promised the creation of a new national oil company and control over it to their new Western patrons.

For America's allies in the Gulf Cooperation Council (GCC), their motives had more to do with the Saudis' and Qataris' long-time enmity against Gaddafi over his years of ridicule for their supplication to Western powers and the Qataris' desire to advance the cause of the Muslim Brotherhood. The Qataris, too, were said to be angry over being double-crossed on an oil and gas deal by the unpredictable dictator.

For McCain and his allies in the Senate, their loud noise in favor of war seemed obviously intended to distract from their previous support for and lobbying of Gaddafi's government. They could have tried to use their unique position to make peace but instead decided to lead the march to war.

Public Choice Theory

The truth is that there is no national interest as it might be conceived of by the average American. There are only the interests of the individuals who run the government departments and agencies. For example, in the Obama administration was the liberal "humanitarian hawk" Samantha Power. Power, a former journalist, had written a book called *A Problem from Hell*, about how the international community, led by the United States, needed to adopt the "Responsibility to Protect" doctrine, given the newspeak brand name "R2P." What the doctrine meant was that when third world countries are engaging in massacres against civilians, such as the Rwandan genocide of 1994, the U.S. and its allies must immediately intervene and not sit around and wait for the worst to be carried out. The truth is that American and other Western intervention in Rwanda and surrounding nations had helped to cause their terrible civil war in the first place, as Helen Epstein shows in her book, *Another Fine Mess: America, Uganda and the War on Terror.*

When the violence in Libya broke out, this was the opportunity Power had been waiting for. The insurgents, sure to provoke a response from Col. Gaddafi's regime, could be saved — by her. Then-UN Ambassador

Susan Rice, who had also been in the Clinton administration, agreed with Power and argued the same position. Never mind Iraq War II having happened in the meantime and everyone learning a thing or two about the danger of creating ungoverned space for radical Sunni insurgents to fight on. No, the only lesson of Iraq was that Bush and his men were just not capable of doing it right. Obama's team was much smarter. Their new war would work out great. So, they decided that the War on Terrorism was over, at least for the moment. Stopping Rwanda-style genocides was what they should be doing instead.

During the 2008 Democratic primary campaign, Power had supported Barack Obama against Hillary Clinton and had made a major political error by calling Clinton a "monster." Once elected, Obama named Clinton secretary of state. Power got a job, but it was an obscure position on the National Security Council. As Michael Hastings reported, by 2011 Power thought she had done her penance for insulting Clinton and was tired of being stuck doing "rinky-dink do-gooder stuff," such as "advocating on behalf of Christians in Iraq." With the uprising in Libya, she saw "a chance to reassert herself within the White House," and win some attention from President Obama. Starting a war was Power's path to achieve it. She then went to Susan Rice. Together they convinced Clinton to lead their effort to get Obama on board. And it worked. After the war was launched, Power was promoted to the UN job, while Rice moved up to national security adviser.

Whatever doubts Clinton may have had about starting this war were evidently dismissed after a single 45-minute meeting with the Libyan version of Ahmed Chalabi, a man named Mahmoud Jibril, leader of the newly invented government-in-exile, the National Transitional Council.

Jibril "said all the right things about supporting democracy and inclusivity and building Libyan institutions, providing some hope that we might be able to pull this off. They gave us what we wanted to hear. And you do want to believe," Philip Gordon, one of Clinton's assistant secretaries, told the *New York Times*.

Secretary Clinton then worked tirelessly to get the administration and America's European and Middle Eastern allies on board for the effort. She also led the successful push to convince President Obama to send weapons to the insurgents. Her director of policy planning, Jake Sullivan — later chosen to be President Biden's national security adviser — wrote up a detailed timeline of the secretary's "leadership/ownership/ stewardship of this country's Libya policy from start to finish." Her friend and State Department consultant Anne-Marie Slaughter enthused, "[Your] turning POTUS [President Obama] around on this is a major win for everything we have worked for."

Reportedly, as they debated it in the White House, Secretary of Defense Robert Gates, Chairman of the Joint Chiefs of Staff Admiral Mike Mullen, National Security Advisor Tom Donilon, his deputy Denis McDonough and even then-Vice President Joe Biden all argued that they should not start this war. Robert Gates later claimed to have repeatedly asked, "Can I just finish the two wars we're already in before you go looking for a third one?" He must have miscounted. It was four, going on five, counting Somalia and Pakistan. But this opposition by Gates and the others should have been all the cover Obama needed to back out of the intervention, but Power, Rice and Clinton talked him into launching it anyway.

Perhaps Obama felt he owed Clinton a favor for becoming his secretary of state instead of attacking him from the senate his whole first term. He had surely promised her he would support her run for president in 2016. As was evident then and confirmed later, Clinton and her team believed that she would be able to run on the short and successful Libyan war in that presidential election, as her unofficial advisers Sidney Blumenthal and Jamie Rubin, as well as her right-hand man Jake Sullivan, enthused in emails later released by the State Department. The fact that Clinton had just lost the presidential primary to Obama mainly due to her hawkishness on Iraq had apparently failed to make an impression on her. By the time the 2016 election came around, the Clinton campaign did not dare bring up Libya as any kind of victory. By then, they clearly hoped everyone would just forget all about it.

According to Secretary Gates, President Obama said that his decision to start the war in Libya was "51 to 49" percent, with Secretary Clinton pushing him over the line. This is nothing less than a confession of a war crime on both their parts. The president was admitting that he launched an unnecessary, aggressive war, a crime under American law as well as the international law America has dictated to the rest of the world for the last 75 years. The fact that the vice president, chairman of the joint chiefs of staff, national security adviser and deputy national security adviser agreed with the secretary of defense that the U.S. should not go to war is more proof that it was absolutely unnecessary. For all of Robert Gates's revisionist history, he was in charge of the defense department. He launched and implemented the war while blaming it on his boss. Gates resigned that summer, but certainly not in public protest against his president's policy and far too late to stop it. The war remains his responsibility as well as that of Barack Obama.

Another Fake Pretext for War

Not only did Obama refuse to consult Congress for authorization, but he was not even in the country when he ordered the attack, which the Pentagon called "Operation Odyssey Dawn." Instead, the president gave a speech from Brazil where he was traveling on unrelated business. In the speech, Obama falsely claimed that Gaddafi had vowed to murder every civilian in the eastern Libyan city of Benghazi and that his forces were already on their way to do the job if the U.S. did not stop them in time. He claimed there were 700,000 "men, women and children" under the threat of imminent extermination and asked Americans to imagine the city of Charlotte, North Carolina being completely wiped out.

The administration also claimed that Gaddafi was bombing peaceful protests and spread the ridiculous propaganda that Gaddafi had given all of his soldiers Viagra so that they could rape every woman and girl they found on their rampage to the east. These were all lies. But they were good enough. The bombs came raining down.

A few weeks after it began, Congress held a series of votes where they refused to authorize the war, but they also refused to specifically condemn or halt appropriations for it. The administration argued that since the enemy could not possibly fight back, this "kinetic action" did not "rise to the level of ['hostilities' or] war for constitutional purposes," as Harold Koh, legal adviser to Hillary Clinton's State Department told Congress.

The Democrats were going to make up for inaction in Rwanda by preventing a genocide from happening in Libya. It was a fun and exciting narrative for the hawks to tell each other, but it was not true. Gaddafi had threatened to hunt down and kill armed insurrectionists, not all civilians nearby them. His forces had already retaken several towns without widespread massacres. He had only sent a force of 2,000 men to Benghazi. How was he supposed to accomplish a Rwanda-style genocide with that?

In fact, the Defense Intelligence Agency predicted that Gaddafi would not engage in any mass slaughter, not that he even had the forces available to use in such a project. They were, the Pentagon concluded, fighting armed insurgents, not massacring civilians. "No intelligence" indicated the opposite, officials told the *Washington Times*. Most civilians had already fled Benghazi anyway.

In 2017, the British House of Commons Foreign Affairs Committee report on the Libyan war admitted this *casus belli* was a hoax and acknowledged the British government knew it too. They quote the Americans saying the choice to start the war was an "intelligence-light decision."

Once the UN Security Council authorized a "no-fly zone" to protect Benghazi, the West's mandate immediately expanded to regime change in

Tripoli. Secretary Clinton, emphasizing the importance of persuading Russia and China to support or abstain on the UN resolution, had promised, "There is nothing in there about getting rid of anybody." But that was just obfuscation. Derek Chollet, a member of Obama's National Security Council, explained, "The mission was civilian protection, but we never defined when that would be satisfied. When we had grounded the air force? When we had decimated the army? Our judgment was ultimately that civilians would not be safe as long as Qaddafi was in power."

According to the *New York Times*, Gaddafi's regime had contacted former British prime minister Tony Blair, retired Gen. Wesley Clark and many others seeking to negotiate a settlement. We know because of the *Washington Times*'s excellent reporting on the subject that the CIA and the Defense Department were actually trying to negotiate a way to stop the war, while the State Department was leading the charge for it and was working to prevent any negotiations with the regime. In fact, General Carter Ham, the new commander of AFRICOM, whom one might think would be most eager for such a major mission, wanted to negotiate too. The Pentagon was talking with Gaddafi's son, Saif, who was widely considered to be a reformer with long-term plans for modernizing Libya and integrating it with the American-led global system. He was just the kind of "moderate reformer" the U.S. should have been able to work with if they really wanted to see Libya transformed into a stable democracy. They at least had an opportunity to force the colonel into retirement and allow his son to attempt to resolve the conflict in a more acceptable way. But Hillary Clinton pulled rank and refused to deal with Saif Gaddafi or allow anyone else to.

Just after the war began, retired Navy Rear Admiral Charles Kubic, then a businessman, was approached by the Libyans with an offer of a 72-hour ceasefire, followed by the elder Gaddafi leaving power. Kubic told the *Washington Times*:

> The Libyans would stop all combat operations and withdraw all military forces to the outskirts of the cities and assume a defensive posture. Then to ensure the credibility with the international community, the Libyans would accept recipients [troops] from the African Union to make sure the truce was honored.

> [Gaddafi] came back and said he was willing to step down and permit a transition government, but he had two conditions. First was to ensure there was a military force left over after he left Libya capable to go after al Qaeda. Secondly, he wanted to have the sanctions against him and his family and those loyal to him lifted and free passage. At that point in time, everybody thought that was reasonable.

However, the *Washington Times* reported, Gen. Ham was ordered to stand down two days after the negotiation began. The orders were given at the behest of Secretary Clinton's State Department, according to those familiar with the plan in the Pentagon. "If their goal was to get Gaddafi out of power, then why not give a 72-hour truce a try?" Kubic asked. "It wasn't enough to get him out of power; they wanted him dead."

Democratic Congressman Dennis Kucinich also spoke to Saif Gaddafi in an attempt to learn enough about the situation to inform the rest of the Congress. Saif immediately compared the pretext for war in Libya with Iraq's weapons of mass destruction, denying false reports that their government was launching airstrikes against peaceful protests. He also warned that the regime's current armed enemies were a small group of bin Ladenite terrorists who were already committing atrocities of their own. He blamed the emir of Qatar as being the main force behind the insurrection. Saif may have been an evil dictator's son, and despot-in-waiting himself, but every word of the younger Gaddafi's recorded diatribe was correct.

The African Union also devised a negotiated settlement, which included plans to hold democratic elections as soon as possible. They submitted it to the UN Security Council, where the major powers ignored it.

Forte wrote that Gaddafi sought negotiations toward the formation of a transitional government. "Indeed, at almost every stage of the conflict, Gaddafi reiterated calls for a peaceful transition, which were always rejected out of hand by the foreign-backed opposition."

But the men the U.S. was backing in the war were no "moderate rebels." The people of far-eastern Libya had sent many young men off to fight against the U.S. and the Shi'ites in Iraq War II, and now they had come home. Even though bin Laden had not yet been killed and U.S. troops were still stationed in Iraq helping fight the last remnants of al Qaeda there, Obama's government chose to take the terrorists' side against Gaddafi in Libya.

The NATO coalition, led by American planes, pounded Libya mercilessly, killing thousands of people. When the "rebels" entered the city of Sirte, they committed atrocities such as the mass execution of prisoners and bombed and burned vast sections of the city to the ground. Forte wrote that when the "popular uprising" came to Sirte, "under the umbrella of foreign intervention, [it] actually became what Western opinion leaders imagined would have befallen Benghazi without foreign intervention."

The CIA and British MI-6 were intimately familiar with the Libyan Islamic Fighting Group (LIFG), whose origins lay in the 1980s Afghan war. The British had attempted to use them to assassinate Gaddafi back in the late 1990s. Hundreds of them had fought in Iraq War II in support of al Qaeda and the Sunni-based insurgency. Many were still living in Manchester, England, where one of their young members would perpetrate the horrific pop concert massacre of 2017. [See Chapter 14.]

But in Libya in 2011, al Qaeda was considered okay by the MI-6 and the CIA.

Just Like Old Times

One might have thought that keeping al Qaeda-types down at all costs would have been the Americans' priority since radical bin Ladenite Islamists had murdered more than 3,000 American civilians at home and helped to kill 4,000 or so American troops as the bloodiest, most radical edge of the Sunni-based insurgency in the last war. No. The Americans and their allies were back to supporting jihadist militias against their enemies like the good old days — as though the bad ones had never happened at all.

Before the war had even started, everybody knew that the Libyan veterans of al Qaeda in Iraq were leading the armed opposition. Gaddafi, whose government had issued the first INTERPOL arrest warrant for Osama bin Laden back in 1998, had warned in his speech of February 22 that al Qaeda was leading the fight against him, seeking to create an "emirate of bin Laden and Zawahiri." He told Tony Blair that

> they [bin Ladenites] want to control the Mediterranean and then they will attack Europe. ... The story is simply this: an organization has laid down sleeping cells in North Africa, called the al Qaeda organization in North Africa. The sleeping cells in Libya are similar to dormant cells in America before 9/11.

Liam Fox, at that time the British defense minister, later conceded that their government knew at the time that the danger of jihadist terrorists embedded among the rebel forces was genuine. The Obama administration was not ignorant of the problem either. Debates in the White House over intervention included the fact of bin Ladenite influence among the rebels. "Are Libyan rebels an al-Qaeda stalking horse?" BBC News asked and answered affirmatively on March 31, 2011.

In the spring of 2011, we still had thousands of soldiers in Iraq fighting the remnants of Zarqawi's group. They would not be withdrawn until the end of the year. But Iraq War II was somehow still not quite over and already ancient history. Efforts against al Qaeda had moved to Pakistan and Yemen. The Obama administration would measure their highest virtue in their refusal to let Bush's Iraq disaster dissuade them from their belief in the efficacy of American military violence. Their capable hands could remake the world in their own democratic image, radical bin Ladenite terrorists fighting on their same side notwithstanding.

Professor Alan Kuperman has shown that the war began not with peaceful liberal protesters, but with al Qaeda fighters, veterans of Iraq War II, in the town of Derna. Their first action was a series of attacks on police stations, seizing arms they then used to attack and seize a military base and its weapons. That is who the regime was targeting, Abu Musab al-Zarqawi's men in the middle of a violent insurrection.

Michael Scheuer, the former CIA analyst, was a guest on CNN in April 2011. He told the anchors that if the men the U.S. government was now supporting were fighting in any other place we would call them "mujahideen" — the enemy. They were the Libyans who had just come home from fighting America in Afghanistan and Iraq War II. He also explained that the CIA can only vet the fighters who would talk to them and that even though the real terrorists would not talk to them, that does not mean they are not the ones with the most to gain from the war America was initiating. The anchors could only scoff. What did the former chief of the CIA's bin Laden unit know about it? The Obama administration must be doing the right thing, or they would not be doing it. Right?

The war was essentially a massive American and NATO air war with U.S., European and Qatari special operations forces leading jihadi militia fighters armed with weapons from Qatar and the UAE on the ground. It lasted for nine months and killed thousands. In the meantime, it was all over the international press who the fighters were, even if the American media would not cover it.

For example, early in the war, the BBC ran a piece about LIFG leader Abdel Hakim Belhaj, who was closely associated with Osama bin Laden and al Qaeda. He had fought in Afghanistan and had been captured by the Americans and the British. From there, he was renditioned from Thailand back to cooperative Gaddafi's Libya to be tortured. Belhaj had been sitting in prison until being released in 2010. When the rebels took Tripoli, it was Belhaj who raced to proclaim himself leader of the revolution on behalf of the Islamists. The so-called moderates in Benghazi were left out. The U.S.A. had scored a huge win for bin Laden's side, just a few short months after he had finally been found and killed. Belhaj is now one of the major leaders of the government in Tripoli. He sued the British government for their role in his torture. They settled.

Abdel-Hakim al-Hasidi was another terrorist. He was happy to give an interview to Italian newspaper *Il Sole 24 Ore* on March 25 — just six days after Obama declared war — where he proudly admitted that he and his men had fought against U.S. troops in Iraq War II.

Sufyan Bin Qumu was an al Qaeda fighter and associate of bin Laden in Afghanistan who had recently been released from the Guantánamo Bay prison. He promptly took up a role leading the al Qaeda-based insurgency under the protection of American planes and special operations forces, fighting at his service. He was profiled by the London *Daily Telegraph*. The role of bin Ladenites in the war was obvious from the beginning to those who were looking critically. What more reason could anyone need to oppose it?

The Americans rationalized that once they parachuted in the long-time CIA asset Khalifa Haftar to join Libyan army defector Maj. Gen. Abdul Fatah Younis in taking control of the revolt, everything would work out fine. Instead, Younis was soon murdered by rivals in the NTC, Clinton's Libyan Chalabi, Mahmoud Jibril, was quickly sidelined and Haftar has been stuck in a mostly stalemated civil war ever since.

Obama's Libyan Klansmen

It turns out that the LIFG and their associated al Qaeda terrorists are also a bunch of horrible anti-black racists. One of the first things they started doing once the war began was rounding up, torturing and murdering sub-Saharan Africans in Libya. They even "cleansed" the predominantly black town of Tawergha, a town of 30,000 people — native Libyans, the descendants of 19th century slaves — many of whom were tortured and killed, their property put to the torch. In Tripoli and Zawiyah thousands of black Libyans and sub-Saharan migrant workers were rounded up and held in camps. Even though Susan Rice, Hillary Clinton and the Democrats lied that Gaddafi was using mass rape as a weapon of war, in fact, it was the jihadis that America and its allies fought the war for who committed mass rapes. David Enders, a journalist then reporting for McClatchy newspapers, went to a refugee camp where the jihadis brutally gang-raped the black women there every night.

Sidney Blumenthal, Hillary Clinton's friend and adviser, sent her a note in March 2011, saying, "one rebel commander stated that his troops continue to summarily execute all foreign mercenaries captured in the fighting." Quickly it became clear that "foreign mercenaries" meant any blacks they could find. Gaddafi had been afraid to keep a large standing army, so he instead had only a small defense force, with some foreign mercenary fighters among its ranks. From that kernel of truth came the accusation that all blacks in Libya, most of whom were simple migrant laborers, were mercenary killers in the employ of Gaddafi's regime. Against this myth, the jihadis took their revenge.

A Turkish construction worker interviewed by the BBC said, "We had 70–80 people from Chad working for our company. They were cut dead with pruning shears and axes, attackers saying, 'You are providing troops for Gaddafi.' The Sudanese were also massacred. We saw it for ourselves."

The *Wall Street Journal* reported, "Some of the hatred of Tawergha has racist overtones that were mostly latent before the current conflict. On the road between Misrata and Tawergha, rebel slogans like 'the brigade for purging slaves, black skin' have supplanted pro-Gaddafi scrawl."

International news channels showed innocent black people rounded up and held in chains in cages at the zoo, with small green flags symbolizing the old regime literally stuffed down their throats.

Economic anxiety, caused by the boom and bust in oil prices and revenue, increased some Libyans' resentfulness of black African migrants, whose presence depressed their wages. The war unleashed their wrath.

As hard as it may be to believe, in the aftermath of the war, when the lack of border controls led to a mass migration movement from sub-Saharan Africa to Europe in the twenty-teens, actual chattel slavery was reinstituted in Libya. This was well-documented by many different news organizations, including the Obama-friendly CNN. Human beings were on sale for $400.

Blumenthal's warning about rebel war crimes came in the spring of 2011, still months before the actual capture and killing of Gaddafi and final destruction of his government. The Americans had every opportunity to call off the war and find a peaceful resolution — even Secretary Gates publicly said so years later — but in 2011, that was out of the question.

August 24, Congressman Kucinich presented still another opportunity to end the war. He sent a letter to Obama and Clinton which said:

> I have been contacted by an intermediary in Libya who has indicated that President Muammar Gaddafi is willing to negotiate an end to the conflict under conditions which would seem to favor Administration policy.

He received no response.

"When Qaddafi himself is finally removed, you should of course make a public statement before the cameras wherever you are, even in the driveway of your vacation home," Clinton's adviser Blumenthal had written to her two days earlier. "You must go on camera. You must establish yourself in the historical record at this moment."

And so she did. "We came, we saw, he died!" Clinton laughed her prepared imitation of Julius Caesar for the camera when news of Gaddafi's murder came in. He had been beaten, sodomized with a bayonet and shot in the side of the head on the side of the road. America was victorious.

Civil War Without End

Secretary Clinton's "victory lap" trip to Tripoli in October 2011 was surely her "Mission Accomplished!" moment, reminiscent of George W. Bush's humiliating premature declaration of triumph aboard the USS *Abraham Lincoln* after the initial toppling of Saddam Hussein's regime in 2003. The war did not create a new democracy to protect freedom and save Libya from tyranny. Instead, it only sowed chaos and far worse violence than could have possibly occurred if the U.S. and its allies had not intervened, instead allowing Gaddafi's regime to put down the short uprising. Instead of the imaginary massacre in Gaddafi's Benghazi attack of the spring of 2011, tens of thousands of people have been killed in the initial foreign intervention and in the endless civil wars raging since that time.

After the U.S.-NATO-GCC war of 2011, the different factions kept their weapons, breaking off into hundreds of warring militias. Elections held in July 2012 only helped to define the battle lines. In 2014, another major civil war broke out with various factions heavily backed by foreign regimes. Perhaps Libya is not really a country at all anymore. Only unified after World War II, it is now divided by two main governments locked in a permanent civil war with competition from hundreds of independent militias, crime rings and bin Ladenite terrorist groups. The Obama administration had no knowledge or concern about the tensions and conflicts between rival militias and tribes from Tripoli, Benghazi, Derna, Misrata and Zintan. Therefore, they had no reason to think that there were such things as factions in Libya, certainly not ones who could ruin the peaceful, democratic future they fantasized was coming.

The House of Representatives (HoR) and its Libyan National Army (LNA) are based in the eastern city of Tobruk. Their leader is the former CIA asset Khalifa Belqasim Haftar. He is now working with the Russians and America's allies, the French, Egyptians, Saudis and UAE. Haftar's forces seized Benghazi and quickly marched on Tripoli in the spring and summer of 2014, determined to depose the Islamist-backed parliament. They have not succeeded yet. According to author Frederic Wehrey, Haftar, unable to defeat the Islamist militias in Benghazi, instead coopted and empowered them while shutting down all of the locally elected town councils under the excuse of protecting their members' security.

The HoR remains at war with their rival government in Tripoli, the Government of National Accord (GNA). They have mostly merged with their former Islamist competition in the west, Belhaj's General National Congress (GNC) and still include violent Islamist groups such as his al Qaeda-connected Libya Dawn. The GNA is backed by America's other allies, the Turks, Italians and Qataris. Close partners, Turkey and Qatar, have a special affinity for the Islamist factions there.

Despite repeated assaults over the years, Haftar's forces have consistently failed to take the capital city. His latest effort in the spring of 2020, backed by Russia, fell short as Turkish troops reinforcing Tripoli helped keep them at bay. However, with Russian mercenary fighters and air support, Haftar's forces were able to halt the GNA's advance and seize the oil in the Sirte Basin. This will deprive the government in Tripoli of their most important stream of revenue and guarantee further conflict in the medium term, at least.

The often-ignored south of the country has largely descended into chaos under the warring militias of local tribal and ethnic warlords, human smugglers and gangsters. It is not so much a third country as just an ungoverned space dominated by criminals. A civil war was fought between opposing tribes in the south in 2014–2016, with one side backed by Belhaj and the other by Haftar.

At one point, the U.S., EU and UN tried to create a "government of national unity" that is hardly worth mentioning.

In 2015, groups declaring loyalty to the Islamic State (ISIS), the al Qaeda break-off group composed of veterans of the wars in Iraq and Syria, seized the Libyan coastal town of Sirte. This led to a joint effort, in 2016, by squadrons of U.S. planes and drones backing up the formerly warring GNA and GNC forces in a massive attempt to roust them back out again. The other Islamist groups, such as Ansar al-Sharia — bin Ladenite perpetrators of the Benghazi massacre of 2012 — weakened after many defected to ISIS in 2015 and 2016, are said to have finally been defeated by Haftar's forces in Derna in 2017.

During a 2016 presidential debate, when she was asked about the chaos reigning in Libya, Hillary Clinton denied any responsibility. It was all Barack Obama's fault — him and his lousy Libyan allies.

> The decision was the president's. Did I do the due diligence? Did I talk to everybody I could talk to? Did I visit every capital and then report back to the president? Yes, I did. That's what a secretary of state does. But at the end of the day, those are the decisions that are made by the president to in any way use American military power, and the president made that decision. And, yes, we did try without success because of the Libyans' obstruction to our efforts. [sic]

Anne-Marie Slaughter explained the secretary's unapologetic thinking to a reporter. "[W]hen the choice is between action and inaction, and you've got risks in either direction, which you often do, she'd rather be caught trying."

Ambassador Power later wrote in her memoir, "We could hardly expect to have a crystal ball when it came to accurately predicting outcomes in places where the culture was not our own." That was not meant as a profound admission of guilt and regret for what she had done. Instead Power was explaining why the results of her war were not her fault. She told Wehrey that, "Much of the instability that Libya is enduring today would've come had Obama decided the other way, not to intervene." If we had not waged the war, its consequences still would have happened anyway, so what difference does it make?

In the real world, the things Ambassador Power did, the choices that she made, helped start a war that has killed tens of thousands of people and displaced literally millions.

Obama himself called Libya a "shit show" and said his failure to implement a massive Iraq War II-style nation-building project there after the war was the greatest failure of his presidency. He said this as though it went without saying that the results, in that case, would have been great. He could never admit that he should not have launched an aggressive war against a sovereign nation for no good reason.

In 2019, when asked about all the chaos in the country since the war began, Jake Sullivan replied, "I've struggled with the question of if we had it to do over again would we have participated in the Libya intervention. And I don't have a definitive answer on that yet." What a light and easy thing it is to be a national security bureaucrat.

In the years since, the U.S. has mostly stayed in the background of the civil war, supporting and then abandoning various groups and governments. After helping oust ISIS from Sirte in 2016, they have launched thousands more airstrikes in the years since, killing hundreds of civilians along with the alleged terrorists and fighters they were targeting.

The massive 2015–2016 Mediterranean refugee crisis and the public relations disaster of new chattel slave markets did not lead to a severe reckoning over another failed American intervention. Instead, the government, media and public mostly turned away — toward the next war.

A Modified, Limited Hangout

Besides the fake excuse for war in the spring of 2011, the other, more famous Benghazi scandal is the murder of Ambassador Christopher Stevens, foreign service officer Sean Smith and two CIA contractors on September 11, 2012. The Republicans' narrative has it that when the American consulate and nearby CIA safe house fell under attack, Obama and his administration left the men there out to dry. They failed to provide adequate security forces, and when the assault began, Hillary Clinton did not take the 3:00 a.m. phone call or do what was necessary to protect her men's lives. The CIA in Tripoli and the military in Italy refused to come immediately to the rescue. Then they lied about the cause of the attack.

There is something to those criticisms, especially on the question of the under-manned and under-motivated security forces who had been hired to protect the consulate building and the Obama administration's blaming of a ridiculous YouTube video for inciting a deadly riot. There had been numerous small attacks against the facility in the months leading up to the one that killed Stevens. He and his team had repeatedly requested better security and had been put off.

The attack began closer to three in the afternoon Eastern time, and all indications are that Clinton and the rest of the administration were aware and concerned if not competent and capable enough to respond effectively. Gen. Petraeus, then director of the CIA, was later criticized by the White House for going to the premiere of the propaganda movie *Argo*, about the 1979 Iran hostage crisis that night when he should have been taking charge of the rescue efforts. To be fair to him, the CIA's co-production of that film was the greatest professional accomplishment of Petraeus's life. It was important that he attend.

Some of the other criticism may partly be based on a Hollywood-created misperception that in such a situation the military would swing into action and send in troops on a daring rescue mission in the middle of a firefight. There was a "stand down" order given to the CIA operatives and contractors at the nearby Benghazi safe house when some of the men wanted to go immediately to the rescue of those at the consulate. But this was apparently a tactical decision by the commander on the scene, rather than an order from Obama or Clinton, and not the massive betrayal as it was portrayed by their political enemies. Benghazi became a mostly manufactured political scandal that dragged on for years after that.

But the popular Benghazi scandal is what President Richard Nixon and his aide John Ehrlichman called "a modified, limited hangout." A *limited hangout* is when a politician or intelligence agency misleadingly makes a big deal about one part of a scandal to obscure the more important truth behind it. To *modify* the limited hangout is to lie about the bit of the story one has confessed to in order to send skeptics off on false trails.

In this case, the rest of the story revolves around the question: what was Ambassador Stevens doing in Benghazi rather than Tripoli in the first place? And why was there a CIA safe house a few blocks away? The answer is that in cooperation with the British MI-6, Saudi Arabia and Muslim Brotherhood-supporting Turks and Qataris, CIA Director David Petraeus was taking jihadis and weapons from Libya and shipping them off to the next conflict in Syria.

Many media reports and documents obtained by the conservative legal foundation Judicial Watch showed this is what was really going on in Benghazi and that it was this operation that had ultimately gotten the ambassador killed. A DIA document read:

During the immediate aftermath of, and following the uncertainty caused by, the downfall of the [Qaddafi] regime in October 2011 and up until early September of 2012, weapons from the former Libya military stockpiles located in Benghazi, Libya were shipped from the port of Benghazi, Libya, to the ports of Banias and the Port of Borj Islam, Syria.

The final report of the House Intelligence Committee claimed that the CIA was only "collecting intelligence" about other "foreign entities" that happened to be shipping weapons off to Syria. But journalist Seymour Hersh later reported that the "rat line" of weapons and fighters from Benghazi to the next war, in Syria, was run by the Americans.

The rat line, authorized in early 2012, was used to funnel weapons and ammunition from Libya via southern Turkey and across the Syrian border to the opposition. Many of those in Syria who ultimately received the weapons were jihadists, some of them affiliated with al Qaeda. ...

A highly classified annex to the [Congressional] report, not made public, described a secret agreement reached in early 2012 between the Obama and Erdoğan administrations. It pertained to the rat line. By the terms of the agreement, funding came from Turkey, as well as Saudi Arabia and Qatar; the CIA, with the support of MI-6, was responsible for getting arms from Gaddafi's arsenals into Syria. ...

The operation was run by David Petraeus, the CIA director who would soon resign when it became known he was having an affair with his biographer.

In January 2013, Senator Rand Paul confronted Secretary Clinton at a foreign relations committee hearing about any knowledge that she had about operations by the U.S. or its allies to ship weapons from Libya to Turkey for use in the Syrian uprising, as reported by the *London Times*. She denied any knowledge and told him that he should direct his question instead to the CIA.

The *Times* story, published just two days after Stevens was killed, said that the Libyan ship *Intisaar* had docked in the Turkish port of Iskenderun, where a fight broke out between the Free Syrian Army and the Muslim Brotherhood over who would take the weapons. "Among more than 400 tons of cargo the vessel was carrying were SAM-7 surface-to-air anti-aircraft missiles and rocket-propelled grenades (RPGs), which Syrian sources said could be a game-changer for the rebels," the *Times* said.

A former bin Laden associate, Libyan Islamic Fighting Group leader and CIA torture victim Abdel Hakim Belhaj traveled to Syria in November to meet with America's so-called moderate rebels, the Free Syrian Army (FSA), as the *Telegraph* reported.

So, what was the real story behind the attack? Remember al Qaeda associate Sheikh Ibn al-Libi, who the CIA had the Egyptians torture into accusing Saddam Hussein of teaching al Qaeda how to hijack planes and make chemical weapons back in 2002? It turns out that his brother, Sheikh Yahya al-Libi, was killed by the CIA in a drone strike in Pakistan in July 2012. Ayman al-Zawahiri, who became the leader of al Qaeda after bin Laden was killed in 2011, put out a recording just before the attack urging friendly forces in Libya to take advantage of the Americans' proximity and to take their revenge. "His blood is calling, urging and inciting you to fight and kill the crusaders." That was the reason that Stevens and the others were killed that night. Just because the Democrats were arming America's enemies did not mean they had bought their loyalty.

It makes sense that the Republicans who supported regime change in Libya and Syria made such a scandal around the lack of security and slow response to the Benghazi attack. They needed to distract from the fact that they had been partially responsible for the situation due to their support for the war in the first place.

"Weapons and fighters were absolutely going to Syria, and the U.S. absolutely knew all about it — though most shipments have stopped since the attack on the American Consulate," a British source living in Benghazi told Fox News. The first part was true. The second was not. Nine months after Stevens was killed, an investigative piece by Reuters and a United Nations report both said that the rat line of weapons and fighters from Libya to Syria was still going strong.

On to the Next One

Despite all the chaos in Libya since then, the real scandal of the war is the way that it spread outside the borders of that unfortunate nation. Syria was only part of it.

Chapter Nine:
Mali

"Timbuktu was sacked many times
before, but we have had no events of
destruction of monuments, mosques
and tombs. It never happened before."
— Shamil Jeppie

Northern Revolt

Before discussing the Libyan war's disastrous consequences for the people of Syria and Iraq, it is important to follow the repercussions of that war for many other nations and individuals in Africa, beginning with Mali and spreading on from there.

One reason black Libyans were persecuted after the fall of Gaddafi was the rumor that they were part of his mercenary forces. Again, they were mostly just migrant laborers, but the bit of truth to that narrative was actually not even about blacks, but about the Tuaregs, who are distinct from Arabs, Berbers, and sub-Saharan Africans. They are their own ethnicity in the western Sahel, the region to the southwest of Libya and Algeria and the vast Saharan Desert, primarily in the northern part of Mali.

When their side lost the war, they took their guns and went home. Northern Mali is approximately the size of Texas. Since independence in 1960, it has been ruled by a relatively small panhandle in the south, which is dominated by French-backed blacks. When the Tuaregs returned from Libya, they decided that the limited autonomy they had accepted from the government in the south for years was no longer good enough. Well-armed from Gaddafi's stocks, they instead decided that the time was ripe to declare independence for their new pseudo-state of "Azawad." They went to war, attacking government positions in the north of the country and scoring major victories against the military.

Unfortunately for the Tuareg fighters, their uprising was short-lived. Libyan and other jihadis came in right on their heels and hijacked their revolution. Fighters from the Libyan bin Ladenite LIFG and Algerian al Qaeda in the Islamic Maghreb (AQIM) allied with Ansar Dine, the worst of the Tuareg groups, and consolidated power over the north. They committed war crimes against civilians and attempted to destroy the shrines and manuscripts at the ancient libraries of Timbuktu. But in early 2013, the bin Ladenites ended up pushing their luck too far, moving down into Mali's southern region, successfully attacking government targets, but provoking a stronger reaction.

Military Coup

Mali had a sort of pseudo-democracy in their capital Bamako. Their government's leader, President Amadou Toumani Touré, was a former military dictator, but he had since stood for election twice, and it appeared that he meant to step down from power on time and leave a new fledgling democratic state in his wake, as Professor Stephen Zunes told the author. But his U.S.-trained military forces, after the loss of the north and the start of assaults on the south, overthrew him in a coup d'état, ending their first real chance at representative government.

The Leahy Law, which forbids military aid to countries guilty of human rights abuses, was considered to be in effect, so the Americans could only give clandestine, deniable Joint Special Operations Command and CIA support to the new coup regime. Secretary Clinton failed to get the Algerians to intervene against the bin Ladenite forces. Finally, the French reinvaded in 2013 and quickly succeeded in driving the bin Ladenites out of the country's south. They crushed the Islamist groups where they could find them in the north, though the counterinsurgency there continues to this day. Deniable U.S. clandestine forces have been documented fighting in Mali as well. The most media attention they received, however, was when three Delta Force operators and their prostitutes were killed in a truck crash and when two American Navy SEALs murdered an Army Green Beret when he discovered they were stealing.

A new civilian government, set up by the French, was overthrown in another military putsch in the summer of 2020. The war rages on.

Spilling Blood

Boko Haram is an indigenous, Islamist insurgent group in Nigeria which established itself toward the end of the first decade of the century. According to numerous reports, including those of British Mali expert Jeremy Keenan, in 2013, they traveled up to Mali, where they received tracts of religious and political indoctrination as well as guns and training in weapons and tactics. That group of now-more dangerous marauders has since taken their battle back to Nigeria, where they continue to wage violent attacks against government targets and atrocities against civilians. U.S. special operations forces have followed them to act primarily as trainers and advisers to the Nigerian army, though retired Brig. Gen. Donald Bolduc told journalist Nick Turse that the U.S. has had combat casualties there as well. "Africa has more named operations than any other theater, including CENTCOM," Buldoc confirmed to Turse.

The terrorists and the wars against them have spread from Libya to Tunisia and Mali, and from there into Mauritania, Nigeria, Chad, Niger, Cameroon, Central African Republic, the Democratic Republic of the Congo and Burkina Faso.

The Army saw the invasion of Africa as a make-work program to stay busy after the drawdowns from the wars in Iraq and Afghanistan. Instead of coming home and getting jobs, they simply found more battles to fight. In the process, they have helped to spread bin Ladenite violence and chaos deep into Africa. It is far from over. [See Chapter 13.]

Chapter Ten:
Syria

"The time is not far off in the Middle East
... when it will be literally 'God help the
Shia.' More than a billion Sunnis have
simply had enough of them."
— Prince Bandar bin Sultan

"Al Qaeda has really got it right."
— Charles Lister

"We thank Allah, who rendered
our enemies imbeciles."
— Ali al-Khamenei

Expediting the Chaotic Collapse

Dick Cheney's Middle East adviser, neoconservative strategist David Wurmser, wrote in his 1996 article "Coping with Crumbling States" that the U.S. should seek to "expedite the chaotic collapse" of Syria as soon as they were done overthrowing Saddam Hussein's Iraq. Unfortunately for Wurmser, the opportunity to destroy Syria did not come until after he was out of power. Americans concerned about bin Ladenite terrorism might have wondered why in the world they should want to spread any more chaos in the region after the catastrophe of Iraq War II.

In an age of international terrorism waged by radical Islamists, Bashar al-Assad was a secularist who shaved his chin every morning, wore a three-piece suit and was an old acquaintance of Secretary of State John Kerry. His father's government had joined George H.W. Bush's coalition against Iraq in 1991 and cooperated with America and Israel at the Madrid and Oslo meetings. Bashar al-Assad had voted for America's UN Security Council Resolution 1441 mandating the return of the weapons inspectors to Iraq. He had also been willing to negotiate with Israel over the Golan Heights in the George W. Bush years, before Secretary of State Condoleezza Rice intervened and forced the Israelis to halt the talks.

Assad was a "reformer," Hillary Clinton had said. Assad's regime had been torturing people for the CIA as part of the "extraordinary rendition" program since her husband's administration in the 1990s. Former CIA officer Robert Baer seemed to be honest about his own role in the program when he told the *New Statesman* that, "If you want a serious interrogation, you send a prisoner to Jordan. If you want them to be tortured, you send them to Syria. If you want someone to disappear — never to see them again — you send them to Egypt." The George W. Bush administration, in a case of mistaken identity, handed an innocent Canadian named Maher Arar over to the Syrians to be tortured.

As revealed in leaked State Department cables, in 2010 Assad's government invited the U.S. to join their efforts against bin Ladenites crossing the border from Syria into Iraq.

Assad was not a full-fledged American sock-puppet dictator like Hosni Mubarak in Egypt, but he had been mostly cooperative in the War on Terrorism and certainly had no love for al Qaeda. Syria had been accused of helping to facilitate the entry of foreign fighters into Iraq earlier during Iraq War II, though it was never proven that his government was behind the jihadists' border crossings. If it were true that Assad had done so, his motives would have been defensive in nature, and understandable, if not justifiable: to get those dangerous terrorists out of his country and help keep the United States bogged down in Iraq before they could move on to the next stage of their publicly stated plan: overthrowing him.

In 2007, House Speaker Nancy Pelosi went to Syria. There she visited the Omayyad mosque in Old Damascus and met with President Assad for three hours, insisting despite the Bush administration's objections that diplomacy with Syria was vital. "We came in friendship, hope and determined that the road to Damascus is a road to peace," she said. In 2011, John Kerry told the Carnegie Endowment that "President Assad has been very generous with me in terms of the discussions we have had. And when I last went to — the last several trips to Syria — I asked President Assad to do certain things to build the relationship with the United States." According to the AP, Kerry listed six requests for Assad, including working together on Iraqi border security and said the Syrians fulfilled them all.

In any case, the Syrian government certainly never attacked or threatened the United States. Intervening in that country did not serve to protect the American people in any way. The hawks would agree and claim this shows that selfless humanitarian concerns were at the core of their policy. The American Superman had to go and save the nice people. But that is not what the U.S. role in Syria was about. The policy was regime change. But after the rise of al Qaeda in Iraq in the aftermath of Iraq War II, the obvious question was if the U.S. did succeed in overthrowing the Ba'athist regime in Syria, what organized force in the country could possibly replace it? The obvious answer was the Muslim Brotherhood if you're lucky. The Brotherhood had posed a major problem for the Syrian government in the past. In 1982, Bashar's father, Hafez al-Assad, had massacred thousands of members of the Brotherhood, their supporters and nearby civilians in the town of Hama to successfully repress a four-year armed Islamist uprising. Though the group remained mostly underground, it was obvious years before the war began that any attempt to overthrow the Ba'athists would benefit the Brotherhood first. The U.S. government knew it too. They did it anyway.

The Redirection

As discussed previously, in direct contravention of its designers' intentions, the second Iraq war (2003–2011) resulted in the installation of Iran's closest allies, the Shi'ite Da'wa Party and Islamic Supreme Council of Iraq (ISCI), in the new Iraqi parliament. Crucially, it also included the creation of the new Iraqi army which drew primarily from the ranks of ISCI's murderous Badr Brigade and other allied Shi'ite militias. The failure of the United States, by increasing of the influence of its major regional competitor, was apparent to neoconservative policy advisers such as Zalmay Khalilzad and Elliot Abrams by 2006, not to mention the outraged

Saudi royals. Even before Hussein's trial was over, some administration hawks were already telling the media it was time to tilt back toward the Sunnis. Khalilzad even pushed for a deal with Sunni tribal leaders and a new effort to turn around and use them against sectarian Shi'ite militias, but was overruled. It was too late for that. But by the end of 2006, the administration did adopt major aspects of Khalilzad's argument for the "Sunni turn."

This policy was the reason for the massive propaganda campaign of early 2007, coinciding with President Bush and Gen. Petraeus's "surge" of reinforcements to Iraq, which blamed all their failures on Iranian intervention and intransigent Shi'ite leader Muqtada al-Sadr. At the same time, Petraeus began bribing the local Sunni tribal leaders with money and weapons to turn against al Qaeda in Iraq, marginalize the most radical and destructive forces in their insurgency against the new Shi'ite regime and promise to cease their attacks against U.S. forces. Petraeus attempted to use this support for some Sunni tribal leaders during the "surge" of 2007 — the so-called "Awakening" movement — as leverage against his own Shi'ite allies, futilely trying to separate the latter from their primary Iranian patrons.

But the policy went much further than that. As journalist Seymour Hersh showed in his articles "The Next Act," "The Redirection" and "Preparing the Battlefield" for *The New Yorker* in 2007, beginning in 2006 the Bush government began backing the bin Ladenite-type groups against the Shi'ites across the region. They began with supporting Fatah al-Islam and Asbat al-Ansar against Hezbollah in Lebanon, a policy which was seen as more urgent after Hezbollah defeated the Israelis when they invaded Lebanon in the summer of 2006. They also backed Muslim Brotherhood groups in Syria; the Party for Free Life in Kurdistan (PJAK), a leftist Kurdish group in Iranian Kurdistan tied to the Turkish sometimes-terrorist organization, the Kurdistan Workers' Party (PKK); as well as Jundallah, an incredibly dangerous group of al Qaeda-connected terrorists in the eastern Iranian Sistan and Baluchistan region. Pentagon reporter Mark Perry wrote in his 2012 piece, "False Flag," for *Foreign Policy* that it was actually the Israeli Mossad posing as CIA that recruited Jundallah to wage attacks against the Iranian military — which they did, including multiple deadly attacks against the Iranian Revolutionary Guard Corps (IRGC), a failed assassination attempt against then-president Mahmoud Ahmadinejad as well as numerous attacks against civilian targets such as Shi'ite mosques.

Hersh wrote in "The Redirection" back in March 2007:

> To undermine Iran, which is predominantly Shi'ite, the Bush Administration has decided, in effect, to reconfigure its priorities in

the Middle East. In Lebanon, the Administration has cooperated with Saudi Arabia's government, which is Sunni, in clandestine operations that are intended to weaken Hezbollah, the Shi'ite organization that is backed by Iran. The U.S. has also taken part in clandestine operations aimed at Iran and its ally Syria. A by-product of these activities has been the bolstering of Sunni extremist groups that espouse a militant vision of Islam and are hostile to America and sympathetic to al Qaeda.

One contradictory aspect of the new strategy is that, in Iraq, most of the insurgent violence directed at the American military has come from Sunni forces, and not from Shi'ites. But, from the Administration's perspective, the most profound — and unintended — strategic consequence of the Iraq war is the empowerment of Iran. ...

The key players behind the redirection are Vice-President Dick Cheney, the deputy national-security adviser Elliott Abrams, the departing Ambassador to Iraq (and nominee for United Nations Ambassador), Zalmay Khalilzad, and Prince Bandar bin Sultan, the Saudi national-security adviser. ...

The new strategy "is a major shift in American policy — it's a sea change," a U.S. government consultant with close ties to Israel said. The Sunni states "were petrified of a Shi'ite resurgence, and there was growing resentment with our gambling on the moderate Shi'ites in Iraq," he said. "We cannot reverse the Shi'ite gain in Iraq, but we can contain it." ...

[T]he U.S. government consultant told me, Bandar and other Saudis have assured the White House that "they will keep a very close eye on the religious fundamentalists. Their message to us was 'We've created this movement, and we can control it.' It's not that we don't want the Salafis to throw bombs; it's who they throw them at — Hezbollah, Moqtada al-Sadr, Iran, and at the Syrians, if they continue to work with Hezbollah and Iran." ...

[T]he Saudi government, with Washington's approval, would provide funds and logistical aid to weaken the government of President Bashir Assad, of Syria. The Israelis believe that putting such pressure on the Assad government will make it more conciliatory and open to negotiations. Syria is a major conduit of arms to Hezbollah.

There it is. This is why the following unbelievable things in this chapter are true. Bush had brought Iran's power in the region up two pegs by installing their best friends in power in Baghdad. So now, realizing his error, he would try to take them down a peg by weakening or overthrowing Iran's ally Assad in Damascus. Remember, al Qaeda hated the U.S. for being too closely allied with their local governments. They did not serve Iran, but radical dissident factions within Saudi Arabia and Egypt, primarily. So overall, many of al Qaeda's regional enemies were the same as those of America and its Sunni alliance system.

To be clear, when President Barack Obama chose the side of al Qaeda terrorists in Libya and Syria, this was not because he was a Muslim terrorist sleeper agent from Kenya, as much of the political right believed. The policy was a reflection of the generations-long Roosevelt-Eisenhower-Carter-Bush Doctrine of support for and deference to the Saudi and other Arabian kings' wishes, and more specifically the continuation of George W. Bush "redirection" in his second term. The primary concern of America's post-Iraq War II Middle Eastern strategy is centered on the question of how to make up for the fact that the U.S. handed Baghdad over to the closest Iraqi allies of our government's main strategic rival, Iran. It was too late to start the Iraq war all over again, turn around and march east to give Baghdad back to the Sunnis, and it was too dangerous to launch another full-scale regime-change war against Iran. So Obama decided that he could instead get a consolation prize by targeting Bashar al-Assad's regime in Damascus.

That was why in 2011, the first year of the Arab Spring, when the U.S. still had thousands of troops in Iraq chasing down the last of the bin Ladenites, it was already siding with them on the other side of the line in Syria. It had been going on for years. As Hersh reported and State Department cables leaked by Spc. Chelsea Manning later proved, the U.S. had been financing the Syrian Muslim Brotherhood's "Movement for Justice and Development" since the redirection began in 2006.

In a spring 2012 interview, the *Atlantic*'s Jeffrey Goldberg suggested to President Obama that, "it would seem to me that one way to weaken and further isolate Iran is to remove or help remove Iran's only Arab ally, [Syria]." The president responded, "Absolutely."

"What else can this administration be doing?" Goldberg pressed.

> Obama: [The Arab Spring is] now engulfing Syria, and Syria is basically [Iran's] only true ally in the region. And it is our estimation that [Assad's] days are numbered. It's a matter not of if, but when. Now, can we accelerate that? We're working with the world community to try to do that. ... [W]hat we're trying to do — and the secretary of state just came back from helping to lead the Friends of Syria group in Tunisia — is to try to come up with a series of strategies that can provide humanitarian relief. But they can also accelerate a transition to a peaceful and stable and representative Syrian government. If that happens, that will be a profound loss for Iran.
>
> Goldberg: Is there anything you could do to move it faster?
>
> Obama: Well, nothing that I can tell you, because your classified clearance isn't good enough. (Laughter.)

Obama's national security adviser Tom Donilon agreed that the "end of the Assad regime would constitute Iran's greatest setback in the region yet — a strategic blow that will further shift the balance of power in the region against Iran." As Reuters reported that August, Obama had signed a new finding — an order to the CIA — to increase support for the insurgents. For more than a year, Americans had helped coordinate the war at a "secret command center" in the Turkish city of Adana, though he could not admit it.

The president's main political opposition in the U.S. Senate could not agree more with the motive for the policy. As Lindsey Graham, Republican of South Carolina, told the *New York Times* just a few weeks before,

> Breaking Syria apart from Iran could be as important to containing a nuclear Iran as sanctions. If the Syrian regime is replaced with another form of government that doesn't tie its future to the Iranians, the world is a better place.

Though Assad is a member of the Ba'ath Party, unlike Sunni Saddam Hussein he is an Alawite, which is Syria's ruling minority sect and closely associated with the Shi'ites. They also have an alliance with Iran. The primary concern of the neoconservatives had always been Syria's role in helping Iran support Lebanese Hezbollah, and they had been pushing for war with Assad's government since after the 2003 invasion. Bush had balked, but Obama gave them half of what they wanted. Not full regime change, but an Israeli-approved policy of prolonging the war for as long as possible.

Neoconservative Max Boot also wrote in 2012 that the "first" reason the United States should attack Assad's government in Syria was to "diminish Iran's influence in the Arab world. … Iran knows that if his regime fell, it would lose its most important base in the Arab world and a supply line to pro-Iranian Hezbollah militants in Lebanon." Oh, and regime change against the Ba'athists will somehow help to diminish, rather than enhance al Qaeda's influence.

It was not just the neocons. Bill and Hillary Clinton's long-time associate, former Assistant Secretary of State for Public Affairs Jamie Rubin, wrote an important memo to Secretary Clinton in April 2012. It outlined why he also thought the U.S. must take the opportunity to hurt Iran and Hezbollah on behalf of Israel by attacking the Ayatollah's Ba'athist allies in Damascus. He later ran a version of the memo as an article in *Foreign Policy* in June 2012, calling it "The Real Reason to Intervene in Syria." It had nothing to do with protecting the safety and liberty of the American people.

It is the strategic relationship between Iran and the regime of Bashar Assad in Syria that makes it possible for Iran to undermine Israel's security — not through a direct attack, which in the thirty years of hostility between Iran and Israel has never occurred, but through its proxies in Lebanon, like Hezbollah, that are sustained, armed and trained by Iran via Syria. The end of the Assad regime would end this dangerous alliance. Israel's leadership understands well why defeating Assad is now in its interests. ...

With Assad gone, and Iran no longer able to threaten Israel through its proxies, it is possible that the United States and Israel can agree on red lines for when Iran's program has crossed an unacceptable threshold. In short, the White House can ease the tension that has developed with Israel over Iran by doing the right thing in Syria.

In the memo, Rubin expressed support for the current operation to help Saudi Arabia, Qatar and Turkey arm and train Syria's Sunni-based insurgency. He also insisted that the U.S. needed to go around the UN Security Council and even its own NATO alliance to team up with Persian Gulf states to launch a major air campaign to quickly oust the Assad government and its forces.

And do not worry, Rubin promised:

Some argue that U.S. involvement risks a wider war with Russia. But the Kosovo example shows otherwise. In that case, Russia had genuine ethnic and political ties to the Serbs, which don't exist between Russia and Syria, and even then, Russia did little more than complain. Arming the Syrian rebels and using western airpower to ground Syrian helicopters and airplanes is a low-cost high payoff approach. ...

Rubin then broke fully into his neoconservative routine, mixing Wurmser's crazy Clean Break policy with Paul Wolfowitz's pipe dreams of being greeted with flowers and candy.

As long as Washington's political leaders stay firm that no U.S. ground troops will be deployed, as they did in both Kosovo and Libya, the costs to the United States will be limited. Victory may not come quickly or easily, but it will come. And the payoff will be substantial. Iran would be strategically isolated, unable to exert its influence in the Middle East. The resulting regime in Syria will see the United States as a friend, not an enemy. Washington would gain substantial recognition as fighting for the people in the Arab world, not the corrupt regimes.

For Israel, the rationale for a bolt from the blue attack on Iran's nuclear facilities would be eased. And a new Syrian regime might well be open to early action on the frozen peace talks with Israel [over the Golan Heights]. Hezbollah in Lebanon would be cut off from its Iranian sponsor since Syria would no longer be a transit point for Iranian training, assistance and missiles.

What, no pipeline to Haifa?

Al Qaeda in Iraq in Syria

Syria is a 70 percent super-majority Sunni country ruled by a minority Alawite elite's Ba'ath Party government. However, the regime is also supported by virtually all the rest of the country's ethnic and religious minorities: Orthodox, Melkite, Armenian, Assyrian and Syriac Christians; Circassians, Jews; Ismailis; Bedouins; (most) Kurds; Druze; Shi'ite Arabs and also a substantial plurality if not majority of the Sunni Arabs, particularly the wealthy business class in the city of Aleppo. The majority of the Syrian Arab Army (SAA) was and is Sunni. But there were major economic problems in the country, including effects of mass immigration to the cities from the countryside after the Turks dammed up the Euphrates River in the 2000s. Syria is also a secular police state and hereditary autocracy, so there was much popular discontent and even room for a significant insurgency to break out. As in Libya, America and Saudi Arabia quickly moved to hijack the Syrian Arab Spring protest movement and turn it into a real civil war.

A National Security Agency (NSA) document from 2013 showed that Saudi prince and then-intelligence director Salman bin Sultan supported and gave direct orders to the so-called moderate Free Syrian Army in this case to "light up Damascus" and "flatten" the airport with rockets in March 2013. Had this document come to light earlier, what it revealed about Saudi control and documented war crimes by America's supposedly moderate rebels may have made a difference in the domestic debate over support for the insurgency. Unfortunately, the *Guardian* and then the Intercept, which received the Edward Snowden leak almost immediately after this event, chose not to publish it for four more years.

It was not just America and their Saudi friends. At the same time that Obama was killing Osama and was running for reelection on his final victory in the War on Terrorism — and still not quite ten years since the September 11th attacks on New York and Virginia — he was taking the enemy's side in Libya and in Syria. His own administration called their tacit support for al Qaeda in Syria "a deal with the devil," according to the *Washington Post*.

Unlike in Iraq War II, where the jihadists were a small subset of the broader Sunni-based insurgency, there was no question from 2011 onwards that the bin Ladenites led the insurgency in Syria. The actual "moderates" wanted to live. They were mostly sitting at hotels in Qatar and Turkey doing just that. In this type of guerrilla war, the fighters are not professional soldiers but terrorists, mercenaries and volunteers who do not mind dying. Hundreds of veterans of Abu Musab al-Zarqawi's al Qaeda in Iraq started coming across the border to take over as soon as the first protests broke out. This was clear to critics from the very beginning of the war, and so was the fact that the U.S. government and its allies were involved in supporting the worst side of it. Just as the Saudis had helped bankroll the Sunni insurgency against the U.S. and Shi'ites in Iraq War II, they began financing the same forces in Syria. Where George W. Bush had turned a blind eye to their treachery, Barack Obama was all in.

Pro-regime change lobbyists in the U.S. tend to accentuate reports of a broader, more peaceful protest movement seeking democratic reforms that took to the Syrian streets in 2011. They also point to the fact that some leftist and other more secular groups did make up a substantial segment of the early armed insurgency. The hawks also claim that much of that insurgency broke out as the result of a heavily armed overreaction on the part of the government to some of the initial demonstrations. There were harsh crackdowns against protesters in some places and reportedly torture of some of those arrested. In the summer of 2011, reporter Reese Erlich met with a group of protesters who said they wanted a parliamentary democracy, though they quickly turned to violence, as Erlich said, with no real political or military strategy.

As Christopher Phillips writes in *The Battle for Syria*, for the first year Assad was hesitant to use force to put down the uprising. The British characterized his actions as "calculated escalations of violence." They were poorly calculated. He did not play nice enough to placate his opposition or crack down severely enough to win. His security forces escalated just enough to be counterproductive. But not all the violence at the early protests was caused by government forces or in reaction to it.

As has been shown by journalists Sharmine Narwani, William Van Wagenen and others, from the very beginning of the uprising that spring, the Islamist group Ahrar al-Sham and other extremists killed cops and soldiers. As Aaron Lund has written, while somehow trying to play it down, Ahrar al-Sham had been founded by first generation al Qaeda members from the 1980s Afghan war or soon after, including Mohammed al-Bahaiyah (a.k.a. Abu Khalid al-Suri). He was accused by a Spanish court of being al Qaeda's paymaster for the 2004 Madrid bombings which killed 193 people. The Free Syrian Army (FSA) had been established in the summer of 2011 and included Iraq War II-era terrorists at the start. Urban liberals may have wanted democratic reforms, but the Western and Persian Gulf powers and fanatical bin Ladenites were determined to have their way. This rendered the concerns, beliefs and motivations of any small, truly moderate groups of protesters and fighters essentially irrelevant. The

Syrian people certainly had the right to protest against or even overthrow their government to better secure their safety and happiness. But this was not that. They were caught between their government and a group of interventionist foreign powers and Islamist terrorists, and that was what really mattered.

It was clear from the very first months of the Arab Spring, in early 2011, that the U.S. and Saudi Arabia were already making their move against Assad in Syria. As early as April 2011, Dick Cheney's former national security adviser John Hannah reported the pertinent facts in *Foreign Policy*. The notorious Prince Bandar bin Sultan had returned to the top rank of Saudi Arabia's intelligence agency, determined to crush the Arab Spring wherever it threatened Saudi interests, such as in Bahrain, and exploit it against their enemies in Libya, and especially in Syria, "Iran's closest ally in the Arab world." As a Saudi official told Hannah, "The king knows that other than the collapse of the Islamic Republic itself, nothing would weaken Iran more than losing Syria." The hawkish Hannah portrayed a hostage situation in which Bandar could start backing terrorists against Iran or even making nuclear weapons due to his lack of confidence in Obama's dedication to Saudi priorities. The "superpower" had better give in to its client state right away and begin a minor war before they declare independence and start a major one. Syria was at the top of the list. The U.S. and the other Western states fell right in line with the Saudi agenda.

That June, syndicated war correspondent Eric Margolis reported that the French were helping to coordinate the uprising in their former colony in cooperation with the U.S., UK, Israel, Saudi Arabia and Jordan, as well as some factions in Lebanon. In October, *Foreign Affairs* published a piece by John R. Bradley explaining that Saudi Arabia was making a massive bet on the Syrian Muslim Brotherhood to overthrow and replace the Assad regime. In November 2011, Alastair Crooke reported in *The Observer* that Bandar was sending jihadist fighters from Saudi Arabia to Syria to oppose Assad. For critics, this showed from the very beginning that the war had nothing to do with protecting Syrians' rights or spreading democracy. It also showed that the insurgents were no "moderates" at all, but bin Ladenite extremists and terrorists in the mold of Abu Musab al-Zarqawi, the founder of al Qaeda in Iraq during Iraq War II.

On December 7, 2011, Reva Bhalla Goujon, vice-president for global analysis for the private intelligence firm Strategic Forecasting Inc. (Stratfor), sent a memo about a meeting she had that day at the Pentagon with strategic planners for the Air Force. It also included one British and one French officer. The memo was later leaked to Wikileaks. She wrote, "After a couple hours of talking, they said without saying that SOF [special operations forces] teams (presumably from U.S., UK, France, Jordan,

Turkey) are already on the ground focused on recce [reconnaissance] missions and training opposition forces." They then told her the plan was to support insurgent attacks and assassinations to try to destroy "the Alawite forces," thus "causing the fall of the state."

Just two weeks later, on December 23, massive suicide truck bombings rocked Damascus, killing dozens.

It has been said a million times over that Obama refused to intervene in the Syrian civil war, leading it to be such a bloody catastrophe. This is wrong. All through 2011, the first year of the Arab Spring uprisings, America and its allies were pouring weapons, cash and "foreign fighter" bin Ladenite terrorists into Syria. They caused the war.

Beginning in 2012, even the *New York Times* would repeatedly admit that Saudi Arabia, Qatar, Turkey, Jordan and the U.S. were all working together to bring weapons to so-called vetted Syrian moderates, but that the extremists were getting the guns and the money every time. Not only that, but they would also admit the truth that al Qaeda's local affiliate, Jabhat al-Nusra, was the dominant force and consistently took control of other groups, their resources and weapons, and directed them on the battlefield. The term "admit" is appropriate since the *Times* still repeatedly spun the dominance of al-Nusra fighters as at-least tolerable in the short term, such as when they warned that

> blacklisting the Nusra Front could backfire. It would pit the United States against some of the best fighters in the insurgency that it aims to support. While some Syrian rebels fear the group's growing power, others work closely with it and admire it — or, at least, its military achievements — and are loath to end their cooperation.

In late February 2012, CBS News interviewed Secretary of State Hillary Clinton. Though she was a hardliner and would spend her last year as secretary pushing Obama to escalate, in this interview she was forced to defend the president's position that he would aid the rebels, but without committing enough resources to ensure their success. Clinton told the CBS reporter:

> We know al Qaeda — Zawahiri is supporting the opposition in Syria. Are we supporting al Qaeda in Syria? Hamas is now supporting the opposition. Are we supporting Hamas in Syria?

Clinton was almost certainly referring to the Reuters article, "Al-Zawahiri Urges Muslim Support for Opposition," which her staffer, and later President Joe Biden's national security adviser, Jake Sullivan, had emailed to her two weeks before, noting, "AQ is on our side in Syria." She clearly understood that "supporting" an insurgency of which al Qaeda is a significant part is essentially supporting them too. Secretary Clinton continued:

> So, I think ... despite the great pleas that we hear from those people who are being ruthlessly assaulted by Assad ... if you're a military planner or if you're a secretary of state and you're trying to figure out do you have the elements of an opposition that is actually viable, we don't see that.

That should have been the end of the argument for intervention. This was only three days after the first "Friends of Syria" meeting. Apparently, the secretary was not inspired. Yet Clinton still insisted on spending the rest of 2012 obstructing UN Secretary General Kofi Annan's efforts at real diplomacy. Her State Department continued to set up "Friends of Syria" conferences in Tunisia and Qatar to organize foreign efforts to create new governments in exile to take over the country, which she had already conceded, when defending Obama's hesitancy, was really an impossible task. As former CIA and National Security Council official Flynt Leverett told the author in the summer of 2012, the U.S. was coordinating the entire international effort against Assad and bore primary responsibility, while Secretary Clinton was refusing to engage in any negotiations that did not include Assad's removal as a poison-pill precondition. They would not settle for a deal. Their forces were already at work on the ground.

The Syrian National Council (SNC) was initially created by Dick Cheney's daughter and now-Congresswoman Liz Cheney when she ran the Iran-Syria Operations Group (ISOG) at the State Department under George W. Bush. The SNC included exiled members of the Muslim Brotherhood and was also the Obama administration's planned government-in-exile, at first. The idea was to install them at the end of an international agreement to be achieved at Geneva in 2012, which never succeeded. In April 2012, State Department spokesmen, when questioned by reporter Reese Erlich, could not name a democratic group within the SNC. "The SNC is faction-ridden. We're trying to find a horse we can ride, but we're not having much luck," a State official admitted.

By October, Clinton officially admitted that the SNC was no longer considered to be credible leaders of the opposition. Its successor, the National Coalition for Syrian Revolutionary and Opposition Forces, fared no better.

As soon as she left office in early 2013, Clinton placed a story in the *New York Times* which criticized Obama for not following through and giving her, Secretary of Defense Leon Panetta and CIA Director David Petraeus the authority they needed to push a real regime change. She made the same complaint in her memoir *Hard Choices*.

However, the month before, in December 2012, even Hillary's State Department declared that Jabhat al-Nusra was an "alias" for al Qaeda in Iraq and added them to the terrorist list. This provoked dozens of other rebel groups to protest that "We are all Jabhat al-Nusra."

Before his death, Osama bin Laden had insisted on a name change in order to make al Qaeda seem more palatable. The same group, after a failed "rebranding" as Jaish al-Fatah and then Jabhat Fateh al-Sham, is now known as Hayat Tahrir al-Sham. They have primarily been financed by the Saudis, Qataris and Turks. Many of them are veterans of Iraq War II, where they fought against U.S. forces. Though terrorist advocates such as the Middle East Institute's Charles Lister sometimes insist it is not so, they are still sworn loyal to Ayman al-Zawahiri and al Qaeda. They publicly insisted so a few days after their leader al-Jolani tried to subtly distance the group from al Qaeda in a TV interview.

"This is just a simple way of returning the favor to our Syrian brothers that fought with us on the lands of Iraq," a Nusra fighter in Syria told the *New York Times*. That April, two months after Clinton acknowledged Zawahiri's interest in Assad's overthrow, the *Wall Street Journal* reported on massive new shipments of communications gear and training for the "rebels" to eavesdrop on government forces. This gave a huge boost to the insurgency.

Foreign Affairs, the flagship journal of the Council on Foreign Relations, ran numerous articles supporting the policy of backing the jihadists, without bothering to couch it as support for the Free Syrian Army. These included "The Moderate Face of Al Qaeda" and "The Good and Bad of Ahrar Al-Sham: An Al Qaeda-Linked Group Worth Befriending." One article was blatantly titled "Accepting al Qaeda." It even featured an old picture of Osama bin Laden and Ayman al-Zawahiri sitting together at the top of the piece to make sure the irony was not lost. "The right Salafis can make all the difference," added the Atlantic Council. The U.S.A. must fight for al Qaeda and those who are sworn loyal to them because we prefer them to Assad. And why? Because Assad is friends with Iran. Not that Iran, Syria or Hezbollah knocked our towers down. But that was their order of priorities. Not only the neoconservatives, but virtually the entire American foreign policy establishment supported this line.

To help illustrate the absurdity of all this, in 2012 the U.S. was still fighting a CIA drone war in Iraq against the last of the Iraqi Sunni-based insurgency, chasing them across the border into Syria where they suddenly became useful "moderate rebels" in the fight against Assad. At the same time, thousands of fighters from Iraqi Shi'ite militias, such as Donald Rumsfeld's old friends in ISCI's Badr Brigade, members of Iraq's ruling coalition, also came to Syria to fight — for the regime, alongside the Iranian Quds Force and Lebanese Hezbollah. The *New York Times* condemned Iraqi PM Maliki for his intervention against al Qaeda in Iraq in Syria.

It was the same thing with the Afghans. Many Taliban fighters fleeing the violence of Obama's Afghan "surge" at the beginning of the decade fled to Syria, where the U.S. was on their side, supporting their fight against the Shi'ite-aligned regime. After ISIS took over western Iraq and the Iraqi Shi'ite militias went home to fight them there. Iran then recruited hundreds of Afghan Hazaras — Shi'ites who largely support the Afghan government in Kabul and in turn have been supported by the U.S. since 2001 — to travel to Syria, to fight for the state in alliance with Lebanese Hezbollah, Shi'ite Iraqis and Iran against the American-Saudi-al Qaeda coalition.

Ahrar al-Sham, the Muslim Brotherhood-associated group mentioned above, was cofounded by Hassan Aboud, whose brother was a leader of Jabhat al-Nusra, according to Michael Jonsson at the Swedish Defense Research Agency. He had been released from prison in a general amnesty granted by Assad under direct pressure from the U.S., its NATO allies and NGOs like Amnesty International. When many of these men, including Aboud, turned out to be terrorist butchers, the hawks then blamed Assad for releasing them, claiming he only did so to make the rest of the insurgency look bad. Though American hawks widely parroted this narrative, it was soundly refuted by scholars and experts such as Joshua Landis and Aymenn Al-Tamimi. It was the "rebels" and the Arab League who had insisted on the opening of the prisons. Assad's May 2011 amnesty was a "key demand of the opposition," even according to the *Washington Post*. Just as with his repeal of the law banning female teachers from wearing headscarves, Assad's release of Muslim Brotherhood and other Islamist figures from prison was an obvious attempt to appease the religious right. It was not some wily scheme to make the protesters seem like extremists by polluting their democratic purity with otherwise-unwelcome terrorists. The protesters never claimed they were being entrapped at the time, only that the early releases were not enough.

In fact, Saudi Arabia was emptying its prisons of both criminals and political prisoners and sending them off to fight in Syria for al-Nusra, which itself had grown out of the American prisons of Iraq War II. Al Qaeda in Iraq, which since 2006 had called itself the Islamic State of Iraq (ISI), was then led by a man named Abu Bakr al-Baghdadi. He and his group of leaders of al-Zarqawi's old terrorist movement had forged their cadre inside the American prison at Camp Bucca in Iraq's south during the war, and had been released in an amnesty by the United States. In the summer of 2011, Baghdadi sent still-current al-Nusra leader Abu Mohammed al-Jolani, who had fought U.S. marines in Fallujah in Iraq War II, across the border into Syria to relaunch their war. During the chaos of the Iraqi civil war, Assad had allowed more than a million refugees into Syria. Many of them later joined in the uprising against him.

As Barack Obama's deputy national security adviser Ben Rhodes later admitted,

> There was a slight absurdity to the fact that we were debating options to provide military support to the opposition at the same time that we were deciding to designate al-Nusra, a big chunk of that opposition, as a terrorist organization. So there was a kind of a schizophrenia that's inherent in a lot of U.S. foreign policy that came to a head in Syria.

But the problem was not that they were supporting terrorists. It was that labeling them as such would make it more difficult to support them:

> Al-Nusra was probably the strongest fighting force within the opposition, and while there were extremist elements in the group, it was also clear that the more moderate opposition was fighting side by side with al-Nusra. I argued that labeling al-Nusra as terrorists would alienate the same people we want to help, while giving al-Nusra less incentive to avoid extremist affiliations.

The administration increased support for the "rebels" in late 2012. After National Security Agency contractor-whistleblower Edward Snowden leaked his cache of documents to the *Washington Post* in 2013, they reported that the CIA was spending a billion dollars per year on the new "Timber Sycamore" program, coordinating this support for the so-called Free Syrian Army with their Middle Eastern allies. This included the Northern Storm Brigade, Nour al-Din al-Zenki, Harakat Hazm, Harakat Shabaab al-Mujahideen, Jaysh al-Islam, the al Hamza Group and others who were fighting essentially as auxiliaries under the al-Nusra Front. A former senior administration official told the *New York Times* it had to be secret because they knew it was illegal, and "We needed plausible deniability in case the arms got into the hands of al-Nusra." America's allies were spending even more.

For years, the media cited this expanded CIA program as though U.S. support for the insurgency began in 2013 even though, as shown above, it started in 2011. Many of the very same outlets had been reporting on covert intervention there since at least early 2012. Four years later, in 2015, after the Pentagon began a short-lived program of backing a small group of so-called moderate fighters, these same media organizations completely ignored all prior knowledge of the CIA programs and pretended to believe this was the beginning of Obama's "minor" intervention in Syria. That military program failed almost immediately because the "moderate" fighters all wanted to fight against the Assad government, not against ISIS.

It is true that the hawks mostly insisted that they supported only supposedly moderate Free Syrian Army forces, but this was only so much deniability and obfuscation. Fighters, money and weapons are all fungible, and as sometimes-Nusra-sympathetic reporter Mitchell Prothero told the author, this new version of al Qaeda had learned the lesson of the local Iraqi Sunnis' "Awakening" betrayal of 2006 and 2007. They had decided instead to "play well" with other insurgent groups. This, combined with their superior financial and military power, meant that from the beginning of 2012 Nusra was the dominant force inside the insurgency. Later, their front Jaish al-Fatah (the Army of Conquest) eventually became the official umbrella organization behind the entire uprising.

More than 10,000 men from dozens of different groups were recruited and trained by the CIA in Jordan and Turkey. Thousands of these went on to join the ranks of the al-Nusra Front, bringing their American TOW anti-tank missiles with them.

A former Obama administration official involved with this policy admitted to journalist Andrew Cockburn, "I would not say that Al Qaeda is our ally, but a turnover of weapons is probably unavoidable. I'm fatalistic about that. It's going to happen." A Free Syrian Army leader told the *New York Times* in 2014, "No FSA faction in the north can operate without Nusra's approval." The reporter explained that "Nusra lets groups vetted by the United States keep the appearance of independence, so that they will continue to receive American supplies."

In 2014 and 2015, two FSA groups armed by the CIA, the Hazm Movement and Syrian Revolutionary Front, were both overrun by their al-Nusra allies who stole all their supplies, including TOW anti-tank missiles. This was revenge for the Obama administration's limited strikes against a small segment of al-Nusra that was accused of targeting the West.

Among the so-called moderate militias was the Northern Storm Brigade. These were the men that Senator John McCain snuck into Syria to meet and pose in a now-infamous photo opportunity with their fighters on the meeting house's front porch. This Syrian militia had fought against U.S. forces as part of the Sunni-based insurgency in Iraq War II and happily admitted it to *Time* magazine in April 2013, a month before John McCain went over to meet with them. It is unknown whether they fought directly for Zarqawi's group, but they certainly would have been considered "foreign fighter" AQI terrorists by the United States military during the second Iraq war.

The Northern Storm Brigade was the same group that three months later kidnapped Israeli-American journalist Steven Sotloff and sold him to ISIS, who then beheaded him. They were already known to be guilty of kidnapping and murdering Lebanese Shi'ite pilgrims before McCain met with them, while insisting that U.S. intelligence could easily "vet" these fighters for the proper amount of "moderation." Inaccurate internet claims that the Northern Storm members pictured with McCain were the leaders of ISIS were widely "fact-checked" and denounced by all good parroting puppets in the media, but they never conceded that McCain's friends really were just one degree of separation away from the worst of the worst, and complicit in their most heinous crimes.

Liwa al Tawheed, Liwa al Islam and Suqor al-Sham were considered good, moderate fighters, backed for two years by the American CIA. They all went over to al-Nusra in the fall of 2013.

The al-Farouq Brigade were also considered liberal moderates worth supporting by the United States. They said they wanted to hold elections and respect minority rights. But then, in 2013, al-Farouq's military commander, Abu Sakkar, was shown on video eating the heart or liver of a dead Syrian army soldier while his men cheered him on. He told the BBC, "If we don't get help, a no-fly zone, heavy weapons, we will do worse. You've seen nothing yet." In truth, they never supported any freedom but the right to install an Islamist dictatorship.

Jaysh al-Islam (the Army of Islam), backed by Saudis, was founded in September 2013. It was led by Zahran Alloush, son of Sheikh Abdullah Mohammed Alloush, a Saudi religious scholar and prominent anti-Shi'ite zealot. According to journalist Reese Erlich, they said they would "wash the filth of the Rashida [an anti-Shi'ite slur] from Greater Syria." They ended up joining the "Islamic Front" that December with Ahrar al-Sham and Jabhat al-Nusra. Later that month, they massacred dozens of Druze and Alawite civilians in the town of Adra.

The Turkish and Qatari-backed Faylaq al-Rahman was another supposedly moderate rebel group. But it turns out that they, too, were murderers. Authors of a United Nations report credibly accused them of indiscriminately shelling civilian neighborhoods in Damascus.

For years, the U.S. supported the group Nour al-Din al-Zenki as part of the Free Syrian Army with massive amounts of money and weapons, including TOW missiles. This continued even after a group of them were caught on camera beheading a 19-year-old Palestinian refugee they accused of fighting with the regime. They held his head up for the camera, laughing, and proudly posted the video of their savagery on the internet. Former Ambassador Robert Ford then warned that "Zenki needs to fairly, publicly hold accountable the killer and his commander. If they lack discipline, they are useless." His line still had not been crossed.

Nobody seems to know of any, but even if there were powerful militias composed of very decent democratic citizens taking part in this war on the insurgents' side, at the end of the day they would still be nothing but a battalion in Abu Mohammed al-Jolani's al-Nusra army. Any victory they accomplished would have ultimately been for Ayman al-Zawahiri.

Over the years, thousands of jihadists, both Syrians and foreign fighters from around the Middle East, fought for different subgroups at different times, mostly depending on who was paying best. The pro-intervention hawk Charles Lister is from the Saudi-, UAE- and Qatari-funded Middle East Institute, and the Qatari-funded Brookings Institute Doha Center. He admitted in 2013 that the American and Saudi "joint operations rooms" in Jordan and Turkey, where they were coordinating the insurrection, could not prevent al-Nusra from vacuuming up all the so-called moderate fighters the allies had been training and deploying in Syria. The *New York Times* also admitted that the CIA could not prevent their weapons and trained fighters from going to al-Nusra. Instead, they saw it as a shame that, "Although the Nusra Front was widely seen as an effective fighting force against Mr. Assad's troops, its al Qaeda affiliation made it impossible for the Obama administration to provide direct support for the group."

But that was not true. In the spring of 2015, Lister admitted that the U.S.-led operations room in Turkey was "instrumental in facilitating" al-Nusra's alliance with the FSA as they launched their successful attempt to seize the Idlib Province with U.S.-provided TOW missiles and suicide truck bombs. As Lister told Congress, "[T]here still remains no better alternative to cooperating with al Qaeda, and thus facilitating its prominence." Jamal Khashoggi, an adviser to the Saudi government who was later murdered and dismembered by Crown Prince Mohammed bin Salman, gave credit to Saudi Arabia and Turkey for the terrorists' capture of Idlib Province. He told the *New York Times* that, "coordination between Turkish and Saudi intelligence has never been as good as now." The extent of Lister's support for Syrian terrorists is detailed in Max Blumenthal's book, *The Management of Savagery*.

As crazy as it was to attack Iraq in 2003, imagine if Saddam Hussein had been right in the middle of trying to put down an al Qaeda-led insurrection at the time, and that instead of helping Hussein, or at least giving him the space to win that fight within his own borders, George W. Bush had instead armed Zarqawi to help AQI defeat the Ba'athists. That was essentially what Barack Obama was doing in Syria. Meanwhile, the leadership of the Republican Party in Congress was egging him on all along to double down and finish the job.

During Iraq War II, the entire Sunni-based insurgency had been labeled terrorists due to the small number of them fighting under Abu Musab al-Zarqawi's group. Now the Zarqawiites were by far the dominant force in the Syrian uprising, but no matter what they did, it seemed there was nothing they could do to discredit the fight against Assad.

In addition to killing or wounding approximately 100,000 Syrian Arab Army soldiers, the various insurgent groups committed war crimes from the very beginning. They murdered children, used suicide car and truck bombs against civilian and military targets, blindly shelled civilian neighborhoods, used torture, carried out mass-executions of captured army soldiers, executed people with crucifixions and beheadings. They also targeted religious minorities, massacring Druze and Christians who refused to convert. They occupied the last ancient towns and villages in the world whose Christian sects still speak ancient Aramaic, killing or displacing the local populations. Bin Ladenites are as they do.

The Mythical Moderates

Barack Obama later admitted that he knew all along that backing the "moderate" rebels could never work, telling the *New York Times*'s Thomas Friedman that Hillary Clinton's preferred policy of arming "moderate" rebels to take over Syria has

> always been a fantasy. This idea that we could provide some light arms or even more sophisticated arms to what was essentially an opposition made up of former doctors, farmers, pharmacists and so forth, and that they were going to be able to battle not only a well-armed state but also a well-armed state backed by Russia, backed by Iran, a battle-hardened Hezbollah, that was never in the cards. There's not as much capacity as you would hope.

Of course, this army of mythical moderates would also be expected to fight the worst part of their own side, al-Nusra, ISIS, Ahrar al-Sham and the rest of the extremists among the rebels. Not that this reality deterred him from funneling in billions of dollars in money and weapons, which virtually all ended up in the hands of the jihadists who tore Syrian society to shreds with them before eventually being defeated anyway.

Senator John McCain of Arizona and 2012 presidential candidate Mitt Romney, could only attack Obama for not doing enough to pursue this disastrous and already-failed policy.

But Obama essentially shared John McCain's doctrine, even if he was afraid to send the B-52s to Damascus. This was the same foreign policy program of Jimmy Carter, Ronald Reagan, George Bush Sr., Bill Clinton and second term-George W. Bush: the U.S.A. backs Saudi terrorists at war with our enemies; the Soviets in Afghanistan, Serbs in the former Yugoslavia, Gaddafi in Libya, Shi'ites in Iran, the Alawites and Shi'ite Ba'athists in Syria, Hezbollah in Lebanon or wherever it is deemed necessary. The American people simply must tolerate the blowback. Obama governed as a conservative Democrat, and a centrist on foreign policy, indistinguishable from Hillary Clinton. Though his actions in Syria were an outright betrayal of the American people, it was not out of disloyalty to the American national security state. That is how Washington, D.C. does business. The government serves its clients. These include arms dealers, spies, foreign princes and prime ministers, but not the American people.

George W. Bush's Iraq War II turned western Iraq into a boiling cauldron of radical Sunni-based insurgency. This was a terrible error. But with the "redirection" policy, he and later Obama decided to double that disaster by going right back to supporting these bin Ladenite mercenaries in Syria to weaken Iran. That was no accident.

The truth is that the Free Syrian Army of so-called moderate rebels was always a sham. Some insurgents had to deal with the Americans to get their money and weapons. But the fight always belonged to al-Nusra, Ahrar al-Sham, Jaysh al-Islam and other terrorist groups, most of whom got their money and weapons directly from America's Persian Gulf allies. They fought "side by side," as people say, for years all across Syria against Assad with U.S. and allied support. As one "activist" who worked with the insurgents in Deraa explained to *The National* out of the UAE,

> The FSA and al-Nusra join together for operations, but they have an agreement to let the FSA lead for public reasons, because they don't want to frighten Jordan or the West. Operations that were really carried out by Al-Nusra are publicly presented by the FSA as their own.

A "leading FSA commander" gave great thanks to al-Nusra for the help and explained that, "The face of al-Nusra cannot be to the front. It must be behind the FSA, for the sake of Jordan and the international community." As William Van Wagenen noted, the American media long went along with this scam, referring to "rebel offensives" and describing al-Nusra and FSA territory as "opposition-held" to obscure the fact that the "opposition" was the enemy from the last war, and they were still head-chopping crazies. Charles Lister conceded to the *New York Times* that "It's inevitable that any weapons supplied by a regional state like Qatar will be used at least in joint operations with Jabhat al-Nusra — if not shared with the group."

The worst of al Qaeda's shills in the American and British media and think tanks, including Lister, the Daily Beast's Michael Weiss and Roy Gutman, the *Washington Post*'s Josh Rogin, the Intercept's Murtaza Hussein, CNN's Bilal Abdul Kareem, Clarissa Ward and S.E. Cupp, Bloomberg News's Eli Lake, Bellingcat's Eliot Higgins, WINEP's Aaron Zelin, Amnesty International's Kristyan Benedict, Ambassador Robert Ford, the Hudson Institute's Michael Doran, former FBI agent Clint Watts, Human Rights Watch director Kenneth Roth and their "emergencies director" Peter Bouckaert, along with all the usual neoconservative suspects such as Max Boot, Bill Kristol and the Kagans, will never live down their disgrace and dishonor. They cry all day about Assad's atrocities in putting down the insurrection, but they will never admit that the war would never have lasted beyond the first year if it had not been for U.S. and allied intervention, which they had no right to do. They only prolonged the conflict that their side inevitably lost, costing hundreds of thousands of innocent civilians' lives. Instead, they continue to insist that the Obama administration had not done enough to win. But they cannot describe what victory would look like beyond vague allusions to "democracy" the terrorists they support would never have delivered.

On the contrary, heroic journalists such as Patrick Cockburn of the *Independent*, Robert Parry and Joe Lauria of Consortium News, Daniel McAdams at the Ron Paul Institute, Bernard from the blog Moon of Alabama, Mark Perry of the *American Conservative*, Sharmine Narwani of Mideast Shuffle, Gareth Porter of Truthout.org, Max Abrams of Northeastern University, authors Christopher Phillips, Reese Erlich, Christopher Davidson, Charles Glass and Mark Curtis, Brad Hoff of LevantReport.com, Professor Joshua Landis of the University of Oklahoma, Justin Raimondo of Antiwar.com, David Stockman of the Contra Corner, Matt Lee from the Associated Press, David Enders of the McClatchey newspaper chain, syndicated columnist Eric Margolis, economist Jeffrey Sachs, Peter Hitchens from the *Daily Mail*, former British ambassador to Syria, Peter Ford, Alastair Crooke of the *Observer* and independent journalist Elijah Magnier saw through the lies and told the truth about this treason in real time. Honorable mention goes to Max Blumenthal of the Gray Zone Project, who admittedly fell for the false narrative for the first couple of years, but later turned around and accomplished important journalism on the war.

Anyone who has told the truth about America's war in Syria has been smeared as an "Assad apologist." This is nonsense. The country is a dictatorship. No one disputes that. Nor does anyone deny the regime and its allies have killed thousands of civilians in its attempt to crush the uprising. But if you listened to the American government and media during this time, they talked about this war as though it began when Assad just decided one morning that he was going to commit genocide against the entire civilian population of his country. And he was doing so just for the fun of it, or perhaps for their daring to show up at a peaceful protest against him. That is why the U.S. and its friends were backing very moderate militia fighters to help defend the country from their leader's aggression. This has been a level of dishonesty that makes the lies about Saddam Hussein's non-existent nuclear bomb project seem believable in comparison.

Former Congresswoman and presidential candidate Tulsi Gabbard, Democrat of Hawaii, served as a major in the National Guard in Iraq War II, stationed at the Balad air base north of Baghdad. This fact alone explains her "controversial" position on Syria. Gabbard had learned the difference between the shirts and the skins in this game. To this day, she supports the permanent drone and special operations wars against the bin Ladenites, broadly defined. But to support those same groups against a secular dictator — especially after the catastrophe of Iraq War II? Why, that would be crazy. This is a woman whose time in the war was spent in a medical support unit, attending to U.S. casualties killed and wounded by al Qaeda in Iraq and their allied groups. Was she supposed to forget their blood for someone else's agenda?

This was the same position as that of Gen. Mike Flynn, President Trump's first national security adviser. He had been the director for intelligence for the top-tier Joint Special Operations Command (JSOC) under Gen. Stanley McChrystal in Iraq War II, as well as McChrystal's right-hand man during the Afghanistan "surge." Flynn is far more of an anti-Iran hawk than Gabbard. He even co-wrote a book with the neoconservative fanatic Michael Ledeen claiming they are the greatest threat in the world. But to support al Qaeda and associated groups against Assad in Syria, just to weaken Iran? No. Flynn did not only oppose the policy in principle. He was the commander of the Defense Intelligence Agency at the time. Flynn's analysts warned in the summer of 2012 that "the Salafists, the Muslim Brotherhood and AQI are the major forces driving the insurgency in Syria." They said al Qaeda could create their own "Salafist principality" in eastern Syria, which was "exactly what the supporting powers to the opposition want, in order to isolate the Syrian regime, which is considered the strategic depth of the Shia expansion (Iraq and Iran)." Flynn's analysts further warned that ISIS even posed a "danger" to western Iraq:

> This creates the ideal atmosphere for AQI to return to its old pockets in Mosul and Ramadi [in western Iraq], and will provide a renewed momentum under the presumption of unifying the jihad among Sunni Iraq and Syria, and the rest of the Sunnis in the Arab world against what it considers one enemy, the dissenters. ISI could also declare an Islamic state through its union with other terrorist organizations in Iraq and Syria, which will create grave danger in regards to unifying Iraq and the protection of its territory.

As Seymour Hersh reported, Gen. Flynn, insubordinate to Obama, started passing intelligence to Assad through Germany to be used to target al-Nusra fighters there. He was fired.

Bill Roggio and Thomas Joscelyn at the Foundation for the Defense of Democracy's Long War Journal are two more anti-Iran hawks who could never bring themselves to support groups who were working directly with and shared the goals of Ayman al-Zawahiri's men just to spite Ayatollah Khamenei.

The CIA and Saudi Arabia's "rebels" would often chant, "Massihiyeh ala Beirut, Allawiyeh ala Taboot!" (Christians to Beirut, Alawites to the grave!) Do those sound like moderate, democratic allies or psychopathic, genocidal bin Ladenites? One could follow a path of headless corpses to the answer.

The Islamic State

The counterfactual is obvious. Barack Obama could have informed our regional allies that he was very sorry about their feelings and agendas, but especially after September 11th and the disaster of Iraq War II, America had only one overriding goal for its entire Middle Eastern strategy: keeping radical Sunni bin Ladenite militias down at all costs. Our first priority then would be to stop creating new, lawless open spaces in which they can thrive. He might have insisted that be their policy too. That would have been consistent with the stated objectives of the War on Terrorism. The U.S. should not be backing dictators. That was a significant part of what motivated the attack on this country September 11th. But our government surely should not be supporting bin Ladenite insurgencies against them either.

"Coordinating our allies' support" for various groups in Syria was the thinnest pretext of plausible deniability. Everyone knew the deal. When asked why the U.S. was unable to prevent tiny client states like Qatar from arming al Qaeda fighters, a former American adviser to one of the Persian Gulf states told Andrew Cockburn, "They didn't want to."

Journalist Ben Swann put it straight to President Obama in 2012:

> You mentioned about al Qaeda during your speech, going after al Qaeda in Afghanistan, certainly going after them in Yemen as well, and yet there's some concern about the U.S. funding the Syrian opposition when there are a lot of reports that al Qaeda is kind of heading up that opposition. How do you justify the two?

The president responded:

> Well, I share that concern, and so what we've done is to say we will provide non-lethal assistance to Syrian opposition leadership that are committed to a political transition, committed to an observance of human rights. We're not going to just dive in and get involved with a

civil war that in fact involves some elements of people who are genuinely trying to get a better life but also involve some folks who would over the long term do the United States harm.

Maybe the president really believed that he had added enough caveats to his orders to the CIA and State Department to make sure that the administration stayed only treason-adjacent rather than admitting to himself that he was putting the American people's security forces directly at the service of their only real enemies in the world. But the results speak for themselves.

After two years of clandestine Western and Arab support for the Sunni insurgency in Syria, in the late spring of 2013 the primary bin Ladenite factions split in a fight over control of eastern Syrian oil resources. The Iraqi-dominated faction, led by Abu Bakr al Baghdadi, which had long-ago renamed itself the Islamic State of Iraq (ISI), now added "and al-Sham" ("the Levant") to the end of their name (ISIS or ISIL in the West; al Dawlah al-Islameyah fi Iraq al-Sham, or *Daesh*, in Arabic). The Iraqis split away from the Syrian-dominated faction, al-Nusra, led by Abu Mohammed al-Jolani, who stayed loyal to al Qaeda leader Ayman al-Zawahiri, who is supposedly still hiding out somewhere in Pakistan. Zawahiri attempted to send Ahrar al-Sham's Abu Khalid al-Suri as an emissary to negotiate a resolution. ISIS leader Baghdadi instead killed al-Suri, consolidated power over the north-central city of Raqqa, and declared a state in eastern Syria. (Raqqa is usually considered to be in Syria's east since it is so far from the major western population centers, and much of the rest of the country's east is barren desert.)

This fight represented a doctrinal split among the terrorists as well. Zawahiri's policy had been to focus on fighting the "Far Enemy," the United States, until the superpower was exhausted and went home like the USSR at the end of the 1980s. Only then, he argued, could they attempt to wage their local revolutions. In the case of opportunities like the war in Syria, he thought they should focus on fighting in the near term and worry about trying to create a new state much later on. What would be the point of carving out fixed positions if the U.S. would just send in the Air Force and Marines to destroy them again? But Baghdadi wanted his Islamic State right then. Zawahiri could write his law, but he could not enforce it. Osama bin Laden and Abu Musab al-Zarqawi's Iraqi descendants would break off and do things their own way. The "Islamic State of Iraq" was no longer a delusional name for a disparate group of defeated insurgents. They finally controlled real territory. Ten thousand foreign fighters — Saudis, Libyans, Egyptians, Tunisians, Chechens, Chinese Uighurs, dozens, possibly hundreds of Americans and thousands of Europeans, sided with ISIS.

Early that summer, Patrick Cockburn reported in the *Independent* that the Shi'ite Iraqi army had mostly deserted their posts in Iraq's predominantly Sunni northwest, leaving it wide open to assault. The chauvinist and exclusivist policies of American-installed Shi'ite prime minister Nouri al Maliki had rendered much of western Iraq an enemy nation, outside of Baghdad's protection or influence. The soldiers stationed in Mosul felt as though they had been abandoned deep inside foreign territory without sufficient force protection. So they fled back to safety behind Shi'ite lines. In Baghdad, politicians told Cockburn they were terrified that U.S. support for the uprising in Syria was "reenergizing" the worst remnants of the previously defeated Sunni insurgency in Iraq and threatened to restart the whole civil war.

Six months later, in January 2014, ISIS temporarily hoisted a black flag above a government building in Sunni Fallujah, just west of Baghdad. Asked about this, President Obama dismissed any concerns about ISIS, calling them the "junior varsity" team compared to al Qaeda, and no threat to Iraq or anyone else.

A few months after that, one of the members of this team of nobodies-to-worry-about, an Algerian who had fought for ISIS in Syria, murdered four people at a Jewish museum in Brussels, Belgium. It was the first of many ISIS terrorist attacks in Europe and the United States in the years to come. But it was merely a hint of the shadow preparing to fall across Iraq just two weeks later.

As was both eminently predictable and predicted by many, in June 2014 ISIS rolled right back into Iraq in Toyota Hilux pickup trucks that were almost certainly some of the very same ones the Saudi princes and Hillary Clinton's State Department had previously given to the Free Syrian Army. ISIS sacked Mosul, Fallujah, Tikrit, Baiji, Samarra and much of the rest of western Iraq within weeks. They seized billions of dollars' worth of U.S. weapons and equipment that Bush and Obama had left behind for the Iraqi army. From the balcony of the Great Mosque of Al-Nuri in Mosul, Baghdadi declared himself the divinely ordained "Caliph Ibrahim," ruler of the new Islamic Caliphate. His forces soon threatened the capital of Baghdad and Irbil in northern Iraqi Kurdistan.

The preposterous war propaganda of the Bush administration and wildest daydreams of Osama bin Laden while locked away in his Pakistani attic exile had actually come true. The terrorists had carved a new Islamist Caliphate the size of Great Britain out of the sands of western Iraq and eastern Syria. He could never have done it without the assistance of the United States of America in the hands of George W. Bush and Barack Obama.

Just two-and-a-half years after U.S. military forces had finally been withdrawn, they were on their way to invade again. Iraq War III had begun.

Chapter Eleven:
Iraq War III

"Daesh is our response to
your support for the Da'wa."
— Saudi Foreign Minister
Prince Saud al-Faisal

"Are we becoming the
Iranian Air Force?"
— John McCain

"It is impossible to
articulate a clear path to
the desired end state."
— Fred and Kimberly Kagan

Another Fake Casus Belli

Even at the height of the Islamic State, after they seized western Iraq in June 2014 and their forces numbered as many as 100,000 men, the U.S. still did not need to intervene. ISIS represented a powerful alliance of ex-Ba'athist army officers and bin Ladenite terrorists. But despite their military successes, the psychotic and chaotic style of the bin Ladenites was always sure to be their undoing. The Islamic State was surrounded by enemies: the Iraqi Kurds and Shi'ites to their east, Saudi Arabia to their south, the Kingdom of Jordan and Ba'athist Syria to their west and Turkey to their north. Turkey and Saudi Arabia together had spent billions in support of the Islamic State but would never have allowed them to invade their territory.

That being the case, the fledgling caliphate made the terrible decision to pick fights with almost all their new neighbors, fights they could not possibly win. For example, at their first opportunity, they threw hundreds of fighters at the now-super-majority Shi'ite Iraqi capital of Baghdad, which they had no hope whatsoever of overthrowing. Ayatollah Sistani called for all able-bodied Shi'ite men to join their local militias, the Popular Mobilization Units (PMUs), to fight the bin Ladenite enemy. It was more than enough to defend the capital. Next, ISIS took on the Iraqi Kurds, who quickly mobilized their *peshmerga* militia forces to prepare for war.

As Patrick Cockburn said, ISIS was sort of an "Islamist Khmer Rouge," comparable to Pol Pot and his insane, auto-genocidal Cambodian Communist revolutionaries of the mid-to-late 1970s. The Islamic State was far too unstable to last in power in such a dangerous region. But that does not seem to be why President Obama delayed intervention for nearly two months after the fall of Mosul. Why did he wait until early August to start the air campaign in support of Iraqi government forces? The fact that ISIS had taken over all of western Iraq was all the cause he needed to begin. Instead, he waited until Baghdad and Irbil were both threatened, seemingly as a bit of extortion, to make them remember why they need us more than their friends next door, the Iranians. They wanted the Iraqis to beg first, push out Prime Minister Nuri al-Maliki — whom Vice President Joe Biden had just intervened to save four years before — and replace him with someone they hoped would be more pliable. Next was Haider al-Abadi, who was also from the Da'wa Party and no less Iran-leaning than his predecessor. The Iraqis, Obama declared, were

> going to have to show us that [they] are willing and ready to try and maintain a unified Iraqi government that is based on compromise. We're not going to let them create some caliphate through Syria and

Iraq. But we can only do that if we know that we have got partners on the ground who are capable of filling the void.

As analyst Ted Snider observed, "That was a clear reference to a new government. Obama used the threat of the Islamic State as leverage for regime change in Iraq." Well, prime minister change anyway.

When the time came to launch the war, the immediate excuse for it quickly fell apart. A small group of Yazidis, a small ethno-religious sect from northern Iraq who remained after Iraq War II, were on the run from ISIS. Obama declared war — again without bothering to ask Congress for authorization — in the name of rescuing the fleeing Yazidis from the top of Mount Sinjar in the Nineveh province. The next day, CNN's Pentagon reporter, Barbara Starr, said that when U.S. special operations forces' helicopters arrived at the mountain, it was too late to save anyone. ISIS had already captured many of them. Everyone left who had wanted to flee had already been rescued by the Syrian Kurdish People's Protection Units (YPG). The rest simply waved the Americans off. They had no intention of leaving the mountain.

Still, as a fake excuse to enter the war, it worked. The next month the U.S. started bombing ISIS targets in Syria too. But President Obama and his administration swore there would be "no boots on the ground."

Israel's Role

The Israeli government and their lobby in the United States pushed hard for intervention against Assad in Syria. As the *New York Times* reported, when Obama increased support for the insurgency with CIA Director John O. Brennan's Timber Sycamore program in 2013, he had done so "because of intense lobbying by foreign leaders, including King Abdullah II of Jordan and Prime Minister Benjamin Netanyahu of Israel."

There is no mystery why. It was the same old strategy since David Wurmser's "Clean Break" and "Crumbling" papers in 1996: separate Iran from Syria to hurt Hezbollah in Lebanon. As former Israeli prime minister and defense minister Ehud Barak explained to CNN in April 2012, regime change against Assad in Damascus,

> will be a major blow to the radical axis, major blow to Iran. ... It's the only kind of outpost of the Iranian influence in the Arab world ... and it will weaken dramatically both Hezbollah in Lebanon and Hamas and Islamic Jihad in Gaza.

In September 2013, then-outgoing Israeli ambassador to the United States Michael Oren explained to the *Jerusalem Post*, "The initial message about the Syrian issue was that we always wanted Bashar Assad to go, we always preferred the bad guys who weren't backed by Iran to the bad guys who were backed by Iran." When the reporter asked him if this was still the case "even if the other 'bad guys' were affiliated to al Qaeda," Oren responded:

> We understand that they are pretty bad guys. Still, the greatest danger to Israel is by the strategic arc that extends from Tehran, to Damascus to Beirut. And we saw the Assad regime as the keystone in that arc. That is a position we had well before the outbreak of hostilities in Syria. With the outbreak of hostilities, we continued to want Assad to go.

Nine months later, a mere two weeks after American support for the jihad in Syria has blown up so badly in everyone's face that the jihadists had conquered all of western Iraq, the just-retired Michael Oren explained at the "Aspen Ideas Festival":

> What I'm going to say is harsh, perhaps a little edgy. But if we have to choose the lesser of evils here, the lesser evil is the Sunnis over the Shi'ites. It's the lesser evil. It's a terrible evil, believe me. Again, they've just taken out 1,700 former Iraqi soldiers and shot them in the field. But who are they fighting against? They're fighting against the proxy [of] Iran, [Assad's government], that's complicit in the murder of 60,000 people in Syria. You know, just do the math. And again, one side is armed with suicide bombers and rockets, the other side has access to military nuclear capability. So, from Israel's perspective, if there's got to be an evil that's going to prevail, let the Sunni evil prevail.

There is no mistake nor moderate rebels here. Oren was referring directly to the new Islamic State that had just conquered western Iraq, including their recent massacre of as many as 1,700 Iraqi Shi'ite air force cadets at Camp Speicher.

Note also that Oren is lying outright. His excuses for this treason — Oren was born in the United States and holds dual citizenship — are first, that Assad is responsible for all deaths on all sides of the war, as though what he really cares about is Assad's human rights record. "Do the math," he says. But the math is that half of those killed were soldiers in the Syrian Arab Army who were fighting to defend Assad's state from the jihadists that America, Israel, Saudi Arabia, Qatar, Jordan and Turkey were supporting against him along with the jihadists' civilian victims. If all casualties on all sides of the war can be blamed on Assad, they could much more easily be put on President Obama, Kings Salman and Abdullah of Saudi Arabia and Jordan, Sheikh al-Thani of Qatar, President Recep Erdoğan of Turkey and Prime Minister Benjamin Netanyahu of Israel. They are the foreign invaders of a sovereign nation. Any one of them, including any American president, would also use violence to put down an armed insurrection, especially one led by al Qaeda. Oren's other excuse, that Iran has a "military nuclear capability," is false. [See Chapter 3.] Even if Iran did have nuclear weapons, it is not clear why that should mandate an Israeli preference for the likes of Baghdadi's Islamic State over Assad's previously stable secular tyranny. The Ayatollah would not start giving nukes he does not have to Syria and Hezbollah to launch a nuclear war he does not want.

Israeli Defense Minister Moshe Ya'alon agreed with Oren. In early 2016, almost two years after the establishment of the caliphate, he expressed what the *Washington Post*'s Adam Taylor called a "widespread belief" among Israeli national security officials at the Herzliya Conference in Tel Aviv, declaring that, "In Syria, if the choice is between Iran and the Islamic State, I choose the Islamic State. They don't have the capabilities that Iran has." Major General Herzi Halevy, the chief of Israeli military intelligence, said the same. He told the conference that Israel "does not want the situation in Syria to end with the defeat of ISIS" since it could cause the major powers to withdraw and leave Israel to face Iran and Hezbollah. Also in 2016, the Israeli Begin-Sadat Center for Strategic Studies argued for stopping short of destroying the Islamic State since it was "taxing" Lebanese Hezbollah, which had come to the defense of the Syrian state. "The Western distaste for brutality and immorality should not obfuscate strategic clarity. Unfortunately, the Obama administration fails to see that its main enemy is Iran."

An Israeli strategist speaking to the *New York Times* was a bit more cautious, saying that as much as they hated Shi'ite power in Syria, being worried about Sunni jihadists meant that they did not want either side to win. Not that they wanted peace. Israel preferred to see the war continue as a stalemate. "Let them both bleed, hemorrhage to death: that's the strategic thinking here."

The British journalist Asa Winstanley from Middle East Monitor collected a master list of important mainstream news articles, especially from the Israeli press, showing extensive Mossad and Israeli Defense Forces (IDF) support for al-Nusra and related fighters in southern Syria. It was shown by the *Wall Street Journal, Foreign Policy*, the *Independent*, War on the Rocks and the Israeli daily *Haaretz*, among others, that Israel's support went far beyond medical care and included financial and material support for as many as 12 different militias. This included paying fighters' salaries and providing weapons, vehicles, fuel and direct air support from Israeli drones. IDF Chief of Staff, Lieutenant General Gadi Eisenkot, after years of official denials, later confirmed it was true. They called it Operation Good Neighbor.

In June 2015, local Druze living in the Israeli-occupied Golan Heights ambushed an Israeli ambulance transporting terrorists, who regularly murdered Syrian Druze, back to the backfield from an Israeli hospital. "Israel stood by our side in a heroic way. We wouldn't have survived without Israel's assistance," Moatasem al-Golani, a spokesman for the insurgent group Fursan al-Joulan, told the *Journal*.

Since near the beginning of the Syrian war, Israel continues to launch thousands of missile and air attacks on regime targets, as well as Iranian and Hezbollah targets in Syria, often in direct support of the insurgency on the ground. Despite all the messaging about the dangers these states and groups pose to Israel, they have done nothing in response.

When asked why Israel gave medical support to Sunni jihadists wounded in the war, but not Shi'ite fighters from the other side, the former director of the Israeli Mossad, Efraim Halevy, explained to a journalist that, "Israel was not specifically targeted by al Qaeda, and therefore it's a different kind of account than we have with Hezbollah."

Apparently, 3,000 dead New Yorkers killed in an attack provoked in-part by Israeli policies and 4,500 dead American G.I.s in Iraq War II fought primarily for Israeli interests do not count for very much in Tel Aviv, or in Washington.

Biden's Half-Truth on Allies and ISIS

To belabor the point since surprising-sounding claims deserve thorough documentation, then-Vice President Joe Biden gave a talk at Harvard University in October 2014 where he explained there was no "moderate middle" among the Syrian insurgency, no "Thomas Jeffersons or James Madisons" hiding behind "a rock or a sand dune," waiting to create a new democratic republic. He did not admit that those merchants and shopkeepers and religious minorities who did make up the moderate middle in Syria supported the current regime, especially in the face of the terrorist opposition. While attempting to deflect blame onto America's clients, Biden still told the truth about the consequences of U.S. policy there:

> What my constant cry was that our biggest problem was our allies. Our allies in the region were our largest problem in Syria. The Turks were great friends, and I've a great relationship with [Turkish President Recep] Erdoğan, who I've just spent a lot of time with, the Saudis, the Emiratis, etc. What were they doing?

> They were so determined to take down Assad and essentially have a proxy Sunni-Shia war, what did they do? They poured hundreds of

millions of dollars and tens of thousands of tons of weapons into anyone who would fight against Assad, except that the people who were being supplied were al-Nusra, and al Qaeda, and the extremist elements of jihadis coming from other parts of the world. If you think I'm exaggerating, take a look. Where did all of this go?

So now what's happening? All of a sudden, everybody is awakened because this outfit called ISIL, which was al Qaeda in Iraq, which when they were essentially thrown out of Iraq, found open space and territory in eastern Syria, work with al-Nusra, who we declared a terrorist group early on, and we could not convince our colleagues to stop supplying them. So, what happened? Now, all of a sudden [now that ISIS has taken over western Iraq] — I don't want to be too facetious — but they have seen the lord.

Now we have — the president's been able to put together a coalition of our Sunni neighbors, because America can't once again go into a [Sunni] Muslim nation and be the aggressor. It has to be led by Sunnis. To go and attack a Sunni organization. And so, what do we have for the first time? Now Saudi Arabia has stopped the funding from going in. Saudi Arabia is allowing training on its soil of American forces under Title 10, open training. The Qataris have cut off their support for the most extreme elements of the terrorist organizations. And the Turks, President Erdoğan told me — he is an old friend — said, "You were right; we let too many people through. Now we are trying to seal the border."

Biden went on to reiterate that there were no reliable "moderate" forces for America to support in Syria and denounced his opponents inside the Obama administration who had favored sending surface-to-air missiles to the insurgents. Biden correctly argued that they would have ended up in the hands of al Qaeda or ISIS, who the United States was at war with by that time.

As truthful as it was, Biden's harangue omitted the most important part of the story. He was trying to create some deniability by blaming the Persian Gulf states and Turkey for their roles, when it had long been public knowledge that David Petraeus and John Brennan's CIA was coordinating the whole project and spending at least a billion dollars a year on it, much more than the hundreds of millions of foreign dollars he mentioned.

Conflict Armament Research (CAR) released a massive study in 2017 in which they traced the majority of the Islamic State's weaponry directly to America and its allies. They were not referring to the weapons the U.S. left behind for the Iraqi army, which ISIS stole after conquering Iraq's west in 2014. These were the weapons America had given their "moderate" terrorist forces in Syria, the weapons they conquered western Iraq with in the first place.

The United States and Saudi Arabia supplied most of this materiel without authorisation, apparently to Syrian opposition forces. This diverted materiel, recovered from IS forces, comprises exclusively Warsaw Pact-calibre weapons and ammunition, purchased by the United States and Saudi Arabia from European Union (EU) Member States in Eastern Europe.

Biden was also wrong to accentuate the role of neighboring Sunni states in this new phase of conflict. Instead, the U.S. would be right back on the side of the Shi'ite Iraqis and their Iranian allies — the same ones they wished they had not fought Iraq War II for — in their fight to smash the Caliphate and liberate western Iraq. The Saudis and Qataris continued to finance the Islamic State, as detailed in an email sent by former Secretary of State Clinton in late September 2014, more than three months after the beginning of Iraq War III. Turkey continued to support them as well.

Another Devastating War

Iraq War III was a disaster for the predominantly Sunni population of western Iraq and eastern Syria. First, they were enslaved by a bunch of bin Ladenite lunatics, and then they were "liberated" by the Americans and their also-Iranian-backed Iraqi Shi'ite allies in the army and PMU militias, the Iranian Quds Force, as well as the Kurdish peshmerga and YPG. The anti-ISIS air war took a devastating toll on civilians in both Iraq and Syria. In what they called "Operation Inherent Resolve," the U.S. and its coalition allies — including Canada, the UK, Australia, Denmark, the Netherlands, France and Belgium — launched more than 30,000 airstrikes on Iraq and Syria from mid-2014 through the end of the war in late-2017. They killed at least 8,000–13,000 Iraqi and Syrian civilians by Airwars.org's very conservative estimate. The western Iraqi city of Fallujah was bombed to smithereens. After an exhaustive on-the-ground investigation of numerous strikes across Iraq and Syria during the ISIS war, the *New York Times* found that civilians were being killed at a rate 31 times higher than the Pentagon would admit.

What explains the fact that almost a year after Iraq War III began, the Obama administration refused to help the western-Iraqi city of Ramadi keep the Islamic State out? The brave war reporter David Enders, previously kidnapped and then thankfully released by al-Nusra in Syria, warned about the coming invasion. Everyone in the government and military were aware as well. Bloomberg News reported that, "The U.S. watched Islamic State fighters, vehicles and heavy equipment gather on the outskirts of Ramadi before the group retook the city in mid-May. But the U.S. did not order airstrikes against the convoys before the battle started."

It makes sense, as administration officials explained, that they were still reluctant to get too bogged down in any more wars. The Iraqi army would have to do all the heavy lifting. But the U.S. ended up bombing the city to bits to drive ISIS out when a little bit of airpower and special operations help could have kept them out in the first place. This was after they had already assisted the effort to drive ISIS out of Hussein's old hometown of Tikrit, and long after they were able to force Maliki from power, so extorting that change was not the answer either. It seems a strange way to fight an ultimately unnecessary war.

The Obama administration was also just starting a brand-new war in Yemen at the same time, so reluctance to get involved in new Middle Eastern quagmires seems like a thin excuse as well. [See Chapter 12.] Maybe the critical difference is that this war was against Saudi Arabia's interests and that one was for them.

Nearly a full year after the declaration of the bin Ladenite "Caliphate," David Petraeus continued to insist that, "the foremost threat to Iraq's long-term stability and the broader regional equilibrium is not the Islamic State; rather, it is [Iraqi] Shi'ite militias, many backed by — and some guided by — Iran." Of course there is something to this, but the United States was in the middle of fighting the second war in a row for these factions. It was Petraeus himself who had built the core of the Iraqi army from the Badr Brigade and helped Maliki finish his sectarian cleansing campaign against the Sunni Arabs of Baghdad back in 2007. This all set the stage for the return of AQI-ISIS to prominence just as the Iraqi government was almost finished eliminating them the first time around.

In March 2015, in Tikrit, the U.S. provided direct air support for Qasem Soleimani's Iranian IRGC along with their allied Iraqi militias in the battle to expel the Islamic State. Chairman of the Joint Chiefs of Staff Martin Dempsey acknowledged that without Iran and the Iraqi militias they supported, the assault on ISIS forces there would have been impossible. The reverse was also true. The U.S. Air Force was again flying in the service of the Ayatollahs. After ISIS fled, the militias took their revenge, destroying hundreds of homes and shops, kidnapping and murdering people. A good portion of the city was destroyed. According to Human Rights Watch, the same kind of revenge attacks were waged against all the smaller towns and villages surrounding the city as well.

As Chris Woods of Airwars.org reported, the town of Hawijah, near Kirkuk, was devastated by a Dutch airstrike on an ISIS bomb factory in 2015. Four or five blocks and entire families were wiped out. A community was destroyed beyond repair. Survivors were never compensated. Few of the houses and little of the infrastructure that was destroyed has ever been rebuilt.

Even supposed "precision" satellite-guided airstrikes cause massive destruction. Targeting can only be as good as the information on which it is based. A bird's eye view can only tell even the best analyst so much. So-called precision strikes also lead to a false sense of confidence on the part of the air forces. They convince themselves they are proceeding at a limited pace and being careful, when in reality they are waging total war. U.S. Army Colonel Amos Fox coined the term "Precision Paradox" when describing America's air war against ISIS, meaning "a situation in which the failed promise of precision strikes — one strike, one kill — generated a creeping wave of destruction across the city" of Mosul.

As many as 12,000 civilians were killed in the battle to expel ISIS from Mosul. The eastern half of the city was captured by the U.S.-Baghdad-Irbil alliance in early 2017. The Old City — old, as in 1,300 years old — as the western half of Mosul was known, was devastated by U.S. and allied airpower in conjunction with the Shi'ite Iraqi army, its associated PMU militias and the Kurdish peshmerga's heavy artillery fire, as well as ISIS's own artillery and armored suicide truck bombers. As many as 5,000 buildings and 130,000 homes were destroyed, decimating Mosul's ancient structures. In one U.S. strike — an attempt to kill two snipers — 105 civilians hiding in a bomb shelter were killed. The last ISIS fighters finally fled at the end of June. A year later, according to Journalist Ben Taub, "journalists were still finding the bodies of women and children on the riverbanks, blindfolded, with their hands tied behind their backs and bullet holes in their skulls." The Mosul morgue had registered nearly 10,000 dead civilians, most killed by shelling and bombing. (They refused to process the corpses of the ISIS fighters.)

In the Islamic State's twin capital city of Raqqa in eastern Syria, the U.S. and allied air and artillery war was just as destructive. In this case, U.S. special operations forces — not wearing boots, but Merrell hiking sneakers — fought with Syrian-Kurdish YPG forces in place of the Iraqi-Kurdish peshmerga and Shi'ite-allied army and militias, since in Syria the Shi'ites were still the U.S.'s primary enemy. A UN study later estimated that 80 percent of the city had been destroyed in what President Trump and Secretary of Defense James Mattis called their "war of annihilation" against the Islamic State and whoever was unlucky enough to have been captured by them. At least two thousand civilians were killed. The city's infrastructure was wrecked. The ruins looked like Dresden, Germany after the allied firebombing of 1945. More than half a million people were forced from their homes.

Russia Returns to the Middle East

In 2017, semi-official CIA spokesman David Ignatius admitted in the *Washington Post*:

> What did the CIA's covert assistance program for Syrian rebels accomplish? Bizarrely, the biggest consequence may be that it helped trigger the Russian military intervention in 2015 that rescued President Bashar al-Assad — achieving the opposite of what the program intended.

U.S. covert action backfiring was not the bizarre part. The details were. America may have been willing to launch Iraq War III to save the Shi'ite regime they wish they had not installed in power in Iraq War II, but even the disastrous rise of the Islamic State was not enough to get President Obama to change his policy in Syria. Weakening the Assad regime was still his primary concern. And while the U.S. might have decided to help the Kurds in northern Syria to resist ISIS, they still would not lift a finger to help the secular Assad government reestablish authority over its own country at the Islamic Caliphate's expense. As the *Los Angeles Times* later wrote about ISIS's invasion of the ancient city of Palmyra in the spring of 2015, nearly a year after the fall of Mosul:

> [A]s Islamic State closed in on Palmyra, the U.S.-led aerial coalition that has been pummeling Islamic State in Syria for the past 18 months took no action to prevent the extremists' advance toward the historic town — which, until then, had remained in the hands of the sorely overstretched Syrian security forces. The U.S. approach in Palmyra contrasted dramatically with the very proactive U.S. bombardment of Kobani during 2014–15 on behalf of U.S.-allied Kurdish militias fending off a furious Islamic State offensive. ...

> In crafting their Syria policy moving forward, U.S. officials face a paradox. They seek to weaken Assad's government, but not so much as to boost Islamic State and other militant factions that initially arose from the chaos of the Syrian conflict. U.S. officials say their goal in aiding rebel factions is not to force a violent overthrow of Assad, but to push his government into negotiating concessions that would ultimately see him leave office.

That was written in March 2016, nearly two full years after support for al Qaeda had already backfired in the form of the Islamic State. Obama's policy was to keep them out of Baghdad and Irbil. But if they could still be used against Assad, then they were still moderate-enough rebels for the U.S. to tolerate and exploit on the western side of the former border. When the Syrian Arab Army (SAA) returned to Palmyra that week with the help of the Russians, State Department spokesman Mark Toner sputtered and stuttered until AP reporter Matt Lee essentially forced him to concede that it was preferable that Assad's government had control of Palmyra rather than the "Caliph Ibrahim," Abu Bakr al-Baghdadi. The director of antiquities there might have agreed, but ISIS had already beheaded him and hanged his corpse from a traffic light.

CIA and allied support for the rest of the insurgency continued as well, as though the absolute worst-case consequences in the creation of the Islamic State had not already taken place. To the hawks, those monsters simply made the rest of the fighters look better. They even continued training insurgents, as was revealed in 2016 when a Jordanian soldier, loyal to ISIS, ambushed and killed three Army Green Berets stationed there on a CIA mission to train "rebels" for the fight against Assad. As September 11th and the Benghazi massacre of 2012 have shown, U.S. support for bin Ladenite mercenaries will never buy their loyalty.

When in the fall of 2015, al-Nusra began to threaten the city of Latakia on the Mediterranean coast, and ISIS threatened to seize the M5 highway between Aleppo and Damascus in preparation for a march on the capital, Vladimir Putin's Russia finally intervened overtly on the side of the Syrian state. They launched massive bombing raids against the CIA's favorite terrorist groups in the country's west, in what was the beginning of the end for the Syrian insurgency. According to the *Washington Post*, the Obama administration had begun to consider cutting support for the insurgency earlier that summer based on the same fear. All the propaganda about the "moderate" FSA aside, at this point their primary role was scoring American TOW anti-tank missiles for al-Nusra. As the *New York Times* admitted, if al-Nusra had not been stopped from taking over Alawite-majority Latakia Province by the Russians, it "almost certainly" would have led to "sectarian mass-murder."

It was ISIS that was threatening to take Damascus from their established position in the Yarmouk Palestinian refugee camp in the capital's suburbs, an area they had seized with the help of the al-Nusra Front.

Thousands of civilians have been killed by Syrian and Russian airstrikes in the war to put down this bin Ladenite insurrection. Chris Woods and his colleagues at Airwars.org have demonstrated that this is so. Casualties have been comparable though to America and its allies' air wars against ISIS in Iraqi cities and Raqqa in Syria's east taking place at the same time. This was terrible, no question, but it shows that it was not true that the Russians were on a mission to help Assad exterminate the civilian population of the country as CNN would have it. They were ruthlessly putting down another part of the same bin Ladenite insurgency that the U.S. had also been fighting for more than a year by that time and in the same manner as the Americans too. Pentagon public relations men like to crow about their high-tech, precision-guided weapons, but as the expert Woods told the author, it is population density, not the type of explosives dropped, which determines civilian casualty rates.

As far as the civilians caught in the crossfire, even then-Secretary of State John Kerry admitted that the Obama administration put those people in that position. The American coalition, in both the pro-terrorist war and the anti-terrorist war in Syria, are responsible for far more deaths and displacement than the Russians.

At least they have been invited by the sovereign government of the country to help defend it from foreign aggression. Even when America has fought against ISIS in Syria, it does so under no legal authorization from the U.S. Congress or the Assad government. As even Obama's special envoy to Syria Michael Ratney explained to Syrian opposition supporters at a meeting in London — where he and Secretary of State John Kerry were secretly recorded — this entire mess was clearly America and its allies' doing. Kerry confessed to Obama's policy but defended it, saying "I think we've put an extraordinary amount of arms in." Ratney added:

> And ... I have to say ... it's a double-edged sword because you give people the ability to defend themselves, but when you pump more weapons into a situation like Syria, it doesn't end well for Syrians, because there is always someone else who is going to pump more weapons in for the other side. The armed groups in Syria get a lot of support, not just from the United States but from other partners.

At this point, Kerry interrupted to state that, "Qatar, Turkey, Saudi Arabia— a huge amount of weapons coming in. A huge amount of money." Ratney then continued:

> But pumping weapons in causes someone else to pump more weapons in and you end up with Aleppo.

(Remember, the names ISIS, ISIL, Islamic State, the caliphate and Daesh all refer to the same group, Abu Musab al-Zarqawi's old al Qaeda in Iraq from Iraq War II.) Kerry then confessed that

> the reason Russia came in is because ISIL was getting stronger, Daesh was threatening the possibility of going to Damascus and so forth. And that's why Russia came in. Because they didn't want a Daesh government and they supported Assad.

> And we know that this was growing. We were watching. We saw that Daesh was growing in strength, and we thought Assad was threatened. We thought, however, we could probably manage. Uh, you know, that

Assad would then negotiate. Instead of negotiating, he got Putin to support him.

There you have it. John Kerry admitted that the U.S. policy of arming the rebels led to the rise of the Islamic State and that even as they were bombing the caliphate in Iraq, they still "thought [they] could probably manage" the terrorists' rise in Syria and use ISIS as leverage to pressure Assad into negotiating his own exit from power. Instead, Assad asked the Russians to help to prevent Abu Bakr al-Baghdadi, ISIS's psychopathic "Caliph Ibrahim," from taking the throne in Damascus.

What kind of crazy thinking is that anyway? If Britain and France had intervened on the side of the South in the American Civil War, would that have put pressure on Abraham Lincoln to negotiate his own resignation in favor of some non-existent replacement to be named by the Europeans? Is it not more likely that it would have motivated him to try more desperately to expand and win the war, perhaps even calling the Russians for assistance? In fact, that is exactly what happened. In response to British and French support for the Southern Confederacy, in 1863 at the height of the Civil War, President Lincoln welcomed Russian Tsar Alexander II's warships to help guard New York and San Francisco Bay against Confederate attack. They had standing orders to fight on the North's side if England and France directly intervened in the war, which may have helped prevent them from doing so. The great American author Oliver Wendell Holmes Sr. even wrote a poem to commemorate the Yankees' gratitude for Russia's friendship. Surely any suggestion that Lincoln should instead have just given up, resigned and let the British pick his replacement to resolve the war would have been greeted with only derision and laughter.

As Christopher Phillips explains in *The Battle for Syria*, Russia had no major interest in the country. They maintained a small base at Tartus of mostly symbolic importance. Arms sales to Syria were modest, and Putin did not have an overly friendly relationship with Bashar al-Assad. His position changed in reaction to the chaos of 2011. Secretary Clinton had promised Foreign Minister Lavrov the new regime would protect Russian interests, but she obviously could not guarantee it. The Libya disaster destroyed President Medvedev's credibility and guaranteed Prime Minister Putin's early return to the presidency in 2012, along with his opposition to U.S. policy in Syria. Putin was worried about the jihadists, especially Russian speakers who were traveling there from the Caucasus region and could pose a significant threat upon return. The Russian Orthodox Church also lobbied Putin to help Assad protect Syrian Christians.

Part of the propaganda campaign against the Syrians and their allies was that they only targeted the "opposition," instead of ISIS, and that in fact, the regime and ISIS had a secret alliance. As discussed above, the story was that Assad had deliberately released dangerous terrorists from prison and refused to attack the worst of them just to make the decent and moderate insurgents look bad. This was political spin. First of all, it was the opposition and their Western government supporters who demanded that Assad empty his jails. The rebels opened more themselves.

Secondly, ISIS was part of the opposition, too, the most ruthless part of it. For years they had dealt severe defeats to the Syrian state, such as when, in a major victory for the insurgency, their suicide bombers made the difference and helped other insurgent fighters take over Menagh Air Base in 2013. Ambassador Robert Ford became very upset that FSA commander Abdel Jabbar al-Okaidi, whom he was closely associated with, had created a "public relations nightmare" for their partisans in the U.S. by appearing on camera celebrating their joint victory with prominent members of ISIS. Incidentally, in that battle, it turned out the ISIS commander, Abu Omar al-Shishani (a.k.a. "Omar the Chechen"), had been trained by the U.S. as part of a former-Soviet Georgian special operations team fighting against the terrorists, as Mitchell Prothero reported. However, at that time, ISIS was tied up attempting to solidify their gains in western Iraq and eastern Syria. So it made sense that the Damascus government and its allies focused on the more significant threat to Syria's major cities, which are almost all in the west of the country. The American hawks gave away the game by refusing to separate Jabhat al-Nusra from the "opposition," the way they did ISIS. No, al-Nusra were "the rebels" whom the Russians were bombing and the Americans were defending. Again, it was the threat ISIS posed to Damascus that finally prompted Russia to intervene overtly in the autumn of 2015.

For a time, it seemed that the most important result of the creation of the Islamic State on the Syrian side of the line in terms of American policy was that it was used as the basis for the further framing of the al Qaeda fighters as the moderates in comparison. The leaders of ISIS were ruthless killers, slaughtering innocents and even beheading Americans they had captured in Syria or bought from John McCain's friends in the Northern Storm Brigade. Though al-Nusra was known to commit atrocities in battle and against civilians under their rule, ISIS was bent on a doctrine of barbarian violence based on the most austere interpretations of Islam. They murdered civilians without mercy, infamously throwing alleged gay men from rooftops, crucifying people in the town square and making clear their genocidal intentions against Shi'ites, Alawites, Christians, Kurds and Yazidis.

But the al-Nusra Front was sworn loyal by blood-oath to Ayman al-Zawahiri, leader of al Qaeda, butcher of New York City, Virginia and Pennsylvania. What difference does it make if Abu Muhammad al-Jolani was a slightly less-psychopathic suicide bomber of civilians and enforcer of Sharia law than his predecessor Zarqawi or counterpart Baghdadi? Many of these same al-Nusra fighters had helped the Sunni-based insurgency kill 4,000 out of the 4,500 U.S. troops who died in Iraq War II. Their Iraqi cousins in ISIS were at that same moment threatening the government America had created during that war. And Jolani was still a cold-blooded murderer. To the hawks in Washington, D.C., this was all irrelevant. Now the Islamic State was considered the worse threat. But there was no denying that al-Nusra was the most powerful force in the country besides the Assad government and ISIS. So, to three-time loser David Petraeus, the by-then disgraced and fired former general and CIA director who had been "instrumental" in the initial weapons transfers to the insurgents at the start of the war, it was time to put arms directly in the hands of al Qaeda to defeat the Islamic State. For example, the *London Times* headline on the story read, "Petraeus: U.S. Must Fund al Qaeda." The Daily Beast's was "Petraeus: Use Al Qaeda Fighters to Beat ISIS":

> Members of al Qaeda's branch in Syria have a surprising advocate in the corridors of American power: retired Army general and former CIA Director David Petraeus.
>
> The former commander of U.S. forces in Iraq and Afghanistan has been quietly urging U.S. officials to consider using so-called moderate members of al Qaeda's Nusra Front to fight ISIS in Syria, four sources familiar with the conversations, including one person who spoke to Petraeus directly, told The Daily Beast.

Fortunately, Petraeus's plan did not gain traction. However, the CIA would continue to back al Qaeda in their fight against the Assad regime. As Ann Bernard reported for the *New York Times* a month after the Russian air force intervened, the U.S. had responded to Vladimir Putin's move by pouring massive amounts of shoulder-fired TOW anti-tank missiles to the Free Syrian Army and, therefore, Jabhat al-Nusra as well. They were immediately put to use by al-Nusra in Hama and Idlib provinces.

In September 2016, the last days of the Obama administration, the president ordered Secretary of State Kerry to make a new deal with Russia to team up in the fight against the Islamic State and, importantly, the al-Nusra Front. Then-Secretary of Defense Ashton Carter had already let his displeasure with this arrangement be known in June to the *Washington Post*. Five days after the deal was signed, the air force "accidentally" wiped out an army position near the eastern Syrian town of Der ez Zour, leading to immediate gains for ISIS and destroying the agreement. Though there is no proof, many took it to be deliberate insubordination and sabotage of the president's policy. The Russians portrayed it as sympathy for the

Islamic State. More likely, Carter's concern was undermining the agreement to protect Jabhat al-Nusra — al Qaeda.

Also in 2016, Obama briefly ordered the Pentagon to target a small subset of al-Nusra that the U.S. calls the "Khorasan Group," which they said was planning attacks on targets in the West. The *Washington Post* news section blasted him: "Obama directs Pentagon to target al Qaeda affiliate in Syria, one of the most formidable forces fighting Assad." Someone waking up from their coma after September 11th or the 2010 Ft. Hood attack might have wondered what in the world was going on.

Thankfully, Obama refused the worst demands of his hawks to escalate the war against Assad to the point of actual regime change. That year, however, Hillary Clinton was running for president on the promise of a "no-fly zone" over Syria, which Chairman of the Joint Chiefs of Staff Joseph Dunford told Congress would have meant war with Russia. At the very least, as she said in one of her leaked Goldman Sachs speeches, it would "kill a lot of Syrians." And all to protect an al Qaeda-led insurgency on the ground below.

She lost the election.

Three Fake Sarin Attacks

The first major false-flag sarin attack in the Syrian war was in the town of Ghouta outside Damascus on August 21, 2013. Despite Secretary of State John Kerry's repeated protestations that "we know" the government of Bashar al-Assad was behind the attack, it turns out, unsurprisingly, that was not true at all. Instead, Barack Obama foolishly announced that he would refrain from full-scale intervention on the side of the insurgency unless the regime crossed his "red line" by using chemical weapons. In doing so, he incentivized the al-Nusra Front to stage just such an attack with help from the Turkish government, as journalist Seymour Hersh reported.

Human Rights Watch first put the launch zones nine kilometers away, a finding supported by Western government-funded war propagandist Eliot Higgins. But the maximum range of the rockets that hit the Zamalka neighborhood was 2.5 kilometers. The rocket that hit the Moadamiyah district at the same time had a nine-kilometer range, but inspectors at one UN lab found no sarin by-products at that scene at all, and the other lab found only a small trace amount in a room where it was claimed an entire family had been killed by it. The UN report also admitted that the crime scene was possibly "manipulated" by unknown actors.

When Higgins later suggested the launch sites were within the rockets' actual range, his assertion of government control over those areas were then debunked by Australian forensic expert Charles Wood, who showed that insurgent groups dominated the areas Higgins claimed were under control of the Syrian military.

Journalist Gareth Porter also concluded that the supposed "smoking gun," the trace presence of the chemical hexamine, was more likely indicative of conventional explosives than proof of sarin originating in the Assad government's stocks.

Seymour Hersh reported that the Defense Intelligence Agency already knew that Jabhat al-Nusra was working on producing sarin gas from precursors they had received from the Turks before the attack took place.

Ake Sellstrom, the head of the UN inspection team, told the *Wall Street Journal* that either side could be the perpetrator. He also pointed out that he and his team had originally arrived in town to negotiate a visit to a separate, lesser-known alleged chemical attack in the town of Khan al-Assal when the Ghouta attack occurred. That original attack had killed an army soldier. Local doctors told the UN it was perpetrated by the insurgency. The Syrian government immediately granted them access to the new sites within a day. The regime was either completely "stupid," as Sellstrom says, or al-Nusra was very smart.

It is worth mentioning that at the time, the war party in America was vanishingly small. TV news and the nations' many neoconservative pundits in the newspapers and magazines were, of course, unanimous. CNN's Jake Tapper framed the question from the point of view of a desperate hawk, hamstrung by the ignorant, reluctant, isolationist masses of flyover country: "How can Obama sway the people" to support the war? But among Washington, D.C. think tanks and lobby groups, things were pretty quiet. Except for the Israel lobby. As *Politico* and Reuters reported, the American Israel Public Affairs Committee (AIPAC) dispatched hundreds of lobbyists to Capitol Hill to try to get them to start another war. But it was not enough.

Obama canceled the bombing campaign against Syrian military forces after British military intelligence reported that the sarin samples from the attack did not match previously known Syrian chemical weapons stocks. Chairman of the Joint Chiefs of Staff Martin Dempsey also issued a public statement, saying he did not see the necessity of the strikes. Then-Director of National Intelligence James Clapper gave Obama a private warning — that was kept from the public for years — that the intelligence linking Assad to the attack was "not a 'slam dunk.'" This was a reference to former CIA Director George Tenet's claims about Iraq's weapons programs, and an implied threat that Clapper would not publicly stand behind the intelligence.

It did not hurt that the British House of Commons had already resoundingly rejected the idea of intervention or that the broad swath of the American right did not trust Commander in Chief Obama to make these decisions. They were right not to since the war, as they complained, would have been fought for the very same sort of bin Ladenite insurgent forces that so many of them had fought against in Iraq War II. Pictures started to be passed around the internet of American soldiers, sailors and marines in their uniforms with paper signs covering their faces which read, "I didn't join the Navy to fight for al Qaeda in a Syrian civil war!" and "I did not join the military to get involved in other countries' civil wars. Stay out of Syria!" Forget Middle America. Obama had lost his own military. Calls to Congress were nearly unanimous. Polls showed public opposition was severe. One showed as much as 74 percent opposition to the strikes.

Instead, the president cut a deal with Russian President Vladimir Putin to ensure that Assad would turn over all of Syria's chemical weapons to the Organization for the Prohibition of Chemical Weapons (OPCW) for destruction in exchange for American restraint.

The second major false-flag chemical attack in the Syrian war was in the town of Khan Sheikhoun on April 4, 2017. The claim was that the Syrian air force had dropped a chemical bomb on this jihadist-controlled town early one morning, leading to the deaths of 89 and the injury of more than 500. This lie was debunked almost immediately. Former Col. Lawrence Wilkerson had the real story, based on intelligence and military sources in the region who had seen the intelligence, on April 7. Journalist Seymour Hersh's later reporting in the German magazine *Die Welt* confirmed it. The Syrians and Russians had been planning on bombing a meeting of leaders of Ahrar al-Sham and Jabhat al-Nusra they knew would be taking place on that day weeks beforehand. They had been surveilling the site with drones and had informed the Americans by way of the usual deconfliction phone calls about the event days before.

They did not know that the fighters' meeting place was being used to store large quantities of ammunition, fertilizers, pesticides and other chemicals. Gareth Porter explains that the cause of poisoning was likely a result of anti-rodent fumigants being exposed to moisture and emitting phosphine gas. Al-Nusra fighters and their MI-6-funded "White Helmet" humanitarian public relations front men quickly improvised and attempted to turn the site into a chemical weapons crime scene with the help of a credulous on-scene reporter for the *Guardian*.

Theodore Postol, professor emeritus of Science, Technology and International Security at MIT, concluded that the munition photographed in a small crater in the street blocks away from the actual bombing site was not delivered by air but planted there.

Donald Trump fell right for the terrorists' lies, ordering cruise missile attacks on regime military bases. His liberal media critics agreed it was his finest hour. According to then-Secretary of Defense James Mattis, Trump even ordered him to assassinate Bashar al-Assad, an order that he claimed to have simply ignored. Trump later confirmed that he had wanted to kill the Syrian leader and that Mattis disagreed.

One year later, it happened again. This time in the town of Douma — then under the rule of the bin Ladenite militia Jaysh al-Islam — at three separate sites. The first was a hospital where a small group of people arrived showing signs of asphyxia from breathing in dust while hiding from shelling in underground tunnels. Once they arrived at the local emergency room, White Helmet public relations men started screaming about "chemicals," spraying the kids down with hoses and shoving albuterol asthma inhalers into their mouths for the cameras. The ridiculous farce was quickly debunked by the doctors at the hospital a few days later when *Independent* reporter Robert Fisk bothered to go and ask them.

The other two sites were both apartment buildings where large yellow canisters were pictured as having landed on an outside balcony and a bed, respectively. The canisters were initially claimed to have been full of sarin gas, though that was later changed to chlorine. The second canister was supposedly explained by a hole in the roof that was not even directly above the bed. At Moon of Alabama, the blogger Bernard debunked the possibility that the scenes portrayed in the pictures were genuine from the very first day. If that metal cylinder fell from a helicopter and punched through a thick concrete ceiling, how could it be undamaged in the photos? Later developments proved him right. Other pictures showed many dead children lying in one of the apartment building's stairways, but there was no apparent cause of death.

Again, Donald Trump bought the narrative surrounding the attacks and ordered more attacks on Syrian military bases. Luckily, as in 2018, the strikes were not extensive, and Russian military personnel were warned beforehand to evacuate the strike zones.

Journalists Peter Hitchens and Aaron Maté made the world aware in 2019 and 2020 of three important whistleblowers inside the OPCW whose original on the ground investigation in Douma was hijacked by the higher-ups in the organization. The bosses rewrote the experts' original report to conclude that the Syrian regime had used chlorine in attacks at the second and third sites even though the original investigation had concluded no such thing. The whistleblowers also exposed the fact that American officials had come to try to persuade them to see the attack their way. Smears against the credentials and credibility of the first two whistleblowers, Brendan Whelan and Ian Henderson, fell flat when they were defended by a third as the best and most experienced experts in their fields and at the organization. Months later, another leak of emails from two top directors of the OPCW was reported by Maté. One signaled agreement with the original inspectors' conclusions, the other at least acknowledged the censorship of the experts' internal complaints regarding the rewriting of the report.

There was no chemical attack in Douma — no sarin, no chlorine. Just as in Ghouta and Khan Sheikhoun, his forces were winning and had no need in the world to resort to such tactics, which could only serve as an excuse for the Western powers to escalate their war against him.

The level of war propaganda surrounding all three of these attacks remain among the all-time worst lies of our era. It is fortunate that Trump and his administration settled for symbolic strikes against Syrian military targets in response to these events. It could have been much worse.

The Syrian Kurds

Syria's ethnic Kurdish minority, approximately ten percent of the population, lived almost entirely in their own enclave in northeastern Syria near the Turkish and Iraqi borders. Before the war, their relationship with the Assad government was less than ideal. They were denied basic citizenship, and after a soccer riot turned into a massacre in 2004, their rights to organize and protest were severely curtailed. Once the war began, they achieved de facto autonomy from the Damascus government, as it was forced to withdraw its forces to protect the major population centers in the country's west. Other than a few skirmishes early in the war, they rarely fought against the central government, if only because they did not have to. Instead, they declared independence for their mini-state of what they called "Rojava." But it would not last.

Once Baghdadi returned to Iraq and declared the Islamic State in 2014, the U.S. decided to ally with the Syrian Kurds. True to their policy of picking fights with far too many enemies simultaneously, the Islamic State attacked the Syrian Kurdish town of Kobani. After the Kurds held out for many weeks against the invaders, the U.S. finally came to their aid, sending in planes and special operations forces to help them repel the ISIS attack. The Islamic State were fools to pick fights with the Iraqi and Syrian Kurds. Both groups would rather have stayed out of it. It was extremely poor savagery management on their parts.

But jihadis are jihadis, so numerous times during the war against ISIS, U.S. military-backed Kurdish "People's Protection Units," or "YPG" fighters — by then renamed the "SDF" or "Syrian Democratic Forces" for public relations reasons — got into major battles with CIA-backed "rebels." This led to some humorous headlines, such as "In Syria, Militias Armed by the Pentagon Fight Those Armed by the CIA," in the *Los Angeles Times* after the SDF took control of the city of Afrin in March 2016.

The U.S. backed the YPG/SDF in their effort to expel ISIS from the city of Raqqa in Syria's east, the Islamic State's last stronghold. However, in doing so, the U.S. was knowingly setting them up to be crushed by the Turks later. Turkey is a long-time NATO ally. Their government hates the Syrian Kurds because they are aligned with the Turkish PKK, a violent leftist Kurdish group considered to be terrorists by the Turkish government. When Rojava declared independence in 2013, Turkey increased its support for al-Nusra.

President Trump said U.S. forces were only there to fight the Islamic State, but his government kept contradicting him, adding enemies to the list and making matters worse. In early 2018, Rex Tillerson, President Trump's first secretary of state, announced that the U.S. would be staying in eastern Syria indefinitely, embedded with the Kurds in order to check Iranian and Syrian government power. Intervening in Syria to check Iran is, in fact, what the U.S. had been doing since 2006. It was fighting against ISIS when they got out of control that was the aberration.

But this sent a signal to the Erdoğan government that the U.S. meant to build up Syrian-Kurdish power at Turkey's expense. As a direct response, he launched a new war against the Kurds. The Turks first hit the town of Afrin in the western part of Syrian Kurdistan, near the border with Turkey. Erdoğan's forces used al Qaeda shock troops armed with CIA TOW missiles to lead the attack. They, of course, committed war crimes against Kurdish civilians as they advanced. Simultaneously, U.S. forces hit the Syrian army after claiming they had attacked some of the same Syrian Kurdish YPG forces that our ally Turkey was then slaughtering without repercussion.

While a small faction of Syrian Kurds joined in attacks against government forces in the early days of the war, for the most part, they did not challenge Assad's power, which for years could not reach their territory anyway. They wanted autonomy and they took it, without getting into a war with Assad. After the war in most of the country wound down, there was an obvious solution to the problem of Turkish paranoia about enhanced Kurdish power in northern Syria. It would have been for the Syrian government to regain control over the border space and promise to prevent the Syrian Kurdish YPG from providing safe haven to any terrorists from the Turkish PKK. For years now the Kurds have talked with the Syrian government about coming back to such an agreement, but the United States continues to prevent it.

Patrick Cockburn reported during the fighting in early 2018 that the Turks were recruiting fleeing ISIS fighters into their ranks to use against the Kurds in Afrin. These were the same ISIS terrorists the American marines and Kurdish YPG had just finished rousting out of Raqqa. A month or so later, our allies, the Turks, were recruiting them to fight against the same Kurds.

That December, Trump's national security adviser John Bolton and special envoy to Syria James Jeffrey announced that the U.S. would stay in Syria until all Iranian advisers and Quds Force members left the country. Evidently feeling cornered on the issue, Trump got angry and ordered a full withdrawal of troops instead, causing his secretary of defense, James Mattis, to resign in protest. The *New York Times, Washington Post, Times of Israel,* Vox.com and the entire establishment howled. America can never leave Syria. That would be bad for Israel. The *Times'*s Bret Stephens, on the occasion of the temporarily announced withdrawal from Syria wrote that "the ultimate long-term threat to Israel is the resurgence of isolationism in the U.S." But he hastened to add that it is an "invidious myth" that neoconservatives such as himself put Israel first. By the end of the month, Trump had backed down anyway.

Events repeated themselves but worse in October 2019, when Trump made an agreement with Erdoğan to withdraw all U.S. troops from Syrian Kurdistan to allow Turkish forces to invade and push the Syrian Kurds more than 30 miles from the border, killing hundreds.

If any third party were responsible for ending the conflict between the Syrian Kurds and the Turks, it would have been the Syrian government in Damascus. Just as in 2018, it would have been easy for President Trump to negotiate exactly that outcome, keeping Turkey at bay by allowing the Syrian army to take back control of the border region. Instead, he quite deliberately stabbed the Syrian Kurds in the back, virtually inviting Erdoğan to smash them and take that territory, using al-Nusra and associated terrorist groups as the shock troops in the attack.

General Salem Idris, the leader of the Supreme Military Council of the Free Syrian Army, who had been directly supported by the U.S. and met with Senator John McCain in 2013, led the attack on the Kurds in 2019. A Turkish think tank later reported that 21 of the jihadist factions who helped with the cleansing campaign against the Kurds had been previously backed by the United States. All the same hawks who had supported these terrorists now complained that Trump had withdrawn from Syria's Kurdish northeast and that the Kurds were being killed, without acknowledging who was killing them. The U.S. had to leave Syria; the sooner, the better. The Islamic State had been smashed. Arresting or destroying the last of their fighters was the responsibility of the Syrian state.

If President Trump had really withdrawn the troops from the entire country, maybe the factions could have worked something out. In fact, it was reported that his administration had intervened to prevent a deal between the Kurds and the Damascus government. But then, on the convoy's way out to Iraq, Trump called the troops back. Soldiers reportedly labeled the exercise "Operation Turn the Fuck Around." They returned to Syria, but to the south of Kurdish territory and out of the Turks' way. At Israeli Prime Minister Benjamin Netanyahu's insistence, they would stay at the al-Tanf military base near the Iraqi border to block Iran's "land-bridge" — as Washington, D.C. insists on calling Highway 2, the road that runs from western Iraq into southeastern Syria that Saddam Hussein's army used to block.

Trump's special envoy James Jeffrey later explained:

> There was never a Syria withdrawal. When the situation in northeast Syria had been fairly stable after we defeated ISIS, [Trump] was inclined to pull out. In each case, we [his staff] then decided to come up with five better arguments for why we needed to stay. And we succeeded both times. That's the story.

He elaborated that even though Trump agreed to only 200 permanent troops in Syria after the aborted withdrawal of 2019, they simply lied to him, leaving "a lot more than" that. "We were always playing shell games to not make clear to our leadership how many troops we had there," Jeffrey said. Why even have elections? Apparently, the bureaucrats can and will do as they wish with impunity.

Turkish forces stopped far short of the full-scale holocaust that was being predicted by the hysterical U.S. media and national security state. But withdrawal from anywhere was tarred with the bad name of "betrayal" of whichever indigenous forces America happens to be backing at any given time.

U.S. troops remain in the way of a peaceful resolution to the Syrian war, still backing the Kurds and occupying oil fields adjacent to their territory. But it is just a matter of time before they are left high and dry again. Nixon and Kissinger betrayed the Iraqi Kurds in the 1970s. Reagan betrayed them in the 1980s. Bush Sr. betrayed them in the 1990s. Bill Clinton supported Turkey's war against their Kurdish population in the mid-1990s, killing hundreds of thousands. Now we have the final Obama-Trump stab in the back of the Syrian Kurds: the U.S. helped build up the ISIS threat against them, then helped them defeat the threat, and then encouraged the Turks to attack and drive them out of Afrin and the northeastern border region with the help of many of those same terrorist groups. If instead the U.S. would withdraw and let the Syrian Kurds make their deal with Damascus, long-term peace would be much better served.

The solution to the problem of ISIS, Turkey and the Kurds, al-Nusra, Syrian dependence on Russia, Iran, and Hezbollah, and relations with Jordan, Iraq and Israel as well, all depend on U.S. withdrawal and its permitting the Syrian state to finally be able to reestablish their monopoly on violent force within their borders and peace with their neighbors.

What About Aleppo?

One of the most egregious propaganda campaigns of the war surrounded the battle for Syria's largest city, Aleppo, in 2016. Jabhat al-Nusra and the FSA first invaded Aleppo in the summer of 2012. One insurgent leader admitted to the *Guardian* at the time that the people of the city did not support them. "Around 70 percent of Aleppo city is with the regime. It has always been that way. The countryside is with us, and the city is with them," he told them. Nevertheless, the al-Nusra Front and Free Syrian Army ruled Aleppo under a combination of austere Sharia law and Afghan mujahideen-style gangsterism for years, with the support of the U.S. and their wealthy Persian Gulf allies. It was these thugs who infamously shot a 14-year-old Aleppo boy in the face for daring to make a joke about how he would not give a customer a free cup of coffee "even if the Prophet himself returns." That was back in the summer of 2013, just after ISIS split from al-Nusra and al Qaeda, one year before the declaration of the "Caliphate" by Baghdadi in Mosul and still four long years before Donald Trump finally called an end to the Timber Sycamore program arming these lunatics in 2017.

Before the war, approximately 250,000 Christians lived in Aleppo. After al Qaeda and their FSA allies took over the town, the Christians fled or were forcibly "cleansed" from their homes. The 100,000 or so that remained lived in the western half of the city which remained under government control.

For a time ISIS was dominant there, but as their fortunes reversed in early 2016, al-Nusra rolled back into Aleppo in force. When the Syrian army and Russians arrived in late summer of that year, one might have thought from watching TV that Baghdadi was right, the end of the world had come. Hundreds of thousands of civilians were being killed, the *Washington Post* claimed, even though there were fewer than 100,000 people left in east Aleppo by that point. "Seventy-nine [people trying to escape the east to 'regime-controlled areas'] were executed at the barricades [by the regime]. The rest — everyone under 40 — were taken to warehouses that look more like internment camps. They face an unknown fate. This morning 20 women committed suicide in order not to be raped," the modern Ministry of Truth known as the Daily Beast uncritically quoted a terrorist spokesman. The story's headline was changed from "Last Rebels in Aleppo Say Assad Forces Are Burning People Alive" to "Women in

Aleppo Choose Suicide Over Rape, Rebels Report." "Belgian Babies on Bayonets Eating Their Hearts Out" could have been next.

The battle was not even depicted as a struggle for power, for control over the city. That would have been far too mundane. No, the secular coalition government had come simply to commit a full-scale genocide against innocent civilians who just happen to be defended by the most sectarian fighters in the world, coincidentally. How long could these moderate rebels heroically continue to defend themselves and the helpless Syrian citizens around them from the rampaging, Russian-backed, Ba'athist monster in Damascus?

Then, once the jihadis fled, all the fighting stopped. The Assad government did not continue to kill civilians at all. In fact, the only civilians left in the eastern part of the city at that point were human shields being held against their will by the Jaysh al-Islam and al-Nusra terrorists. As soon as the city "fell" to government forces, in the words of the American government and media establishment, the civilian population rushed to return home and celebrate Christmas in peace in areas under Syrian army control. On American TV, the issue was dropped.

Iraq War III 1/2 Still Rages

Iraq War III came to an end in 2017 after the liberation of the Islamic State's twin capitals, Mosul in northwestern Iraq and Raqqa in eastern Syria. The Islamic State was destroyed. Thousands of their fighters were killed in the war, eventually including their leader al-Baghdadi in a raid by the Delta Force in 2019. The *Washington Post*'s Joby Warrick mourned the mass-murderer, terrorist and enslaver in his obituary, "Abu Bakr al-Baghdadi, Austere Religious Scholar at Helm of Islamic State, Dies at 48."

In western Iraq, U.S. special operations forces are still embedded with the Shi'ite Iraqi army and continue to go out on missions against the remnants of the ISIS insurgency, which does not appear to be going anywhere. When the fall of the Islamic State came in 2017, many fighters put down their rifles and went home to wait for the opportunity to rejoin the permanent insurgency against Shi'ite power in Iraq, an opportunity whose time has already come.

After President Trump's assassination by drone of Iranian Quds Force leader Qasem Soleimani in January 2020, the Iraqi parliament voted unanimously to demand the U.S. finally withdraw combat forces from their nation. Trump threatened them with massive sanctions and the confiscation of all their gold stored at the Federal Reserve in New York if they did not back down. Trump said the real reason U.S. forces remain in

Iraq is to "keep an eye on Iran," although American troops are still fighting ISIS in alliance with the same government in Baghdad that Iran supports.

The long-term fate of the predominantly Sunni western regions of Iraq remains an open question. Have the Iranians and their favored Iraqi Shi'ite factions come to terms with the fact that cutting the Sunnis adrift after the 2000s-era civil war had left half of the country wide open to invasion and overthrow by bin Ladenite forces? Do they understand that a more compromising posture will be necessary to maintain the peace for the long term? It does not look good. Though the major cities seem to have been brought under the "protection" of government forces, there have been numerous reports of brutal reprisals by Shi'ite forces against accused ISIS fighters and sympathizers. Ben Taub wrote of the aftermath of the battle for Mosul:

> ISIS fighters who surrendered were executed on the spot. Iraqi security forces filmed themselves hurling captives off a cliff, then shooting them as they lay dying on the rocks below. Helicopters buzzed the Tigris, bombing people as they tried to swim across. The troops assumed that anyone still living in the Old City sided with the Islamic State. For the rest of the month, corpses bobbed downstream, dressed in civilian clothes.

> "We killed them all — Daesh, men, women, and children." ... As he spoke, his colleagues dragged a suspect through the streets by a rope tied around his neck. "We are doing the same thing as ISIS. People went down to the river to get water, because they were dying of thirst, and we killed them."

The government holds rapid mass show trials with little evidence, often against obviously innocent men, leading straight to executions. Beyond that, Shi'ite forces commit widespread lynching, torture and murder, including beheadings, of those suspected of association with the defeated Islamic State. A senior Iraqi intelligence official admitted to Taub that most of the imprisoned never even see the inside of their show-trial courtrooms. "A few of the suspects are sent to court, but only to maintain the illusion that we have a justice system." He continued, "[M]ost of the Arab foreign fighters do not make it to court. We do not tell their governments what happens to them, and their governments do not ask." As Amnesty International detailed, refugee camps are filled with the widows, sisters and mothers of these ISIS fighters and their children, many the product of mass rapes by their guards in the Iraqi Shi'ite army, police and militia forces.

Human Rights Watch said in 2019 that 1,500 Sunni minors were being held and tortured by the Iraqi state into "confessing" their previous membership in ISIS. The judges hold fake five-minute trials with no defense lawyers and then throw away the key. Even in the cases where it may be technically true, these boys were conscripts, essentially enslaved by the Islamic State to fight. But George W. Bush put the Da'wa Party in charge of Iraq's government, and they care about rights and freedom and fairness about as much as his father's old asset Saddam Hussein did. Even Muqtada al-Sadr and Ayatollah Ali al-Sistani have spoken out against unjust arrests, sectarianism and revenge killings, to little effect.

The rebuilding of western Iraq's cities, devastated by allied airstrikes and artillery in Iraq War III and still littered with unexploded ordinance of all kinds, has not happened in many places. Much of Mosul is still in ruins. The rebuilding that is taking place is getting done with little help from the national government in Baghdad, beyond the restoration of basic services like water and electricity. If the Da'wa and ISCI-based government wanted to be good sports and finally take the opportunity to be gracious in victory and embrace their estranged countrymen, presently would be a good time. Otherwise, Ayatollah Khamenei, the Supreme Islamic Council, and Joe Biden and Antony Blinken's plan to divide Iraq will have succeeded. But who will govern western Iraq? If Baghdad's "protection" of the predominantly Sunni western provinces amounts to nothing more than revenge, torture and murder, and if the tribes and the Ba'athists are all unacceptable, then support for a bin Ladenite-type insurgency against the Shi'ite government, and their inevitable counter-reaction will continue indefinitely.

Journalist Shelly Kittleson has written that there is a strong movement based in the western Anbar Province, including Fallujah, pushing for a new strong federalism program of their own. In theory, they need independence from Baghdad's tyranny if they are ever to prosper in peace and out from under the thumb of the Shi'ites and the jihadists. But if "federalism" means building their own new Sunni army, it will only lead to further conflict.

Allegedly, Shi'ite militia forces almost caused a war between the United States and Iran in early 2020. On December 27, 2019, U.S. forces at K-1 Air Base in Kirkuk Province came under rocket attack. An American contractor was killed, and four U.S. and two Iraqi army soldiers were injured. Iraqi journalist Suadad al-Salhy told the author the attack was in an area where it could just as easily have been launched by ISIS fighters or other Sunni insurgents the soldiers were already fighting. But the Trump administration chose to blame Khatib al-Hezbollah, an Iraqi Shi'ite militia group unrelated to the Lebanese group with the similar name, though also backed by Iran. Trump responded by launching air raids against their bases and associated militia targets in Iraq and Syria that killed 25 fighters. Next, Khatib Hezbollah militiamen staged a riot at the U.S. embassy in Baghdad's Green Zone. Trump then escalated by assassinating Iranian

Quds Force commander General Qasem Soleimani in a drone strike at the Baghdad airport. After Iran responded by firing missiles at an empty corner of a U.S. air base in Iraq, Trump thankfully let them have the last word, refusing advice to take the country to war. Tragically, a panicky Iranian anti-aircraft missile operator shot down a Ukrainian airliner on takeoff from the Tehran airport a few hours after their missile volley launched toward Iraq, killing all 176 civilians onboard.

In March, the American in charge of the ongoing Iraq war, Lt. Gen. Robert White, sent a sternly worded memo to then-Secretary of Defense Mark Esper. It explained that the U.S. was in a de facto alliance with these Shi'ite militias, who are fighting ISIS in support of the Iraqi army the same as our troops are. Turning around 180 degrees and starting a war against those same Shi'ite militias would require thousands more troops since it would also mean taking on the Iraqi army the U.S. had been fighting the last 17 years to build up to rule that country. They truly were facing an Order 66-type situation where the Iraqi army soldiers would almost certainly turn on their American partners, leaving them stranded or dead in the field if they had escalated further against the militias or Iran itself.

Just because the ruling Iraqi parties are those most favored by Iran does not mean that they are or wish to be completely under Iranian control, nor does their shared religious sect mean that the people of southern Iraqi Shiastan favor Iranian domination of their country. In fact, Trump's attack on Gen. Soleimani in Iraq brought what had been widespread protests among Iraqi Shi'ites opposing Iranian influence to an abrupt end. The U.S. strikes, rather than limiting Iranian influence in favor of the Americans — a contest Bush lost back in 2007 — instead only pushed the two countries' people and governments closer together. Still, the Baghdad regime is such a corrupt and incompetent kleptocracy that anti-Iranian sentiment remains high among Iraqi Shi'ites, many of whom evidently blame them for foisting the parties in power onto their country.

In December 2020, Muqtada al-Sadr himself announced that he would be seeking a seat in Parliament, and subsequently the Prime Ministership in the June 2021 elections. The sounds of knives being sharpened could be heard around the world.

The Next Generation

As previously mentioned, covert support for the insurgency against Assad continued for three full years after ISIS conquered western Iraq and declared their "Caliphate" in Iraq and Syria. President Trump finally canceled the program in July 2017. "Trump Ends Covert CIA Program to Arm Anti-Assad Rebels in Syria, a Move Sought by Moscow," the

Washington Post headline blared, essentially accusing the president of treason for ending support to al Qaeda terrorists.

The *New York Times* news section was also emotional about this supposed betrayal. "[T]he president said many of the CIA-supplied weapons ended up in the hands of 'al Qaeda' — presumably a reference to the al Qaeda-affiliated Nusra Front, which often fought alongside the CIA-backed rebels," Mark Mazzetti and his co-authors wrote, annoyed that the president had correctly identified "al Qaeda's largest affiliate" as a major beneficiary of this material support. But still, Mazzetti insisted, "Unlike other al Qaeda affiliates such as Al Qaeda in the Arabian Peninsula, the Nusra Front has long focused on battling the Syrian government rather than plotting terrorist attacks against the United States and Europe."

Who cares if these violent men are declared enemies of the American people? Right now, they are too busy being useful against Iran's friends to attack us. That is all that mattered to the *Times* and the U.S. foreign policy establishment opinion-makers they echoed.

Trump and then-CIA Director Mike Pompeo may have ended support for the Syrian insurgency in the summer of 2017, but U.S. forces remain in eastern and central Syria to keep the oil out of the hands of the central government. The new strategy is to deliberately, rather than accidentally, increase Syrian dependence on Iran. While this may give Iran more influence in Syria, the reduction of which was the motive for the entire project in the first place, it still costs Iran hundreds of millions of dollars. This contributed to the Trump administration's policy of "maximum pressure" against Iran, their attempt to force them into accepting stricter terms in a new nuclear deal or weaken their regime to the point of collapse.

In 2020, Trump's Syria envoy James Jeffrey defended U.S. forces' continuing presence after the caliphate's defeat. "This isn't Afghanistan. This isn't Vietnam. This isn't a quagmire." Then he added, echoing Jimmy Carter and Osama bin Laden decades earlier, "My job is to make it a quagmire for the Russians." Thomas L. Friedman had previously written in the *New York Times* that the U.S. should not fight ISIS in eastern Syria at all for the same reason:

> Trump should want to defeat ISIS in Iraq. But in Syria? Not for free, not now. In Syria, Trump should let ISIS be Assad's, Iran's, Hezbollah's and Russia's headache — the same way we encouraged the mujahideen fighters to bleed Russia in Afghanistan.

In 2014, the State Department's "Country Report on Terrorism" for Syria noted:

> The rate of foreign terrorist fighter travel to Syria [in 2014] — totaling more than 16,000 foreign terrorist fighters from more than 90 countries as of late December — exceeded the rate of foreign terrorist fighters who traveled to Afghanistan and Pakistan, Iraq, Yemen or Somalia at any point in the last 20 years.

The ones who were not killed are either holed up in Syria's northwestern Idlib Province or, following the pattern of previous bin Ladenite radicals after the 1980s Afghan war and 2000s Iraq War II, returned home to nations around the Middle East, North Africa and Afghanistan. When ISIS killed 17 Iranians in 2017, Republican Congressman Dana Rohrabacher praised the attacks and said he hoped that the Trump administration was behind it:

> Isn't it a good thing for us to have the United States finally backing up Sunnis who will attack Hezbollah and the Shi'ite threat to us? Isn't that a good thing? And if so, maybe … this is a Trump strategy of actually supporting one group against another.

It looks like Rohrabacher was pretty close. Saudi Crown Prince Mohammed bin Salman had said just before the attack that, "We know that the aim of the Iranian regime is to reach the focal point of Muslims [Mecca] and we will not wait until the fight is inside Saudi Arabia and we will work so that the battle is on their side, inside Iran, not in Saudi Arabia."

In 2015, it was reported that ISIS fighters from the Syrian war were fighting with the neo-Nazi-infested Ukrainian military in what they called the Dudayev Battalion against Russian-backed separatists in that country's far eastern Donbass region.

Reversing Hillary Clinton and David Petraeus's ratline, in 2019 President Erdoğan of Turkey started sending down-and-out jihadists in the Idlib Province to Libya to fight for the Government of National Accord (GNA) against former CIA asset Khalifa Haftar.

In late 2020, numerous reports showed that the Turks were transporting some of these fighters to Azerbaijan to use as shock troops against the Armenians in their war over the disputed territory of Nagorno-Karabakh. Thousands of Europeans and at least a few hundred Americans traveled to Syria to fight for al-Nusra, ISIS or other insurgent groups during the more than seven years of war there. The FBI admitted that they were not keeping track of which Americans had traveled to Turkey and on to Syria to fight for the insurgency.

Now, all we have is the same government that created this mess to keep these men from coming back and committing acts of terrorism here. Repatriation of former Syrian fighters is currently a major political issue in some European countries. Out of the tens of thousands of new bin

Ladenites forged in the fires of America's 21st century Middle Eastern wars, there will remain some incorrigibles who will not be placated by America's inconsistent backing any more than bin Laden was by Bill Clinton's support for the KLA in Kosovo. Men who fought on the terrorists' side in Syria have already committed atrocities in Belgium, France and England. [See Chapter 14.]

As of this writing, tens of thousands of these al-Nusra, ISIS and other fighters still control Syria's northwestern Idlib Province in alliance with the Turkish army, which continues to hold the terrorists over the heads of the Syrian government and the Kurds. In the summer of 2020, when Assad's forces advanced into the province, U.S. ally Turkey prevented them from destroying the remaining al Qaeda forces there. However, that fall, the Trump administration started attacking al Qaeda targets with drone strikes. The CIA occasionally singles out the so-called "Khorasan group" and a faction calling themselves Hurras al-Din or "Guardians of Religion" as "bad al Qaeda" in Idlib, implying that Jolani and his renamed al-Nusra, Hayat Tahrir al-Sham, are the moderate ones by comparison. Again, this is not because they are moderate by any measure. It is only because they are currently focused on fighting the government in Damascus.

For a few years, ISIS was able to have their "Caliphate." But when America helped the Iraqi Shi'ites and Kurds smash the Islamic State, our government proved that Zawahiri's strategy was right. As long as the American empire is the dominant force in the Middle East, they will never be able to create their caliphate, because the U.S. will come and bomb it off the face of the earth again.

Just like overthrowing the elected government in Egypt made it seem that al Qaeda was right to criticize Islamists for naïvely participating in democracy, Iraq War III would seem to have proven their doctrine right again: the Americans must be bled all the way to bankruptcy and forced out of the region entirely. Only then can they create their Islamist caliphate. We can anticipate more terrorist attacks against the United States for that reason.

When the George W. Bush administration started this war, there were only 400 al Qaeda fighters hiding in Afghanistan and not many more spread throughout the region. Now, there are many thousands more. The consequences are only beginning to be revealed.

Chapter Twelve:
Yemen

"It may be dangerous to be
America's enemy, but to be
America's friend is fatal."
— Henry Kissinger

"Obama is helping them
to kill us, unfortunately."
— Nasser Arrabyee

CIA Drone War

One of the worst American wars of this century has been the war President Barack Obama launched in cooperation with Saudi Arabia and the United Arab Emirates (UAE) in 2015 against Yemen. As of early 2021, this brutal campaign against the civilian population of that country continues. But the CIA's drone war against al Qaeda was just the beginning.

The U.S. had supported the dictator Abdullah Saleh for decades. With the beginning of the War on Terrorism, President George W. Bush sent the CIA and special operations forces to Yemen to set up a base, train local forces, track and kill members of al Qaeda in the Arabian Peninsula (AQAP or Ansar Al-Sharia). In November 2002, the CIA bombed an SUV carrying al Qaeda members, including the naturalized American citizen Kamal Darwish, with a Predator drone. They then outsourced most of the rest of the mission against al Qaeda to the Yemeni government.

When Obama came to power in 2009, he started paying off Saleh with money and weapons to let the CIA wage its Predator and Reaper drone war against AQAP targets in the country's southeast. Saleh had told Obama's assassination supervisor John Brennan, "I have given you an open door on terrorism. So I am not responsible." AQAP, of course, traced their origins back to the Arab-Afghan jihad against the Soviets in Afghanistan in the 1980s. They had been attacking U.S. targets for years, including against Americans at a Yemeni hotel in 1992, the 1998 African embassy bombings, the attack on the *USS Cole* in 2000 and they had played a role in coordinating the September 11th attack. Since then they had attacked the U.S. embassy in Sana'a in 2008, played a role in the murder of two Army soldiers in Little Rock, Arkansas in June 2009 and in Nidal Hasan's attack at Ft. Hood, Texas that November.

When Obama declared the beginning of his Afghan "surge" in December 2009, he announced escalations in both Somalia and Yemen as well. The bombing had already started weeks before. That Christmas Day, the underpants bomber, Umar Farouk Abdulmutallab, recruited by Yemeni al Qaeda, tried but luckily failed to blow up a Northwest Airlines flight over Detroit, Michigan. An American lawyer named Kurt Haskell was eyewitness to unknown officials' intervention to help Abdulmutallab change planes in the Netherlands. State Department official Patrick Kennedy later admitted to Congress that U.S. intelligence officers deliberately let him into the country because they were trying to track him and see who he talked to. They apparently did not know he had a bomb in his pants. That a terrorist tied directly to AQAP, whose own father warned the CIA about how dangerous he was, could slip through the net and attempt to attack the U.S. in this way was so inexplicable to President Obama that he sent a friendly journalist, Richard Wolff, to go on MSNBC and relate the president's concerns. He thought that some in the intelligence community may have let this happen deliberately to tarnish the record of rival agencies or individuals within them at the expense of the security of the American people.

The underpants bomber's failed attack became the reason for the drone war, according to the media, even though it had already begun months before. The State Department cables leaked by Chelsea Manning and published by Julian Assange's Wikileaks in 2010 revealed a secret agreement between the Obama and the Saleh governments. The American role would remain deniable, while Saleh would take responsibility for the bombings, although the Yemenis and American skeptics saw through the deception from the beginning.

The drone war against AQAP in Yemen, sold as a comparative anti-terrorist "scalpel" using "surgical" strikes that could target only the bad guys with a minimum of collateral damage, predictably resulted in the deaths of hundreds of civilians. This only generated more support for the bin Ladenites. Journalist Jeremy Scahill wrote in 2010 about a local tribal elder who was trying to marginalize al Qaeda. He and some associates had gone to meet with the terrorists to warn them to get out of town and stay out. The Americans dropped a 500-pound bomb on the whole meeting, killing a few lower-level terrorists along with those most able to stand up against them. The U.S. was only creating more reason for new people to join the terrorists' cause. Obama's drone war was strengthening al Qaeda, who have continued to attack the United States. They were behind the package bomb plot of 2010, the foiled underpants bombing of 2012, and various other plots against the U.S. and our European allies, including the 2015 *Charlie Hebdo* attack in Paris, France and the Naval Air Station attacks of 2019 and 2020 in Pensacola, Florida and Corpus Christi, Texas. [See Chapter 14.]

Former CIA officer John Kiriakou explained:

> Well, the truth of the matter is that the drone program is probably the most potent recruiting tool that foreign terrorist groups have. I can tell you that I interrogated dozens of al Qaeda fighters in my CIA years, and to a man they all said that they had no beef with the United States, they had no personal problem with the United States, until we rocketed their villages with drones, and we killed their cousin or their parents or their brother and sister or whatever it was — and they were compelled to take up arms against the United States. So, there are people in countries all over the region — not just the Middle East but South Asia and the Horn of Africa — that otherwise would never have had reason to take up arms against us and did so solely because of the drone program.

In 2013, former CIA director and then-outgoing Secretary of Defense Leon Panetta was questioned by a reporter about Gen. McChrystal's concerns about new resentments created by seemingly easy drone wars: Have "we opened a Pandora's Box that we may regret in twenty years?" Panetta could only stammer that, "in the end, [we are] using what we have to use against the enemies of the United States."

Picking a Fight with Ansarullah

While the CIA was targeting AQAP, Saleh took the money and weapons Obama had given him to launch his own attacks against a group called Ansarullah (a.k.a. Ansar Allah or often "the Houthis" after the family and tribe which leads them). The Houthis are a political faction of Zaidi Shi'ites based out of the Sa'ada province in the far north of Yemen, near the Saudi border. The Houthis had formed decades before as a reaction against Saudi Arabia's attempt to export radical Wahhabist Islam to their region.

Their more recent fight with the central state began as a consequence of Iraq War II. The Houthis had humiliated Saleh by chanting anti-American slogans to his face at a mosque in 2003, mocking him for his alliance with the U.S., when it invaded Iraq. This enraged Saleh, who vowed to punish them for their obstinance. Also, under pressure from the Bush administration to attack AQAP, Saleh used his ginned-up crisis with the Houthis to avoid doing so, which would have alienated him from important political allies.

But as with America's drone war against AQAP, every time Saleh attacked the Houthis — six different times — it backfired. They only grew stronger in response.

Not only was Saleh empowering the Houthi movement every time he failed to destroy them, but he was also helping to build up al-Islah, Yemen's branch of the Sunni-Islamist Muslim Brotherhood, and by some reports, even some AQAP factions to use against them. According to Yemeni political analyst Abdul-Ghani Al Iryani, Saleh was also sending arms to his enemies the Houthis to wear out his own military forces along with al-Islah, who were growing too powerful while fighting for him. And we think the curved daggers of American politics are sharp.

A Bogus Election

When the 2011 Arab Spring revolutions began, there quickly emerged an Egypt-like consensus of virtually all different factions that Saleh must step down from power. There were two assassination attempts against him, the second of which wounded him. This gave the Americans, Saudis and United Nations an opportunity to push Saleh out in favor of his vice president, Abd Rabbo Mansour Hadi, thus preventing the people of Yemen from coming to their own consensus about how to proceed. Instead, they held an "election" with only Hadi's name on the ballot. Secretary Clinton declared his victory the advent of Yemeni democracy.

But Saleh refused to retire to a life of farming or quiet study. Instead, once he recovered from his injuries, he went away mad and took much of his army with him. Saleh then allied with the Houthis in the north. Ignorant U.S. policymakers belatedly discovered he was a Zaidi Shi'ite like them, just not a Houthi.

Meanwhile, Hadi was terrible at being a democratic president. After two years, he refused to hold new elections as promised and unilaterally prolonged his term in power. He replicated Saleh's previous failed attempts to use al-Islah fighters to attack the Houthis, which only provoked them. He then announced a strong federalism plan which would have hardened provincial borders, cutting the Houthis off from the Red Sea. Finally, he abolished gasoline subsidies, severely disrupting the economy and causing riots. With that, what little support he had was gone.

The Houthis Take Over

At the end of 2014, the Houthi-Saleh alliance marched into the capital of Sana'a. Hadi fled south to Aden, then soon after to Saudi Arabia. According to the *Wall Street Journal*, the military had no problem with the Houthis and was instead happy to have motivated enemies of al Qaeda to work with in Yemen. The Houthis' hate for al Qaeda was defensive since AQAP considered the Shi'ite Houthis to be heretics worthy only of death. At that time, the man who later became President Biden's first secretary of defense, General Lloyd Austin, was commander of Central Command. Austin started sharing intelligence with the Houthis, which they began to use to target al Qaeda forces there. The *Journal* reported:

> The U.S. has formed ties with Houthi rebels who seized control of Yemen's capital, White House officials and rebel commanders said, in the clearest indication of a shift in the U.S. approach there as it seeks to maintain its fight against a key branch of al Qaeda.
>
> American officials are communicating with Houthi fighters, largely through intermediaries, the officials and commanders have disclosed, to promote a stable political transition as the Houthis gain more power and to ensure Washington can continue its campaign of drone strikes

against leaders of the group al Qaeda in the Arabian Peninsula, officials said. ...

U.S. officials said they also are seeking to harness the Houthis' concurrent war on AQAP to weaken the terrorist organization's grip on havens in Yemen's west and south. ...

Houthi commanders, in recent interviews conducted in Yemen, asserted that the U.S. began sharing intelligence on AQAP positions in November, using intermediaries, as the conflict in the country intensified. They specifically cited a Houthi campaign against AQAP positions in western Al Baitha province as one such operation.

One Houthi commander said the U.S. provided logistical aid to the militants and exchanged intelligence on AQAP to support the Houthis' operations against the group and pinpoint drone strikes. The Americans passed on all this information, the officer said, through Yemeni counter-terrorism officials.

Journalist Barbara Slavin wrote of an appearance by then-Deputy Secretary of Defense for Intelligence Michael Vickers at the Atlantic Council explaining the same:

Senior U.S. intelligence official Michael Vickers said Jan. 21 that the United States is continuing attacks on al Qaeda in the Arabian Peninsula (AQAP) despite ongoing violence in the Yemeni capital, Sana'a, and has an intelligence relationship with the Houthi insurgent group that has seized much of the capital since September. ...

Vickers, a special forces veteran and current undersecretary of defense for intelligence, presented a more nuanced view of the Houthis' recent advances and aims than has been reported in much of the Western and Sunni Gulf media. ...

Vickers, in response to a question from Al-Monitor, stated, "The Houthis are anti al-Qaeda, and we've been able to continue some of our counter-terrorism operations against al-Qaeda in the past months." Asked after the public event whether that included lines of intelligence to the Houthis, Vickers said, "That's a safe assumption."

Of course, Austin and Vickers's drone war was also brutal and counterproductive. Yet this shows that the Houthis were no enemies of the United States. Instead, they were our allies — for a little while. Two months later, President Barack Obama stabbed America's new partners in the back and took al Qaeda's side against them.

Obama's Green Light

Once the Houthis took control of the capital, they made moves to create a representative government and come to an understanding with the Saudis. They created the "people's transitional council" to join the government as a lower house better representing the people of the south, women and the youth. They declared their intention to propose a new constitution and hold elections. The UN envoy on Yemen, Jamal Benomar, told the UN Security Council that rival Yemeni groups were about to sign a peace deal before Saudi Arabia launched their first airstrikes in March 2015. The Houthis explicitly said they wanted normal relations with the United States and Saudi Arabia. The United States and Saudi Arabia launched a war against them anyway.

The Saudis wanted the Shi'ite Houthis ousted immediately and Mansour Hadi returned to power. The Obama administration gave them permission to launch the war with promises of full U.S. support. In their very first air raid, the U.S.-Saudi alliance bombed a civilian neighborhood, killing 14 children. Obama immediately authorized new sales of bombs and spare parts for the Saudis' American-made F-15 fighter-bombers. He also sent civilian and military intelligence assets to set up a "joint coordination planning cell" to pick targets and run the logistics of the entire war. U.S. contractors take care of all the maintenance of the Saudis' planes and other equipment. For the first four years of the war, U.S. Air Force refueling tankers helped the Saudis reach distant targets and loiter in place looking for new ones until the Saudis gained their own refueling capability. U.S. satellites and drones provide real-time and after-action surveillance of Yemeni targets.

In place of a declaration of war by the elected Congress of the world's oldest constitutional republic, on March 25, 2015, National Security Council Spokeswoman Bernadette Meehan released a written statement:

> In support of GCC actions to defend against Houthi violence, President Obama has authorized the provision of logistical and intelligence support to GCC-led military operations. While U.S. forces are not taking direct military action in Yemen in support of this effort, we are establishing a Joint Planning Cell with Saudi Arabia to coordinate U.S. military and intelligence support.

The Obama administration put a piece in the *New York Times* explaining they knew the war would be "long, bloody and indecisive." But they said they had to help launch it anyway because they had to "placate the Saudis" while pursuing the Iran nuclear deal. This is mildly ironic since the 2015 nuclear deal secured Saudi Arabia's military interests by guaranteeing Iran will not attempt to develop nuclear weapons by locking

241

down and inspecting Iran's civilian nuclear program far more than ever before. But in the larger scheme of things, the deal seemed to open up the possibility of a real rapprochement between the U.S. and Iran. The Saudis should have known that Obama had no intention of tilting back toward the Persians. He was only trying to take the threat of war over their nuclear program off the table. That was all. He was barely able to get the deal past Congress as it was. But the Saudis panicked that they were now going to lose their place in the American-dominated order in the Middle East. So, to make the princes feel better about the situation, and although they knew that there was no "realistic endgame," the Obama administration helped launch an orgy of mass killing as bad as the horrors of Iraq War II or Syria.

"We're doing this not because we think it would be good for Yemen policy; we're doing it because we think it's good for U.S.-Saudi relations," Ilan Goldenberg, a former Obama administration official, told the *L.A. Times*.

From the very beginning, the administration knew the war could not succeed. Gen. Lloyd Austin, then commander of Central Command, admitted, "I don't currently know the specific goals and objectives of the Saudi campaign, and I would have to know that to be able to assess the likelihood of success." As the *Wall Street Journal* reported, "The Obama administration is skeptical the airstrikes will reverse the Houthi gains. Worried by the risk of more direct intervention by Iran, U.S. officials say they are urging the Saudis to set their sights more narrowly on halting rebel advances and reaching what amounts to a battlefield stalemate that leads all sides to the negotiating table." That was in 2015.

The British and French have been happy to help — and cash in — as well. The UK's Special Air Services (SAS) has been documented fighting with Saudi forces against the Houthis on the ground in Yemen. "The Saudi bosses absolutely depend on BAE Systems," John Deverell, a former defense official and attaché to Saudi Arabia and Yemen, told the *Guardian*. "They couldn't do it without us." The Royal Air Force provides training for pilots and targeters. Their Special Boat Squadron (SBS) has provided training for Saudi-backed mercenary fighters, reportedly including child soldiers; that is, slaves.

After a British court ruled that continued weapons transfers were illegal due to the war crimes being committed with them, a special review by the Ministry of Defense decided that these ongoing atrocities were merely "isolated incidents" and bomb sales could resume.

As Yemen's "pen-holder" on the UNSC, Britain has never committed to a real attempt at ending the war but reserve to themselves the right to initiate one, at least on that level. So nothing happens.

Former Obama administration officials Robert Malley and Stephen Pomper later wrote in most comedic and tragic fashion:

Why the U.S. got entangled in this war — and why a president so determined to keep the country out of another Mideast military mess nonetheless got caught in this one — makes for a painful story. In March 2015, Saudi Arabia came to the U.S. with a request for support in a campaign it vowed to conduct regardless. After that, and although events took place a mere four years ago, memories blur. In our conversations, many former U.S. officials found it hard to recall what precisely the Saudis asked for, what specific commitments the administration made in response, and when certain types of assistance started to flow. Some, including one of us who attended the deliberations, recall a deeply ambivalent president who greenlighted U.S. support but insisted it be confined to the defense of Saudi territory and not extend to the war against the Houthis. Others don't recall hearing about that instruction, and struggle to reconcile it with what the U.S. actually did during the war — including refueling coalition sorties and replenishing weapons stocks.

Yet all agree the decision ultimately came without much debate. The reason, at bottom, was straightforward: Here was a partner (Saudi Arabia) seeking help in restoring a government (that of President Hadi) the U.S. regarded as legitimate and a loyal ally in the war against al Qaeda. That government had been toppled by an insurgent group (the Houthi or Ansar Allah); although the extent of its ties to Iran was debatable and debated, their existence was indisputable. Plus, all this came at a time when relations between Washington and Riyadh already were deeply damaged by disagreements over the Obama administration's response to the Arab uprisings and, even more so, its negotiations over a nuclear deal with Tehran. As Riyadh saw it, doing nothing would mean permitting control by a Hezbollah-like organization of its southern border [sic], ensconcing a perpetual threat. Rebuffing the Saudi request at any time likely would have provoked a serious crisis in Saudi/U.S. bilateral relations. Doing so while the U.S. was seeking a landmark agreement with the kingdom's sworn enemy could have brought them to breaking point. That was a risk even a president skeptical of the wisdom of Saudi policies and willing to call into question elements of the relationship was not prepared to take.

"Doing nothing" was a "risk" Obama "was not prepared to take." America must stay at war to serve not even the interests, but the emotions of the leaders of its client states... or else what? They never explain that part very well.

Iranian Foreign Minister Javad Zarif revealed to former ambassador Ann Wright that during the 2015 nuclear talks, he and Secretary of State Kerry had worked out a side-deal to end the war in Yemen. The Saudis at first agreed to it, then quickly reneged. Obama blamed Iran.

MBS's War

Regional politics aside, one reason why the Saudis attacked Yemen came down to palace intrigue within the royal family. Mohammed bin Salman (MBS), the now-infamous killer of *Washington Post* writer Jamal Khashoggi, had just been named defense minister and deputy crown prince at the age of 29. Bin Salman thought he needed to shore up his support inside the royal family by acting tough and launching a war. He had an agenda, since successfully carried out, to arrest his cousin Mohammed bin Nayef and take his place as crown prince and de facto king, since his father, King Salmon, is quite elderly and reportedly has dementia. Launching the war seems to have been part of his plan for political success. Though there have been some rumblings of discontent over his incompetence, his failure to accomplish the war's stated goals after six years has not seemed to hurt him very much within the royal court.

Obama's deputy national security adviser Ben Rhodes later said that it was bin Salman's mentor, the United Arab Emirates' Mohammed bin Zayed, who first came seeking to "sell" the war to them.

It's Treason, Then

The Saudis and United Arab Emirates launched "Operation Decisive Storm" that March, with Obama's explicit permission and participation. Al Qaeda quickly became a part of what has since been called the "Saudi-led coalition," leading the initial resistance against the Houthi takeover of the capital. For a time, AQAP succeeded in seizing what Reuters called a "mini state." Their territory included military bases, weapons depots and as many as six towns, including the entire port city of Mukalla, along with al Shihr, Ja'ar, Zinjibar, Azzan, Habban, Mahfad, Saqra, and Ahwar, their tax bases and oil revenues, as well as vast tracts of Yemen's eastern countryside.

Not long after the war began, Pentagon reporter Mark Perry spoke to generals at CENTCOM and the U.S. Special Operations Command (USSOCOM) who were livid that Obama had turned their policy around so severely. He reported that they had argued strenuously against it. Perry also spoke to Yemen expert Michael Horton from the Jamestown Foundation (no relation to the author). Horton denounced Senator McCain's hawkish stance in support of the war. "This is a guy who complained that we were Iran's air force in Iraq. Well, guess what? Now we're al Qaeda's air force in Yemen."

It does sound too crazy to be true, or perhaps, like some sort of partisan attack. So here is the Obama-friendly *New York Times* from June 10, 2015, conceding the plain, awful truth:

> In recent weeks, the al Qaeda affiliate in Yemen has allied with armed tribes to fight Iranian-backed Houthi rebels, putting that alliance on the same side of the country's civil war as the United States and Saudi Arabia. In Syria, al Qaeda-allied fighters are important members of a rebel coalition against President Bashar al-Assad that includes groups supported by the West.
>
> This strategy has clear benefits for a group that has long been near the top of the United States's list of enemies by allowing it to build local support while providing some cover against the threat of foreign military action.

The U.S.A. was openly siding with al Qaeda in two simultaneous wars. The terrorist group was now considered to be only "near the top" of our government's enemies list. Tell that to the survivors of the thousands of American civilian and military victims murdered by these terrorists in the last 30 years. Well, they did tell them, right there in the newspaper of record.

And that was back in 2015. The situation has only gotten worse. In 2016, Reuters, reporting from the city of Mukalla, explained:

> If Islamic State's capital is the Syrian city of Raqqa, then al Qaeda's is Mukalla, a southeastern Yemeni port city of 500,000 people. Al Qaeda fighters there have abolished taxes for local residents, operate speedboats manned by RPG-wielding fighters who impose fees on ship traffic, and make propaganda videos in which they boast about paving local roads and stocking hospitals.
>
> The economic empire was described by more than a dozen diplomats, Yemeni security officials, tribal leaders and residents of Mukalla. Its emergence is the most striking unintended consequence of the Saudi-led military intervention in Yemen. The campaign, backed by the United States, has helped Al Qaeda in the Arabian Peninsula (AQAP) to become stronger than at any time since it first emerged almost 20 years ago. ...
>
> A senior Yemeni government official said the war against the Houthis "provided a suitable environment for the ... expansion of al Qaeda." The withdrawal of government army units from their bases in the south allowed al Qaeda to acquire "very large quantities of sophisticated and advanced weapons, including shoulder-fired missiles and armed vehicles."

Since then, AQAP has withdrawn from the cities and have focused on fighting the Houthis. While the UAE claimed to be fighting al Qaeda, they instead bought them off and integrated AQAP into the UAE's mercenary forces on the ground, as the Associated Press and UK's *Independent* revealed in 2018. "Key participants in the pacts said the U.S. was aware of the arrangements and held off on any drone strikes," the AP reported.

In 2019, CNN revealed that the Emiratis had even given al Qaeda American MRAP armored personnel carriers to use in battle. Terrorists straight from the U.S. Treasury Department lists, such as Islah Party leaders Abdallah al-Ahdal and Al Hassan Ali Abkar and Hadi government advisers and officials like AQAP's Nayif Saleh al-Qaysi, Abd al-Wahhab al-Humayqani, Abdul Majeed al-Zindani and Shaykh Abu al-Abbas, receive backing from the Saudis and UAE and support the so-called Hadi "government" in return. In a very real sense, Presidents Obama and Trump have again put the U.S. Army, Air Force, Navy and special operations forces at war in the service of al Qaeda leader Ayman al-Zawahiri.

Yemeni journalist Nasser Arrabyee emphasizes that the small group declaring itself loyal to ISIS in Yemen is mostly aligned with al Qaeda, rather than their deadly rivals, as is the case in Syria. The previous drone war had "decapitated" enough of the old leadership to end any rivalry and allow them to fight together.

The rise of the Houthis has helped to mainstream AQAP as the vanguard force against them. In a remarkable monograph for Joint Special Operations University in 2018, called "The Enemy is Us: How Allied and U.S. Strategy in Yemen Contributes to AQAP's Survival," Dr. Norman Cigar writes:

> Absent foreign intervention in 2015, the Ansar Allah-Saleh alliance would probably soon have fallen apart and a reconfiguration of a new domestic balance of forces among the country's many players would have developed. Instead … [L]ocal commanders and government officials reportedly have often welcomed AQAP as a cobelligerent against the Ansar Allah, according to a Popular Committee commander and former AQAP member, and have diverted arms meant for the committees to AQAP. Conversely, AQAP apparently has long found opposition to the Ansar Allah a useful vehicle to ingratiate itself with the tribes, and in 2012 ordered its members not to clash with or otherwise alienate the tribes in the interest of a united front against the Ansar Allah.

He also wrote that "waves" of Yemeni al Qaeda fighters who had gone to Syria to fight Assad were returning home, first to avoid the Nusra-ISIS split, then for their own safety as the Islamic State collapsed. Now they were battle-hardened, back home and again ready to help America and its allies take on the dreaded Shi'ite menace.

Iran's Role

A major excuse for Saudi and American intervention against the Houthis in Yemen is that they are backed by Iran. As President Donald Trump explained at a cabinet meeting in January 2019,

> Iran — when I became President, I had a meeting at the Pentagon with lots of generals. They were like from a movie. Better looking than Tom Cruise, and stronger.

> And I had more generals than I've ever seen, and we were at the bottom of this incredible room. And I said, "This is the greatest room I've ever seen." I saw more computer boards than I think that they make today. And every part of the Middle East, and other places that was under attack, was under attack because of Iran. And I said to myself, "Wow." I mean, you look at Yemen, you look at Syria, you look at every place. Saudi Arabia was under siege. They were all. I mean, they wanted Yemen because of the long border with Saudi Arabia, and that's why they're there, frankly. But every place was under siege.

Former Secretary of Defense James Mattis claimed, "Everywhere you look, if there's trouble in the region, you find Iran. What we're seeing is the nations in the region and others elsewhere trying to checkmate Iran and the amount of disruption, the amount of instability they can cause." Gen. Mattis helped to lead the invasion of Iraq, which deposed Saddam Hussein for the Ayatollah, and he had just finished up fighting Iraq War III against ISIS for him too, so perhaps he was covering for his own embarrassment on that front.

In fact, the Ansarullah movement (the Houthis) was only friendly with Iran and not dependent on their support at the beginning of the war, nor did they take orders from Tehran. For example, the Iranians had warned the Houthis repeatedly not to march into the capital city of Sana'a and the southern port of Aden because it would be sure to provoke a terrible Saudi response, as Obama himself admitted. His government knew it too. "It remains our assessment that Iran does not exert command and control over the Houthis in Yemen," NSC spokeswoman Bernadette Meehan told reporters in April 2015. "It is wrong to think of the Houthis as a proxy force for Iran," another U.S. intelligence official said.

Charles Schmitz, an expert on Yemen at the Middle East Institute (which is funded by co-belligerent, the UAE), told Slavin, "From 2004 to

2010, the Houthis won wars against the Yemeni government without Iran. Iran's role now is non-essential, and the Houthis won't take orders from them." Immediately after the war began, U.S. officials started complaining. The *Wall Street Journal* wrote that "American intelligence officials had long thought that the Saudis overstated the extent of Iranian support for the Houthis, and that Iran had never seen its ties to the rebel group as more than a useful annoyance to the Saudis."

Yemen is a nation so awash with weapons, before and after President Obama shipped hundreds of tons over there, that this whole time they have continued to be small arms exporters, even during the war. Far from depending on Iran to ship them weapons, on average per capita, Yemenis are more heavily armed than Texans, with almost all households owning fully automatic AK-47 rifles and better.

Journalist Gareth Porter has repeatedly debunked false news stories about the Iranians shipping arms to the Houthis. In one case, the ship did not have any guns on it. The other one did have guns aboard, but it was on its way from Yemen to Somalia. Accusations abound, but they never hold up. Numerous experts have written at length about the vast political and religious differences between the Houthis and the Iranians. The Zaidis are an entirely different sect of Shi'ite Islam than that of the Iranians, so Ayatollah Khamenei has no religious authority over them. As the analysts Joost Hiltermann and April Longley Alley wrote in *Foreign Policy*, "the Houthis are not Hezbollah."

The limited amount of support Iran has given to the Houthis over the course of the war, include radio equipment, training and supposedly a 3D printer and schematics for building drones. One thing is certain about their relationship, and that is they are closer now than ever before. In the late summer of 2019, Iran's mullahs finally officially recognized the Houthis as the government of Yemen. The country is under a near-total blockade, with their ports and airports shut down or under Saudi and United Nations' control. It is hard to see how Iran could provide much support under current circumstances beyond money in the form of discounted oil sales, weapons designs or technical advice to the Houthi government.

The Houthis seem to have an ever-increasing inventory of anti-tank missiles, but these are more likely being sold to them by disgruntled proxy forces when the Saudis and UAE do not pay on time, Yemen expert Michael Horton told the author.

Former United Nations ambassador Nikki Haley put on a big show in late 2017, displaying the remains of a Yemeni missile that had been fired at Riyadh, claiming that it must have been given to them by Iran. This was not true. The industry journal *Jane's Defense Weekly* debunked the story a year before it even came out, writing that the Yemeni

> Burkan-2 appears to use a new type of warhead section that is locally fabricated. Both Iran and North Korea have displayed Scud derivatives with shuttlecock-shaped warheads, but none of these match the Yemeni version. The range of the Burkan missiles also appears to have been extended by a reduction in the weight of their warheads.

It was a modified Russian-made Scud-B missile, the source being either North Korea or the old Soviet Union and modified by the Yemenis themselves. The Houthis got them from the Yemeni army, which had at least 300 Scuds before the war ever started, as the AP reported.

The Bab el-Mandeb, the gate of the Red Sea to the Gulf of Aden, the Arabian Sea and then the broader Indian Ocean, is a potential choke point in world trade and naval mobility. It makes sense that the U.S. would be concerned about an Iranian-friendly power controlling the nation of Yemen, but that could in no way justify their brutal treatment of the people these past years. For decades, the Saudis simply bribed the different Yemeni factions to behave. Why could they not just go back to that?

After six years, the war has solved nothing. The Saudi puppet Hadi is essentially on house arrest in Riyadh, not even in the country of Yemen at all. There is no chance that he will ever be the president of a united Yemen again. The stated goal of the war cannot be accomplished. If by some miracle the U.S.-led coalition did succeed in ousting the Houthis from power in Sana'a, as Senator Rand Paul once explained to Neil Cavuto on Fox News, that could mean al Qaeda and the Muslim Brotherhood taking over the capital instead. Cavuto got the lesson. It is simple enough.

Yet the coalition continues to bomb them — and everybody else.

The Worst Humanitarian Crisis in the World

The American-Saudi-UAE war against Yemen is plainly criminal. Barack Obama sought no authorization from Congress, dressing up the war as a Saudi-led effort. "Leading from behind," they call it. But who is the superpower, and who is the client state? In 2019, Major General David C. Hill, deputy commander of CENTCOM, confirmed to the AFP that the U.S. was still helping the Saudis with targeting in their air war.

Aside from the war never being authorized, the coalition has been committing war crimes since the beginning. For years, the Saudis have deliberately bombed the country's infrastructure and other civilian targets such as the electricity, water and sewage works, schools, hospitals, factories, bridges, farms, markets, car and truck dealerships, fishermen in their boats, weddings, funerals, civilian apartment buildings, refugee camps and even near-ancient homes that had been passed down within families for centuries.

Michael Knights, from the usually hawkish Washington Institute for Near East Policy (WINEP), accused the Saudis of waging a campaign of "terror bombing" over the northern city of Sa'ada in 2015 and 2016. "You couldn't have hit more civilian targets," he told Arron Merat of the *Guardian*. The Saudis "worked their way down a list of all the national infrastructure targets like we did [during Iraq War I in 1991.] That meant everything: cranes, bridges, ministries ... water treatment plants."

The U.S.-Saudi coalition launched 18,000 strikes by the fall of 2018, "one-third of which have hit non-military targets," according to Frank McManus of the International Rescue Committee.

The Saudis have been credibly accused of illegally using white phosphorus incendiary bombs in civilian areas. They also drop massive 2,000-pound bombs and anti-personnel cluster bombs in populated areas when 500-pound bombs are bad enough. Innocent people are killed every day. Journalist Nicolas Niarchos wrote about some of them:

> In the rubble outside, Sabrah saw what he described as "bits and parts" of human beings. "A woman used to live with her children in one floor of the building. They used to get up in the morning and sell boiled eggs," Sabrah told me, his anger rising. "What danger did these children pose to the coalition? What danger did they pose by selling eggs in the street?"

> When I asked Sabrah how he felt about U.S. involvement in the war, he replied, "America is the main sponsor of all that is happening to us." He had reached this conclusion only recently. "The Gulf countries are merely tools in its hands."

According to Yemeni reporter Nasser Arrabyee, the people of the capital Sana'a have long called it the "American-Saudi war," appropriately placing blame on the real power behind the satellites' aggression.

There was an important meeting scheduled between tribal leaders to attempt to settle the civil war at a funeral in Sana'a in October 2016. In Yemeni culture, funerals are a traditionally neutral meeting ground for dispute resolution. The Saudis bombed it, killing 140 people, including many tribal leaders, and prolonged the conflict in perhaps the ultimate example of the counterproductivity of targeted assassinations, unless that was the point.

In August 2018, the world was horrified when the Saudis bombed a school bus full of young children on a field trip sponsored by the UN, killing all 40 of them. Local activists showed from the wreckage that it was a Lockheed bomb, made in America.

A couple of months later, 30 former Obama officials signed a public letter saying they regretted giving an American blank check of support for the Saudis to wage war on Yemen. It was far too little too late. None of them left their cushy think tank and consulting jobs to help distribute food and clean water to the innocent people whose lives they destroyed with the war they helped launch. But at least it showed that they knew what they had done.

Economist Martha Mundy did a lengthy study for the Fletcher School of Law and Diplomacy at Tufts University showing Saudi Arabia's targeting of Yemeni farms. Their jets bomb the grain silos, flocks of sheep in the fields, horses in their stables, irrigation systems, work trucks and every aspect of the process of food distribution that they can. It is a deliberate medieval-style siege campaign against a civilian population, a genocide. That may sound like hyperbole, but many military and humanitarian experts have said the same for years. What do you call it when one nation, or a group of nations, deliberately inflict famine on another — one that had never attacked or even threatened them? Participation in the Yemen war is a moral war crime and a profound violation of the Geneva Conventions and the American War Crimes Act, among others. Lawyers in both Obama and Trump's State and Defense Departments have written memos expressing their concern that administration officials could go to prison for violations of these laws in this war. Despite it being laughable that under our system, anyone at that level of power could ever be held accountable for serious crimes they commit on the job, it does again reveal that they know perfectly well what it is they are doing.

Yemen is the poorest country in the Middle East. Due to previous IMF machinations, they had reduced the production of sustenance crops like sorghum and millet and instead focused on growing more coffee and cotton for export. This made sense in a globalized economy where a nation can import food with the money they make selling their specialty. When the war began in 2015, Yemen was importing 80 to 90 percent of their food. But once the Americans and the Saudis put a naval blockade on their country, cutting them off from international trade, and for long periods, even aid from the UN and related humanitarian groups, they were ruined. For years, the port of Hodeida on the Red Sea, which supplies Sana'a and everything in the north of the country, was completely shut off to international trade. Scott Paul of the aid group Oxfam International told the author that even when the port is open, the Saudis often deliberately enforce an inspection regime that takes so long much of the food is spoiled before it gets to the hungry.

In 2016, pro-Hadi and Saudi forces moved the central bank to the southern port city of Aden, cutting all civil servants in the north off from their salaries. This compounded the deliberate targeting of infrastructure in airstrikes by causing the repairmen to all be laid off, along with garbagemen, doctors and other essential workers, leading to even more economic and health problems for the people there.

Since 2017, there have been massive outbreaks of cholera and diphtheria each year. Thousands of people have died from them, most of them children under five years old. Cholera is actually a quite treatable bacterial infection. Most of the time antibiotics are not even required, just a steady supply of clean water. But without that, people die, mostly the very young. Quite literally, this means tiny babies and toddlers, thousands and thousands of them — American victims all — are dying of dehydration from uncontrollable vomiting and diarrhea.

For more than four years, Western media and politicians clung to the old and immediately outdated UN statistic from early 2017 that 10,000 people had died in the war. How could the war still be going on, and the casualties never increase? The answer was the UN did not have the ability to collect the data to update their statistics and the media were either lying or too partisan or too lazy even to try to find or determine more recent calculations. The number is more than twenty times that by now, possibly much higher. Jamie McGoldrick, the United Nations resident coordinator for Yemen told the author in 2018 that since half of the hospitals were destroyed or otherwise closed, many people who had been killed or died as a result of the fighting were never counted. He also admitted that the 10,000 number still being cited was surely long out of date.

Millions of Yemenis lack clean drinking water and access to the necessary calories to survive and thrive. The group ACLED Data said in early 2020 that 112,000 people, including approximately 13,000 civilians, have been killed in "targeted attacks." These are precise counts of reported and confirmed deaths of individuals and are certainly the most conservative numbers available. In 2019, the United Nations finally increased their numbers, estimating that 233,000 had been killed, 100,000 in direct violence, the other 130,000 from deprivation caused by the war. Sixty percent of the dead were children under the age of five. The group Save the Children counted 85,000 dead children in this deliberately inflicted famine back in the fall of 2018. In October 2020, the UN warned that another 100,000 children were at risk of dying due to malnutrition.

Until the statisticians can measure the excess death rate in future surveys, no one can really know how many people have started to death, or died of otherwise treatable diseases because they were so hungry and malnourished that they succumbed to minor infections. But we will almost certainly find out that it has been half a million or more civilians who have been killed by this war, beyond the tens of thousands killed in direct violence.

At the end of his presidency, Donald Trump and Mike Pompeo added the Houthis to the State Department's international terrorists list over the objections of humanitarian organizations, who protested that to do so would not hurt the Houthi regime but would make it impossible for them to deliver food aid to Yemen's starving civilians.

United Arab Emirates Murderers

The UAE has its own interests in the war. Their major ally has been the Southern Transitional Council (STC), a leftist governing faction that rules the port city of Aden, though at times they have fought each other as well. The STC has also fought against al Qaeda. They have not sought to defeat the Houthis, but instead to secede from their rule and recreate the pre-1990s North and South Yemen divided arrangement.

While the Saudis have focused on waging their war crimes from the air, their UAE partners focused more on the ground war, sending in their U.S.-trained army and hiring a vast militia of terrorists and mercenaries. UAE forces have been repeatedly caught committing the war crimes of rape, torture, disappearances and murder, including by roasting their victims on spits over open fires to death. This reporting in the Associated Press might be dismissed as war party propaganda if it were directed at an enemy nation as part of a case for intervention. In this case, it was the western media reluctantly casting doubt on the wisdom of partnering with such barbarians. Thus "against interest," the reporting seems more credible. United Nations reports have made similar, credible accusations against the Emiratis for rape, torture and murder. The UAE has largely integrated AQAP into its mercenary force, rendering the supposedly ongoing CIA and special operations war against them a farce. They have also hired former U.S. military officers, troops from Senegal and child soldiers from Sudan to serve in their militia force, who remain in Yemen even after the Emiratis withdrew the bulk of their army in 2019.

In 2020, the socialist-separatist Southern Transitional Council government, in alliance with the UAE, seized power from the Saudi-backed government on the Yemeni island of Socotra in the Gulf of Aden. U.S. marines quickly set up shop there as well.

Saleh's Last Mistake

In December 2017, the former dictator Abdullah Saleh attempted to cut a deal with the Saudis at the expense of the Houthis. The Houthis turned around and killed him first. If he had worked well with the Saudis for 30 years and had been partners with the Houthis more recently, then perhaps if he had not gone behind their back, a real compromise could have been made. We will never know.

The Houthis quickly consolidated their power in the capital and over the military and have held their enemies at bay. War, unless you lose, is the health of the state. Factions who never had cause to ally with the Houthis support them now, far beyond their Sa'ada Province home in the north. The international relations experts call it the "rally around the flag effect." Americans who came to revere their government after September 11th may be able to relate.

The Saudis and UAE have also had significant differences over who to back and what their policies should be. Saudi Arabia, which hates the Muslim Brotherhood in Egypt, favors their party, al-Islah, in Yemen. And though the Saudis often support al Qaeda forces, such as in Iraq War II and in Syria, in Yemen, they have mostly left AQAP to the UAE.

Yemen may end up divided between north and south as it was until Saleh unified the country 30 years ago. While the UAE-aligned separatist, socialist "Southern Transitional Council" is attempting to make their own state centered in the southern port city of Aden, the Houthis evidently lack the ability to stop them.

Long, Bloody and Indecisive

In late 2017, nearly three years into the war, the Brookings Institution, a Democratic Party-aligned think tank, raised a vital question with their article, "Who Are the Houthis, and Why Are We at War with Them?" It was a decent piece by the former CIA officer Bruce Riedel, who is fairly interventionist. But the article and its title must amount to some sort of existential remark on the state of our society.

President Trump stepped up the war against al Qaeda in Yemen too. As Airwars.org showed, especially in 2017, his administration increased JSOC night raids and CIA drone strikes against them, although they mostly succeeded in killing civilians as the journalist Iona Craig has documented. And where Obama drone-bombed Anwar Awlaki and his son, both U.S.-born American citizens, Trump's forces killed Awlaki's eight-year-old daughter Nowar in a JSOC raid. She reportedly bled out over four hours after being shot in the neck. Despite this escalation of the drone and night raid war and some successes against al Qaeda leaders, the bulk of AQAP and ISIS fighters have simply joined the UAE's mercenary army where they are protected from American strikes.

Though all of Western media continue to refer to the Ansarullah regime in Sana'a as Houthi "rebels," as of this writing they have ruled the capital city and the north of the country with no real challengers for over six years. There is no indication they are leaving any time soon. It seems the Saudis' plan is to keep fighting until Hadi is back on the throne, which will never happen. It has been the war that has solidified Houthi power in Sana'a, and it may be the primary factor in continuing popular support for their minority faction in power. Under Donald Trump, there was no serious pressure by America or its allies to end this war any time soon. Perennial attempts to start real peace talks have gone nowhere.

In 2018 and 2019, the Houthis showed that with a combination of missile and drone attacks, they have little trouble destroying targets in Saudi Arabia, including inside Riyadh, and with precise targeting, such as with the drone assassination of a top Saudi general and oil refinery facilities.

Remarkably, in 2019, after the scandal of bin Salman's brutal murder of Jamal Khashoggi, both houses of Congress passed resolutions invoking the War Powers Resolution of 1973 to force President Trump to end U.S. participation in the war. However, it was a "continuing" rather than a "concurrent" resolution, providing him the opportunity to veto, which he did. They could have refused to finance any U.S. participation in the war, but those amendments to the National Defense Authorization Act were killed in conference committee. When they did pass a measure to restrict new bomb sales, Trump's State Department under Mike Pompeo declared that the sales were an "emergency" so they could continue.

"People make miscalculations all the time," Steve Pomper, a former Obama NSC official, told the *Times*. Of course this is true. Who among us has not accidentally started a war against a government that they were working with against their actual al Qaeda enemies from time to time, right? This was Obama's third. "But it was striking to me as I reflected on my time in the Obama administration that it wasn't just that we embarked on this escapade — it's that we didn't pull ourselves out of it." For two years, they helped to murder tens of thousands of innocent people in a war they had just accidentally stumbled into, and yet, somehow, they could not bring themselves to stop. That is rather striking.

At the very end of his term, Obama symbolically suspended new arms sales to Saudi Arabia. It meant nothing. The Trump administration went right on ahead at full steam. Trump justified the continuation of this tragedy for one reason only: money. He ludicrously claimed that the Saudis are pledged to spend $450 billion on American weapons in the near future. This is little more than a hoax. It would take decades for the Saudis to spend that much money on U.S. weapons at the current rate. Trump claimed a "million" American jobs depend on arms sales to Saudi Arabia, but defense expert William Hartung found that "actual, paid-for deliveries of U.S.-produced arms for Saudi Arabia have averaged about $2.5 billion per year over the past decade, enough to support at most 20,000 to 40,000 jobs, some of which are located overseas." From a narrower view, Raytheon alone has made more than $3 billion in arms sales to Saudi Arabia between 2015 and 2020. According to the *New York Times*, their lobbyists went to "great lengths" to influence officials in the Trump administration, particularly trade adviser Peter Navarro, to pressure Trump to veto Congress's various invocations of the War Powers Resolution to stop the war.

American arms manufacturers are in the perfectly deniable position of fulfilling U.S. government demand. Therefore, they may hold themselves not responsible for any innocent people who are killed with their weapons. For example, missile maker Raytheon does not comment "on the military actions of our allies or customers." Arms sales to Saudi Arabia only "reflect the foreign policy and national security interests of the United States government and are in compliance with U.S. law." That is all they need to know. Of course, when it is time to pay up to the think tanks who write the studies justifying the policy or cozy up to the president's trade adviser, they are the first ones in line.

There is no question that it means a lot to them. Trump made their top lobbyist, Mark Esper, the secretary of defense. Biden's first defense secretary is former general Lloyd Austin, who has been sitting on the board of Raytheon ever since he helped Obama and bin Salman start this phase of the war back in 2015.

But even a few hundred billion dollars amounts to chump change compared to the overall American economy. The nation does not need Saudi investment to sustain us one bit. Lockheed Martin, Raytheon, Northrop Grumman, General Dynamics, United Technologies, Boeing, Booz Allen Hamilton, BAE Systems, and the politicians they support might need the princes, but they are not us. And even if somehow the U.S.A. was genuinely dependent on that revenue, then we, of course, would still have to do without because killing people for money is wrong.

You could even ask Donald Trump. He would tell you the same thing.

Chapter Thirteen:
War All the Time

"We have done a tremendous disservice
not only to the Middle East — we've
done a tremendous disservice to
humanity. The people that have
been killed, the people that have
been wiped away — and for what?
It's not like we had victory. It's a mess."
— Donald Trump

"Don't kid yourself. You do have
a Military-Industrial Complex.
They do like war."
— Donald Trump

"I want Boeing and I want Lockheed
and I want Raytheon to take those
orders and to hire lots of people to
make that incredible equipment."
— Donald Trump

"I would leave troops
in the Middle East."
— Joe Biden

Maximum Pressure

Donald Trump unnecessarily escalated tensions with Iran back to the level of the bad old days under George W. Bush and early Obama. Trump claimed Obama's nuclear deal was the worst deal in all of history, citing the fact that the JCPOA did not include restrictions on Iranian ballistic missiles and contained some relatively short-term sunset provisions.

In 2018, Israeli Prime Minister Benjamin Netanyahu gave Trump a presentation claiming that Israeli spies had somehow seized a warehouse full of Iranian nuclear weapons secrets. Most of these happened to be the same ones his predecessors, Ariel Sharon and Ehud Olmert, pushed in the form of the fake Iranian scientist's "smoking laptop." Netanyahu pulled the same stunt publicly a few weeks later. The only new claims were an order by the defense minister, which was supposedly overheard being discussed by others, and an alleged blueprint for the program's future. There were no markings or official stamps on any of the documents nor any other indication they were real. Trump withdrew the U.S. from the deal shortly after.

Trump had also been somewhat humiliated by the poison pill provision in the American law ratifying the deal that said he would have to certify Iranian compliance every 90 days. Luckily, Iran has officially stayed in the agreement with the rest of the UN Security Council powers, though they have ceased to abide by some of its restrictions on the size of their stockpile of low-enriched uranium and heavy water. Though this may sound like a violation, this limited response to America's withdrawal is actually stipulated in the deal itself.

Leaving the nuclear deal was just the beginning of the Trump administration's "maximum pressure" campaign against the government in Tehran, a strategy which mostly consisted of another brutal regime of "strongest sanctions in history," as Secretary of State Mike Pompeo called them. This was meant to either force the Ayatollah to accept new, stricter terms in the deal or to weaken his state so much that local forces could overthrow it. "After our sanctions come in force, it will be battling to keep its economy alive."

Trump's administration could not launch a CIA coup or military invasion. However, his policy amounted to one of backing the mullahs into a corner where they have no way to compromise further while still saving face. Pompeo's list of demands in his May 2018 Heritage Foundation speech were clearly designed to be impossible for the other side to meet. That is no way to make a deal. It did not work, though the sanctions have virtually halted international trade to and from Iran and induced mass suffering and deprivation on the part of the civilian population. It could very well have led to war.

Competing tensions over influence in Iraq especially have led to repeated violent clashes, including the American missile attack on Iranian Quds Force leader Gen. Qasem Soleimani in January 2020 and an Iranian missile volley directed at an American base in Iraq in response. [See Chapter 11.]

In July 2020, a reported joint Israeli-American sabotage campaign hit the Natanz nuclear enrichment facility, a pipeline and some ships at port in the Persian Gulf, among other targets. The supposedly fanatical maniac, the Ayatollah Khamenei, did not respond in kind.

There is a better way. Dick Cheney himself promoted it back in the 1990s when he was the CEO of Halliburton, the Texas oil services company. In comments he made to the Cato Institute in 1998 blasting Bill Clinton's sanctions policy, including against Iran, Cheney said, "The good Lord didn't see fit to put oil and gas only where there are democratically elected regimes friendly to the United States. Occasionally we have to operate in places where, all considered, one would not normally choose to go." The U.S. has nothing to lose, Cheney had explained:

> I think it is a false dichotomy to be told that we have to choose between "commercial" interests and other interests that the United States might have in a particular country or region around the world. Oftentimes the absolute best way to advance human rights and the cause of freedom or the development of democratic institutions is through the active involvement of American businesses. Investment and trade can oftentimes do more to open up a society and to create an opportunity for a society's citizens than reams of diplomatic cables from our State Department.

If there was anything positive about the election of Joe Biden to the presidency from a foreign policy perspective, it is the reasonable chance that he will reenter the nuclear deal with Iran and the other members of the UN Security Council. After the election, the Iranians released a statement saying they would be happy to return to its restrictions if the U.S. were to return to the deal.

Two weeks later, with a green light from the Trump administration, the Israelis assassinated the prominent Iranian scientist Mohsen Fakhrizadeh in an attempt to constrain Biden's ability to rejoin the 2015 nuclear deal and the Ayatollah's continuing willingness to cooperate. Israel's policy, which insists that there be no uranium enrichment for Iran whatsoever, is ironically the single most likely thing to cause Iran to attempt to make nuclear weapons and therefore, an American war to try to stop them. The lesson of Moammar Gaddafi's murder by Obama and the U.S. withdrawal from Obama's nuclear deal by Trump, for Iran, North Korea or any other government the U.S. opposes, is that no American administration can be trusted to keep their word. The next president can overturn any deal his predecessor made on a whim. And if you want to be safe: obtain nuclear weapons, or at least the technology to make them.

Israel's assassination may have worked. Jake Sullivan, Biden's incoming national security adviser, gave in on behalf of the president-elect before November was even over. He told the *New York Times* the U.S. would return to the JCPOA "[i]f Iran returns to compliance, for its obligations that it has been violating, and is prepared to advance good-faith negotiations on these follow-on agreements." America has altered the deal. It may be deliberate sabotage.

Rolling the Presidents

All of the presidents of the War on Terrorism era have run for election partly on the notion that the United States has been doing too much in the world and needs to dial its interventions back for its own good. It was what they knew the people wanted to hear.

George W. Bush campaigned on the doctrine of a "humble foreign policy." He told the American people in his second debate with then-Vice President Al Gore in 2000, "If we don't stop extending our troops all around the world in nation-building missions, then we're going to have a serious problem coming down the road. I'm going to prevent that." In the next debate, he claimed, "I'm going to be judicious as to how to use the military. It needs to be in our vital interest. The mission needs to be clear, and the exit strategy obvious."

Barack Obama famously ran on his early opposition to the "dumb war," the 2003 invasion of Iraq. "I don't want to just end the war, but I want to end the mindset that got us into war in the first place. That's the kind of leadership I intend to provide as president of the United States," he claimed.

Donald Trump ran against the Bush-Obama legacy of permanent war, saying, "We never should have been in the Middle East. It was the single greatest mistake in the history of our country." And further, "We are spread out all over the world. We are in countries most people haven't even heard about. Frankly, it's ridiculous." He sometimes talked as though he really meant to bring the troops home. "Our current strategy of nation-building and regime change is a proven failure." Under a Trump administration, he promised, "the era of nation-building will be brought to a swift and decisive end."

Bush started three wars. Obama started six. Trump famously did not start any new wars, but neither did he end any. U.S. troops still fight in Afghanistan, Somalia, Libya, Syria, Iraq and Yemen, as well as their various special operations missions throughout Africa. The drone war in Pakistan is one that thankfully has all but ended, with Trump ordering his last airstrike there in 2018.

Trump does deserve credit for his deal to get out of Afghanistan. It was his greatest accomplishment in foreign policy. However, he severely set back Iran relations with his unwise and unnecessary "maximum pressure" campaign. He also made the denial of independence for the Palestinians a foregone conclusion by moving the U.S. embassy to Jerusalem. This implies American recognition of Israeli sovereignty over the entire city, making it impossible for East Jerusalem to serve as the future capital of a Palestinian state. Trump also reversed official U.S. policy, which had recognized Israeli colonies in the West Bank as illegal. And he ignored the rights of the Druze living under occupation in the Golan Heights, whose official annexation was recognized by the Trump administration in 2019. All of this must have seemed necessary for Trump to gain the financial support of Zionist activists like the late casino mogul Sheldon Adelson and legions of evangelical Republican voters for his reelection campaign in 2020, but he lost anyway.

Trump's 2020 "peace deals" between UAE, Bahrain, Sudan and Morocco and Israel were not really peace deals at all. None of these countries were at war with Israel, nor threatening it. Sudan is the only one who ever fought Israel, but that was more than 50 years ago. What these deals really represent is a further marginalization of Israel's Palestinian victims. These Arab states had always withheld official recognition of Israel until Palestinians in the West Bank and Gaza Strip were given independence or equal rights. Now even that negligible effort is being thwarted as they turn their back on the Palestinians in exchange for money and weapons.

In 2020, Bob Woodward reported that former Trump officials boasted to him about their effective "strategy" of "scaring the shit out of the president." They would tell him that he would look "weak like Obama" if anything bad happened after he withdrew troops from anywhere. Of course, no matter what catastrophes take place where U.S. forces are stationed, those must always be taken as happening despite their best efforts and are no mark against intervention at all. From a short-term political point of view, in a country where few support the wars but even fewer actively oppose them, the safe political bet has been to let the Pentagon run on autopilot and hope the public does not pay too much attention. Obama had made the same calculation in his time.

It is too bad because, in his 2016 campaign, candidate Trump repeatedly got it right that Obama had helped "found" the Islamic State, by backing the jihadists in Libya and Syria and then also pulling the last troops out of Iraq, so they were not there to protect Mosul when the terrorists rolled into town in 2014. Trump later seemed to forget the first part of that story and allowed the generals to threaten him with a lightning fast ISIS takeover of anywhere he considered pulling back. So, he escalated. Not only did Trump loosen the rules of engagement at the end of Iraq War III in Iraq and Syria, but he kept the troops there after the war. In his last two months in office, he passed on a chance to do anything but reduce troop levels in Afghanistan and Iraq to 2,500 each. This was only a reduction of 500 men in the case of Iraq and about 1,000 in Afghanistan. Trump continued to wage the drone war in Somalia, Libya and the horrific slaughter in Yemen, while sending thousands of troops back to their bases in Saudi Arabia and continued spreading special operations forces and CIA drones to the four corners of the earth.

If one needs an indication of the state of politics inside the Democratic Party in this era, Joe Biden's 2020 campaign barely bothered to criticize America's "forever wars." They were far more determined to cast Trump not as a belligerent prosecutor of unnecessary wars, but rather some kind of "isolationist" whose policies required the new president to take significant steps to "once more have America lead the world." After all, "the world does not organize itself."

In his hilarious and terrifying article for *Foreign Affairs* in January 2020, Biden promised to lead the world into a brave new democratic future free of corruption and violence. He evidently has no idea why that would sound ridiculous to any person with a satellite TV or internet connection anywhere on this planet. The senator from Delaware, the most corrupt, corporatist state in the Union, who supported or failed to prevent somewhere in the neighborhood of eight to ten wars in his political career so far, is going to lead the world toward transparency, peace and democracy? We will have to wait and see. Not until paragraph 27 did Biden promise to end the Middle East wars. But then he did not really promise that at all:

> It is past time to end the forever wars, which have cost the United States untold blood and treasure. As I have long argued, we should bring the vast majority of our troops home from the wars in Afghanistan and the Middle East and narrowly define our mission as defeating al Qaeda and the Islamic State (or ISIS). We should also end our support for the Saudi-led war in Yemen. We must maintain our focus on counter-terrorism, around the world and at home, but staying entrenched in unwinnable conflicts drains our capacity to lead on other issues that require our attention, and it prevents us from rebuilding the other instruments of American power.

Bringing the "vast majority" of U.S. troops home means, of course, bringing a small percentage of them home with no overall change in strategy for the War on Terrorism. As he makes clear, Biden's intention is not to abandon the empire to save the republic but to abandon those American wars that serve as the worst distractions to the larger mission of building up the U.S. government's power over the other nations of the earth.

Biden intends to leave forces in Afghanistan and the Middle East indefinitely. His vice president, Kamala Harris, promised in 2020 that the U.S. was going back to supporting the terrorists in Syria at their first opportunity, promising to "increase pressure" to "secure some dignity, safety and justice for the Syrian people." Apparently, regime change against secular dictators is still not off the table in the new administration.

The only good things Biden promised in Middle East policy were to end the war in Yemen and rejoin the nuclear deal with Iran. But we can always count on politicians to forget all their good promises and keep all their bad ones. There are certainly no guarantees. As late as June 2020, Biden's national security adviser Jake Sullivan endorsed the Yemen war in remarks to the *Washington Post*, "I think we should deepen our support for Saudi in terms of the legitimate threats it faces. ... I think the United States should go even deeper from the point of view of its technical assistance and security cooperation on that set of issues," he told them. Activists in and out of Congress are ready to force the issue but need overwhelming popular support to see both of these things through. Israeli Prime Minister Benjamin Netanyahu forbade a return to the Iran deal soon after the U.S. presidential election of 2020. "There must be no return to the previous nuclear agreement," he declared.

Biden must feel badly burned after the disaster of Iraq War II. He was a comparative voice for restraint in the Obama government. But his initial picks to fill national security positions in his first cabinet are not promising for peace. As previously discussed, Antony Blinken, Jake Sullivan, Lloyd Austin, Susan Rice, Samantha Power, Tom Donilon and John Kerry all have terrible foreign policy records. If Biden has learned any reluctance to fight after supporting so many failures, it sure does not show in his national security staff.

Invading Africa

Since the French and Americans followed the consequences of their war from Libya to Mali, the terrorists and the drone and special operations forces that follow them have also spread into Chad, Niger, Burkina Faso, Nigeria, Cameroon and Tunisia.

As previously mentioned, Boko Haram, the indigenous Islamist insurrectionist group in Nigeria, has reportedly traveled up to Mali to receive indoctrination and training in weapons and tactics. They have taken their battle back to Nigeria, having been made that much worse for the experience. After the Obama administration added them to the international terrorist list in 2014 they declared their loyalty to the Islamic State, thus supposedly justifying the presence of the Special Operations Command for the indefinite future. In the book *Shadow Wars*, Christopher Davidson makes a compelling case that since 2014 Boko Haram has received massive funding and possibly technical assistance from the Saudis and Qataris. Though it gets very little coverage, U.S. forces have been killed fighting Boko Haram in Nigeria, as army Gen. Donald Bolduc confirmed to journalist Nick Turse.

Turse has become an indispensable source about the expansion of the U.S. African Command (U.S.-AFRICOM) and of American power and influence on the continent, especially in the form of deployed special operations forces. Mostly this means training and equipping current standing armies. It also includes combat missions against armed groups of all descriptions on behalf of friendly governments. As of early 2021, there were 29 bases across Africa, and missions in far more, including Somalia, Kenya, Tunisia, Libya, Mali, Niger, Chad, Nigeria, Cameroon, Central African Republic and Burkina Faso. This does not include the U.S. presence in places like South Sudan, which they do not pretend falls under the category of the War on Terrorism.

The military's AFRICOM and USSOCOM have a massive vested interest in finding armed groups to hunt down and fight. Lucky for them, the 2011 war in Libya and its aftermath have provided plenty.

General David M. Rodriguez, fresh from losing the war in Afghanistan under generals McChrystal and Petraeus, promoted to the new head of the Africa Command, told the Congress in 2013, "[W]ith the United States military out of Iraq and pulling out of Afghanistan, the army is looking for new missions around the world." Army sources were enthusiastic to Defense News as well.

> Based at Fort Riley, Kan., the "Dagger Brigade" will be the first regionally aligned brigade the Army will field as part of a new initiative to keep non-deploying units engaged globally now that rotations to Iraq have ended, deployments to Afghanistan are winding down and the service is looking for ways to stay globally engaged.

But what right does America have to pick and choose political winners and losers in Africa? If our troops side with the actual least-worst faction — or even just the most pro-American one — in any given country, that is just as likely to backfire and generate support for the groups our government is trying to suppress. It remains unlikely that America's best and brightest could ever have good enough information to know who deserves American support and what the likely consequences of giving it will be. This is a continent where European imperialists drew almost every national border in the 19th and 20th centuries for the deliberate purpose of dividing and conquering some indigenous groups and grouping together other competing ones. In other words, many of the lines do not conform to the wishes of the local populations. This means there will be quarrels, secessions and attempted secessions, and conflicts between majority and minority groups from now into the indefinite future. American bureaucrats do not know how to solve these problems.

Take a look at the Philippines, where U.S. special operations forces have been stationed on and off for the past 19 years, helping the central government fight against the Islamist group Abu Sayyaf. Their origins date back to Carter and Reagan's 1980s jihad in Afghanistan. Abu Sayyaf now supposedly pledges its loyalty to ISIS. Our troops are still there, and so are they. If anything gives them local legitimacy, it is that the U.S. takes them seriously enough to send special operations forces after them and that they are the ones to defend the territory from the Americans when they come.

However, all current informed forecasts predict U.S. Army and special operations forces will continue to expand their presence as trainers and on missions throughout the African continent, chasing real and imaginary consequences of their previous actions for the foreseeable future.

In Tunisia, they have been dealing with the jihadist aftermath of the war in Libya next door. But the Americans who created the crisis are here to help. In 2019, at least 150 American soldiers and marines were stationed there, training the locals and assisting them on missions against AQIM. The *New York Times* says our troopers maintain a drone base outside the town of Bizerte, even though they would have preferred to have been stationed further south near Tataouine.

AFRICOM's project, the "G5 Sahel Joint Force," a joint counter-terrorism force, made up of 4,500 troops from Burkina Faso, Chad, Mali, Niger and Mauritania, began operations in 2019.

The Americans have built a massive drone base in the city of Agadez and have also deployed hundreds of special operations forces to Niger since 2002. Everything got more violent after the Libya war in 2011. In October 2017, four U.S. Special Forces soldiers were killed in a firefight during a mission against local militiamen said to be "loyal" to ISIS. One of the U.S. Senate's leading hawks, Lindsey Graham of South Carolina, admitted that he had no idea U.S. forces were even in Niger. The public was just as unaware. But the war continues. American and French troops train, advise and also go out on combat missions against a local group calling itself the "Islamic State in the Greater Sahara," doubtless for the Saudi money. Local politicians complain that American troops are driving radicalization and making terrorism in the area worse.

The United States has been working with the military in Chad since the beginning of the War on Terrorism. Their army also helped the French roust Ansar Dine and AQIM from northern Mali in 2013. The U.S. now has an air base near the capital of N'Djamena, which they have used in the fight against Boko Haram in Nigeria. Nearly 100 of their troops were wiped out by Boko Haram in a major battle near Lake Chad in 2020. Their troops then withdrew from Nigeria but still fight in Mali and Burkina Faso.

In the latter country, jihadists from the war in Mali have begun to pose a huge problem, waging devastating attacks against civilian targets and massacring Christians. They have turned a stable if poor country into a killing field. Almost a million people have been displaced as the terrorists and American-trained army take turns committing atrocities against the civilian population in the name of their war against each other. U.S. Green Berets are there in force, too, training the locals how to deal with the trouble America has created for them in the first place and how to make more. They have also recently embarked on a mini-counterinsurgency campaign, passing out medicine and financial aid to poorer parts of the country in the hopes of turning them away from militant groups. Chances that there will be further repercussions for these interventions are likely greater than zero.

There was one massive attack by al Qaeda in the Islamic Maghreb (AQIM) in Algeria in 2013, waged by former assets of their intelligence services, but they seem to have gotten a handle on the problem since then.

The White House and the military have made the obvious clear for everyone. Just as in Central Asia and the Middle East, great power competition with China lies at the heart of American strategy in Africa. Rifle-toting insurgents reacting to the intrusion simply serve as the perfect excuse.

The military is on the record repeatedly trying to justify their expansive new Africa policies under the excuse of limiting competition from the Chinese. But the average American does not have a thing to lose if China brings African oil to the world market. For that matter, even in a real war, no one doubts the U.S. Navy's ability to limit the shipment of Chinese oil supplies. The whole thing amounts to a make-work program for the Special Operations Command at the expense of the civilian population of that vast continent.

Great Power Politics

The War on Terrorism continued throughout Donald Trump's term in office. But from the very beginning, his staff, led by his first secretary of defense, James Mattis, worked to reorient American military strategy away from patrolling Pashtuns in their poppy fields to "Great Power Competition" with Russia and China. The new National Security Strategy announced in 2018 said that "Inter-state strategic competition, not terrorism, is now the primary concern in U.S. national security." They have done this even though America's Cold War against the great Communist powers ended 30 years ago and 45 years ago, respectively. There is no one else left to fight. Though it makes sense in terms of American domestic politics for the Democrats to demonize Russia and the Republicans to scapegoat China, neither is a threat to their neighbors, much less the United States of America. It is the U.S. government that seeks "full-spectrum dominance" over the planet, in the words of perennial defense department official Michèle Flournoy.

The Russians did nothing as the Americans expanded their NATO military alliance across Eastern Europe, right up to Russia's western border. This was in direct violation of the solemn promise made to Soviet Premier Mikhail Gorbachev by President George H.W. Bush and our Western European allied states' leaders as the USSR dissolved. The Russians reacted by giving speeches as the U.S. overthrew numerous Russian-allied governments through the CIA and National Endowment for Democracy's "Color-Coded revolutions" in the Bill Clinton and George W. Bush years. The Russians' intervention in Ukraine in 2014 and 2015, like it or not, was defensive in nature after the U.S.- and neo-Nazi-backed violent street putsch of February 2014. This was organized by Victoria Nuland, who was assistant secretary of state for European and Eurasian affairs and wife of notorious neoconservative theoretician Robert Kagan, along with then-Vice President Joe Biden. The Russians seized back the Crimean Peninsula without killing a single person in a successful *coup de main* to protect their essential strategic asset, the warm water naval base at Sevastopol. Putin then provided special operations assistance to the people of the eastern Donbass region, who were defending themselves from military assault by the U.S.-backed Kiev government. It had attacked them after they refused to recognize what they considered to be an illegitimate coup junta. When the people of the Donbass voted to join the Russian Federation, they were denied by Moscow, which had no intention of enlarging Russia's borders beyond taking back Crimea, even when the opportunity was being handed to them. Just as in Syria, this does not necessarily mean that what Russia did was right, it just means that this was all, in fact, a reaction to terrible interventionist policies by the U.S., rather than an aggressive expansionist move on their part.

The Democrats, especially, attack Russia, but perhaps they should take responsibility. Secretary of State Clinton leaned hard on then-Russian President Dmitry Medvedev after their mutual "reset" to get his government to abstain while the UN Security Council voted for the no-fly zone in Libya in 2011. She then humiliated him by quickly switching to a policy of regime change in Tripoli. This reportedly encouraged Vladimir Putin's early return to the presidency from the prime ministership where he had been temporarily cooling his heels and helped to further estrange his government from ours. Yet, Putin still helped Obama avoid full-scale war against Assad's government in Syria and helped pressure Ayatollah Khamenei to support his president's efforts to negotiate the nuclear deal of 2015 with the U.S. and UN Security Council powers.

Despite all the Democrats, CIA, FBI counter-intelligence division and media's preposterous lies about Donald Trump's subordination to Russia's government and its goals, as president, he was either an absolute anti-Russia hawk or had no control over the Pentagon's foreign policy whatsoever. The man who campaigned on "getting along with Russia," added two new members to the NATO alliance, Macedonia and Montenegro. He sold arms to Ukraine, which Obama had rightfully been reluctant to do. He pulled America out of Ronald Reagan's Intermediate Nuclear Forces (INF) treaty of 1987, which kept medium-range missiles out of Europe for more than 30 years, and the Open Skies treaty, which the U.S. and Russia each use to reassure themselves that the other is not mobilizing for war. Trump also abandoned all efforts to preserve the New START treaty, the last standing treaty between the U.S. and Russia limiting overall numbers of deployed and stockpiled strategic nuclear weapons. Trump's government also unnecessarily escalated with provocative bomber flights over the Baltic, Black and Okhotsk seas in attempts to survey Russian defenses. He did this all while continuing Obama's massive project — projected to cost three trillion dollars and rising — to completely rebuild and revamp America's entire nuclear weapons industry and arsenal. Trump's government also spent four years threatening and sanctioning Russia's allies in Syria, Iran and Venezuela.

Biden has vowed to reinforce America's "sacred" commitment to the NATO alliance in Europe to roll back "Russian aggression," though at least he has promised to negotiate an extension of the all-important New START treaty. A *New York Times* headline from the end of 2020 says it all. "NATO Needs to Adapt Quickly to Stay Relevant for 2030, Report Urges." They do not even know to be embarrassed. This is what they mean by "self-licking ice cream cone." If the NATO alliance is not relevant, then why do we have it at all? How can their mission be "sacred" when they had to hold an emergency study group to decide what it is? The answer they came up with? China. The North Atlantic Treaty Organization's new reason for existing is China. Maybe someone at their headquarters finally got the memo: Russia is not coming.

This is how the Bush and Obama governments talked about the Afghanistan war as well. It was a "team-building exercise" for the Atlantic alliance. In other words, these policies exist because all the vested interests want to stay paid without having to get a real job. It is understandable but unacceptable.

China's real sin in the U.S. government's eyes is that they "threaten U.S. domination of the Pacific," in the words of Rex Tillerson, the former Exxon CEO and Trump's first Secretary of State. Is the entire Pacific Ocean an American lake, or only 99 percent of it? And how many sailors are we willing to send to the bottom to find out? China does not threaten American forces in the region, much less our actual country. Their entire military doctrine is defensive in nature: "Anti-Access, Area Denial," or "A2-AD" in U.S. military-speak. But China does not seek to shut down international shipping. Nor have they denied passage to the world's navies. It seems the most important factor driving this policy is the increase in money, power and influence to be gained by the U.S. Air Force and Navy and their associated contractors. They have found that they can use China's rising military strength to justify a massive new arms build-up against them. We will see your A2-AD and raise you an "Air-Sea Battle"! And if their missiles make our ships obsolete, we will just have to build more long-range bombers.

The think tanks and war hawks in and out of government will go on and on for years about all their different strategies for how to fight future wars against Russia and China — oftentimes in ways that make the threat of violent conflict sound very real and inevitable in the near term. Yet, from the way they talk, you would think they have forgotten that Russia and China are both armed to the teeth with hydrogen bombs and could permanently erase our entire civilization from the face of the earth in about half an hour. The Russians have many thousands more than the Chinese, but just a few hundred thermonuclear-tipped missiles are more than enough. This means that no matter what, we can never, must never fight them. Perhaps we should also prioritize keeping the people on our side who would consider war with nuclear-armed states a reasonable option far away from the levers of power before it is too late.

If the military and its assorted industrial complexes need something to do, let them get work providing goods and services in the market like everybody else.

If we leave the decisions to the self-interested authors of the Long War doctrine, we will be fighting hot and cold wars against what the Pentagon calls the "4 + 1 Threats" — Russia, China, North Korea, Iran and terrorism — until America finally destroys itself in the process.

Chapter Fourteen:
A Choking Life

"The spirit of this country is totally
adverse to a large military force."
— Thomas Jefferson

"From whence shall we expect the
approach of danger? Shall some trans-
Atlantic military giant step the earth and
crush us at a blow? Never. All the armies
of Europe and Asia could not by force
take a drink from the Ohio River or make
a track on the Blue Ridge in a trial of a
thousand years. No, if destruction be
our lot we must ourselves be its author
and finisher. As a nation of free men
we will live forever or die by suicide."
— Abraham Lincoln

"You're just angry because you
don't have an enemy anymore."
— Mrs. McMaster to H.R.

Backdraft

Remember, if *blowback* means the long-term consequences of secret foreign policies that come back to haunt the American people while leaving them ignorant of the actual context of what is going on, then *backdraft* means the short-term consequences of overt policies blowing up right in our face. We previously discussed two backdraft terrorist attacks, the attempted Times Square bombing of 2010 and the San Bernardino massacre of 2015. [See Chapter 6.]

Our government said if we gave them the writ to bring the bad guys to justice, they would do just that and keep us safe. But they never meant it, and they sure have not done so. It is worth citing a few more of the many examples here. Terrorism is no small price to pay. Take, for example, the Manchester massacre. On May 22, 2017, a bin Ladenite suicide bomber named Salman Abedi attacked a concert by the American singer Ariana Grande at an arena in Manchester, England, slaughtering 22 people, including little girls, and wounding hundreds more.

While the usual suspects rushed to blame faith in Islam for the attack, they should have been blaming the lily-white, Anglican MI-6 and their allied intelligence agencies long before the teachings of an ancient Arab prophet. The Libyan Islamic Fighting Group (LIFG) had its origins in Carter and Reagan's secret war in Afghanistan in the 1980s. When it was over, they came home to be brutally suppressed by Gaddafi's regime. As exposed by the MI-5 whistleblower David Shayler, in 1996, MI-6 attempted to use the LIFG in a failed plot to assassinate Moammar Gaddafi. Some of the conspirators were then provided safe haven in Manchester.

One of the LIFG jihadists that the British imported was an associate of Osama bin Laden named Nazih Abdul-Hamed Nabih al-Ruqai'i (or Anas al-Libi), who in turn was close friends and allies with Ramadan Abedi, the eventual Manchester attacker's father. Many of the LIFG members living in England were not religious fundamentalists at all. They were political radicals opposed to Gaddafi first and foremost.

When the Arab Spring broke out in Libya, MI-6 went right back to their old ways, recruiting heavily from the Libyan expatriate community in Manchester for the new war. The pipes were calling. Ramadan Abedi and his sons Salman and Heshem quickly answered and traveled to Libya to fight. Eventually, they joined Katibat al-Battar al-Libi (KTB), a group of Libyans who went on to fight in the CIA's covert war against Assad in Syria.

Abedi stopped in the Libyan town of Sabratha on his way home to England, which was infested with Libyan ISIS members at that time. He met with them before returning to Manchester. By the time of his massacre, the UK had mostly switched sides in the war in Syria, along with the U.S. and France, attacking the new so-called "Caliphate" established by ISIS. Like many, but by no means all young Muslim terrorists of our era, the young Abedi was reportedly a religious fundamentalist, but that is not why he killed those little girls.

As Abedi's sister explained, "I think he saw children — Muslim children — dying everywhere and wanted revenge. He saw the explosives America drops on children in Syria, and he wanted revenge. Whether he got that is between him and God." After a friend was killed on the street in England and another was killed by a U.S. drone strike in the anti-ISIS war in Syria, he decided to take his revenge.

A week and a half after the Manchester bombing, another fighter who had fought under Abdel Hakim Belhaj in Libya and the main al Qaeda affiliate in Syria, along with two others, waged a truck and knife attack at London Bridge, which killed seven people and wounded 48.

Just as with the original al Qaeda war against the U.S., the fact that western nations continue to support these groups provides them no immunity from their despicable violence.

In December 2009, just after President Obama announced the launch of the Afghan "surge," journalist Patrick Cockburn explained that the continued occupation of Afghanistan, rather than preventing terrorist attacks by denying our antagonists safe haven, actually increased the likelihood of attacks in Western countries. Just a month before, a U.S. army major named Nidal Hasan, due to deploy to Afghanistan and upset about the reports of war crimes being committed against civilians there, along with the prospect of being made to kill fellow Muslims himself, instead killed 13 soldiers and wounded 30 others in a massacre at Ft. Hood in central Texas. It was later revealed that Hasan had been in contact with prominent American al Qaeda preacher Anwar al-Awlaki. The Obama administration, insistent on pretending they had won the War on Terrorism, and anxious to deny that backdraft from U.S. policies were to blame for this "lone wolf" attack, tried to spin the entire thing as "workplace violence," as though Hassan had "gone postal" under the work-a-day pressures of his job. The Republicans said this was ridiculous. They instead blamed "radical Islam."

Dzhokhar Tsarnaev, co-conspirator with his brother Tamerlan in the deadly 2013 Boston Marathon attacks, told investigators they were motivated by the U.S. wars in Iraq and Afghanistan. Then-Marine Sergeant Thomas Gibbons-Neff wrote in response to the Boston attack:

> While I was deployed, I went to bed at night believing that I was protecting the homeland because coming after me and my fellow Marines was a much easier commute for those so hell-bent on killing

Americans. But that argument no longer makes sense if my war has inspired enemies at home.

Omar Mateen, the American-born perpetrator of the horrific Orlando Pulse nightclub massacre of June 2016, explicitly told witnesses he was taking revenge for the continuing U.S. war in Afghanistan, the country of his family's origin. "When I saw his picture on the news, I thought, of course, he did that," a co-worker of Mateen told *Newsday*. "He had bad things to say about everybody — blacks, Jews, gays, a lot of politicians, our soldiers. He had a lot of hate in him. He told me America destroyed Afghanistan."

A young woman named Patience Carter, who was shot in the leg by Mateen and held hostage in the bathroom of the club for three hours with the gunman, said, "The motive was very clear to us who are laying in our own blood and other people's blood, who are injured, who were shot. Everybody who was in that bathroom who survived could hear him talking to 911, saying the reason why he's doing this is because he wanted America to stop bombing his country."

In the middle of committing his atrocity — Mateen slaughtered 49 people and wounded 53 — he stopped to post on his Facebook page: "You kill innocent women and children by doing us airstrikes ... now taste the Islamic state vengeance." [errors in original] The transcript of his call to 911, released much later after all the attention died down, is more explicit. As Mateen declared his loyalty to the leaders of ISIS, he explained his demands:

> [Y]ou have to tell America to stop bombing Syria and Iraq. They are killing a lot of innocent people. What am I to do here when my people are getting killed over there? You get what I'm saying? ... You need to stop the U.S. airstrikes. They need to stop the U.S. airstrikes, okay? ... You have to tell the U.S. government to stop bombing. They are killing too many children, they are killing too many women, okay? ... I feel the pain of the people getting killed in Syria and Iraq and all over the Muslim [world]. A lot of innocent women and children are getting killed in Syria and Iraq and Afghanistan, okay?

As it turns out, the government lied like the Devil that Mateen was a repressed, closeted homosexual struggling under the tyranny of his fundamentalist religion, causing him to lash out at this gay nightclub. His attack had nothing to do with that completely false narrative. Only when the feds attempted to prosecute his wife did the truth come out that Mateen was not gay but had simply picked that nightclub for his massacre from the top of Google's search results after deciding that Disney World's security was too tight.

Mateen had chosen to sign on with the agendas of al-Nusra and the Islamic State and attacked a crowded nightclub as a strike against the United States on their behalf. (The cowardly Orlando police waited outside for hours as people bled to death inside the nightclub. After the cops finally breached the wall, they opened fire, killing even more innocent people trying to escape. No one was ever held accountable.) In the meantime, millions of people were led to believe that a bin Ladenite terrorist had just massacred 49 people because of how much Muslims hate gay people, and how much this one hated himself. The reality was that he was angry that Obama had built an Islamic caliphate and then started bombing it. Mateen was avenging the innocent people caught in the middle. It is certainly no excuse for killing innocent people, but that makes Mateen's atrocity his and Obama's responsibility, not the religion of Islam or Freudian sexual repression.

Long-time Afghan-war partner Germany was hit a month after the Orlando attack when a young Pakistani refugee, Riaz Khan Ahmadzai (a.k.a. Mohammed Riyadh), who by all accounts had been adjusting quite well to his new life in Germany, took out a hatchet and started attacking people on a train in northern Bavaria. He then attacked one more woman during his attempted escape, wounding a total of six people, several of them severely. It was, police said, revenge over a friend who had recently been killed by an airstrike in Afghanistan. In a video released by the Islamic State soon after the attack, Ahmadzai says, "I am one of the soldiers of the Islamic Caliphate, and I am going to conduct an attack in Germany. It is about time to stop you from coming to our homes, killing our families and getting away with it. Our apostate politicians have never tried to stop you, and Muslims have never been able to fight you back or even speak against what you do. But these times are gone now."

In September 2016, an Afghan-born U.S. citizen named Ahmad Khan Rahami set off two bombs on public streets, one in New York and one in New Jersey — thankfully, again, killing no one. Just like Shahzad before him, Rahami seemed to be happy and well-assimilated into American culture. His family owned a small restaurant in New York, and he spent most of his free time souping up and racing Honda Civics. Then he traveled to Afghanistan and Pakistan. It is unknown whether he had any actual contact with members of al Qaeda or Taliban faction while there, but he reportedly came back a changed, much more "serious" man and soon went to war on their behalf.

On June 21, 2017, a Canadian Muslim named Amor M. Ftouhi attacked and wounded a police officer at a Michigan airport with a knife but was thankfully subdued by other police and a maintenance man before he could grab the cop's gun and do any more damage. According to police, during the actual stabbing the attacker yelled, "You have killed people in

Syria, Iraq and Afghanistan and you are going to die." He also yelled "Allahu Akbar," ("God is Great") while he was being taken down. The latter statement received far more media attention.

In December 2019, Saudi Air Force Second Lieutenant Ahmed Mohammed al-Shamrani killed three men at the naval air station in Pensacola, Florida. Senator Rick Scott said he must have either been under the influence of "radical Islam" or perhaps was "mentally unstable." The reality was that the perpetrator knew exactly what he was doing and said so in the last post to his Twitter account. It read:

> I'm not against you for just being American, I don't hate you because your freedoms, I hate you because every day you [are] supporting, funding and committing crimes not only against Muslims but also humanity. I am against evil, and America as a whole has turned into a nation of evil. What I see from America is the supporting of Israel which is invasion of Muslim countries. I see invasion of many countries by its troops, I see Guantánamo Bay. I see cruise missiles, cluster bombs and UAVs.

> Your decision-makers, the politicians, the lobbyists and the major corporations are the ones gaining from your foreign policy, and you are the ones paying the price for it.

> What benefit is it to the American people to suffer for the sake of supporting Israel?

> Do you expect to transgress against others and yet be spared retribution?

> How many more body-bags are American families willing to receive?

> For how long can the U.S. survive this war of attrition?

> The U.S. Treasury spends billions of dollars in order to give Americans a false sense of security.

> Security is shared destiny.

> You will not be safe until we live it as reality in Palestine and American troops get out of our lands. [Spelling errors corrected for clarity.]

Every time this happens, foreign policy hawks and social media commentators announce that their biased expert opinions have been confirmed again: Islam makes people into insane killers. The deeper their religious devotion, the more dangerous they are. But people can only persist in this belief as long as they presume, even after 20 years of war, that it is impossible that anyone on America's side could do anything to provoke such hatred, a premise that cannot withstand honest scrutiny of U.S. intervention or the words of our enemies: killing them makes their survivors want to kill us.

The U.S. government is perfectly content to blame foreign policy blowback, even for ISIS attacks, rather than religious extremists' hatred of freedom, when the victims are from countries that are designated American adversaries, sometimes going so far as to imply that the innocent victims deserved it. In one example, after the killing of 224 people in the October 2015 bombing of Russian Metrojet flight 9268 out of Sharm El Sheikh, Egypt, U.S. officials "delighted" in its destruction, according to their friends at the Daily Beast. After the June 2017 attacks on Parliament and the Ayatollah Khomeini's tomb in Tehran, Iran, the Trump administration's official statement read, "We underscore that states that sponsor terrorism risk falling victim to the evil they promote."

A 2011 report written by the Los Angeles office of the FBI determined that an increase in attacks against U.S. targets was due to "a broadening U.S. military presence overseas and outreach by Islamist ideologues." The outreach they refer to was the propaganda of those like Anwar Awlaki, who consistently framed terrorism as a defense against the U.S. military waging war in the Mideast.

To be sure, when the FBI launches an entrapment sting on a target here in America, they virtually always prey on their victim's sympathy for people dying in the wars overseas — and desperate need for money. Never in the history of all 800-plus terrorism cases the U.S. government has successfully prosecuted since September 11th has anyone claimed to have been motivated by a hatred of the freedom and innocence of the American people. They only cite the U.S. government's tyranny and violence in their countries.

As Dr. Ron Paul famously instructed former New York City mayor Rudy Giuliani at a Republican Party presidential candidate debate in 2007, "If we ignore this, we ignore it at our own risk. If we think that we can do what we want around the world and not incite hatred, then we have a problem."

A Police State

Osama bin Laden did want to destroy our freedom, not because he hated or was jealous of it, but because he knew that we loved it. He warned that "The U.S. government will lead the American people — and the West in general — into an unbearable hell and a choking life." His bet was that at some point we would force our government to withdraw from the Middle East if losing our freedom was the price we had to pay to maintain military dominance there. Essentially, bin Laden was attempting to blackmail or extort the American people into telling our government to abandon its Middle East project.

The real assault on our freedom began when Senator Joe Biden's USA-PATRIOT Act passed right after the September 11th attacks, which included a massive expansion of power for the Department of Justice, its FBI and other agencies. President George W. Bush soon signed orders authorizing the illegal National Security Agency spying programs, CIA torture at "ghost prisons" and "black sites" in countries like Poland, Romania, Morocco and Thailand. He also ordered the establishment of the lawless detention camp at Guantánamo Bay, Cuba, where many were tortured, at least four were murdered and 40 men remain imprisoned to this day. His government, led by Vice President Dick Cheney along with his lawyer and adviser David Addington, made it deliberate policy to push against the Constitution's constraints on the president's powers until "some larger force makes us stop," as Addington told White House lawyer Jack Goldsmith. Their respect for the sacred oath they took to protect it was not enough. Cheney and his lawyers pushed what they called the "new paradigm." They introduced the "unitary executive" theory of power which holds that in wartime, the "commander in chief" clause of Article II grants the president "inherent" and "plenary" power which allowed him to essentially override any law, treaty or even other parts of the Constitution to wage war in any way he sees fit, even without an official declaration of war by the Congress. Thankfully, in three major decisions, the Supreme Court made it clear that the powers of the president do not include the authority to hold people outside the law. Courts have also ruled that the NSA programs exposed by the *New York Times* and National Security Agency contractor whistleblower Edward Snowden were illegal and unconstitutional. Of course, the government found ways around the courts' constraints in both cases.

In 2013, Snowden revealed that the NSA — which is officially part of the military — had been keeping records of all Americans' phone calls and cell phone location data. The documents he provided to journalists showed the NSA is able to hack into systems of virtually every kind and to warrantlessly investigate Americans beyond the wildest dreams of the East German Communists or science fiction writers of the 1980s. This includes the ability to tap directly into the most powerful technology firms' databases, intercept and store all individuals' text messages, emails, visited internet addresses and search terms, and even log all their keystrokes remotely. With the help of the whistleblower William Binney and others, the great journalist and author James Bamford had already told much of the story, but the Snowden documents proved it beyond doubt. The

Foreign Intelligence Surveillance Court (FISC) had issued general warrants on the entire American population.

The "Vault 7" leak to Wikileaks showed that the CIA has a spying apparatus nearly as extensive as that of the NSA, including the ability to spy on people through their television sets, just like in George Orwell's totalitarian dystopia, *1984.*

In 2002, Bush created the new Department of Homeland Security (DHS), combining dozens of agencies together into a new leviathan including the Transportation Security Administration (TSA), which specializes only in radiating and sexually assaulting children and grandmothers, and like their parent organization, has never stopped a terrorist attack.

As journalist Trevor Aaronson has shown, the Justice Department has prosecuted more than 340 fake entrapment terrorism cases over the past two decades. Well-paid informants trick idiots into saying they love Osama bin Laden, or yes, they would like to buy some illegal guns. Then off they go to the maximum-security dungeon, complete with anti-terrorist "Special Administrative Measures" meant to deny them virtually all access to the outside world. Some of the more famous of these stings include the Liberty City 7 supposed-plot against the Sears Tower, the Fort Dix Pizza plot, the New York subway and synagogue plots, the JFK Airport fuel storage plot, the remote-control plane attack on the Pentagon plot, the Portland, Oregon Christmas Tree plot and the supposed "material support" given by poor Hamid Hyat of Lodi, California to terrorists who existed entirely in the minds of the FBI agents and informants who framed him.

These cases were all lies made to scare your family into supporting the wars and big FBI budgets. It is as simple as that.

At least one entrapment job backfired. The 2015 attack on the Mohammed cartoon contest in Garland, Texas was spurred on by an FBI agent-provocateur who told the perpetrators to "tear up Texas," but nevertheless failed to prevent the armed shooters from attacking the event. Though the federal agent in question was standing right there, it was a local off-duty cop who shot and killed the assailants, though not before they shot and wounded a civilian security guard who luckily survived.

The Boston Marathon bombing was not a sting operation, but as Aaronson showed, the Boston FBI might have stopped that real plot if they had not been too busy chasing their tails entrapping some other fool at the same time instead.

Obama's CIA and Air Force used Predator and Reaper drones to carry out his policy of targeted assassinations, including at least three American citizens. Much of the supposed legal reasoning behind the program remains secret.

In 2011 Obama signed the National Defense Authorization Act (NDAA) of 2012, which contained a provision that allows for the abduction of "U.S. persons" — including U.S.-born and naturalized American citizens — to be held indefinitely without charges by the military. This law, the ultimate violation of Article One, Section Nine and the 5th and 6th Amendments to the U.S. Constitution, remains on the books. It has not been implemented yet. But the power is there, waiting for the next major attack to be used.

The militarization of federal, state and local police since the dawn of the War on Terrorism has also gotten completely out of control. According to the ACLU, there are now, on average, more than 60,000 SWAT raids on American civilian homes per year. These are mostly paramilitary night raids equivalent to those done by the Delta Force and Navy SEALs in Iraq and Afghanistan. That is more than 1,000 night raids per week, every week of the year, mostly to enforce contraband "offenses" against poor people. Even local traffic cops and sheriffs' deputies run around dressed up in their paramilitary "tactical pants" and black military-style fatigues instead of traditional slacks with blue or brown work-dress shirts. The bleed-through of the military mentality of engaging against "enemies" among the public are all too real. Many of the weapons and other equipment given to our domestic police have come from military surplus from the War on Terrorism. Since 2003, through the Department of Homeland Security and military 1033 programs, the federal government has distributed more than 1,000 massive MRAP land mine-resistant armored personnel carriers to state and local police. Predator and Reaper drones patrol the U.S.-Mexico border, help monitor forest fires and circle above leftist and right-wing protests in American cities. Austin, Texas police were the first ones to use a drone for surveillance on a SWAT team raid. Police in Dallas, Texas were the first to use a wheeled robot with a bomb to kill an armed suspect. There are plans to establish a permanent presence for drones with "Gorgon Stare" technology made to surveil entire cities at a time.

There has also been established a new "veteran to police pipeline," where soldiers promised a higher education and purpose in life are instead more likely to become a local sheriff's deputy. Many see their daily patrols through the same eyes as they needed to stay alive during the military occupations of Iraq and Afghanistan, and they act like it. Ironically, actual U.S. soldiers have far stricter rules of engagement determining when they may fire their weapons against presumed enemies in foreign nations. But American cops need only cry that they saw a "furtive" movement and felt afraid to justify killing anyone according to laws that have been entirely made up by unelected federal judges. Currently, American cops kill on average more than two Americans every day of the year.

In 2010, the *Washington Post's* Dana Priest and William Arkin published a series called "Top Secret America," which later became a book. Their thesis was that since the dawn of the War on Terrorism, the old national security state and military-industrial complex were now complemented by their domestic mirror image: the Homeland Security State and its own related industrial-complex, feeding off of massive new anti-terrorism budgets. This means a million new vested special interests from the local sheriff's deputies to the holster, bayonet, ammunition and armored personnel carrier manufacturers, and especially an entire new generation of top-secret clearance-holding intelligence and military contractors of every description. It amounts to nearly a million economically worthless new rent-seekers who protect no one but are determined to keep the entire fraud going as long as they can. A Senate staffer described the beast as "a living, breathing organism," out of control. "How much money has been involved is just mind-boggling. We've built such a vast instrument. What are you going to do with this thing? ... It's turned into a jobs program." Nothing beats a captive market like the Congress and the departments it creates.

There are fewer separations of police power than ever in the United States, as the different levels of government join together in multi-jurisdictional task forces, fusion centers, information sharing and military training programs. Meanwhile the federal courts typically uphold this dismemberment of constitutional federalism and the Bill of Rights in the name of the emergency.

Even worse, the FBI and CIA, agencies supposedly subordinate to the president and the Congress, and described nowhere in the U.S. Constitution, now act as though they are separate and co-equal branches of government, or better. A critical example of this was in 2014, when Senate Intelligence Committee Chairwoman Dianne Feinstein's staff was investigating the CIA's Bush-era torture program. Someone in the CIA leaked or accidentally turned over to the staffers a secret internal study of the torture program higher-ups never meant for them to see. Director John Brennan then turned to the FBI and Justice Department and attempted to have the Senate staff indicted for hacking into the CIA's computers and stealing the report, which was an obviously false accusation. Under the rule of law, someone of Brennan's station would not have dared to come after the chair of the Senate Intelligence Committee in this way. But we are an empire now. This is the reality that they have made.

The most important recent example of the national security state's supremacy was when the FBI's counter-intelligence division and CIA helped to frame Donald Trump, at that time the already-nominated major-party candidate for president of the United States, and his associates for acts of treason with the Kremlin, of all things. It just was not true. For one example, consider the case of former general Michael Flynn, Trump's designated incoming-national security adviser. He was accused of making a promise to the Russian ambassador on an intercepted phone call that he would lift sanctions against Russia once Trump was sworn into office. In fact, the eventually released transcripts showed that he had only asked the Russians not to respond to Obama's sanctions in a negative way and had promised nothing. Rather than receiving instructions from the Russians, the only collusion with a foreign power revealed in the call was Flynn's intervention on behalf of Israel. He had attempted to convince the Russian ambassador to veto a UN Security Council resolution condemning the illegal Israeli settlements in the West Bank. He refused. The resolution passed. The FBI knew this all along and yet let the American people believe that Flynn was a traitor, instead of just a dangerous pro-Israeli and anti-Iranian ideologue.

A second example is that of American oil industry consultant Carter Page. The FBI knew that he was a loyal CIA asset who always briefed his handlers whenever approached by powerful or suspicious Russian characters. They were only pretending to believe he might be an agent of the Russians as the basis for a Foreign Intelligence Surveillance Act warrant and a phony predicate for a continuing investigation into the entire Trump campaign. An FBI lawyer was eventually convicted for censoring the information about Page's relationship with the CIA from their application for the FISA warrant. And again the American people were led to believe for years that a patriot was a traitor in furtherance of this false narrative.

Not only that, but the Department of Justice pretended to "investigate" this ridiculous hoax for two-and-a-half years, including the appointment of a special counsel and talk of using the 25th Amendment to force the president from office over it just weeks into his presidency. Reasonable people who heard about the Russiagate investigation may have assumed in good faith that where there's smoke, there's fire. Why would the Department of Justice be investigating Trump and all these people for colluding with Russia if they had no basis for it? It was because they decided they had to "rein him in," as the FBI told CNN. "God bless the 'deep state,'" wrote the *Washington Post*. In the spring of 2019 they finally gave it up. The special counsel reported that there had been no "collusion" between Trump or his campaign with Russia after all.

No matter what anyone's opinion of Donald Trump is, the question here is who the hell do these people think they are? The FBI and CIA were acting like secret police in this case, unleashing a COINTELPRO-type subversion campaign against a sitting president. It was not much different than the kind of propaganda the same government agencies used against

Saddam Hussein and their other foreign enemies to start the wars. After years of getting away with murder, people like John Brennan seem to think they can do anything they want, including frame an elected president for treason. They did all this because Trump said he was opposed to the new Cold War with Russia, which he evidently never meant anyway.

Chalmers Johnson, one of the last great defenders of the old republic, said we will have to either give up our empire or live under it ourselves. Do we really want to let the government destroy our hard-won freedoms when all we have to do to guarantee our safety is to call off its unnecessary interventions, especially in the Middle East? The U.S. should not capitulate to the demands of terrorists. But that is, ironically, exactly what the government has done in waging this war, provoking so many new enemies and destroying so much of our privacy and freedom they claim to be fighting to protect.

It is the right thing to stop doing the wrong thing, and ceasing intervention is the best first step in deterring the terrorist attacks that have cost so many lives and driven so much of the government's expansion of powers in recent years.

Support the Troops

Almost 7,000 U.S. soldiers, marines, sailors and airmen have been killed in the War on Terrorism, hundreds of contractors with them. Tens of thousands more have been wounded. Iraq and Afghan war veteran suicide rates are far higher than the rest of the population due to their health problems, injuries and their dependence on the government's Veterans Administration for help. While some of the VA's facilities are reportedly very good, there have also been terrible backlogs with care being rationed or even denied and more than a few anecdotes about frustrated soldiers giving up the fight to survive altogether after trying to deal with its bureaucracy. Beyond direct wounds in combat, U.S. troops have been inflicted with post-traumatic stress disorders, "moral injury," and high rates of cancers and other diseases caused by the burn pits used by the military outside their bases. There is every reason to believe that the brain cancer that killed President Biden's son Beau was caused by the chemicals he was exposed to in the war his father lied us into, as shown in the book *The Burn Pits*, by Sergeant Joseph Hickman, U.S. Army (ret.).

As the outraged, decorated Iraq War II Marine captain and later Afghan war whistleblower Matthew Hoh put it, when railing against the unnecessary loss of more than 9,000 Iraq and Afghan war veterans to suicide, "Sacrifice does not confer sanctity."[*]

In recent years, polls have shown that veterans of Iraq War II and Afghanistan oppose continuing the wars there in greater proportions even than the rest of society. A 2019 Pew Research survey found 58 percent of veterans thought the war in Afghanistan was not worth fighting, while 64 percent say the same about Iraq War II. Fifty-seven percent of veterans think the U.S. should be "less engaged in military conflicts overseas." Full withdrawal from Iraq has 71 percent support, and full withdrawal from Afghanistan, 73 percent. These veterans also opposed intervention in Syria and supported efforts to negotiate with Russia and North Korea.

That should be it. The argument is over. It has not been so much won by antiwar forces as finally lost by its proponents. Who could look at the calendar and argue that the project to defeat terrorism is on target and on schedule? Who could support the wars if the soldiers who fought them do not? If the war party has lost the troops, they have lost more than just "Middle America," but the very men upon whose will they depend on to do the fighting for them. Reaper drones can kill people, but they cannot hold ground. Nor apparently, can they be effectively used to accomplish truly productive reductions in the power of the terrorist groups targeted with them.

For years we were told that it was wrong to criticize the wars because it was betraying the soldiers and marines. To "support" the troops meant to support whatever mission some think-tank eggheads and corrupt, insecure politicians decided to send them on, no matter how blatantly unnecessary or dangerous the strategy was. That was wrong. The critics were right on each and every one of these wars.

Groups like Veterans for Peace and Iraq Veterans Against the War have been joined by the new Concerned Veterans of America and

---

[*] Asked about mental health support for U.S. vets, Matthew Hoh writes: "First is Veterans Crisis Line, 1-800-273-8255, https://veteranscrisisline.net. The crisis line is not reserved only for individuals who are about to kill themselves, it is for anyone in a crisis, for anyone looking for help, who needs to reach out and talk. It is a really good place for anyone to start, a safe place for someone to speak anonymously with someone who is compassionate, who will care and who can give qualified answers. The crisis line can also make referrals and consultations to the VA on behalf of people who are calling into the crisis line. Here is the site for the VA PTSD program: https://www.ptsd.va.gov. I recommend everyone go to the VA. The VA PTSD program is the best thing we have. There are a lot of other programs out there, but, honestly, a lot of them are niche, tailored, advanced, or quirky. The results from the VA suicide treatment have been good, not great, but good. And it is free. Most of the guys who have problems, who need the most help, by the time they are willing to get help, may not have the money or the health insurance to get the help. Which is why this is also a good program: https://giveanhour.org. This program matches up veterans in need with health professionals who are willing to donate their time. I also recommend this program as a program for veterans and their families to go to for general forms of assistance: https://semperfifund.org. They are not as well-known as some of the larger veteran's charities, but Semper Fi Fund has been around for a while now, is administratively sound and they do solid, good work that is actually needed by veterans and their families."

BringOurTroopsHome.us, groups led by conservative and libertarian combat veterans of our recent wars. They are making a huge difference in showing people that all partisan politics aside, our current policy of attempted dominance of the Middle East is not worth the cost to our nation in terms of body, dollar and spirit. Of course, they all still remain tough guys and patriots. But now they have gotten smart and know better what is to be done and what should not be. And they do speak for the vast majority of veterans of America's wars of this century.

War is Bad for the Economy

According to Catherine Lutz at the Cost of War Project, America's Middle Eastern wars have cost $6.4 trillion over the last 19 years. That estimate includes the costs of all the deployments, equipment, spent ammunition, replenishing of weapons stocks, caring for all the wounded at the Veterans Administration and the rest.

Readers may remember when the George W. Bush administration claimed Iraq War II would be cheap and easy. The people will greet us as liberators and the oil will pay for the whole war, Paul Wolfowitz promised. When they announced the first appropriation of $87 billion for the occupation, the American people were shocked: "What?! $87 billion?! But you said the war would pay for itself." That was six and a half trillion dollars ago.

On top of that, for more than a decade now the federal government's defense budget has been approximately a trillion dollars per year. This only includes the costs of the wars when it comes to the replenishment of equipment. But most of the war budget comes from a separate account. The vast majority of the total budget is for arms far beyond what is used in the War on Terrorism: the military departments and their massive fleets, squadrons and divisions of armor and men, new nuclear weapons, the Energy Department's maintaining of the nuclear stocks, and the Veterans Administration and the billions it costs to care for the veterans of current and past wars and their families.

What is lost is not just the opportunities for productive investment, but all the new wealth and further capital for investment that would have been created instead of blasted into oblivion. You could also include all the wasted engineering and organizational skills and sheer manpower blown on this misbegotten mission. Six or seven trillion dollars is the least of it.

Another critical but little-discussed aspect of the consequences of American militarism is that the central bank, the Federal Reserve System, holds interest rates to artificially low levels to make the economy boom and the wars seem free. This has happened over and over again since the

Fed was created: during World War I, World War II — not so much during Korea — but absolutely in Vietnam, the Reagan-era nuclear arms build-up, Bill Clinton's global expansion and the entire War on Terrorism since then. The real costs of the wars are disguised and delayed by monetary inflation. The citizenry also pays the price later with their time spent in the unemployment line or when they cannot afford a good education or a safe neighborhood for their children or healthcare for their spouse when prices are rising. It is even worse once the inflation-generated bubbles pop and the economy crashes. The associated suffering is the public's share of the cost of the war. The loose monetary policy to disguise the costs of the wars is the core cause of price inflation at the supermarket and the painful and destabilizing boom and the bust "business cycle" that causes the economy to crash every 10 or 12 years. This is why the economy "cratered" in 2008 and why working people, knocked back a few steps with every crash, can never seem to keep up with rising prices. The stock market rides high on injections of new cash by the government. Then, just as regular people are starting to get their feet back on solid ground, the rug gets pulled right back from under them again.

In 2002 and 2003, the Bush administration had the IRS send taxpayers "rebate" checks of $300 and $400, as though they were dividends from the profits being made from the invasion of Iraq. It was just an illusion. Iraq War II was a massive sinkhole for the American peoples' wealth. The only way the government could pull off such a trick was by borrowing and inflating the money supply, disguising the costs and making it seem like war is good for the economy when, in fact, it is not. The illusion finally caught up with Bush when the markets came crashing down in 2008. Since then, the government has only inflated another massive set of bubbles. When they will burst, nobody knows. That they will is assured beyond doubt.

The Imperial Court

A major reason why the United States government is so invested in protecting the interests of Saudi Arabia is that the Saudi royals spend hundreds of billions of dollars on American debt. The deal struck between Richard Nixon's government and King Faisal bin Abdulaziz Al Saud in 1974 stipulated that the U.S. would protect Saudi Arabia's interests if they would promise to recycle their petrodollars into U.S. Treasurys and military hardware. This policy then carries through to the rest of the OPEC cartel, ensuring that virtually all international oil transactions are denominated in American currency.

This politically fixed demand helps to prop up the value of the U.S. dollar. Though it does not appear to be the primary motive for their removal, Saddam Hussein and Moammar Gaddafi had both signaled their intent to begin denominating their oil sales in euros and a new gold dinar, respectively, before being attacked by the United States. As economist Ryan McMaken has pointed out, "Other regimes that have called for abandoning the petrodollar include Iran and Venezuela. The U.S. has called for regime change in both these countries."

"The real Great Game" of course concerns arms sales and control of the American defense budget. Not that the U.S. government needed much persuasion beyond attacks from bin Laden's minions to justify diving headlong into the Middle Eastern quagmire. But then came legions of New York- and Washington, D.C.-based pressure groups subsidized by American tax dollars laundered through defense firms like Lockheed Martin, Northrop Grumman, Boeing, Raytheon, General Dynamics and General Atomics. These companies recycle a small fraction of the money they make from weapons contracts in the form of donations to think tanks full of experts from the "foreign policy community," who then write up endless studies, rationalizations and justifications for staying the course in the War on Terrorism. Near the end of 2020, the University of Pennsylvania's Go To Think Tank Index ranked the top think tanks in America and found their budgets over five years are only in the low millions of dollars, even for the big ones like the Center for a New American Security (CNAS), the Atlantic Council, New America Foundation and the Council on Foreign Relations. They then promote the policies that make these companies hundreds of billions of dollars. The various Gulf sultanates play the same game, spending just a little bit of money for major influence over American foreign policy. Ben Freeman from the Center for International Policy showed how Saudi Arabia was buying senators' votes on the Yemen War Powers resolutions for small donations of just a few thousand dollars each.

A great example of how the system works is shown by the career of former Lockheed Martin vice president Bruce Jackson. As Richard Cummings wrote in his excellent piece "Lockheed Stock and Two Smoking Barrels," Jackson set up and financed the 1990s Committee for NATO Expansion (later renamed the U.S. Committee on NATO), whose entire purpose was to find new customers for Lockheed jets. In the early 2000s he set up the Committee for the Liberation of Iraq, which spent millions of dollars propagandizing about Hussein's human rights abuses in the run-up to Iraq War II. The committee's board included Richard Perle, Jeane Kirkpatrick and James Woolsey. His "point of contact" at the White House was Stephen Hadley, who had been a lawyer for a firm that represented Lockheed. A neoconservative leader described Jackson to a journalist as the "nexus between the defense industry and the neoconservatives. He translates us to them, and them to us." Jackson also bankrolled the neoconservatives' influential Project for a New American Century (PNAC) and *Weekly Standard* magazine in support of the second Iraq war. The government then spent hundreds of billions of dollars on Lockheed weapons and equipment for use in the same war.

Millions of dollars are also spent directly lobbying Congress to support these policies which keep the arms manufacturers in business. CNN's Wolf Blitzer was incredulous when confronting Senator Rand Paul about his opposition to the war in Yemen:

> So for you, this is a moral issue? You know that there are a lot of jobs at stake. If a lot of these defense contractors stop selling war planes and other sophisticated equipment to Saudi Arabia, there's going to be a significant loss of jobs, of revenue here in the United States. That's secondary from your standpoint?

The U.S.A., land of liberty, is nothing more than a land of mercenary killers, in the eyes of the "liberal" American establishment. They appear not to even know that it is wrong.

This system is beyond the proverbial lobbyist-bureaucrat "conflict of interest" or "revolving door." It is the "Iron Triangle," or "Deep State," of military and intelligence officers, arms manufacturers and the congressmen, lobbyists, public relations flacks and news media stars who keep the whole project going. It is the very same post-World War II National Security State, or Military-Industrial Complex that President Dwight D. Eisenhower helped to construct and then belatedly warn the American people about, and that has never been tamed in all the decades since. It seems the national security bureaucracy replaced much of America's constitutional form of government at a point long past. Their priorities now vastly outweigh those of the civilian population, just as Eisenhower had cautioned. The necessity of emergency has been their mandate to maintain power, and it appears that they will never let it go.

As James Madison, the principal author of the Constitution, once wrote,

> Of all the enemies to public liberty war is, perhaps, the most to be dreaded, because it comprises and develops the germ of every other. War is the parent of armies; from these proceed debts and taxes; and armies, and debts, and taxes are the known instruments for bringing the many under the domination of the few. In war, too, the discretionary power of the Executive is extended; its influence in dealing out offices, honors, and emoluments is multiplied; and all the means of seducing the minds, are added to those of subduing the force, of the people. The same malignant aspect in republicanism may be

traced in the inequality of fortunes, and the opportunities of fraud, growing out of a state of war, and in the degeneracy of manners and of morals engendered by both. No nation could preserve its freedom in the midst of continual warfare.

None of these wars have anything to do with helping the people of the Middle East or even securing real American national defense interests there. Instead, the economics of politics create a conspiracy of a thousand separate interests and motives, none of them significant enough to justify the policy on their own, yet they somehow add up to a bureaucratic inertia that has thus far proven impossible to restrain.

After all these years of war, Congress is now full of hawkish war veteran Republicans, such as Sen. Tom Cotton and Rep. Dan Crenshaw. This now includes a new generation of so-called "CIA Democrats," such as Jason Crow, Abigail Spanberger and Elissa Slotkin, who came to power in the elections of 2018. They have prioritized working with Republican hawks like Liz Cheney to keep us at war at all costs. For example, they joined with her in June 2020 to pass a resolution to forbid Trump from withdrawing from Afghanistan until all of her father's failed conditions are somehow finally met after *New York Times* reporter Charlie Savage published an obviously fake story, which he later walked back, accusing the Russians of paying bounties for the killing of U.S. troops in Afghanistan.

The NSA, Gen. Mackenzie, commander of CENTCOM, Gen. Miller, commander of the Afghan war, Gen. Milley, the Chairman of the Joint Chiefs of Staff and Mark Esper, the secretary of defense, all backed down from the claims within a week. The allegations against the Russians kept getting more vague and the disclaimers more severe in the *Times*'s follow-up stories too. Language including, "Such a possibility, if true, would be" and "Thus far, there is no conclusive evidence linking the deaths to any kind of Russian bounty" was added. A follow-up piece admitted that even the CIA analysts actually only had "medium" confidence in their own spies' lies, while the NSA and military dissented entirely. Savage's co-author admitted on MSNBC that the premise of the entire story was false, telling the anchor, "The funds were being sent from Russia regardless of whether the Taliban followed through with killing soldiers or not. There was no report back to the GRU about casualties. The money continued to flow." That is not a bounty. And there is no reason whatsoever to believe it has anything to do with the killing of American soldiers and marines. Russia pays the Taliban for the same reason JSOC flies as their "air force": to kill ISIS. But the morally bankrupt CIA stenographer Savage refused to concede that he or the *Times* were backing down from his claims at all. As he told the author in an email exchange, "in this case 'real' = the CIA really did assess this, put it in the PDB, there was an NSC meeting about it,

Trump WH authorized no response." Referring to the author's public ridicule of his assertions that his story had been "confirmed" by the *Wall Street Journal* and *Washington Post*, Savage said their reporting

> confirmed that the CIA did, in fact, make that assessment and we didn't garble the story as sometimes happens when scoops can't be matched. That was what I was saying; you leaped to the conclusion I was instead saying that these matching stories proved that the CIA's assessment was itself accurate, which I was not.

Who cares whether or not it is true that the Russians are paying these bounties for American scalps? Who cares if the entire foreign policy establishment, Democratic Party, cable TV news and the general public get the impression that the *New York Times* said that the Russians had done this, or see their reporters congratulating themselves on the internet for having their scoop confirmed by others? What does it matter if the Congress passes an amendment forbidding the removal of troops from the country based on this obvious hoax? All Charlie Savage said was that there was a CIA report that said that it might have happened. That is solid reporting on the existence of an unconfirmed rumor. If you and the rest of America read more into it than that, then that is your problem. It is not Savage's job to make sure the top story above the fold of the most important newspaper in the country does not leave anyone with the false impression that he or his colleagues had verified that it was true, even if it was claims about a nuclear power murdering Americans or the president had been indicating he might withdraw the troops before the election. He wrote:

> Your reasoning proves too much. It negates the legitimacy of 99 percent of news about foreign policy and national security. Its implication is that journalism in which reporters convey information they gather from the government (whether from a press release or by piecing together classified info) is not reportable news unless the reporters also first are able to go out and independently prove the information to be true.

> Indeed, it negates the legitimacy of ordinary crime and courts reporting about what FBI agents and even local police detectives are investigating or even the fact that prosecutors have charged someone with a crime, unless reporters have first independently proven that the government's accusations are true.

> I think you have overlearned the lessons of the pre-Iraq War reporting failures — almost 20 years ago now — and see that dynamic as the norm rather than the aberration that it was. All systems carry risks and tradeoffs and will sometimes not result in a good outcome. Yours

would prevent an Iraq WMD debacle, or a Richard Jewell [the heroic security guard the FBI falsely accused and smeared for the 1996 Olympic Park bombing in Atlanta, Georgia].

Your alternative, to guard against the risk that people are told something that could be false because government officials got something wrong or was engaged in a conspiracy, would eliminate most of how the public is able to learn about what is (actually in fact) happening outside of public view, day in and day out — a cure that is worse than the disease, or destroying the village to save it, or pick your cliché.

Passing on unconfirmed CIA rumors about Russia killing American soldiers in the most important paper in the country to help thwart a possible withdrawal from Afghanistan is the same thing as the local TV news reporting that someone has been arrested and charged with a crime. That is the way it has to be, and if you cannot accept that, then you will not have the privilege of being told anything at all. Savage is probably the second or third least-worst reporter at the *Times*, too. At least Savage admitted that your author's way would have prevented the greatest catastrophe of our era while his newspaper laundered the lies that helped cause it. May America finally "overlearn" the lessons of Iraq War II.

The CIA's gambit worked. The withdrawal was delayed. After the election, when Trump announced his cowardly decision at the end of 2020 to only "draw down" to 2,500 troops in Iraq and Afghanistan each — after 30 and 19 straight years of bombing those nations respectively — the government and media still howled with rage. These are "dictator moves!" a current Defense Department official told CNN. His supposed ally, Republican Senate Majority Leader Mitch McConnell, said this was a "hasty withdrawal" which would "hurt our allies and delight the people who wish us harm." Democratic Senator Tammy Duckworth said of rumors of withdrawal, "We want our troops home, but let's not bring them home in body bags." We are supposed to believe that it is now more dangerous for soldiers to fly home from a war than for them to stay and fight in it. "Why now? Dismay as U.S. Considers Troop Pullout from Somalia," the Associated Press cried. No one thought the senators, TV or major print media were speaking for the American people. They represent the point of view of those who have a vested interest in continuing the wars.

Of course, as ever, the National Security State had nothing to fear from the supposed "isolationist," President Donald Trump, even on his way out the door.

Spreading Liberty

There is plenty to criticize about societies in the so-called "Islamic world," especially the epidemic of child rape in Afghanistan Pashtun culture, lynchings over religious conversions in Pakistan, female genital mutilation among Kurds and east Africans and executions over vices and superstitious crimes in Saudi Arabia. But things are much better in Malaysia and Indonesia — the most populous Muslim country in the world — and many other predominantly Muslim countries. While there is plenty wrong with the state of things in many of these nations, Americans would be in a better position to criticize if our government were not responsible for the worst things about these places in the current era: the massive violence taking place in them.

Some people say what Islam really needs is a "reformation." God help us. This is not the time to get back to fundamentals and original interpretations. We want an Enlightenment, where, as with Judaism and Christianity in the West, the more superstitious and intolerant aspects of the religion could be deemphasized, and these cultures could then join the rest of us in the modern era. The scholar Mustafa Akyol has argued that the secularist backlash against the Islamists' chaotic resistance to the West is already coming due. One should hope so, though it sure is the long way around to the gains we could have achieved through peace and commerce in the first place.

This is what we could have had in the 21st century if we had not had George W. Bush and Dick Cheney as the rulers of the American superpower just as the current era was beginning. If only George W. Bush had hired a couple of generic Republican senators to be vice president and secretary of defense and had kept Colin Powell's counsel on how to handle foreign policy, none of this would have ever happened. To be sure, the wars were Powell's fault, too, since he decided to be a good soldier and go out there and help lie the American people into them. But if it had just been up to him, it is a near certainty that even if they had still gotten bogged down in Afghanistan, Iraq War II and the rest of this nightmare that followed from it would never have happened. Instead, Bush, Cheney and Rumsfeld, with the help of Paul Wolfowitz, Richard Perle, David Wurmser, Douglas Feith and the rest of their neoconservative group ruined everything. They got this entire century off to a bad start.

If they had meant what they claimed about wanting to help mankind and deliver free markets and self-government to the people of the world, they could have demonstrated it by working to make America a society where freedom is held as the highest political value and showing the people of the world what that really looks like in practice. They might have made some real progress in convincing people to embrace the best aspects of our ways. The war party claimed to be spreading freedom and protecting us from threats. But they were the greatest danger all along.

The success of market capitalism around the world since the end of the first Cold War with Russia 30 years ago has been remarkable. All across Asia and Africa, poverty levels are falling to their lowest proportions in history. Though the Communist Party still rules China, they abandoned Marxist starvation for a corporatist-style "mixed economy" decades ago and have the most growth in the shortest time in world history to show for it. Middle-rank powers like India and Brazil are also rising in influence. This all means that America's "unipolar moment" is over. Other countries have a greater relative ability to resist American dictates than they have since the end of World War II. Trying to dominate the planet is a lost cause. Why should we not just let them have their independence? What have the American people gained from a permanent policy of running roughshod over other nations in ways that would drive our people to the most extreme violence if it were done to us? Our government is still bombing people in a dozen countries, mostly over one massive, horrific attack on New York and Virginia 20 years ago. Just think what we would do if another nation actually meddled in our elections, overthrew our leaders in a violent coup, stationed combat forces in our country to attack our neighbors or started launching airstrikes against what they consider high-value targets in our hometowns on a regular basis.

Even disregarding Mullah Omar's various offers to negotiate the extradition of al Qaeda to the U.S. after September 11th, the mission to kidnap or kill bin Laden, Zawahiri and their few dozen leaders at the top of the al Qaeda organization could have been over by Christmas 2001. America could have shown the world how restrained we were in applying our power and proved that our society is the exception because we really do believe in liberty and justice, not because of some invented "exceptionalism" that grants our government the right to break the law and commit atrocities. If that had been how America had chosen to "lead" the world into the 21st century, we would almost certainly be making more progress than with the current set of policies.

Then again, spreading democracy and freedom was only a smokescreen anyway. The giveaway is that our government only seeks regime change in countries they do not control, rather than ones that deny their people the vote. They will support a king or sultan any day, and a military coup in a heartbeat, if it is to overturn the results of an election which the wrong side won, such as in Algeria in 1993, Gaza in 2006 and Egypt in 2011. This is not to mention all the coups in Russia's near-abroad or the continuing series of U.S. interventions in Latin American elections, such as Honduras in 2009 and Bolivia in 2019.

As many as two million Iraqis, Afghans, Pakistanis, Somalis, Libyans, Syrians and Yemenis have been killed in these wars. Their countries have been completely destroyed. The famines in Somalia and Yemen are on Bush, Obama and now on Trump as well. They are not responsible for bad weather, but the chaos of their wars is responsible for the inability of people to make up for the droughts. Of course, in Yemen, targeting food supplies has been a deliberate strategy of the U.S.-led coalition all along. Helpless civilians are still dying in large numbers. More than 37 million people have been internally and externally displaced by the wars, more than in any crisis since World War II. Nobody knows how many widows and orphans have been created, nor how many new enemies.

After all that has happened, how could any American claim the position to lecture other people about their systems' faults when our government, not theirs, is the greatest purveyor of violence and injustice in the world today? What is the average Earthling supposed to think about the world's oldest republic, born in bloody secession in the name of liberty from the British Empire, which now invades country after country to spread democracy while standing behind the Israelis' merciless 50-year-long military occupation of the people of Palestine and the Saudi Kingdom that murders people for the crimes of adultery, "witchcraft" and "sorcery"? The Saudi royals' religious henchmen impose this totalitarian state based on the most pious interpretations of scripture while everyone inside and outside of Saudi Arabia knows their princelings live the high life in private jets, abusing drugs and prostitutes and otherwise exemplifying the lowest corruption of the characters of men with unlimited wealth and power.

In 2005 on Fox News, Sean Hannity interviewed a Protestant Christian missionary whom he had interviewed at least a few times before. The missionary desperately told Hannity what he was not at all prepared to hear. He had just gotten back from East Asia and felt that the U.S. had to call the Iraq war off immediately because everywhere he traveled to spread the Gospel, people would react and say that what they knew about Christianity was that it was the religion of the Americans who attacked Iraq and that they were not interested. Of course, to the missionary this was intolerable. How could the Gospel of "democracy spreading" through war possibly be more important than saving men's very souls through preaching from the Bible? The same sort of thing has happened to all sorts of ideas and brands that are associated with the United States and the West. We had our "unipolar moment," and sure blew it alright. "Freedom" in the American style is now far more strongly associated with licentiousness in war and business as well as culture; liberty meaning only the right to exert power over others.

Thomas Friedman, one of the most influential writers at the *New York Times*, has claimed that sustainable globalization still requires a stable, geopolitical power structure, which simply cannot be maintained without the active involvement of the United States. ... [The] world [is] stabilized by a benign superpower, with its capital in Washington, D.C.

The hidden hand of the market will never work without a hidden fist — McDonald's cannot flourish without McDonnell Douglas, the builder of the F-15. And the hidden fist that keeps the world safe for Silicon Valley's technologies is called the United States Army, Air Force, Navy and Marine Corps.

But other than Tom Friedman and the author's junior college sociology professor, says who? Milton Friedman (no relation to the former), the influential capitalist economist from the University of Chicago, never maintained that a world empire was necessary to have a capitalist economy in America or trade between nations. Nor did any other major American free-market economist of the post-World War II era.

But this is what the people in charge of the American government and its foreign policy believe, and it is how they behave. No wonder the world is turning back toward nationalism and socialism if this is what liberalism and democracy have to offer.

Leaders of the Western nations have claimed they are attempting to initiate a new Enlightenment era of democratic values in the Arab and Muslim worlds. Perhaps trying to live by our highest principles and leading by example — promoting natural, individual rights and self-government in the free market of ideas — might be a more effective strategy than the current policy of propping up some of the world's most repressive governments, while launching invasions and carrying out regime change operations against others. As Alan Bock and Aldous Huxley taught, violent and destructive means determine violent and destructive ends.

It has been argued that the key to the American "crusader state" lies in the doctrines of the Declaration of Independence itself. If all men and women are born naturally free, then everywhere that people's civil rights and liberties are not being protected to our standards, our country must claim the right to invade to secure these rights for the people. But Thomas Jefferson, who wrote those lines about mankind's natural rights, believed in revolution in one country. He did not seek to export the American Revolution to Europe. Thomas Paine and a few of the other American founders did believe in the gospel of universal revolution, but they were by far in the minority. Nor does the U.S. Constitution grant our government the authority to guarantee a republican form of government to any nation on the planet.

If we want to be free, we have to recognize that any government powerful enough to give anyone in the world what they want is powerful enough to destroy everything they have and take from us everything we have to do so. As the libertarian economist and theoretician Murray N. Rothbard wrote, our doctrine must be one of "universal rights, locally enforced" from the bottom-up wherever possible. Secretary of State John Quincy Adams, in his Independence Day address of 1821, explained the United States' position regarding the outbreak of a republican revolution in Greece and whether their efforts deserved U.S. government support:

> [America] has abstained from interference in the concerns of others, even when conflict has been for principles to which she clings, as to the last vital drop that visits the heart. She has seen that probably for centuries to come, all the contests of that Aceldama the European world, will be contests of inveterate power, and emerging right.

> Wherever the standard of freedom and Independence has been or shall be unfurled, there will her heart, her benedictions and her prayers be. But she goes not abroad, in search of monsters to destroy.

> She is the well-wisher to the freedom and independence of all. She is the champion and vindicator only of her own. She will commend the general cause by the countenance of her voice, and the benignant sympathy of her example.

> She well knows that by once enlisting under other banners than her own, were they even the banners of foreign independence, she would involve herself beyond the power of extrication, in all the wars of interest and intrigue, of individual avarice, envy, and ambition, which assume the colors and usurp the standard of freedom.

> The fundamental maxims of her policy would insensibly change from liberty to force. The frontlet upon her brows would no longer beam with the ineffable splendor of freedom and independence; but in its stead would soon be substituted an imperial diadem, flashing in false and tarnished lustre the murky radiance of dominion and power. She might become the dictatress of the world: she would be no longer the ruler of her own spirit.

> Her glory is not dominion, but liberty. Her march is the march of the mind. She has a spear and a shield: but the motto upon her shield is, Freedom, Independence, Peace. This has been her Declaration: this has been, as far as her necessary intercourse with the rest of mankind would permit, her practice.

Of course, the hawks continue to bring up Adolf Hitler and the German Third Reich of the 1930s and 1940s because using the exception to the rule to establish a new rule of perpetual war is their only option. The Nazis are the last refuge of a bankrupt warmonger. Without Hitler, who would H.R. McMaster invoke when trying to scare the American people about Trump signing a deal with the Taliban? Pashtun militiamen are not so scary. Chamberlain and Hitler at Munich it is again then.

Meanwhile, even in the West, liberalism and democracy broadly defined are being discredited by the consequences of the terror wars. The number of democracies in the world is now in decline. The disasters of the wars include the lives and money wasted, the corrupt crony capitalism, the economic devastation of the American-led financial crisis of 2008 and the mass refugee crisis of the twenty-teens in which hundreds of thousands of people fled the devastation of America and its allies' Middle Eastern wars to head to Europe. These crises have shattered other populations' and governments' faith in the American-led "liberal" international order. They have not only undermined American hegemonic power — power it should never have sought — but also have helped to undermine the ideas of free people and self-government that our so-called moderates have invoked as their excuses for inflicting the horrors of these mostly unprovoked wars. The foreign policy professionals blamed President Donald Trump for being rude to Germany's Chancellor Angela Merkel, but the damage was done before he arrived. The rise of the right in the European Parliament and the UK's vote to leave the European Union in 2016 preceded and presaged Trump's victory later that year.

That is what the American people have allowed our government to do to our civilization. They have marred it and tarred it as being nothing but a bunch of self-serving hypocrites who talk all day about human rights but, in fact, jump at any chance to deprive people of them in the most brutal fashion and for the slightest cause. The national security state never even stops to take a break. They just move on from one disaster to the next in an unending chain. Thirty years since the end of the Cold War with the Soviet Union and two decades into the 21st century, America has just about screwed up everything. The U.S. government is responsible for most of the worst things happening on this planet right now, and all in the name of making it better and keeping us safe.

Just Come Home

So, the U.S. government got us into this mess by backing a massive Islamist terrorist movement, then enraging it and turning it against the American people with Iraq War I and the decision to stay in Saudi Arabia to enforce the blockade and patrol the Iraqi "no-fly zones" in the 1990s. Even while al Qaeda was already targeting us, the government continued to back them in minor missions in the Balkans and Caucasus while failing to protect the American people from the danger they had made. They then exploited their creation's violent revenge against us and used it as an excuse to expand America's military "footprint" in the Middle East even further than before with the launch of Iraq War II. This set off a massive regional sectarian war where the Americans first took the side of their regional adversaries, the Iranian Shi'ites, and then switched back to their traditional allies, the Saudis, the Gulf Cooperation Council (GCC) and their intelligence agencies' bin Ladenite terrorists. This led directly to the catastrophe of the war in Syria, the rise of the Islamic State "Caliphate," and then to Iraq War III — again on behalf of the Shi'ites they hate — to destroy it. The American war for al Qaeda in the Arabian Peninsula against their Houthi enemies rages on.

After the killing of bin Laden in 2011, the late, great Navy commander turned antiwar humorist, Jeff Huber, wrote a piece called, "Osama bin Laden: Dead and Lovin' It!!"

> Alexander the Great, eat your heart out. Et tu, Julius Caesar. The same goes for you, Charlemagne. Dead or alive, Osama bin Laden is the greatest military and political strategist in human history, bar none.

> Neither Alexander nor Caesar nor Charlemagne managed, as bin Laden has, to lure the best-trained, best-equipped military of the world's all-time mightiest nation in a series of inescapable goat-rope entanglements without so much as an army or a navy or an air force of his own.

> Osama bin Laden … couldn't have picked a better stratagem than the 9/11 attacks to goad us into becoming the victim of our own military-industrial establishment, the one that President Dwight Eisenhower warned us in 1961 would take over if we didn't stay on guard against it.

In every American-Middle Eastern conflict this century, whether they were actually trying to fight against al Qaeda or indirectly backing them, only the conservative Shi'ite theocracy in Iran and our shared enemy, the radical bin Ladenite Sunni extremist fighters and terrorists, have gained. And all at the expense of the people of the Middle East and our own society in America. Not only have they increased their numbers, but the U.S. has helped them to accomplish many of their goals, such as the overthrow of Saddam Hussein, Moammar Gaddafi and Abdullah Saleh. America has helped to destabilize the region economically, radicalize the population politically and in religious terms, discredit and destabilize its client regimes, completely blown our country's reputation, discrediting our highest ideals, helped to increase division between Islamic societies and the West and spent seven trillion dollars that we did not have and could not afford on the whole endeavor.

The American government has created the violent, stateless territories where bin Ladenite forces have thrived. In Iraq, Somalia, Libya, Mali, Syria and Yemen, all the United States has done is make our bin Ladenite terrorism problem worse to almost unbelievable degrees. We are already on our second generation of returning jihadis in the last 19 years, mostly from the wars in Iraq and Syria. No one knows what the future holds for Yemen, even if President Biden does follow through on his dubious campaign promise to end the war against the Houthis. Al Qaeda in the Arabian Peninsula is stronger than ever. Yet every nation in the region has a reason to keep these men on a very short leash at worst, so they do not fall victim to their violence. The most important thing the United States could do to fight bin Ladenite terrorism in the Middle East would be to stop knocking over their governments and creating these massive, lawless spaces where their fighters can thrive.

Long after the American people have wised up, the establishment hawks still say U.S. forces can never withdraw without causing "power vacuums" and terrorist attacks against us. But getting out of the way of governments like that of Bashar al-Assad in Syria so that they can reestablish control over their own territory is a much more straightforward and obvious way of denying it to al-Nusra and ISIS than the American military occupying the desert out there indefinitely.

Even where significant concentrations of bin Ladenite terrorists still exist, such as in Syria's Idlib Province and southern Yemen, the safe-haven myth is still just that. Terrorist attacks can be planned in an apartment or during a walk in the park. There is nothing special about Iraq, Syria, Afghanistan or Yemen that provides unique access to the United States. The September 11th attacks were planned and coordinated in Malaysia, Germany, Spain, California, Florida, New Jersey and Maryland — just down the street from and right under the nose of National Security Agency headquarters, as journalist James Bamford has shown. Virtually all of the attacks against the United States in the years since have been planned here, with the shoe and underpants bombers being the only notable exceptions. It is staying in the wars because of the safe-haven myth that is more likely to get America attacked again.

Proponents of American global dominance declare that all they ever seek or create is peace and "rules-based" order. But that is not true. They have run the American republic into the ground trying to maintain their world empire. They have already failed. But it could be worse. For all great civilizations, overextended empire is the last stage before it finally dies. In a perverted mirror image of our al Qaeda enemies, America is committing murder-suicide on a mass scale.

The debt is already nearing 30 trillion dollars. Our government can only sell so many bonds, especially when their brilliant plan is to borrow enough from China that they can dominate central Asia to limit Chinese power and influence there. How long can Beijing be expected to continue to finance that?

But the American people do understand. We must make the American government give up this project to dominate Eurasia. The U.S. is going broke, losing all our freedoms and destroying whatever was valuable and worth conserving about our society in the attempt. Nor can we allow our government to insist on additional time and chances to "tie up loose ends" and leave the Middle East and Central Asia "responsibly." These wars are already lost. There is no victory or stable peace to be had in any of them. If the U.S. must stay until its goals have been accomplished, then that is not opposition or skepticism, but a blank writ for another two decades of war. None of Joe Biden's best national security staffers know how to tie up the loose ends of these wars just right so that we can then call it off. They see the project has already failed. That is why they no longer speak even of "success" in the wars. Like Zawahiri says, just keep fighting.

Again, this is not to say that the American people should give in to extortion by terrorists. Of course we should not. But the U.S.A. is not supposed to be a world empire anyway. Our Constitution describes a limited republic, under the rule of law, and which holds the rights and safety of the people actually under its jurisdiction paramount. You cannot have it both ways. Besides, the rest of the world does not want or need the United States to "lead" them in the first place. Some relatively tough nationalists are coming to power all around the world now, not in spite of America's best efforts to "spread democracy," but because of them.

One of the major causes of the crisis of confidence in our system, which is now leading the population to move further to the socialist left and nationalist right, was the centrist-liberal establishment's disastrous Middle Eastern foreign policy over the last two decades, in which the American people and military have made vast sacrifices in exchange for nothing. How could anyone believe our leaders know what is best? They clearly do not. Barack Obama was elected over Hillary Clinton and John McCain because people falsely believed that he was from outside of the establishment and therefore might care more about people like them. And he sometimes talked a good game about ending the wars. Trump was elected because he really was from outside of the American political establishment, but he never had the principle, focus, wherewithal or allies to follow through on his pledges to end the wars either.

It was not just Hillary Clinton's character, but the entire Bush-Clinton post-Cold War consensus of the last 30 years that was defeated in 2016. The establishment's return in the form of Joe Biden's presidency, over the bungling failures of management and character under Donald Trump, is no vindication of their previous stewardship. The fact that Trump was nearly reelected against such an establishment stalwart as Biden is surely a damning indictment against their authority. The Democrats' and national security state's insistence that Trump was only elected due to Russian intervention in the 2016 election and the refusal of Trump's base to concede his loss to Biden in 2020 has more Americans discussing and predicting secession in the face of the other sides' obstinance. This reflects a notable if not severe declining faith in the U.S. constitutional order to survive for the long term.

At the dawn of the War on Terrorism, now-*Washington Post* columnist Max Boot wrote in the *Weekly Standard*, "The Case for American Empire." His colleague, David Brooks, declared that America needed a grand new project, something that we could all be excited about together to help forge a new "National Greatness." Iraq, as his friend Christopher Beam wrote, "fit the bill." More than four years into Iraq War II, Brooks was still carrying on about how the war was "one of the noblest endeavors the United States, or any great power, has ever undertaken." This was all delusional madness. These neoconservatives and the men who listened to them ruined everything.

A few of America's worst hawks have learned an important lesson. In January 2020, Martin Indyk, the man who had insisted on Clinton's "dual containment policy" against Iraq and Iran from bases in Saudi Arabia that caused al Qaeda to turn their war against America, finally threw in the towel. He wrote in the *Wall Street Journal* that "The Middle East Isn't Worth It Anymore." Rather than dominating Middle Eastern oil supplies to compromise major competitors, Indyk says that since the U.S. is again a hydrocarbon exporter, "China and India need to be protecting the sea lanes between the Gulf and their ports, not the U.S. Navy." And Israel, due to American "largess," can "defend itself by itself."

Before he died in 2016, even establishment oracle Zbigniew Brzezinski finally became convinced that America had overreached in the Bush and Obama years and desperately needed to retrench, cooperate with Russia and China and deputize more of the imperial law-enforcing to smaller allied nations before the entire thing fell apart. The quest for empire only pushes other nations away. Even from the point of view of those who built it, the whole project is counterproductive. It wastes our money and diminishes our influence in the long term.

In January 2021, the influential foreign policy theorist Walter Russell Mead wrote in *Foreign Affairs* that the entire post-World War II, U.S.- and UN-based international order is over. He correctly identified Bush's Iraq War II and Obama's war in Libya, the 2008 financial crisis and other examples of elite American and Western incompetence which have undermined the U.S. elite's rule over the American people and the rest of the world. What will it take to get the remainder of the American establishment to realize that their insistence on dominating the world has been the very key to the undoing of their power? Perhaps Ron Paul is right that they will never learn until the dollar breaks.

But the American people understand that it is time just to call the whole thing off. When the American empire finally does come home from the Middle East, we will find that anti-American terrorism will dry up anyway. The last few revenge-obsessed bin Ladenites out there could be taken care of with simple police and intelligence work. If America is no longer dominating the Middle East, then we no longer are a target for those who are trying to kick us out. The American people gave our government the mandate to hunt down the men responsible for the September 11th attack and "bring them to justice." They have proven that they cannot and will not abide by the limits of that narrow authority. Our government simply cares too much about its special interests and their wants to prioritize the American people's security.

There is no real danger of the future creation of new bin Ladenite states in the Middle East in America's absence, at least outside of the Idlib Province, where our allies, the Turks, still protect al Qaeda. But they have no hope of overthrowing the governments of Arabia, Jordan or Egypt. Even if they could, the Islamic State has shown us how incompetent these men are. No group promising purity by forcing people to live as they did in the 13th century will get very far or last very long in the 21st. Where they can get a foothold, let them put themselves out of business and prove to their own people what failures they are.

Our leaders say we are facing generational war — the "Long War," they call it — and they mean it. As David Petraeus says, "we will be fighting this for the rest of our lifetimes for the rest of our children's lifetimes." Petraeus is also implicitly admitting that he personally lost both Iraq War II and Afghanistan, or else we would not have to fight there anymore at all. Perhaps other people more qualified to comment should be heard in his place.

The U.S. backed the Arab-Afghan mercenaries and terrorists and then fought them; backed Saddam Hussein and then fought him; backed the Taliban and then fought them; worked for Sadr, then fought him; fought al Qaeda in Iraq, backed them, and then fought them again; worked with Gaddafi, Assad and the Houthis against al Qaeda, and then fought all of them too — for al Qaeda. Does that sound right to you?

Just as the enemy planned, the U.S. government has accomplished almost all of Osama bin Laden's original goals. They have destabilized many of our allies' regimes, radicalized the entire region in terms of politics and religion, discredited those Arabs who have tried to participate in American-style democratic elections, such as Hamas in the Gaza Strip and the Muslim Brotherhood in Egypt, and diminished overall American influence in the region. The extremists' enemies, the actual moderates, have been ruined.

The "gray zone," as the Islamic State refers to it, is diminished. In America, Muslims are mostly well assimilated, educated professionals. They earn advanced degrees, own property and prosper. But both al Qaeda and ISIS have made it clear that they hate that. The terrorists cannot abide Western liberty because it undermines their narrative of our evil. How is that for a realistic take on al Qaeda hating us for our freedom? They cannot stand that we allow Muslims to live at peace in our super-majority Christian society, with no history of pogroms against them. If millions of Muslims live in America in peace and prosperity, that ruins the terrorists' narrative that we hate them for their faith and represent an irreconcilable evil. ISIS commands its followers to attack the U.S. for the explicit purpose of driving our government to crack down upon and alienate innocent American Muslims. This is supposed to marginalize them and remove that gray zone where both so-called sides can live together in peace, to "sharpen the contradictions," as the Communist terrorists of previous eras used to say. But it is just another example of how doing the right thing in the first place, such as clinging to our respect for freedom of religion in the face of all the anti-Muslim hype, is the best way to diminish support for the terrorist threat anyway.

Since September 11, 2001, America's wars have helped to increase the ranks of the bin Ladenites from 400 to about 40,000 at the height of the Islamic State. They are now spread throughout the Middle East and North, West and East Africa. The jihadists the U.S. backed in Syria created their own Caliphate for a few years, and remain in force in the Idlib Province. Because of George W. Bush's Iraq War II, the "Shi'ite Crescent" now includes Baghdad, and the policy to make up for that fact by seeking regime change in Syria has also blown up in America's face, leaving Iran and Hezbollah with more influence in Damascus than ever before. Tensions between the U.S. and Iran have brought us to the brink of war as recently as 2020.

On top of all that, the Russians have now returned to the Middle East when they had been content to sit out for the last generation, since the fall of the Soviet Union.

Our government continues to levy massive economic sanctions on Iran and Syria and threaten both of them with regime change. Osama bin Laden would have wanted to see both of these governments overthrown. He would also have been outraged at the devastating effects the sanctions are having on the innocent civilian population of both countries. In Syria's east, the Kurds, under U.S. control, hold the oil and much of Syria's wheat hostage. *Foreign Policy* magazine reports that Syrians are starving as the situation begins to look like Iraq under President Bill Clinton's blockade in the 1990s. Just as during Iraq War I, the policy remains regime change. Syrian civilian suffering is a deliberate result of America's economic war, as a means, no matter how unrealistic, to that end:

> Senior Western diplomats have told *Foreign Policy* on many occasions that sanctions are the West's last leverage against Assad to pressure him to ... agree to a political reconciliation that, if carried out sincerely, would eventually mean him leaving power. They insist that paying for Syrian reconstruction, including infrastructure like power plants and irrigation systems that are necessary for the country's food security and daily life, will end up strengthening the regime's oppression. They say they have no intention of letting Assad succeed in that, at least not unless he makes significant concessions.

There is nothing the U.S. could do better for the enemy other than putting al Qaeda leader Zawahiri himself on the throne in Cairo.

Iranians are also dying of easily treatable diseases because international trade to their country has been all but eliminated. Even exempted items like medicines do not get through the sanctions regime because international shippers do not want to take the risk of crossing the U.S. Treasury Department. So, they sail on to safer harbors.

The first step in ending the terrorists' war against the United States is to stop supporting them directly and indirectly as our government has in Libya, Syria, Yemen and Iran, since the redirection began. Then we must forever foreswear the policy of regime change, especially in the Middle East, where all of our wars in this century have only created wide-open spaces where bin Ladenites and other violent extremists can thrive.

As we have seen, in the very few cases where the War on Terrorism has actually focused on al Qaeda, such as in the Pakistani and Yemeni drone wars, they succeeded only in causing worse consequences. It led to the rise of Afghan ISIS in the first case and helped grow AQAP into a massive force to be reckoned with in the second. The U.S. can claim very few real successes in the War on Terrorism. They helped the Tripoli government destroy the ISIS stronghold in Sirte, Libya in 2016, though obviously the American war five years before, and the then-still ongoing support for the insurgency in Syria, was the only reason ISIS existed at all, much less in Libya. They also helped to win Iraq War III — including in eastern Syria — where they again were only cleaning up their own mess and helping the Iranian-backed Iraqi Shi'ites win the war. American special operations forces are still fighting Iraq War III 1/2 in western Iraq, but there is no doubt that what is left of ISIS there has so many enemies to deal with that they no longer pose a threat to the United States, or even our "interests" broadly defined, at all.

The Biden-Harris administration cannot, nor can any other American government, be trusted to fight a war only against al Qaeda and do so effectively. The date on the calendar proves the case. We just have to call the whole thing off. Ceasing intervention and relying on the thorough vetting of those who enter our country to make sure they never worked for the U.S. or our allies as paid mercenary terrorists will have to do.

Whoever said that the U.S.A. had a mandate to dominate the world was wrong. The evidence is in. But it does not have to be this way. To begin to make it right, the American people must demand an end to the War on Terrorism.

Appendix I:
Counting Iraq Wars

- Iraq War I (1990–1991): "Operations Desert Storm," a.k.a. The Gulf War
- Iraq War I 1/2 (1991–2003): 12 years of blockade and bombing from bases in Saudi Arabia. At least 300,000 killed.
- Iraq War II (2003–2011): "Operation Iraqi Freedom," George W. Bush's invasion and occupation of Iraq resulting in Iran's friends being empowered in the east, al Qaeda in the west, a million killed.
- Iraq War III (2014–2017): "Operation Inherent Resolve" the war against the Islamic State in Iraq and Syria a.k.a. ISIS, ISIL, Daesh.
- Iraq War III 1/2 (2017–∞): The indefinite mopping up of Sunni insurgency in western Iraq, in alliance with the Iraqi army.

Appendix II:
Middle East Alliances

Of course, there are major differences between Turkey and Saudi Arabia and Qatar and so forth as well.

America's Sunni alliance is:
U.S.A.
Saudi Arabia
Egypt
Jordan
UAE
Turkey
Israel (The "Jewish state")
Kuwait
Bahrain
Qatar

The Iranian Shi'ite alliance is:
Iran
Iraq (since 2003)
Syria
Hezbollah
Supposedly the Houthis
And, in the case of Syria, Russia

Appendix III:
The Bin Ladenites

In Afghanistan:
Then: al Qaeda; now: ISIS-K, a.k.a. Islamic State Khorasan Province

In Iraq:
Al Qaeda in Iraq, a.k.a.: Jama'at al Tawhid w'al Jihad, AQI, Ansar al-Islam, the Islamic State of Iraq (ISI), later ISIS, the Islamic State, the Caliphate, al Dawlah al-Islameyah fi Iraq wal-Sham, Daesh

In Libya:
The Libyan Islamic Fighting Group (LIFG), Ansar al-Sharia, Libya Dawn

In Mali:
Ansar Din, Al Qaeda in the Islamic Maghreb (AQIM)

In Syria:
Jabhat al-Nusra a.k.a.: Hayat Tahrir al-Sham, ISIS, Ahrar Al-Sham, a hundred more.

In Iran:
Jundallah

In Somalia:
Al-Shabaab

In Yemen:
Al Qaeda in the Arabian Peninsula (AQAP), ISIS

Appendix IV:
The Iraqi Shi'ite Factions

The Supreme Council for Islamic Revolution in Iraq (SCIRI) is led by the al-Hakim family. After the invasion, it was renamed the Islamic Supreme Council of Iraq (ISCI) or Majlis al-A'la. Their militia is the Badr Brigade, a.k.a. Badr Corps or Badr Organization. Prime Minister al-Mahdi came from ISCI.

The Da'wa Party was founded by Iraqis, including Mohammad Baqir al-Sadr, Muqtada al-Sadr's father-in-law. They provided three of the five of Iraq's post-2005 prime ministers: al-Jaafari, al-Maliki and al-Abadi.

Both of the above groups fled to Iran and took their side when Iraq invaded Iran in 1980. They returned to Iraq to seize power on the heels of the U.S. invasion of 2003.

Then there's Muqtada al-Sadr and his powerful Mehdi Army militia based in eastern Baghdad and Najaf.

They were the big three Shi'ite factions whose United Iraqi Alliance took over the new state.

Since then, they have split and renamed and reorganized somewhat. For example, the Badr Brigade is now also a political party and Maliki created his own State of Law party, etc.

There have also sprung up numerous semi-independent Shi'ite militias, some allied with Iran, such as Khatib Hezbollah and Asa'ib Ahl al-Haq.

Appendix V:
Lying Us Into War

Articles about how the neoconservatives lied us into Iraq War II:

"The Israel Lobby and U.S. Foreign Policy" by John Mearsheimer and Stephen Walt

"The Men from JINSA and CSP" by Jason Vest

"The Lie Factory" by Jason Vest and Robert Dreyfuss

"Agents of Influence" by Robert Dreyfuss

"The Spies Who Pushed For War" by Julian Borger

"The Man Who Sold the War" by James Bamford

"Selective Intelligence" by Seymour Hersh

"The Stovepipe" by Seymour Hersh

"In Rumsfeld's Shop" by Karen Kwiatkowski

"Conscientious Objector" by Karen Kwiatkowski

"Open Door Policy" by Karen Kwiatkowski

"The New Pentagon Papers" by Karen Kwiatkowski

"Soldier for the Truth" by Marc Cooper

"Pentagon Office Home to Neo-Con Network" by Jim Lobe

"How Ahmed Chalabi Conned the Neocons" by John Dizard

"Special Pentagon Unit Skirted CIA on Iraq" by Greg Miller

"Abusive Tactics Used to Seek Links" by Jonathan S. Landay

"Lockheed Stock and Two Smoking Barrels" by Richard Cummings

"How Neoconservatives Conquered Washington and Launched a War" by Michael Lind

"Practice to Deceive" by Joshua Micah Marshall

"Iran-Contra II?" by Joshua Micah Marshall (I know, he's just horrible now, but these two are old and good.)

Appendix VI:
Benghazi Scandals

March 2011: The Obama government pretended to believe that Moammar Gaddafi was going to murder every civilian in the eastern Libyan city of Benghazi as his false *casus belli* to launch his regime change war there.

September 11, 2012: The CIA and Qataris were working with terrorists to ship guns and fighters off to the war in Syria. This blew up in their face when local al Qaeda fighters took revenge for another compartment of the CIA's killing of their friend Sheikh Yahya al-Libi — brother of Sheikh Ibn al-Libi, the man Dick Cheney had tortured into accusing Saddam Hussein of helping train al Qaeda in hijacking techniques and chemical weapons manufacture — in a drone strike in Pakistan. They killed Ambassador Chris Stevens and three others.

Appendix VII:
Acronyms and Initials

AEI — American Enterprise Institute
AFRICOM — African Command
AIPAC — American Israel Public Affairs Committee
AMISOM — African Union Mission in Somalia
AQAP — al Qaeda in the Arabian Peninsula, Ansar Al-Sharia
AQI — al Qaeda in Mesopotamia (or Iraq)
AQIM — al Qaeda in the Islamic Maghreb
CFR — Council on Foreign Relations
CIA — Central Intelligence Agency
COIN — Counterinsurgency
CNAS — Center for a New American Security
CSP — Center for Security Policy
DIA — Defense Intelligence Agency
EFP — Explosively Formed Penetrator
FBI — Federal Bureau of Investigation
FEWSNET — Famine Early Warning Systems Network
FSA — Free Syrian Army
GCC — Gulf Cooperation Council
GID — Saudi General Intelligence Directorate
GNA — Government of National Accord
GNC — General National Congress
HoR — House of Representatives
IAEA — International Atomic Energy Agency
ICU — Islamic Courts Union
IDF — Israeli Defense Forces
IED — Improvised Explosive Device
INC — Iraqi National Congress
INR — Bureau of Intelligence and Research
IRGC — Iranian Revolutionary Guard Corps
ISCI — The Islamic Supreme Council of Iraq
ISI — Pakistan's Inter-Services Intelligence
ISIS — Islamic State in Iraq and Syria
ISIS-K — Islamic State in Iraq and Syria, Khorasan Province
ISOG — Iran-Syria Operations Group
JCPOA —Joint Comprehensive Plan of Action ("the nuclear deal")
JINSA — Jewish Institute for National Security Affairs
JSOC — Joint Special Operations Command

LIFG — Libyan Islamic Fighting Group
LNA — Libyan National Army
MBS — Mohammed bin Salman
MEK — Mujahideen-e-Khalq
NED — National Endowment for Democracy
NIC — National Intelligence Council
NIE — National Intelligence Estimate
NGO — Non-Governmental Organization
OPCW — Organization for the Prevention of Chemical Weapons
OSP — Office of Special Plans
PCTEG — Policy Counter-Terrorism Evaluation Group
PMU — Popular Mobilization Unit
PNAC — Project for a New American Century
SAA — Syrian Arab Army
SAS — British Special Air Service
SBS — British Special Boat Service
SCIC — Supreme Council of Islamic Courts
SCIRI — Supreme Council for Islamic Revolution in Iraq
SDF — Syrian Democratic Forces
SNC — Syrian National Council
SOFA — Status of Forces Agreement
TFG — Transitional Federal Government
UAE — United Arab Emirates
USSOCOM — U.S. Special Operations Command
WHIG — White House Iraq Group
WINEP — Washington Institute for Near East Policy
YPG — People's Protection Units

About the Author

Scott Horton is director of the Libertarian Institute, editorial director of Antiwar.com, host of Antiwar Radio on Pacifica, 90.7 FM KPFK in Los Angeles, California and podcasts the Scott Horton Show from ScottHorton.org. He's conducted more than 5,400 interviews since 2003. He's also the author of *Fool's Errand: Time to End the War in Afghanistan* (2017) and editor of *The Great Ron Paul: The Scott Horton Show Interviews 2004–2019* (2019).

His articles have appeared in the *American Conservative, The National Interest,* Antiwar.com, the History News Network and the *Christian Science Monitor.*

He lives in Austin, Texas with his wife Larisa Alexandrovna Horton.

Acknowledgments

Sincere thanks to Joanne McKenzie, Steve Woskow, Mike Swanson, Mike Dworski, Aaron Keith Harris, Hunter DeRensis, Eric Schuler, Thaddeus Russell, A.J. Van Slyke, Sheldon Richman, Gareth Porter, Brad Hoff, Ed Huff, Sam Hage, Christopher West, Jared Wall, Zooey Greif, Gus Cantavaro, Andrew Harrison, Tom Woods, Dan Sanchez, Jeremy Diehl, Louis Grilli, Adam McDonald, Andrew Messer, Erik Koth, Monty Ellis, Adam and Jennifer Haman, Tim Dryden, Rebecca Berthold, Shauna Lynch, Rick McGinnis, Mike Marion, Louis J. Vandenberg, Alan Minsky, Ricky Herrera, August Wagele, Mark Jokel, Matt Barganier, Aaron Vaughan, James Jenneman, Robert Gaines, Matthew Hoh, Danny Davis, Anthony Walker, Braden Chapman, Adam House, Danny Sjursen, Dan McKnight, Anne Frost, Anthony Gregory, Justin Zelinsky, Matthew Hampton, Noah Pugsley and my wife, Larisa Alexandrovna Horton.

Special thanks of course also to the staff of Antiwar.com:
Eric Garris, Malcolm Garris, Justin Raimondo (RIP), Jason Ditz, Dave DeCamp, Kyle Anzalone, Angela Keaton, Margaret Griffis, Michael Austin, Alexia Gilmore, Colin Hunter, Mike Ewens, Brandon J. Snider, Andrew Phillips and M.K. Lords.

And I'd like to give my extra thanks to the great Grant F. Smith, founder and director of the Institute for Research: Middle Eastern Policy, irmep.org. Without his production help, none of the Libertarian Institute's books would have ever made it to print. Like all of his great work, it is truly appreciated.

Thank you also to all the donors and supporters of the Libertarian Institute, especially:

A.J. Ellis, Eric Sammons, Nathan Pablo Juarez, Kevin Stever, Gavin Luckett, Casey Johnson, Samuel Mourani, Remy Demarest, Chad Wilson, Derek M. Smith, Andreas Brekken, Brian Mooney, Jared Wall, Wayne Harley, Brian Miller, Nolan Miller, Daniel Rice, Joseph M. Stivaletta, Lawrence M. Ludlow, Theodore Wray, Gary Clouse, The Radical Elijah Minton, Mark Lewis Owens, Shawn Ansley, Charlie St. James, Daniel Malouf, Dan Higgins, Matthew Allen, Shardan Radmanesh, Greg, Ashley Mitchell, Justin Moore, C. Jacobs, Andrew W. Cleveland III, M.D., Andrew Ranta, Eric Keisler, Fergus MacDonald, Elissa Kao, Margaret Bowman and James McMahon.

The Scott Horton Show and
The Libertarian Institute

Listen to *Antiwar Radio* every Sunday morning on 90.7 FM KPFK in Los Angeles and sign up for Scott's daily email and the *Scott Horton Show* podcast feed, and check out the full interview archive, at scotthorton.org. To interview Scott, email his producer Ed Huff, ed@scotthorton.org.

Regular donors of $5 or more per month by way of Patreon or Paypal get access to the /r/scotthortonshow group on Reddit.com. Info at scotthorton.org/donate.

Also, check out The Libertarian Institute at libertarianinstitute.org. It's Scott Horton, Sheldon Richman, Pete Quinones, Kyle Anzalone and the best libertarian writers and podcast hosts on the internet. We are a 501(c)(3) tax-exempt charitable organization. EIN 83-2869616.

Help support our efforts — including our project to purchase wholesale copies of this book to send to important congressmen and women, antiwar groups and influential people in the media. We don't have a big marketing department to push this effort. We need your help to do it. And thank you.

libertarianinstitute.org/donate or

The Libertarian Institute
612 W. 34th St.
Austin, TX 78705

Check out all of our other great Libertarian Institute books at libertarianinstitute.org/books:

> *Fool's Errand: Time to End the War in Afghanistan* by Scott Horton
> *The Great Ron Paul: The Scott Horton Show Interviews 2004–2019*
> *No Quarter: The Ravings of William Norman Grigg* edited by Tom Eddlem
> *Coming to Palestine* by Sheldon Richman
> *What Social Animals Owe to Each Other* by Sheldon Richman

Selected praise for Scott Horton's previous book Fool's Errand

"Scott Horton's *Fool's Errand* is a deeply insightful and well-informed book on America's longest war, explaining why it remains as unwinnable as it ever was." — Patrick Cockburn, Middle East correspondent for the *Independent*, author of *The Age of Jihad: Islamic State and the Great War for the Middle East*

"An incisive, informative analysis of the Afghan fiasco and how we got there, scrubbed clean of propaganda and disinformation. Horton captures the situation very well indeed. I much enjoyed reading it." — Eric S. Margolis, author of *War at the Top of the World: The Struggle for Afghanistan, Kashmir and Tibet* and *American Raj: Liberation or Domination? Resolving the Conflict Between the West and the Muslim World*

"Scott Horton's *Fool's Errand: Time to End the War in Afghanistan* is a definitive, authoritative and exceptionally well-resourced accounting of America's disastrous war in Afghanistan since 2001. Scott's book deserves not just to be read, but to be kept on your shelf, because as with David Halberstam's *The Best and Brightest* or Neil Sheehan's *A Bright Shining Lie*, I expect Horton's book to not just explain and interpret a current American war, but to explain and interpret the all too predictable future American wars, and the unavoidable waste and suffering that will accompany them." — Capt. Matthew Hoh, USMC (ret.), former senior State Department official, Zabul Province, Afghanistan

"*Fool's Errand* is a hidden history of America's forgotten war, laid bare in damning detail. Scott Horton masterfully retells the story of America's failed intervention, exposes how Obama's troop surge did not bring Afghanistan any closer to peace, and warns that the conflict could go on in perpetuity — unless America ends the war. Horton shows why the answer to a brutal civil war is not more war. *Fool's Errand* is a scintillating and sorely needed chronicle of the longest war in American history." — Anand Gopal, journalist and author of *No Good Men Among the Living: America, the Taliban, and the War Through Afghan Eyes*

"Scott Horton's *Fool's Errand: Time to End the War in Afghanistan* is a brilliant achievement and a great read. I recommended it to the faculty at the Army Command and General Staff College to be part of the course work. It's that important." — Col. Douglas Macgregor, U.S. Army (ret.), author of *Warrior's Rage: The Great Tank Battle of 73 Easting*

"A lot of people think of the war in Iraq as the bad war, but Afghanistan as the good and justifiable war. That convenient view does not survive Scott Horton's careful and incisive demolition." — Thomas E. Woods Jr., author of *Nullification: How to Resist Federal Tyranny in the 21st Century* and *Rollback: Repealing Big Government Before the Coming Fiscal Collapse*

"America's longest war — in Afghanistan — has until now been among America's least documented. Horton brings together far more than 16 years of conflict, drawing in sources from well before most Americans even heard of Osama bin Laden to show how the Afghan quagmire's roots are deep. The title tells it all, however: this war cannot be won, and 'victory' will be in the form of escape. Meticulously researched and footnoted, *Fool's Errand* is required reading." — Peter Van Buren, retired foreign service officer and author of *We Meant Well: How I Helped Lose the War for the Hearts and Minds of the Iraqi People* and *Hooper's War: A Novel of WWII Japan*

"Why is the United States still fighting in Afghanistan? In this timely new book, Scott Horton explains why America's longest war is strategically misguided and why getting out would make the United States safer and advance America's broader national interests. Even readers who do not share Horton's libertarian world-view are likely to find themselves nodding in agreement: the war in Afghanistan has indeed become a 'fool's errand.'" — Stephen M. Walt, professor of international affairs, Harvard University, co-author of *The Israel Lobby and U.S. Foreign Policy*

"Scott Horton's *Fool's Errand* makes a well-researched and compelling case that American policies in Afghanistan were ill conceived from the outset and doomed to fail. Chronicling one unsuccessful American initiative after another in a seemingly endless war, Horton argues that our continued military efforts now yield little more than revenge-minded blowback. There is no light at the end of the tunnel, and no one can imagine realistically that one will appear. It will no doubt be a bitter pill to acknowledge that the Beltway fantasy of a united, democratic, pluralist and feminist Afghanistan will never be achieved, but it is one we will have to swallow eventually. Since the cost of pursuing unrealistic goals is exorbitant in blood and treasure, the sooner our failure is faced up to, the better." — Scott McConnell, founding editor of *The American Conservative* magazine

Learn more about *Fool's Errand: Time to End the War in Afghanistan* at foolserrand.us.

318